Wrestling with

ROWAN WILLIAMS

Wrestling with Angels: Conversations in Modern Theology

Edited by
Mike Higton

scm press

© Mike Higton 2007

The Author has asserted his right under the Copyright, Designs and Patents Act, 1988, to be identified as the Author of this Work

British Library Cataloguing in Publication data

A catalogue record for this book is available from the British Library

Cover picture: Detail from the nave mosaics of the Basilica in Monreale, Sicily; late 12th-century, probably Venetian. The mosaics encircle the whole church and systematically tell the story of creation and redemption. The mosaics of the centre nave are devoted to the Old Testament, from creation to the Jacob's struggle with the angel after which he was renamed Israel.

ISBN 978-0-334-04095-8

First published in 2007 by SCM Press
9–17 St Albans Place,
London N1 0NX

www.scm-canterburypress.co.uk

SCM Press is a division of
SCM-Canterbury Press Ltd

Typeset by Rowland Phototypesetting Ltd,
Bury St Edmunds, Suffolk
Printed and bound in Great Britain by
William Clowes Ltd, Beccles, Suffolk

Contents

In loving and grateful memory of
Dewi Phillips (1934–2006)

Chronological Listing of Sources and Acknowledgements

1979

Chapter 1

'The *via negativa* and the foundations of theology: An introduction to the thought of V.N. Lossky', in Stephen Sykes and Derek Holmes (eds), *New Studies in Theology* 1 (London: Duckworth, 1979), pp. 95–117.

Chapter 7

'Barth on the triune God', in S.W. Sykes (ed.), *Karl Barth: Studies of his theological method* (Oxford: Clarendon, 1979), pp.147–93.

1982

Chapter 6

'Balthasar and Rahner', in John Riches (ed.), *The analogy of beauty* (Edinburgh: T & T Clark, 1982), pp. 11–34.

1984

Chapter 12

'"Religious realism": on not quite agreeing with Don Cupitt', *Modern theology* 1.1 (October 1984), pp. 3–24.

1988

Chapter 8

'Barth, war & the state', Oxford Conference in Commemoration of the Centenary of the Birth of Karl Barth, 18–21 September; reprinted in Nigel Biggar (ed.) *Reckoning with Barth* (Oxford: Mowbray, 1988), pp. 170–90.

Chapter 10

'The suspicion of suspicion: Wittgenstein and Bonhoeffer', in Richard Bell (ed.) *Grammar of the heart: New essays in Moral Philosophy and Theology* (San Francisco: Harper and Row, 1988), pp. 36–53.

1989

Chapter 9

'Violence, society and the sacred', a lecture delivered at St Antony's College, Oxford, 26 October 1989, OPPS paper 18 (Oxford: Oxford Project for Peace Studies, 1989).

1991

Chapter 4

'Between Politics and Metaphysics: Reflections in the Wake of Gillian Rose', *Modern Theology* 11 (January 1991), pp. 3–22.

1992

Chapter 2

'Hegel and the gods of postmodernity', presented at The shadow of spirit: contemporary western thought and its religious subtexts, King's College Cambridge, 1988, and in Philippa Berry and Andrew Wernick (eds), *Shadow of Spirit: Postmodernism and Religion* (London: Routledge, 1992), pp. 72–80.

Chapter 14

'Doctrinal criticism: some questions', in Sarah Coakley and David A. Pailin (eds) *The making and remaking of Christian doctrine: Essays in honour of Maurice Wiles* (Oxford: Clarendon Press, 1992), pp. 239–64.

1993

Chapter 11

'The necessary non–existence of God', in Richard H. Bell (ed.) *Simone Weil's philosophy of culture: Readings towards a divine humanity* (Cambridge: CUP, 1993), pp. 52–76.

1996

Chapter 13

'Reply: Redeeming sorrows', paper presented at 15th annual conference on philosophy of religion, Claremont, February 1991; printed in D.Z. Phillips (ed.) *Religion and morality*, Claremont Studies in the Philosophy of Religion (New York: St Martin's Press, 1996), pp. 132–48.

1998

Chapter 3

'Logic and spirit in Hegel', in Phillip Blond (ed.), *Post–secular Philosophy: Between Philosophy and Theology* (London: Routledge, 1998), pp. 116–30.

Chapter 5

'Afterword: Making Differences', in Lucy Gardner, David Moss, Ben Quash and Graham Ward (eds), *Balthasar at the End of Modernity* (Edinburgh: T&T Clark, 1998), pp.173–9.

Author's Introduction

Ronald Knox, the Roman Catholic scholar and satirist, once remarked that he usually had two sensations when he read pieces he had written years earlier – first, how bad they were, second that he couldn't even do them *that* well now. Many will feel some sympathy for that; and a volume whose contents go back over some thirty years is a prime candidate for such reactions. But what has been intriguing in reading over these pieces has been the experience of watching arguments develop even when the author wasn't really aware of them. There are some continuities emerging here that have been surprising.

The first piece contained in this collection is the earliest to be written – substantially a chapter from a doctoral thesis on the early twentieth-century theologian, Vladimir Lossky. As the chapter argues, the tradition of 'negative theology' in Christian thinking needs to be understood not just as a corrective but as something of definitive importance in itself. It is not just that theologians make positive statements and then add, 'Mind you, this only applies in a rather extended sense, not too literally.' It is rather that both the subject matter and (for lack of a better word) the style of good theology insist upon a radical change of attitude. A doctrine like that of the Trinity tells us that the very life of God is a yielding or giving-over into the life of an Other, a 'negation' in the sense of refusing to settle for the idea that normative life or personal identity is to be conceived in terms of self-enclosed and self-sufficient units. The negative is associated with the 'ek-static', the discovery of identity in self-transcending relation. And accordingly, theology itself has to speak in a mode that encourages us to question ourselves, to deny ourselves, in the sense of denying systems and concepts that are the comfortable possession of individual minds. This means both that theological language has to open out on to a sort of darkness – not the darkness of obscurity or confused ignorance, but the darkness of sheer resistance to the finite mind on the part of the divine. And at the same time, theological language must be the language of a community of persons actively engaged in the common life of building the Body of Christ. Doctrinal formulae are neither a set of neat definitions nor some sort of affront to the free-thinking soul; they are words that tell us enough truth to bring us to the edge of speech, and words that sustain enough common life to hold us there together in worship and mutual love

That basic duality can, I think, be traced in all the essays here presented. As the reader will see, it finally led me to a re-examination of Hegel, who receives a rather summary treatment in some of the earlier pieces. I had begun by taking very much for granted the view of Hegel that treats him as a thinker obsessed with final reconciliations and total intellectual schemes. I learned to read him more sympathetically partly through the brilliance of a former student, Andrew Shanks (who has made outstanding contributions to British theology), partly through the friendship and intellectual companionship of the late Gillian Rose (one of the foremost minds in Britain in her generation). Between them, these two persuaded me to rethink Hegel and to grasp that what he was concerned with was not a system that could be projected on to some detached reality 'out there', but a habit of thinking that always sought to understand itself as a process of self-questioning and self-dissolution in the process of discovering *real* language – and thus real thinking. Here too negation is not a corrective or a passing moment – though that's an easy misunderstanding of Hegel: it is the energy of surpassing the settled individual self in the journey to truth and community. And as such it shows us that thinking itself is the clue to what can be said and known about God. The essay on Gillian Rose's own work spells out some of the implications of this in the world of public and political negotiation. But it also underlines the Hegelian point (as I understand it) that meaning does not come in the gaps between words or things, but in the way in which the structure and the surface of the world and speech can be so read and heard as to lead us into new and strange configurations of understanding – how words and things always deliver more than themselves, more than a series of objects and labels, and so both undermine and re-establish appearances.

Hans Urs von Balthasar, undoubtedly the most original of Roman Catholic theologians in the later twentieth century, developed an aesthetic of extraordinary depth in which some of the same themes may be discerned. His 'dramatic' construal of the world is meant to remind us that we do not start from intuitions of spiritual truth and then embody them in some way in practices and words. First we are addressed and engaged by what is utterly outside our capacity; we are forced towards new horizons. This is intrinsic to the experience of beauty; but as beauty itself deepens, the conventional standards disappear – negation again – until, in the Christian narrative, the ultimately beautiful can appear in its full freedom only in the disfigurement of the crucified Jesus. For Balthasar, this is how we establish on the firmest basis the recognition of the gap between what we can achieve or understand and what God makes known to us. He refines this conviction in his long debate with Karl Rahner, the other great giant of twentieth-century Roman Catholic thought, who had argued with immense philosophical subtlety for a fundamental disposition of the human spirit towards the unconditional, which constituted an indestructible element of openness in humanity towards God. In exploring the tension between Balthasar and Rahner, I did less than justice to the latter, I think; more recent studies (for example by Karen Kilby) have strongly challenged my reading of Rahner. But what remains distinctive to Balthasar is the paradox of beauty's freedom to appear in the horror of the crucified. This becomes the central point for a theology of revelation.

Balthasar wrote a fine book on Karl Barth, the dominant Protestant thinker of the age and an excellent match for his capacities. It was Barth who most spectacularly put revelation back on the map of theology, insisting on the same point as Balthasar, though in a wholly different, Reformation, idiom: God is free from obligation to our good deeds, free from confinement in our categories; God defines who he is by what he says and does, by revelation. And the doctrine of the Trinity, so far from being a speculative addition to the real essence of doctrine, is basic to all Christian discourse because it sets out what revelation means: it declares that God is a God who chooses to make himself known. The long essay on Barth's trinitarian theology looks at how this theme is developed in the early sections of the *Church Dogmatics*, and identifies some of the problems that arise when the emphasis is so heavily on the *knowledge* of God rather than the transforming relation with God that a fuller doctrine of the Holy Spirit might suggest. Although this discussion makes too little use of some of the ways in which Barth himself corrects some of the imbalance in later parts of the *Dogmatics*, it does pinpoint a difficulty felt by many in reading Barth: that the doctrine of the Spirit and the Church are less than completely developed. Yet Barth's view of the Church emerges powerfully when we look at his own actual witness in relation to the Confessing Church in the thirties and in his postwar writing about Church and state. A little to the surprise of some, he took a strong position against German rearmament, and voiced uncompromising opposition to atomic warfare. The exploration of this theme opens up some wide-ranging issues around political justice and order in relation to the Kingdom of God and offers a challenging test case for the renewal of a Calvinist political ethic in modern circumstances.

The question of violence and social order has only recently begun to receive the level of real theological engagement that it deserves, from some outstanding thinkers like Oliver O'Donovan, John Milbank and Stanley Hauerwas. One of those who opened up the question in a completely fresh way was René Girard, whose work was beginning to make a serious impact in Britain by the 1980s. The essay on Girard in this volume was written as an introduction to his thinking, and not as a full-scale critical engagement; and some of its conclusions are challengeable – such as the ascription to Girard of a too 'Protestant' emphasis on (once again) saving knowledge rather than saving relation. As in the case of Barth, I now think this is balanced by other factors – though not completely offset. What emerges from this sketchy discussion, though, is a strong caution against simply writing off the Enlightenment heritage of 'critique' – of the scrutiny of metaphysical and moral claims to discern what hidden interests lie beneath them. And the study of Wittgenstein and Bonhoeffer draws this out to suggest that the proper inheritance of this suspicion in the 'late modern' period is to turn suspicion against itself – to grasp that searching for a single concealed agenda that can be unmasked by the triumphant modern interpreter is to remain as much in thrall to crude models of power as any pre-modern thinker. This suggests that contemporary philosophical and religious wisdom involves a return to 'surfaces' or appearances, conscious of the irreducible elements of history and contingency in the formation of knowledge and religious faith. Central to the argument here is a theme that has become of increasing importance in some other things I have written, which is the inescapable significance of *time* as a correlate of bodiliness.

It is the lack of reconciliation with time and the body that causes unease with the brilliant speculative adventures of Simone Weil, as set out in the next essay. Weil can be seen as an exponent of negative theology in its sharpest form: for her, the only way of talking truthfully about God is the unequivocal and undialectical negation of the human 'I'. Whatever is said about God thus becomes necessarily about a non-existent God, the God who can be spoken of. This is a powerful insight, but its outworking unavoidably suggests something too close to self-loathing. One theme that recurs here and there in these papers is the risk of a theology that does not really accept the doctrine of creation – that the sheer material obstinacy of the world is 'desired' by God, not an accident, not a catastrophe. There are moments when Barth comes uncomfortably near blending creation and fall; Weil goes well beyond, and it leaves her profundity and poignancy as a thinker deeply shadowed by the suggestion that the world – and the human person – *cannot* be willed and therefore valued by God. Weil's religious thought is poised between the Christian affirmation (that we become ourselves in self-giving) and a sort of Buddhist conviction (that there can be no self that ought to be affirmed). If she were really a Buddhist, this would mean detachment from all levels of the self's life and equally an acceptance of the interdependent complex that constitutes what we think of as personality. Part of Weil's difficulty is that she brings to her 'Buddhist' concern to avoid mythology and sentimentality about the self a very Christian passion to dissolve the self not as illusory but as intrinsically sinful.

It does not at all mean that she is a weak or unprofitable thinker; quite the contrary. She is one of those of whom you can say that their errors are more fruitful than the right answers of others. And the discussion of Don Cupitt's first essays in 'non-realist' theology arises out of something of the same exasperated gratitude and respect. The response to Cupitt outlined here picks up (or anticipates, since it was written earlier) some of the themes of the Bonhoeffer–Wittgenstein paper in challenging the notion that there is a single hidden script at work in the surface language of religious faith, and also pleads against the strongly voluntarist language of 'creating' values and beliefs in the face of a perceptible world that is composed of matter and the Void. This has its own mythology and its own moral ambiguities. But here more than anywhere, the reader needs caution: Cupitt has gone on to write an enormous sequence of fairly brief, intense, imaginative books in which the voluntarism is steadily burned away and the non-realist picture becomes more and more associated with the serious play of French postmodernism and many other aesthetic and philosophical currents in the contemporary world. My discussion of his work here is at best a snapshot of problems at a particular stage of his intellectual evolution. But I still hold to the questions I wish to put to this or any other form of non-realism – questions mostly based on the difficulty of claiming that religious language has a 'true' meaning that can be decoded in the face not only of what it purports to say, but of how and where it is used (as it might be used by a martyr who is manifestly not dying for a choice she or he thinks of as having been constructed out of nothing).

Realist theology is by no means as crude as Cupitt tries to portray it; but it does inevitably make some claims about God as *active*. The penultimate essay begins from the difference of views between the Marilyn McCord Adams and the late Maurice Wiles over divine agency. This paper expresses dissatisfaction with both – agreeing with Adams that a theology like that of Wiles which seems to conceive of God as incapable of specific action and yet finding Adams' own language, which ascribes to God a (variable) *policy* of non-intervention based on the calculation of achievable goods, deeply problematic as applied to theodicy. Adams is one of a number of highly sophisticated philosophers of religion in recent decades who have done remarkable work on the logic of doctrinal statements, yet have not (in my view) done justice to the sort of point that I think Lossky and Barth in their divers ways are making – that talking about God requires a recognition that we cannot simply give him a 'biography' of plans, experiences and feelings like some inhabitant of the universe. Again, the reader should be aware of the detailed response to my criticisms that was made by Professor Adams, and of the much richer and more extended statement of her position in her book on theodicy.

Wiles himself is the subject of the final essay in this sequence, an essay written for his Festschrift and resting on a deeply felt respect and affection for a colleague of rare human quality. The discussion begins from an unease about the way in which the category of 'doctrinal criticism' created by Wiles begs extensive methodological questions. And, appropriately perhaps, it points back to the first essay. *If*, as Wiles often appears to think, you think that doctrinal formulae are rather poor attempts to solve intellectual questions that we no longer ask, then you will inevitably wish to relativise them if not abandon them. If, on the other hand, they are shaped by the desire to find the least problematical way of holding a profoundly elusive truth, and by the impulse to push towards the edge of what can be said and to impel a kind of 'emptying out' of personal and intellectual assertion, they will be viewed differently and will not so readily be brought before the supposedly impartial tribunal of ahistorical modern reason. The conclusion presses on a Christological point echoed in several other essays directly or indirectly: is the person of Jesus an illustration of something we could know by other means? Or the phenomenon that ultimately demands and moulds a new language for itself? The latter is the presupposition of traditional doctrinal theology, and, as will appear, it is a presupposition that I share. Trying to do without it leaves theology without what I have sometimes called salutary difficulty – the sense of 'wrestling', if you will, with angels or whatever else.

These comments may help the reader trace a path through this book. In the nature of such collections, they do not offer a continuous argument, but I hope they may suggest some continuities in the search for ways of theologising about time, materiality and community within the context of a classical trinitarian and Christological faith. In one way, these pieces can be read as vastly overblown footnotes to the more general and constructive essays collected some years ago as *On Christian Theology*; they show the sorts of 'conversation' that were going on in the background of other work. And both books are footnotes to a good many other much slighter volumes, most recently my short introduction to Christian teaching called *Tokens of Trust* (Canterbury Press, 2007). These essays were mostly written for a rather specialist readership, and their style is accordingly condensed and sometimes technical; I apologise in advance for any undue cleaving to jargon and any unnecessary obscurity or compression. But the point of all of these pieces is to understand a little better what other theologians want to say about the simplest yet most inexhaustible of all subjects, the life upon which all life depends and the embodiment among us of that life in a human life and human words, in the person of Jesus of Nazareth.

I am deeply grateful to Mike Higton for initiating and carrying through this collection; it is both an honour and an embarrassment to realise that someone knows far better than you what you've written (and frequently what you mean as well). His has been an exemplary work of selflessness. But I must also thank all who contributed to these essays in whatever way – students who heard some of the ideas, colleagues who read and criticised, friends and audiences. Particularly I must acknowledge the stimulus and help of Richard Bell, David Ford, Fergus Kerr, Nicholas Lash, Andrew Louth, John Milbank, Oliver O'Donovan, Stephen Sykes and, of course, Jane Williams. Finally, several of these pieces owe a great debt to the late Dewi Z. Phillips, dear friend and fellow-townsman; to his memory I gladly dedicate this volume.

Rowan Williams

Archbishop of Canterbury
Lambeth Palace, Passiontide 2007

Editor's Introduction

Rowan Williams has been engaging with the writings of modern theologians since the very beginning of his academic career, and this book is a collection of fourteen previously published articles in which his negotiating skills are displayed. The chapters cover roughly two decades of his life, from the late 'seventies to the late 'nineties, but engage with theologians spread over nearly two centuries, from Hegel to Marilyn McCord Adams.

One could think of this book as an accompaniment to Williams' earlier collection, *On Christian Theology*[1] though it is not quite the same kind of book. Although the two have much in common, the articles in the present book do not set out Williams' theological vision as directly as did the chapters of the earlier collection. As a first approximation, one might instead think of this book as showing us more of Williams' *workings*, the processes of reading and interpretation that have helped to form his theological vision. That won't quite do, however, if it suggests that the processes of engagement shown here are simply superseded by the results displayed in *On Christian Theology*, and therefore of interest only to those concerned with intellectual archaeology. One could equally well see the vision displayed in *On Christian Theology* as the product of deliberate pauses in the ongoing journey of negotiation and discovery embodied here – pauses to take stock, or to take in the view from the point that the journey so far has reached. In that light, the chapters of *On Christian Theology* might look more like a *commentary* upon the evolving and unending conversation that is partially displayed here.

So this is not a systematic collection, with a clear topical organisation. It is, rather, a set of notes from a voyage, albeit one whose story is held together by resemblances and recurrent themes. I have chosen to arrange the book so as to highlight some of those unsystematic continuities, rather than in chronological order either of writing or of subject matter. That is, I have tried to arrange it so that, if read from start to finish, the reader might be aware of being taken on a wandering and circuitous but continuous journey.

That there is not a single, clear system of theological ideas in this book is itself of substantive theological importance. Williams' engagement with the various modern theologians he treats cannot be seen simply as the judgment of those authors against a standard already in his possession. He does not render these authors and their texts down until he is able to find secreted within them a basic agreement or disagreement with his own existing vision, or until he distils some truth or falsehood already well understood. Rather, his approach to these authors and texts is marked by attentive negotiation. Many of these chapters begin with what might be seen a form of method acting: lengthy passages of exegesis in which Williams performs other theologians' scripts, having found out how to speak their words in a way that is meaningful, plausible, and inhabitable. He takes on each theologian's voice, rolls his or her words around on his tongue, and presents the author's work not as a distant spectator might, but as if he had, for a time, become that theologian's representative. This is, to use a term that crops up in several of these chapters, a process of 'ecstatic' attentiveness: Williams goes out from himself, and dwells for a while in foreign territory. He is, for a while, beside himself. The performances of these texts that emerge from this process are, nevertheless, always clearly Williams' own. One hears the recognisable tones of his voice, even when he is speaking for Karl Barth or for Simone Weil or for Don Cupitt. The *ecstasis* involved is not a matter of the disappearance or obliteration of his own position and history: it is a matter of negotiation, a struggle to find a way in which *he* can speak *their* words.

In part, Williams' performances of interpretation are to be judged by their fidelity to the texts that he reads. If we think not of an actor's performances but of a musician's, we will recognise that a performer may be criticised if she simply plays the wrong notes, or – more interestingly – if her performance makes it hard for us to hear the riches of a piece that other performances have shown us. Just so, these chapters can properly be questioned for the accuracy and sensitivity of their reading, and there are places where Williams might well now play differently in that regard, were he writing the pieces again. He might now, say, produce a performance of Karl Barth's music that is less marked by the influence of Gustav Wingren's performances, or a performance of Karl Rahner now inflected by Karen Kilby's playing.

The appropriateness of this kind of criticism is not, however, a sign

xxii

that Williams is simply trying to 'get these authors and their texts right', and to produce faultlessly accurate performances. It is appropriate because it is by struggling for this kind of fidelity that the otherness or resistance of these texts is most fully registered. Fidelity makes the ecstatic journey possible. To engage in this kind of exegesis of a text is to trust that it is, as Williams puts it,

> sufficiently solid, sufficiently realized in itself or worked through, that it resists being mastered and made to serve some function in our mental programme. It invites us to take time...[and] we do not know what time is demanded of us, nor what it will issue in. We respond to the work as to a claim on our attention, of indeterminate scope; a presentation of multiple possibilities for assimilation and action.[2]

The concern for fidelity is, therefore, at the same time a concern for the *generativity* of these texts. Williams' aim is not to provide a reading that will end in a full stop, enabling us finally to grasp what the author meant and rest content with it. A performance is a proposal for continuation:

> Understanding, explaining, interpreting are not efforts of an individual to penetrate a surface: they are *social* proposals for common reading and common, or at least continuous, activity (a gesture or performance that in some sense goes on with or takes up from mine). They do not, therefore, see what is to be interpreted as setting a problem to be solved: interpretation is not designed to put an end to puzzlement for good and all, though it may remove specific puzzles.[3]

A proposal for continuation: that is the deeper way in which these chapters should be judged. Do you go home from the performance and find yourself whistling the tunes? Are they readings that provoke not 'Aha!' experiences, but 'Ah, yes, but...', 'Of course; and...' or even 'Well, no – although...' experiences – experiences, that is, that both involve some level of recognition *and* make you want to respond? Does Williams' performance of these texts allow you to return to them in your own way, and continue the process of struggling to perform them for yourself, in a way that will inevitably differ from Williams but will now have echoes of his tones? Does it enable you to hear these texts as challenge and as gift, so that you will find your way ahead reshaped by what you have heard?

That Williams' attempt to inhabit these texts is a matter of negotiation is shown by the way in which his exegeses naturally segue into judgment. Perhaps the most obvious example is chapter 12, the subtitle of which is 'On not quite agreeing with Don Cupitt'. Williams' attempt to perform Cupitt's texts leads him to a point where he can find no way in which *he* can speak some of Cupitt's words with integrity – and he must say 'No', and a quite definite and trenchant 'No' at that. As a reader who has already been shaped within a certain complex of traditions, some of Cupitt's thoughts are simply unthinkable for him.[4]

Such judgments emerge because Williams is, finally, interested in coherence – but it is not the coherence of what he reads with his already fixed and settled opinions that moves him, but a hoped-for, promised, and as-yet-unfinished coherence. When in his exegeses he asks how *he* can play *this text*, he is asking what kind of future is possible for him and the author to share, and his judgments about the challenges that the text offers to him and that he offers to the text are attempts to grasp what change might be needed on both sides for such a future to be possible. That future is genuinely future, however, for 'we do not know what time is demanded of us': Williams' reading of these modern theologians is a reading that *waits* upon peace – not the peace of some silent Spring in which each has agreed to differ with each, but a musical peace, the peace of a common good that will be shaped by the goods that each person, community and tradition embodies – a peace of harmonious difference without violence. The negotiations in which Williams engages in this book are serious, therefore, because they are seriously hopeful: they are serious negotiations conducted in the hope of that peace of God that is and remains beyond his grasp and ours.

Notes

1. Oxford: Blackwell, 2000
2. Below, p.198.
3. Below, p.190.
4. In its original context, in the first volume of *Modern Theology*, the article was followed by a response from Cupitt, in which Cupitt as it were whistles his

tune again, and asks Williams whether, now that he hears it clearly and cleanly, he can really find it so impossible to play. Don Cupitt, 'A Reply to Rowan Williams', *Modern Theology* 1.1 (1984): 25–31. 'So I appeal to Rowan Williams to consider changing sides . . .' (31).

Lossky, the *via negativa* and the foundations of theology

Vladimir Lossky is now widely recognised as perhaps the most creative theological mind among the younger generation of Russian Orthodox *émigré* writers who made such an impact on Western European religious thought in the years before and after the Second World War. His tragically early death in 1958 left a great gap in the ranks of Orthodox thinkers; it also meant that he left no work of mature theological synthesis. His great essay on *The mystical theology of the Eastern Church* is, deservedly, a classic; but there is evidence from late and unpublished material that he would have wished to extend and deepen, perhaps even revise, some of its arguments. The present paper is an attempt to examine some of Lossky's basic assumptions about theology and theological method, in the light of this later material as well as of his published work, and to elucidate the sense in which he considered apophasis, 'negative' theology, as normative in Christian dogmatic reflection.

I

Lossky's earliest published article, on negative theology in the *Corpus areopagiticum*[1] was to set the tone for a very large part of his subsequent work and thought: it represents the first fruits of the lifelong academic absorption which finally issued in the posthumous publication of his monumental work on Eckhart. Few scholars of this century have provided so painstaking and nuanced an analysis of the historical expressions of the *via negativa*. Lossky recognised two highly significant and commonly neglected features of this history: first, that apophasis is not coterminous with 'mysticism' (however defined);[2] and, secondly, that the use of apophasis in the history of Christian thought is anything but homogeneous, that the scholar must 'in every work regard the writer's end', must attempt to discern what it is that apophasis is being used *for*. His concern for both these points is expressed in his insistence that apophasis is not in itself revelation: it is a means and not an end, a receptacle, the necessary condition for the apprehension of revelation.[3] Furthermore, if apophasis has this character as, in its own right, 'pro-paedeutic' to revelation, the conventional Western view[4] of the apo-phatic method as essentially a corrective to cataphatic theology, a qualification which acts as a necessary dialectical stage between the *via affirmativa* and the *via eminentiae*, is a misunderstanding of its real nature.[5] Apophasis is never, for Lossky, a move in a conceptual game: it is the μετάνοια of the intellect, and indeed, not only of the intellect, bound up as it is with the μετάνοια of the whole human person.[6] In this sense, as Lossky made clear in *Spor o sofii* (*The Sophia debate*), his early polemical essay on Bulgakov's theological speculations, apophasis is 'not a branch of theology', but an attitude which should undergird *all* theological discourse, and lead it towards the silence of contemplation and communion.[7]

In what way, then, is apophasis not the same as the mystical ascent? The answer is not simply 'it depends what you mean by "apophasis"'. It lies, rather, in the simple recognition that apophasis in itself can never be more than the verbal symbol of encounter with God. We do not, after all, encounter God primarily through language or through the contemplation of words allegedly referring to him, and it makes little difference to the experience of encounter whether such words are prefaced with – as it were – a plus or a minus sign. In any Christian theology which is serious about the transcendence of God, there is bound to be present a sense of 'check', of limitation, if it is not to remain 'dans les limites d'une théologie naturelle, en faisant de la voie d'éminence et du principe d'analogie un moyen de signaler, dans les conceptes mêmes dont elle se sert, la transcendence d'un Dieu qui échappe à la connaissance conceptuelle'.[8] Thus understood, apophasis is seen to be not merely the exclusive preserve of a more or less Chris-tianised Neoplatonism, of the tradition which exalts God above 'being' (and therefore above conceptual predication); it is 'impliquée dans le paradoxe de la révélation chrétienne: le Dieu transcendant devient immanent au monde, mais dans l'immanence même de son économie ... il se révèle comme transcendant'.[9] At this fairly basic level, even Aquinas can be described as, in some respects, an 'apophatic' theo-logian, having applied to the Dionysian terminology a 'correction prudente' which does not involve the location of God above and beyond *esse*.[10] And only at this level, Lossky maintains, is Augustine a practitioner of apophasis: since God is, to Augustine, 'Being itself', it is possible to have some kind of intellectual knowledge of him – the 'reverse side' of our positive intellectual knowledge of created being.[11] God is not apprehended in a mystical *ignorantia* which is beyond the activity of the intellect: *sufficit ut attingat*. Such is the experience so unforgettably described in the *Confessions*, the so-called 'vision' at Ostia; beyond such experiences, our discourse about God can be characterised only by *docta ignorantia*, as we press forward to transcend the inadequacy of all our language about him.[12] For Augustine, it seems that ignorance finally issues in knowledge; whereas for Dionysius it is knowledge that issues in ignorance, in an absence of concepts which is an authentic but non-intellectual, non-ratiocinative, knowledge of God. Augustine's intellect may be transfigured, but it is not transcended: it is enabled to 'hear (God) speaking, not by any tongue of the flesh or by an angel's voice ... but in his own voice, the voice of the one whom we love in all these created things, and to know itself to have reached out in thought and touched the eternal Wisdom'.[13]

The Dionysian ἔκστασις, on the other hand, is a state beyond *any* kind of intellection, 'negative' no less than 'affirmative'; and it is described in terms of 'darkness' and 'unknowing', because it can only be spoken of in the language of dogmatic speculation or, better, dogmatic *metaphor*.[14] This is what we find in Gregory of Nyssa; for him, the fundamental datum is encounter with God, and the goal, perfect but non-conceptual knowledge of him. Union is higher than (conceptual) knowledge, the latter being finally rendered impossible by the 'inadéquation radicale' between Creator and creature. In this union, the heart 'sees' the divine light; but the quality of the vision, its inexhaustible, incircumscribable character, never totally possessed or assimilated by man, can be expressed only in terms of darkness and ignorance. Dionysius must be interpreted along these lines, as postulating a union beyond the level of the νοῦς, by means of a dialectical interplay between images of 'light' and 'darkness', 'knowledge' and 'ignorance', 'affirmation' and 'negation'. It is not that darkness, ignorance and negation represent a 'higher stage' in the knowledge of God, superseding that of light, knowing, and affirmation; but rather, that true encounter with God is a reality beyond both sets of terms.[15] In this sense, and this sense only, apophasis may be said to have a 'corrective' function: it exposes the inadequacy of the language of 'light' and 'knowledge', but at the same time confesses its own. And no conceptual *via eminentiae* intrudes with a facile synthesis, to reassure us that only a mode of predication is really in question.[16] Apophasis is 'the perfect way, the only way which is fitting in regard to God', not because it is itself *communion* with God, but because, in its refusal to limit God with concepts, it stands closer to and points more clearly towards the summit of theology, 'the level of "mysterious revelation" in the strict sense, that is "mystical theology" or the self-revelation of God in silence', that knowledge which knows nothing at all of concepts.[17] The true relation between apophasis and 'mystical theology', encounter and union with God, is well expressed by Lossky in his discussion of whether Eckhart, in his treatment of a certain theological problem, writes as a 'mystic' or a 'dialectician': 'Loin de s'exclure mutuellement, l'intuition mystique et la pensée dialectique non seulement peuvent coexister, mais doivent être indissolublement liées dans un esprit tendu vers une réalité metalogique.'[18] As we have seen, negative theology of a sort may exist in the absence of a mature doctrine of the human person's encounter with God; but it is most truly *theology* when it is related to such a doctrine, as it is in Gregory of Nyssa and Dionysius. To recognise the distinction between formal apophaticism of any kind, and 'the self-revelation of God in silence' is indispensable to an understanding of the *proper* use of apophasis, and of the radically non-conceptual nature of that true knowledge of God to which apophasis should point.

Historically, however, what Lossky considers to be the most authentically Christian style of apophasis developed only gradually, in the face of strong competition from the perennially seductive intellectualism of Middle Platonism and Neoplatonism on the one side, and an excessively 'economic' idea of God's trinitarian being on the other. The former led to the union of the νοῦς with a God with whom it is 'connatural', in a perfect intellectual apprehension, the latter, to a communion, bestowed by grace, indeed, but with the 'abyss of the Father' only, transcending the 'economies' of the Father's manifestations in Son and Spirit – an approach exemplified in many ante-Nicene Fathers, notably Clement of Alexandria. Lossky argues at length in 'L'apophase et la théologie trinitaire', and in less detail elsewhere, that apophatic theology, if it is truly Christian, must point beyond the intellect to the *personal* mystery of the Trinity which encounters the human person in the act of revelation.[19] The opposition is between an extreme intellectualism and an extreme agnosticism: in his earliest article, Lossky examines this opposition, taking Clement as the arche-

4

typal agnostic and Origen as the archetypal intellectualist, and suggesting that the Cappadocians, and Dionysius in their wake, offer a mediating position. Clement argues that the divine names have no real reference, and are used only to avoid 'less proper' ones: the achievement of the Cappadocians and Dionysius is the securing of a real informative content for these names.[20] This necessary mediating position is, in Lossky's view, the basis of the 'essence–energies' distinction, without which Dionysius is sure to be misunderstood as a 'pantheist' or 'emanationist'.[21] The importance of Lossky's treatment of the question in this early essay is very great: already he is looking to the Cappadocians and Dionysius as providing a normative theological *via media*; he dissociates the authentic vision of God from the activity of the νοῦς; and the idea of orthodoxy as a mediant between extreme intellectualism and extreme agnosticism is a theme which he developed in the last years of his life in his 'Two monotheisms' theory. Already the 'Palamite synthesis' holds pride of place as the interpretative key to the patristic debates; and it is precisely this which enables Lossky to see the Cappadocian and Dionysian schemes as a *via media*, the high road of orthodoxy leading onwards into the Byzantine period.

Here we have in outline that approach to the history of Christian spirituality which is finally and most systematically developed in the lectures which grew into *La vision de Dieu* (posthumously published in 1962), and which may be traced in the first three essays included in the posthumous edition, *A l'image*; an approach dependent upon the acknowledgement that the transcendent incomprehensibility of God is not reducible to a consequence of the limitations of finite intellect, but is, in some way, a characteristic of God in himself.[22] Hence the importance for Lossky of Dionysius' break with Plotinian intellectualism: the Areopagite does not regard τὸ ἕν as an adequate description of God, nor does he identify ecstasy with ἅπλωσις, the purging of 'multiplicity' from the intellect.[23] Even if we arrive at an 'intellectual monad' by some *via remotionis*, the God of revelation is still beyond. This looks back to Clement, for whom knowledge of God is ultimately a ἕξις γνωστική bestowed by God's grace.[24] Yet, even for Clement, Plato does not finally yield to Moses: language about God-given 'faculties' in the soul, effected by θεία μοῖρα, is wholly Platonic. At the crucial moment, Clement reverts to intellectualism; 'Knowledge is beatitude'. Further, even such a statement must be qualified when we recognise that, for Clement, knowledge of God and eternal salvation are at least conceptually separable. It is not really a matter of personal fellowship with a personal God: the terminus of our relation with God in Clement's system, the βάθος τοῦ Πατρός, is really, Lossky suggests, exactly what would later be designated as the divine οὐσία. We shall see later how the practice of such an 'essentialist' mysticism is one of the most weighty charges laid against Western Christendom by Lossky. Again, since the ἕξις γνωστική is mediated to man by the Son and the Spirit in order to lead to the Father, the 'gnostic' finally transcends Son and Spirit in his knowledge of the Father. Thus the system is not trinitarian but *triadic*, 'dans la mesure où elle implique la notion des trois personnes qui ne sont pas supprimées par la *via remotionis*', and ultimately 'elle n'est determinée que par l'hypostase du Père, la seule vraiment transcendante'.[25]

Clement, then must be adjudged to be outside the authentic mainstream of Christian spirituality, because, on the one hand, he offers an attenuated and impoverished view of man as a being whose last end is related, not to his whole existence, but exclusively to his intellectual faculties; and because, on the other hand, he refines away the idea of God's personal being first to the Father's hypostasis alone and then to the content, the βάθος, of that hypostasis, an impersonal or subpersonal object of intellection. Clement's orthodox rejection of 'natural' intellectualism, the natural ability of the νοῦς to encounter God, is vitated by his capitulation to what might be called a 'revealed' intellectualism. In contrast, Origen insists on the συγγένεια of the νοῦς with God from the first, and it is for this reason, not for any alleged subordinationism, that he fails as a Christian theologian.[26] Especially in the Commentaries and Homilies, there are moments when 'the Greek intellectual sometimes disappears in the face of the disciple of Jesus'; but in the greater part of Origen's work there is a pervasive 'spiritualism' which refuses to treat man as anything other than a νοῦς, temporarily and regrettably bound to matter, and finding its destiny in contemplating the simple monad of the divine nature.[27] In this context, apophasis is seen primarily as a stripping-away from theology of language relating to matter and to multiplicity, in order to reach an object of which 'the One' is a satisfactory conceptual account, in a full-blown Plotinian manner.[28] Origen transforms theology into a 'religious philosophy',[29] a manipulation of conceptual counters on an exclusively intellectual board, blocking the way to any real union between man and God. For although the doctrine of συγγένεια postulates an intimate natural bond between the soul and God, in giving such priority to the νοῦς it preserves for all eternity the cognitive distance between man and his Creator, absolutising the subject–object relation between them in a positively academic kind of beatitude.[30] Evagrius, the great popular-iser of Origen in monastic circles, gives a similar account: 'le dualisme platonicien s'introduit ici dans la spiritualité pré-byzantine'.[31] Evagrius does not consider God to be unequivocally transcendent to the intelli-gible, as to the sensible world. The subject of contemplation is the νοῦς γυμνός, the intellect purified to absolute simplicity; there is no ἔκστασις from or of the νοῦς, no 'knowledge through ignorance'.[32] Lossky con-nects Evagrius' shortcomings in this respect with the influence upon him of Gregory Nazianzen, whose doctrine of contemplation is in many ways imprecise and unsatisfactory, especially in its failure to give positive content to γνόφος, darkness, in man's meeting with God.[33] Thus Evagrius combines Gregory's attitude to γνόφος and ἀγνωσία with Origen's estimate of the dignity of the νοῦς, and produces almost an unqualified intellectual maximalism.

In such a picture, Lossky maintains, contemplation can have no degrees; it is 'undifferentiated'.[34] Progress and growth in the knowledge of God are excluded: once the νοῦς has realised its συγγένεια with God and confronted the divine essence in immediate and perfect vision, nothing can change. There can be no sense of an inexhaustibility in God, a depth which can never be sounded by the finite subject. The perspective of genuine transcendence is lost, the cleavage between sens-ible and intelligible replaces the more radical gulf between created and uncreated.[35] The superiority of Gregory of Nyssa and Dionysius is evident in this, that 'darkness' and 'ignorance' are, for them, expres-sions of precisely that dynamic, 'progressive' aspect of the knowledge of God which is denied by all forms of Origenism. 'Par delà Origène, qui n'avait pas insisté sur cet aspect, Grégoire retrouve en Philon la tradition de la mystique nocturne qu'il va à son tour transmettre à Denys.'[36] The researches of H.-Ch. Puech, confirmed and extended by Daniélou (whose edition of Gregory's *de vita Moysis* is several times referred to in *The mystical theology of the Eastern Church*), provided a firm scholarly foundation for Lossky's emphasis on the relative nov-elty of Gregory's (and Dionysius') approach, its peculiarly Christian, non-Hellenic, non-Platonic character.[37] The reaction of all the Cappa-docians, in their different ways, to the Eunomian *reductio ad absurdum* of Origenist intellectualism marks a turning-point in the history of Christian devotion, as Lossky sees it, something of a rediscovery of the biblical conception of the knowledge of God, preserved by Irenaeus, and subsequently obscured.[38] It is a conception in which intellectual knowledge *becomes* ἀγάπη, as it does for Gregory.[39] 'An object is known; this is an imperfect knowledge in which there is no reciprocity; where there is reciprocity of knowledge, knowledge signifies a relationship between persons, it is determined by ἀγάπη.'[40] Gregory, in turning his back on a static intellectualism, has reopened the way to an understanding of man's knowledge of God as a personal encounter, to which conceptual affirmation and negation are alike alien; and so we are returned to the notion of the true character of apophasis as the expression of *encounter* with the inexhaustible personal being of God.

The significant fourth-century development which precludes the Cappadocians from regarding God as an intellectual monad is the maturation of trinitarian theology, the final agreement that between the ὁμοούσιον and pure Arianism there was no middle way. Clement's solution thus ceases to be an option; and Origen's attempts to modify this by speaking of a vision of the Father 'in' and 'with' the λόγος, while continuing to treat 'the Father' as coterminous with 'the divine simplicity',[41] is equally inadmissible. Once it is firmly established that the three persons of the Godhead are in all respects equal, there can be no doubt that 'to see God is to contemplate the Trinity'.[42] So when Dionysius speaks of God's ὑπερούσια, he obviously means the Trinity of persons; and the τῶν ὀνομάτων σεπτότατον is the name 'Trinity'.[43] The God of the Areopagite, exalted above τὸ ἕν, is clearly and unmistakeably the triune God of revelation; Dionysian apophasis never leads to a level of divine existence superior to the three persons.[44] It may lead us to deny that notions of 'paternity' and 'sonship' are properly applicable to God, since Dionysius' principle of the 'non-opposition des contraires' in theological dialectic will not permit us to think of the Trinity in terms of such relations of logical opposition; the identity-in-distinction of the divine persons is utterly beyond logic, since it is *absolute*, and so irreducibly personal, although no merely human language about persons can be adequate to the divine reality.[45] 'La théologie négative ne va jamais jusqu'à la négation des personnes';[46] how could it, indeed, if apophasis is truly a vehicle for the expression of personal encounter? The 'personalism' of Dionysius is, Lossky argues, further developed in his adoption of the conviction of the Antiochene school that, in the beatific vision, our transfigured senses perceive the Incarnate Word as he was seen by the apostles at his own transfiguration; there is a '*visible* theophany' (ὁρατὴ θεοφάνια),[47] as well as an illumination of the intellect, although the union of the whole person with God is deeper and other than either of these.[48] Again, we have a theme grounded in scripture, maintained by Irenaeus, and obscured

8

by Alexandrian 'spiritualism', coming to the surface in the *Corpus areopagiticum*, purged by Antiochene naturalism – the theme of the significance of the body in the economy of grace.[49] 'With Dionysius we enter the world of truly Byzantine theology':[50] the way is open for the Christocentric syntheses of Maximus and Damascene, and for the final systematisation of the tradition by Palamas, in a theology which is apophatic (and therefore personalist), scriptural, trinitarian, and incarnational; the whole man, body and soul, confronting the revelation of the divine ἐνέργειαι, 'the glory of God in the face of Jesus Christ', the revelation of the inexhaustible transcendence of God's three-personed being.[51]

II

Such in brief is Lossky's account of the development of early Christian and Byzantine spirituality. It is a view developed partly (as he explains at the beginning of *The vision of God* and of 'Le problème de la "vision face à face"') by way of response to the sixteenth-century scholastic critique of the Eastern spiritual tradition. Lossky does not undertake a point-by-point refutation of say, Vasquez's complaint that the Greek Fathers exaggerated the incomprehensibility of God:[52] his aim is, rather, to demonstrate that the Eastern tradition has an inner consistency and continuity deriving from a firm scriptural foundation, and is therefore not patient of interpretation or criticism in terms of the alien categories of scholasticism. The defence of this position involves a rebuttal of the assertions of scholars such as Martin Jugie that Palamism represents a 'heretical innovation'.[53] And it is this concern in particular which tends to make Lossky's treatment of the early centuries a little too schematic: for Palamas and Dionysius to be seen as offering an orthodox middle way, an equilibrium position, it is necessary sometimes to exaggerate the 'wrongness' of, for instance, Origen. In *The vision of God*, Lossky admits the importance of ἀγάπη in Origen's thought, the inseparability of γνῶσις from ἀγάπη, and Origen's use of nuptial imagery to evoke the soul's union with Christ; yet Origen must be characterised as an 'intellectualist', *tout court*, and these aspects of his system must be relegated to insignificance.[54] Gregory of Nyssa, on the other hand, belongs to the mainstream that flows into Palamism, since he rejects Origen's brand of intellectualism; yet, while Lossky rightly identifies Origen's attitude to matter, indeed, to created being in general, as the most ambiguous area of his theology, he ignores or glosses over the degree to which the same ambiguity is characteristic of Gregory. We may agree with Daniélou that Gregory's conviction that beatitude is progress without limit, the eternal journey of the soul towards God,[55] is an authentically Christian and non-Hellenic viewpoint; but Daniélou himself questions whether Gregory's doctrine of the 'spiritual senses' goes any further than Origen's virtually identical teaching in allowing a truly positive role to man's biological existence.[56] When Lossky does discuss Gregory's anthropology, especially his view of the relation of body to soul, he shows some understandable embarrassment, and is clearly reluctant to admit that Gregory was seriously in error in this matter.[57] The desire to present a clear and straightforward evolution in the history of Eastern spirituality towards Palamite apophaticism and incarnationalism coexists a little uneasily with the demands of strict scholarly justice.

Similarly in the case of Dionysius: in several places, Lossky lays a good deal of emphasis on Dionysius' one solitary reference to the Transfiguration, arguing that it implies a developed doctrine of the 'spiritual senses' and the transfiguration of bodily vision in the vision of God.[58] This is by no means clear, and it is just as probable that the passage is no more than a rhetorical flourish. And more dubious still is Lossky's claim, already mentioned, that τὸ τῶν ὀνομάτων σεπτότατον of *De div. nom.* XIII refers to the Trinity, a claim for which the context provides only the slenderest support. It is undeniable that *De div. nom.* in several places implies that there is no difference in *kind* between the trinitarian hypostases and the natural πρόοδοι of the Godhead.[59] Again, what are we to make of Dionysius' assertion that God is, ultimately, οὐδεμία δὲ μονὰς ἢ τριάς?[60] Lossky argues, in 'L'apophase et la théologie trinitaire' that, although Dionysius denies Paternity and Sonship as such in the supersubstantial Godhead, he is still faithful to the idea of a Trinity, though it cannot be said *at all* what its 'threeness' means: God *is trias*, but οὐδὲ τριὰς ἡ πρὸς ἡμῶν.[61] But this avoids the issue: a few pages earlier in the same article, Lossky says quite clearly that God is not knowable outside of his revelatory economy, although this economy leads beyond itself to the confession of the unknowability of the transcendent God-in-himself.[62] If this is so, it makes no sense to follow Dionysius in postulating what seems like a total discontinuity between the 'immanent' and the 'economic' Trinity, a discontinuity which Lossky elsewhere is anxious to avoid.[63] If we have to abandon completely the hypostatic γνωρίσματα of the three persons, characteristics which themselves, as Gregory of Nyssa makes clear,[64] have only a negative role in trinitarian theology, we are left with a thoroughly abstract (and potentially impersonalist) apprehension of the Trinity in itself. In attempting to secure Dionysius' orthodoxy, his position as 'father of Byzantine theology', Lossky is unavoidably led into confusion and contradiction, and something dangerously near to misrepresentation: his passion for schematising is often imperfectly controlled.

III

The problem of the distinction between God *in seipso* and God *ad extra* is, of course, the central issue for Palamism, with its separation of the absolute, unknowable, imparticipable οὐσία of God from the relational, knowable and participable divine ἐνέργειαι. As we have noted, Lossky insists that Dionysius, and, presumably, the tradition behind Dionysius, can only be rightly understood in the light of this separation.[65] The Dionysian πρόοδοι are that-of-God in which creatures partake, and are, as such, the ground of all knowledge of God; and, in union with God, we are united to these πρόοδοι, and never to the οὐσία or ὕπαρξις of God.[66] πρόοδοι (or δυνάμεις, or ἐνέργειαι) *are* God, but they are not the οὐσία of God; as the outgoing of God in and to creation, they make possible cataphatic theology, the 'naming' of God, but, 'in themselves' they are unified and simple, and are apprehended as such in apophatic theology.[67] But here is a further and almost insupportable complication. The comparatively simple idea that the distinction of πρόοδοι from ὕπαρξις in God corresponds to the distinction of cataphatic from apophatic theology seems to have vanished: our ultimate encounter is not *with* the οὐσία through the πρόοδοι,[68] but with the πρόοδοι or ἐνέργειαι 'in themselves', whatever that may mean. The question is not only how far Palamas and Dionysius are consistent, but how far Palamism, *stricto sensu*, is consistent with itself; but this is a very involved problem, which demands far fuller treatment.[69] Enough for the present to note this as a further instance of a point of dubious coherence in Lossky's thesis.

The main features of the synthesis towards which Lossky is working are these: an unequivocal Trinitarianism, not confined to any 'economic' level; a positive evaluation of the role of the body in the plan of salvation, with special reference to the Transfiguration; an insistence on both the transcendence and the immanence of God, expressed by the οὐσία/ἐνέργεια distinction, in some form or other; and finally, the identification of our final encounter with God as a supra-intellectual ἔκστασις, a personal meeting with the inconceptualisable personal being of God. I have suggested that the first three of these characteristics are not so uniformly and unambiguously affirmed in the tradition as Lossky would have us believe; but the fourth is, I believe, more genuinely and consistently significant, and more capable of use as some sort of criterion for differentiating between fundamentally Hellenic, Platonic, or intellectualist doctrines of the knowledge of God, and a more radically Christian view. A problem immediately arises, however: Plotinus has a highly developed doctrine of ἔκστασις; how are we to rule this out from the Christian ambience? Lossky's answer is an exposition of Plotinus' conception designed to show that it simply obliterates subjectivity altogether. In the Plotinian ἔκστασις, the soul undergoes a process of ἅπλωσις, in which νοῦς is transcended, and the barrier between the created subject and the infinite subject vanishes, the soul is absorbed into the One.[70] If this is so, Lossky alleges, it is in no sense *knowledge*: the soul in ecstasy – by definition, one might say – knows nothing, and only outside ecstasy can the experience be identified.[71] For the Christian, on the other hand, knowledge of God is a *conscious* relation: the subject is not annihilated, does not cease to be a subject, but is purified in order to be more truly a subject, a person, fulfilled in its relation to divine subjectivity. In fact, once again, Lossky has exaggerated a genuine difference into an absolute polarity: especially in his last years, when he was developing a general theory of monotheistic religion, he assimilated Plotinus' views to an 'absorption-mysticism' of the classical Hindu variety.[72] This not uncommon approach to Plotinus has been questioned by one of the foremost British exponents of Neoplatonism, A. H. Armstrong; and, more recently, J. M. Rist has strenuously denied any close parallels between the 'Enneads' and the 'Upanishads'.[73] Yet even Armstrong grants that Plotinus' conception of ecstasy does appear to rule out any awareness of the separateness of subject and object in the experience: there is little room for the idea of encounter. And it is essential to Lossky that the subject should not only know, but *know that he knows* in the fulness of communion with God.[74] Insofar as ecstasy, in the usual sense of an interference with 'normal' personal consciousness, is a part of the ascent to God, it characterises only the earliest stages; and even then, the sense of separateness never disappears.[75] Ecstasy is the issue of a personal act, 'dans laquelle l'être créé cherche à se depasser, en s'ouvrant infiniment aux participations déifiantes',[76] the immediate response to the revealed 'darkness' of God's infinity. It is a state of self-forgetfulness which is the precondition for the subject to be filled with the grace and love of God, the 'kenosis' which precedes exaltation.

The source and end of apophatic theology for Lossky is, therefore, a fully conscious (though non-intellectual) relationship of personal confrontation between man and God in love; and the importance of ἔκστασις in the attainment of this relationship is very great. 'La personne', says Lossky, 'est une sortie de soi-même'.[77] The distinctiveness of man's existence as personal is in this freedom from the determinateness, the mere givenness, of 'nature', in his capacity for – to use an overworked and not very satisfactory term – 'self-transcendence'; in his capacity, we might equally well say, for 'ecstasy'.[78] The person is a reality beyond the bondage of a closed conceptual system; and thus its proper activity is apophasis. Apophasis is not the same thing as ecstasy, but they are intimately connected as two manifestations of that which makes personal reality what it is. When Dionysius speaks of God as 'beyond being', and insists that man, to meet God, must equally go 'beyond being', this presupposes the freedom of the human subject from 'being', understood as the given, determined order of nature. The renunciation of conceptual activity is the renunciation of a world of determined 'essences': Lossky quotes with approval the Cappadocian view that, ultimately, not even finite essences can be exhaustively described by the conceptual analysis of their properties.[79] 'There will always remain an "irrational residue" which escapes analysis and which cannot be expressed in concepts, it is the unknowable depth of things, that which constitutes their true, indefinable essence.' Creation is more than the 'being' which can be expressed in our intellectual constructs, and our awareness of creation is not restricted to these constructs. *A fortiori* then, the human subject and God are 'beyond' the level of manipulable notions. The human person is always subject and never object of rational enquiry, not identifiable with any 'thing' in the world, not reducible to an individual of a certain type.[80] The root of sin is the confusion of personality with individuality, regarding personal being as a bundle of repeatable, natural characteristics deployed by a controlling independent ego which is defined in terms of its opposition to and exclusion of other egos.[81] Strictly and inevitably, this cuts man off from communion with his God, because it denies his freedom to go beyond 'being' or 'nature', it denies what we might call his 'apophatic dimension', and so denies his capacity for encounter with God. To say that

13

God is known only in the ignorance attained on the far side of ecstasy is emphatically not, for Lossky, a speculation about the higher levels of the mystical ascent, peripheral to the central areas of theological discourse: it is the foundation of a whole dogmatic system. If man's last end is θέωσις, the perfection of communion with God, and if this is realised only through the 'ecstatic' self-transcendence of human person, then the capacity for ἔκστασις must be written in to the formulations of Christian anthropology as fundamentally and normatively important. The unity between ascetical and dogmatic theology which Lossky is so eager to recover could hardly be more firmly and rigorously grounded.[82]

Hence theology itself must be ascesis, even crucifixion. This appears most clearly in some passages in *The mystical theology of the Eastern Church* on the trinitarian dogma, 'a cross for human ways of thought',[83] a doctrine which is the most radically inaccessible of all to the speculations of the discursive reason, the most totally given of dogmas. 'The revelation of the Trinity shines out in the Church as a purely religious gift, as the catholic truth above all other'.[84] The trinitarian dogma demands not ratiocination but contemplation, such as is made possible only by the redemptive death and resurrection of Christ, and by the gift of the Holy Spirit, 'the Mystagogue of the apophatic way'.[85] Apophatic theology is an aspect of life in grace: only in the communion of the Spirit does ἔκστασις, openness to fellowship with God, become a reality, because only in the Spirit is man's personal character fully realised.[86] In this sense, apophasis is anything but a decorative importation from the world of Hellenistic religiosity: it is the fruit of the graceful indwelling of the Holy Ghost, the fulfilment of the evangelical commendation of losing one's life in order to save it, a taking-up of the cross to follow Christ.

It is essential for Lossky to stress the role of the cross in this context, since it is in the cross that we see the revelation of what it is that characterises God's personal being, and so also of what is possible for man: the cross reveals personality as 'kenotic'. This is a theme which was to play an increasingly large part in Lossky's later work. For the present, however, I wish to consider it mainly as it finds expression in *The mystical theology of the Eastern Church*. The chapter in that book on 'Image and likeness'[87] establishes personality in man (in the sense already outlined, of free self-transcendence) as constituting the *imago Dei*: the renunciation of existing-for-oneself is man's most authentically personal act and so also man's most *Godlike* act. The following chapter,

'The economy of the Son',[88] then sets out to explain how such an act can be recognised as 'Godlike', in the light of the Incarnation. Christ's incarnate life is apprehended by the believer as the life of God in the flesh; but it is a life of rejection and agony, lived in the total self-renunciation of absolute obedience to the Father.[89] This obedience leads us to see salvation as the common will and act of the *whole* Trinity; and the second person is perfectly manifested to us in a life utterly devoid of selfish, *individual* will: 'This renunciation of his own will is not a choice, or an act, but is so to speak the very being of the persons of the Trinity who have only one will proper to their common nature'.[90] This revelation of humility and self-renunciation in the heart of the Godhead is further confirmed by the 'kenosis' of the Spirit. His work is to witness to the Son while his own person remains hidden: he draws each unique human person in a unique and personal way to the contemplation of and participation in the Godhead imparted to humanity in the Incarnation, but conceals his own person in order to manifest and communicate only what is common to the whole Trinity.[91] Thus the trinitarian dogma proposes a model of personal being which radically challenges the assumptions of the fallen human mind: thought itself must be turned upside down by grace if we are to grasp the mystery in any way. The dogma is 'a cross for human ways of thought' because it demands a belief that the abnegation of self and the absence of self-assertive, self-interested 'individualism' are the fundamental notes of personal existence at its source, in God. In its fallen and encapsulated condition, the individual human subject cannot accept this: only in the life of the Spirit, who transforms the whole of human being, is faith in the trinitarian dogma possible. This faith is not a matter of indifference, of taste or distaste, for the Christian: it is a mark of the transformation accomplished by the Spirit, it is inseparable from soteriology, indeed from anthropology as a whole.[92] The 'apophatic attitude' is the primary expression of trinitarian faith, of the profound disturbance in thinking which is created by the manifestation of God as personally suffering death and the 'abyss of hell'.[93]

All this has important repercussions for other areas of theology, most notably the doctrine of creation. *The mystical theology of the Eastern Church* contains, as I have indicated, quite a developed 'kenotic' interpretation of the Trinity and the Incarnation, but its corollaries are not fully explored in the chapter on 'Created being'.[94] Lossky has a good deal to say about the freedom of God's creative act, and creation as the positing of a new and totally 'other' subject outside of God; and later chapters (especially 'Image and likeness', and 'The economy of the Son') emphasise God's condescension to the liberty, the 'otherness', of man.[95] But this is not linked with the idea of self-renouncing humility in the Trinity. However, when Lossky returns to the question in his last years, the connection is made a little clearer. 'Dieu est sorti, pour ainsi dire, de lui-même, pour créer. Il y a un moment . . . d'une certaine humiliation, d'une kenose; qui est plus grande que cette théologie qui veut toujours être fixée sur la majesté de Dieu.'[96] In creating free personal beings, God voluntarily limits his own omnipotence: there is a sort of *risk* involved, God making himself impotent before man's freedom.[97] The summit of God's exercise of his omnipotence is precisely his abnegation of power over his free creatures. We should note that, here, the language of 'sortie de soi-même' is applied to God: creation is seen as *God's* 'self-transcendence', a 'transcendence of transcendence'.[98] However, as Lossky never follows Dionysius to the extent of speaking directly of God's ἔκστασις,[99] presumably because he connects ἔκστασις with the salvation of *man* from his selfish individuality, so that the application of such language to God would sound rather misleading, he does adopt Dionysius' view of creation as 'a hierarchy of real analogies', with the extension of this by Maximus into a theory of the 'divine ideas' as the creative λόγοι of the divine λόγος; and in his lectures he further enlarges on this by emphasising the dynamic character of the λόγοι, and pointing out that the notion of λόγος itself implies a kind of 'sortie de soi-même' of the subject.[100] Thus the divine ideas, so frequently associated with a static, 'essentialist' cosmology, a world of eternally determined substances, come to be seen as a further expression of the creative, personal outgoing of God.

IV

This examination of Lossky's conception of the nature and function of apophatic theology suggests several considerations about the method, presuppositions and concerns of his theology as a whole. In the first place, it is clear that Lossky's theological thought evolved out of a 'dialogue' with the Fathers in the context of a conscientious and scholarly investigation of the history of Christian spirituality. It is not a byproduct of his scholarly activity, however; several of his articles are fairly clearly written to provide a historical grounding for various theological theses. His aim is, it seems, to discover the criteria within the tradition, even within a particular writer's work, by which deviations and distortions can be recognised as such. Thus, for example, he does not criticise Origen so much for having failed to Christianise his Hellenism as for initiating such a process and failing to carry it through consistently. Origen introduces the biblical ἀγάπη into his Platonic world, and comments with depth and perception on the work and words of the Incarnate God, yet fails to see that this subverts and renders ultimately untenable his spiritualist and intellectualist ideas of salvation. It is when we see the more complete baptism of Hellenism in the Cappadocians, Dionysius, and the Byzantines that we discover wherein Origen – or Clement, or Evagrius – fails. The criticism is in terms of the tradition itself as a living and developing reality.[101] Lossky is attempting to identify a *via media* in the tradition, which is sensitive to the concern expressed in and exaggerated by distorted statements, and applies the same basic principles as do such distortions with greater clarity and fidelity, so that an authentically and peculiarly Christian synthesis develops. The synthesis comprising Irenaeus, the Cappadocians, Dionysius, Maximus, Symeon the New Theologian, and Palamas does not reject the whole of the theology of Clement, Origen, the Antiochenes, and Evagrius, but sets their true insights in a more precise and more comprehensive and balanced scheme. This search for a *via media* is not, therefore, an attempt to force a system out of recalcitrant and not very homogeneous material, but is, far more, a historian's essay in identifying what it is that gives a group of very diverse thinkers at various periods such homogeneity as they have, and in assessing how successfully various of them balance fidelity with 'creative reinterpretation', and assimilate material from outside the tradition. Thus the Eastern spiritual and theological tradition cannot legitimately be criticised on points of *detail* by the Western: as Lossky makes perfectly plain in the introduction to *The mystical theology of the Eastern Church*,[102] the two must confront each other as systematic and consistent *units*, alternative Christian world-views.

However, Lossky obviously does not imagine that the historical position of equilibrium which he identifies can simply be adopted, more or less unaltered, for use at the present time. It is an indispensable foundation for dogmatics, the clarification of a language and the definitive exclusion of certain options: theology cannot go behind the Fathers, cannot attempt to reconstruct *ab ovo* this groundwork, but it must go beyond them. Hence Lossky is able to develop his emphasis on personal encounter in the knowledge of God in a way which at times seems consciously and deliberately to echo philosophers like Sartre. My purpose in this article has been to trace the connections between Lossky's interpretation of apophatic theology as a historical phenomenon and his use of it in the construction of his own system: the connections are real, but they are, indisputably, subtle and complicated, and it is clear that there is a move from the purely historical to the dogmatic at many unexpected points. It is hard to draw a line between the two levels: what seems like arbitrary or over-schematic exegesis on a historical plane may, arguably, be a legitimate hermeneutical contribution to a dogmatic theology, so that the criteria by which Origen is excluded from and Gregory of Nyssa included in an 'orthodox mainstream' are far from straightforward. The whole idea of a coherent orthodox tradition is one that is neither purely historical nor purely theological: hence our problems with Lossky's judgments. Similar problems arise with several theological themes in Lossky's work; the question constantly recurs of how it can be confidently asserted that a certain point of view is faithful to 'what the Fathers really meant'. Sometimes, indeed, it is possible to see how Lossky has grasped the inner logic of his patristic data in an unusual and valuable way (much of the material discussed in this paper shows, I believe, an insight of this kind). Yet the question obstinately remains of how far the foreshortening of historical perspective can go before it becomes sheer distortion, ignoring real ambiguities, differentations, and developments in the tradition. These are issues which any consciously traditionalist theology must face, and Lossky does not emulate Florovsky in developing a philosophically systematic defence of his position,[103] so that the student of Lossky is obliged to be alert to unresolved puzzles in Lossky's attitudes to some points in patristic thought, as also in his attitudes to Western Christendom.

The final point which emerges from this survey is the remarkable degree to which Lossky's system is *unified*; no one area can be revised without the whole structure being called in question. A certain approach to the knowledge of God is demanded by a certain approach to anthropology and soteriology, which is in turn grounded in a particular understanding of the Incarnation, which itself implies a certain kind of trinitarian doctrine. The unifying theme is what might be called 'personalism': admittedly a rather vague term, which I use to indicate that the central and controlling idea of the system is that of the personal subject in the context of its relations with other subjects. In theology, it expresses a view which locates all dogmatic construction and reflection in the context of living personal experience, encounter with the personal God, in the Christian community. My contention in this paper has been that an understanding of Lossky's 'personalism' requires an appreciation of the fundamental importance for him of apophasis, regarded as the expression of the foundation of all theology in the 'self-revelation of God in silence', the meeting of human and divine persons in a direct confrontation that does not require the mediation of any image or concept. At the heart of his theology lies the denial that the essence of Christian belief can be stated in terms of precise logical categories – not that he favours irrationalism or incoherence, as is evident from the rigour and consistency of his work; but he sees the ultimate consistency of belief in the 'personal consistency' of man's response to God and fidelity to God within Christian tradition and Christian community. Theology rests upon God's self-giving in revelation: man is called to 'mirror' this in his ἔκστασις, his exercise of the faculty of 'self-transcendence' which constitutes him as personal. And so one of the primary tasks of theology is to expound how it is that man is capable of thus reflecting God's act.

If we are to speak in terms of a theology for which ἀπόφασις, ἔκστασις, and κένωσις are determinative ideas, we must ground this in a serious consideration of the well-worn theme of God's image in man. One of Lossky's major contributions to dogmatic theology is his remarkably fresh and suggestive treatment of this subject, seeing man as *imago trinitatis* not in virtue of the structure of his interiority, but because of his capacity for 'kenotic' relationship with his fellows. But that is matter enough for another and a long paper. My hope is that these pages may have shown Lossky's theological seriousness and significance to be far greater than might be thought from the limited extent of his published writings. As can be clearly seen, there is much in his work for those struggling to achieve some kind of rapprochement between systematic theology and what is so inadequately called 'spirituality'; and that in itself may be commendation enough.

Notes

1. Vladimir Lossky, 'Otritsatelnoe bogoslovie v uchenii Dionisiya Areopagita' ('Negative theology in the teaching of Dionysius the Areopagite'), *Seminarium Kondakovianum* 3 (1929), 135–44; French translation in *Revue des sciences philosophiques et théologiques* 28 (1936), 204ff.

2. See, e.g., Vladimir Lossky, *The mystical theology of the Eastern Church* (London: James Clarke, 1957), 38–9; 'Théologie négative dans le pensée de Saint Augustin', in *Augustinus magister* I, Supplement of *L'année théologique Augustinienne* (Paris: Études Augustiniennes, 1954), 575–81; 'Ténèbre et lumière dans la connaissance de Dieu', in *A l'image et à la resemblance de Dieu* (Paris: Aubier-Montagne, 1967), 32–3 (cf. the English translation, 'Darkness and light in the knowledge of God', in *In the image and likeness of God* (New York: St Vladimir's Seminary, 1974), 31–44). Cf. Gregory Palamas, *Triads* 1.3.19.

3. E.g., Vladimir Lossky, 'Théologie dogmatique A', *Messager de l'exarchat du patriarche russe en Europe occidentale* 46–7 (1964), 88–9.

4. And, to a greater extent than Lossky might have cared to admit, the conventional *Eastern* view: see, e.g., Timothy Ware, *The Orthodox Church* (London: Penguin, 1963), 217; G. Habra, 'La significance de la transfiguration dans la théologie Byzantine', *Collectanea cisterciensia* 25 (1963), 119; and, for an insistence that apophatic theology be seen as 'corrective' rather than 'programmatic', see T. Stylianopoulos, 'New theology and the Orthodox tradition', *Saint Vladimir's theological quarterly* 14 (1970), 136–54, esp. 139.

5. Lossky, *The mystical theology of the Eastern Church*, 26–7; 'La notion des "Analogies" chez Denys le pseudo-Areopagite', *Archives d'histoire doctrinale et littéraire du moyen-age* 5 (1931), 279–309; 'L'apophase et la théologie trinitaire', in *A l'image*, 20 (cf. the English translation, 'Apophasis and Trinitarian theology', in *In the image and likeness of God*, 13–31); see also *Théologie négative et connaissance de Dieu chez Maître Eckhart* (Paris: J. Vrin, 1960), 37–9.

6. Lossky, *The mystical theology of the Eastern Church*, 37–9, 42, 238–9; 'L'apophase et la théologie trinitaire', 7; 'Théologie dogmatique A', 85–8.

7. Lossky, *The mystical theology of the Eastern Church*, 42, 231–2; 'Foi et théologie', *Contacts: revue trimestrielle de l'Orthodoxie française* 31 (1961), 163–76.

8. Lossky, 'Théologie négative dans le pensée de Saint Augustin', 575; cf. 'L'apophase et la théologie trinitaire', 7–8.

9. Lossky, 'Théologie négative dans le pensée de Saint Augustin', 575–6; cf. 'L'apophase et la théologie trinitaire', 8; 'La notion des "Analogies"', 280–1; *The mystical theology of the Eastern Church*, 25; cf. 'Foi et théologie', 163–76.

10. Lossky, *Théologie négative et connaissance de Dieu chez Maître Eckhart*, 23; 'Théologie négative dans le pensée de Saint Augustin', 575.

11. Lossky, 'Théologie négative dans le pensée de Saint Augustin', 567–70; see also the admirable essay of J. Anderson, *St Augustine and being* (The Hague: M. Nijhoff, 1965), esp. 5–8 and 35ff.

12. Augustine, *Confessions* IX.10; Lossky, 'Théologie négative dans le pensée de Saint Augustin', 580–1; on the expression *docta ignorantia*, see 578, esp. the reference to Ep. 130.

13. Lossky, *The mystical theology of the Eastern Church*, 25. See Augustine, *Confessions* (London: Penguin, 1961), 198, my emphasis.

14. Lossky, 'Théologie négative dans le pensée de Saint Augustin', 575; 'Ténèbre et lumière', 32, 37.

15. 'Beyond affirmation and negation', as Dionysius says in *Mystical theology*, V (*PG* 3, 1048AB).

16. Lossky, 'Ténèbre et lumière', 33; 'L'apophase et la théologie trinitaire', 20; 'Théologie négative dans le pensée de Saint Augustin', 575; 'La notion des "Analogies"', 281–2; 'La théologie de la lumière chez St Grégoire Palamas', in *A l'image*, 47 (cf. the English translation, 'The theology of light in the thought of St Gregory Palamas', in *In the image and likeness of God*, 45–70).

17. Edith Stein, 'The knowledge of God', in *Writings of Edith Stein* (Westminster: Newman, 1956), 95 – an exceptionally illuminating introduction to Dionysius. Cf. Lossky, 'Foi et théologie', 163; *The mystical theology of the Eastern Church*, 25; Palamas, *Triads* 1.3.19; 2.3.26.

18. Lossky, *Théologie négative et connaissance de Dieu chez Maître Eckhart*, 38; cf. 'Otritsatelnoe bogoslovie', 139.

19. Lossky, 'Ténèbre et lumière', 34–5; 'La notion des "Analogies"', 283; *The mystical theology of the Eastern Church*, 43 and ch. 3, esp. 49–51, etc.

20. Lossky, 'Otritsatelnoe bogoslovie', 133–4; cf. Clement, *Strom.* 1.V.xi.

21. Lossky, 'Otritsatelnoe bogoslovie', 137, esp. n. 34; cf. 'La notion des "Analogies"', 281–2.

22. Vladimir Lossky, *The vision of God* (London: Faith, 1963); 'L'apophase et la théologie trinitaire' (c. 1953?), 'Ténèbre et lumière' (1952) and 'La théologie de la lumière' (1945), in *A l'image*; cf. 'Otritsatelnoe bogoslovie', 133–4; *The mystical theology of the Eastern Church*, 30–3, 37–8; 'Théologie dogmatique A', 8–9.

23. In *Mystical theology* V (*PG* 3, 1048A), Dionysius says that God is οὐδὲ ἕν, οὐδὲ ἑνότης; cf. *The mystical theology of the Eastern Church*, 30–1.

24. Lossky, 'L'apophase et la théologie trinitaire', 11–16; *The vision of God*, 39–46.

25. Lossky, 'L'apophase et la théologie trinitaire', 16.

26. Lossky, *The vision of God*, 49; cf. 'La théologie de l'image', in *A l'image*, 123–37, esp. 135–7, translated as 'The theology of the image', in *In the image and likeness of God*, 125–40; 'Théologie dogmatique B', *Messager de l'exarchat du patriarche russe en Europe occidentale* 48 (1965), 218–33, esp. 225–6. Lossky is inclined to minimise Origen's subordinationism; see *The vision of God*, 53–4.

27. Lossky, *The vision of God*, 54–6.

28. Lossky, 'Otritsatelnoe bogoslovie', 133–4; *The mystical theology of the Eastern Church*, 32.

29. Lossky, *The mystical theology of the Eastern Church*, 42.

30. Lossky, *The vision of God*, 56, referring to Origen's description of the earthly paradise as *locus eruditionis* and *auditorium vel scola animarum* (*PG* 11, 246A); Lossky agrees with Puech and Lieske against Völker on the question of the eternity of distinct personal consciousness in Origen's system on the grounds that his intellectualist view of beatitude demands an eternally distinct subject (*The vision of God*, 52–3).

31. Lossky, 'La problème de la "vision face à face" et la tradition patristique de Byzance', *Studia Patristica* 2 (1957), 512–37.

32. Lossky, *The vision of God*, 88–9.

33. Ibid., 89, cf. 68–70; 'Ténèbre et lumière', 30. Polycarp Sherwood, discussing *The vision of God* in 'Glorianter vultum tuum, Christe Deus', *St Vladimir's Theological Quarterly* 10 (1966), 195–203, actually considers that

Lossky underrates the ambiguities of Evagrius' scheme, but excuses him on the grounds that he was writing before Guillaumont's publication of the complete version of Evagrius' *Centuries*.

34. Lossky, *The vision of God*, 90; 'Ténèbre et lumière', 30.

35. Lossky, 'La problème de la "vision face à face"', 526.

36. Jean Daniélou, in his introduction to *La vie de Moïse*, *Sources Chrétiennes* I bis (1942) XV.

37. H.-Ch. Puech, 'La ténèbre mystique chez le pseudo-Denys l'Areopagite et dans la tradition patristique', *Etudes Carmélitaines* 23 (1938), 33–53; Daniélou, introduction to *La vie de Moïse*, xix; cf. his *Platonisme et théologie mystique* (Paris: Editions Montaigne, 1944), 291–307.

38. Lossky, *The vision of God*, ch. 2.

39. Ibid., 74; 'Ténèbre et lumière', 31.

40. Lossky, *The vision of God*, 26, referring esp. to 1 Cor. 8.2–3.

41. Ibid., 53–4.

42. Ibid., 68.

43. Ps-Dionysius, *Mystical theology* I.1 (*PG* 3, 997); *The divine names* XIII.3 (*PG* 3, 981A); cf. Lossky, 'L'apophase et la théologie trinitaire', 20–1; *The mystical theology of the Eastern Church*, 31; *The vision of God*, 101.

44. Lossky, 'L'apophase et la théologie trinitaire', 23.

45. Ibid., 20, 22; *The mystical theology of the Eastern Church*, 44.

46. From an unpublished lecture delivered by Lossky on 24 November 1955; transcript collected by A. M. Allchin.

47. Ps-Dionysius, *The divine names* I.4 (*PG* 3, 592C).

48. Lossky, *The vision of God*, 103–4; 'La problème de la "vision face à face"', 533.

49. Lossky, *The vision of God*, ch. 5; on the Antiochenes, see esp. 76–80.

50. Ibid., 104.

51. Ibid., ch. 9.

52. Ibid., 20; on Vasquez in particular, see esp. 12–14; cf. 'La problème de la "vision face à face"', 513–16.

53. Lossky, *The vision of God*, 125; cf. 'La théologie de la lumière', 39–40. See also the articles by Martin Jugie on Palamas and the Palamite controversy in the *Dictionnaire de théologie catholique* (Paris: Letouzey et Ané, 1909–1950), vol. 11.

54. Lossky, 'La théologie de la lumière', 48, 50–2.

55. See, e.g., *De vita Moysis* (*PG* 44, 300D; *Sources Chrétiennes*, I bis (1942), 3), 'Ἐπὶ δὲ τῆς ἀρετῆς παρὰ τοῦ Ἀποστόλου ἕνα τελειότητος ὅρον ἐμάθομεν, τὸ μὴ ἔχειν αὐτὴν ὅρον.' On ἐπέκτασις as a theological concept original to Gregory, see Daniélou, *Platonisme et théologie mystique*, 291–307; note the connection suggested with Paul's use of ἐπεκτείνω in Phil. 3.13.

56. Danielou, *Platonisme et théologie mystique*, 225, 229.

57. Though see Vladimir Lossky, 'La notion théologique de la personne humaine', in *A l'image*, 117–18 (cf. the English translation, 'The theological notion of the human person', in *In the image and likeness of God*, 111–24).

58. Lossky, 'Otritsatelnoe bogoslovie', 144; 'Ténèbre et lumière', 35–6; 'La problème de la "vision face à face"', 533; *The vision of God*, 103; see Ps-Dionysius, *The divine names* I.4 (*PG* 3, 592C).

59. See esp. Ps-Dionysius, *The divine names* II.3 (*PG* 3, 646BC); cf. Lossky, 'La notion des "Analogies"', 282–3.

60. Ps-Dionysius, *The divine names* XIII.3 (*PG* 3, 981A).

61. Ibid., 980D.

62. Lossky, 'L'apophase et la théologie trinitaire', 9.

63. Cf. e.g., Lossky, *The vision of God*, 66.

64. Gregory of Nyssa, *Quod non sint tres dei* (*PG* 45, 133B–136).

65. Lossky, 'Otritsatelnoe bogoslovie', 137, n. 34.

66. Ibid., 142; cf. 'La notion des "Analogies"', passim.

67. Lossky, 'Otritsatelnoe bogoslovie', 136, 142, 145–6; 'La notion des "Analogies"', 286.

68. As Lossky, *The vision of God*, 104 and 108 suggest.

69. I have attempted a longer discussion in 'The philosophical structures of Palamism', *Eastern Churches review* 9 (1977), 27–44; see also the response by K. T. Ware in the same issue, 45–63.

70. See Plotinus, *Enneads* 5.5.4.8.

71. See Lossky, *The mystical theology of the Eastern Church*, 29–31; 'Théologie dogmatique A', 86.

72. Lossky, 'Théologie dogmatique A', 85. In this text, Lossky expounds his theory of the 'two monotheisms', Platonic-Oriental and Hebraic, the former preoccupied entirely with the divine nature, and so impersonalist, the latter overemphasising the divine personality and the unpredictable character of man's existential meeting with God, at the expense of any idea of the real deification of man's *nature* in union with God's. This scheme is also important in Lossky's analysis of Roman Catholicism and Protestantism.

73. See *The Cambridge history of later Greek and early medieval philosophy*, ed. A. H. Armstrong (Cambridge: Cambridge University Press, 1967), 258–63, and Armstrong's introduction to the Loeb edition of Plotinus (Cambridge, MA: Harvard University Press, 1969), vol. 1, xxvii–xxviii; J. M. Rist, *Plotinus: the road to reality* (Cambridge: Cambridge University Press, 1967), ch. 16, esp. 225–9.

74. See, e.g., Lossky, *The mystical theology of the Eastern Church*, 215–16, 229–30. Here as elsewhere, Lossky's paradigm case of ecstasy is the transfiguration of St Seraphim of Sarov during a conversation with Motovilov, his disciple.

75. Ibid., 208–9, 229–31, 68–9.

76. Lossky, 'Ténèbre et lumière', 31–2, referring to Gregory of Nyssa; but see also *The mystical theology of the Eastern Church*, 208, on the characteristic *passivity* of 'ecstatic' states.

77. From an unpublished lecture delivered by Lossky on 8 March 1956, transcript collected by A. M. Allchin.

78. See, e.g., Lossky, *The mystical theology of the Eastern Church*, 122.

79. Ibid., 33.

80. See, e.g., ibid., 53–4; *A l'image*, 115–16, 185–6; 'Théologie dogmatique A', 96–7.

81. Lossky, *The mystical theology of the Eastern Church*, 121–2.

82. Ibid., ch. 1.

83. Ibid., 66 and ch. 3.

84. Ibid., 66; cf. *A l'image*, 75–6, 83–5.

85. Lossky, *The mystical theology of the Eastern Church*, 66, 239.

86. Ibid., chs 8 and 9; cf. 'Rédemption et déification' and 'La tradition et les traditions', in *A l'image*, 95–106, 139–66 (cf. the English translations, 'Redemption and deification' and 'Tradition and traditions', in *In the image and likeness of God*, 97–110, 141–68).

87. Lossky, *The mystical theology of the Eastern Church*, 114–34.

88. Ibid., 135–55.

89. Ibid., 144–5.

90. Ibid., 144.

91. Ibid., ch. 8, esp. 168–70.

92. Ibid., 238.

93. Ibid., 66.

94. Ibid., 91–113.

95. Ibid., 92–3, 114–34.

96. From an unpublished lecture delivered by Lossky on 12 January 1956, transcript collected by A. M. Allchin.

97. Lossky, 'Théologie dogmatique B', 229.

98. In unpublished lectures delivered by Lossky on 17 and 24 November 1955 and 25 October 1956; transcripts collected by A. M. Allchin. Note also that von Balthasar draws attention to Maximus' understanding of the revelation of omnipotence in kenosis in *Liturgie cosmique: Maxime le Confesseur* (Paris: Éditions Montaigne, 1947), 191–2; this French translation of the first German edition was the version used by Lossky.

99. See Ps-Dionysius, *The divine names* IV.13 (*PG* 3, 712AB); cf. Walter Völker, *Kontemplation und Ekstase bei pseudo-Dionys der Areopagit* (Wiesbaden: F. Steiner, 1958), 202: 'Diese "Ekstase" Gottes mutet schließlich wie ein Spezialfall eines Grundgesetzes an ... wobei Ekstase wiederum das Aus-sich-Heraustreten bedeutet.'

100. From an unpublished lecture delivered by Lossky on 12 January 1956, transcript collected by A. M. Allchin; cf. *The mystical theology of the Eastern Church*, 94–100.

101. There is something of a contrast here with Georges Florovsky's critique of Origenism (see, e.g., 'Protivorechiya Origenizma' ('The contradictions of Origenism'), *Put'* 18 (1929), 107–15) which is cast in more general and schematic theologico-philosophical language.

102. Lossky, *The mystical theology of the Eastern Church*, 7–22, esp. 11–14, 21–2.

103. See, for instance, the final chapter of Florovsky's *Puti Russkago Bogoslovija* (Pathways in Russian Theology) (Paris, 1937) and 'The predicament of the Christian historian', in W. Leibrecht (ed.), *Religion and culture: essays in honour of Paul Tillich* (New York: Harper and Bros, 1959), 140–66.

2

Hegel and the gods of postmodernity

As this ludicrously ambitious title indicates, I shall be offering no more than a sketch for an argument which I hope may turn out to be worth pursuing more carefully; an argument which attempts to identify an area of ambiguity in certain kinds of theological reception of Derridean themes, and to raise, yet again, the overworked spectre of Hegel in order to question and explore this ambiguity. My attention will be directed not so much to the primary texts of deconstruction as to certain discussions of their problematic by writers in theology and religious studies; but my final aim is to raise an issue for some of the rhetoric of postmodern performance itself.

I

Briefly then: in spite of Derrida's disclaimers, it has proved very hard for religious writers *not* to read the language of trace and *différance* as a negative theology. For Derrida himself, it is reasonably clear that 'God' is an 'effect of the trace': to speak of God is to try to put a face upon that which haunts language – what is over the shoulder, round the corner, what is by stipulation not capable of being confronted, being *faced*. Thus to speak of God is to try and erase the genuine trace; and negative theology (like the negativity of all dialectic) simply affirms the possibility of a state devoid of this haunting, since it *identifies* trace and *différance* with a kind of subject, with what is ultimately, despite all theological evasions, presence. However, the response of a good many writers (J. D. Crossan,[1] John Caputo,[2] and Kevin Hart,[3] among others) has been to say, in effect, that Derrida has assumed too hastily that negative theology is a merely dialectical move in an unreconstructed metaphysical (or, if you insist, onto-theological) framework. Negative theology, as practised by an Eckhart or a John of the Cross, is a prohibition against *any* thematizing of divine presence, any ultimate

25

return to an analogy of being between God and the subject. Kevin Hart, in particular, at the end of his admirably clear study, suggests that a negative theology that has learned its proper task under Derridean probing is the only thing capable of stopping theology's constant and compulsive sliding back towards a metaphysic of presence.

Hart and Caputo – and I think Joseph O'Leary[4] as well – repudiate a theology of divine presence but seem eager to hold to a theology of divine *grace*. Other theological or quasi-theological receptions of Derrida evidently see this as a failure to understand the seriousness of Derrida's challenge. Cupitt's reading of Derrida[5] supports what still appears as a powerfully voluntarist account of the speaker's confrontation with the world, and pays little attention to the question of trace; since nothing in Cupitt's writing can be put down to carelessness, we must suppose that this is a conscious strategy to block any attempt at slipping an 'objective' God in through the back door of the *via negativa*. In other words, he rejects in advance the retrieval and radicalization of negative theology by Caputo, Hart and others. Mark Taylor, on the other hand, has tackled the question directly, and – notably in his *Tears*[6] – developed an aesthetic of 'non-absent absence' (Blanchot's term), the inscription (not representation) of *différance* in a manner which does in some sense make of *différance* an occasion of 'grace'. The art of 'non-absent absence' is the art of the sacred; taking the sacred to be the interruption of ordinary 'exchange', 'the circulation of knowledge'.[7] Thus, for art to be grace-full, it must *defer* presence; which means deferring, indefinitely, the end of time, and thus dissolving time as *a* system or *a* story. In Taylor's own idiom, his a/theology is 'anachronistic': it is the refusal alike of origins and ends. The grace or gift of art, what it is that locates this or that work in the arena of the sacred, is an overthrowing of the normally prevailing alliance of time and understanding. Time as history is spoken of as a linear movement; it cannot avoid the suggestion of ends, and so of *parousia*, the manifestation of what's hidden. It is thus appropriately bracketed with understanding, whose task is 'reducing difference to identity and returning otherness to same'.[8] The sacred interrupts as 'Absolute Paradox' (Taylor is here working through Kierkegaard's *Philosophical fragments*); yet, although it is a rupture it is also the desire of understanding itself. Language wills its own downfall: this is what it is to say with Derrida that language itself announces the non-originary origin, *différance* as such, that without which (only it is not an 'it' or a 'that') there would be no speech.

What interests me in all this is the clarity with which the sacred, the order of grace or liberation, is assimilated to absence, rupture. Taylor is more consistent here than the negative theologians, for whom some sort of gracing agency seems still to be in the background: for Taylor, who is here, I think, profoundly faithful to Derrida, grace can only be the effect of the irruption, both unpredictable and unavoidable, of the empty purity of *différance* 'surrounding' the practice of speech. For Derrida, of course, it is *writing itself* that irrupts, breaks through the presence of the spoken word. There are no *words* of grace, except in so far as the writer or, for Taylor, artist deploys signs in the direction of the saving absence, the trace; nor can there be a narrative of grace, since the holy is the timeless – not simply the *discontinuous* in time, but the pure negation of successiveness as such, chronological successiveness and the 'succession' of thinking and speaking. There is the world of exchange, in which (to pursue the figure of 'exchange') utterances are convertible, in that they provide material for a hearer's or reader's utterance in response; and there is pure, unanswerable 'tearing'. (I suspect that 'exchange' is being given more malign connotations as well, in terms of the endless substitutability of signs in an advanced credit economy.) It is hard to avoid the conclusion that the exchange of language, as a communal and temporal practice, is necessarily an extinguishing of true or final otherness: the otherness of linguistic intercourse inevitably falls under the condemnations of totalizing dialectic, the other becoming *my* other, defined in relation to my (self-)presence, a resolvable, confrontable difference. And this in turn bears out Peter Hodgson's judgement in a recent book[9] that the theology or a/theology of postmodernism is fundamentally tragic and ironic: it leaves the speaker and what speech cannot master eternally divided. Writing/art remembers what speech forgets, precisely by *dis*membering (the idiom is infectious) direct utterance, speech coming from a tangible source. It 'reminds' speech of its contingency, of the illusoriness of presence, transparency, authorship/authority.

Writing for Derrida, the art of dismemberment and silence for Taylor, are occasions of grace presumably because they constitute an end to illusion by locating language vis-à-vis what makes language what it is – which is not a cause or source, an *archē*, but the very fluidity and play of language itself. Direct, 'convertible' utterance conceals this. My question here, chiefly to Taylor but to some extent also to Derrida, is to do with the *pathos* of this model, the pathos of the 'veiled truth', of a diurnal or primitive perception in need of dismantling. A string of dualisms opens up in the background: the intelligible and the mysterious, speech and silence, the inside and the outside, the apparent and the real, the speaking ego and the speechless void, even – dare I evoke it? – spirit and nature. The sacred, the liberative, is here the second set of terms – the ineffable, the outside, the eternal. My anxiety is to do with the relegation to profanity of the temporal, the communicative, the implied devaluation of 'exchange', or, to adapt an idea of Hodgson's, 'followability'. If the sacred is innately alien to 'exchange', the tragic quality of such thinking is not only a matter of abstract dualism between speech and void but also affects the valuation of human corporateness. Take 'exchange' to designate the whole range of *negotiated* human activity, from plain conversation to political activity, all those contexts in which resistance and misunderstanding have to be overcome, concealed interests and agenda drawn out and confronted, the implicit or explicit refusal of a voice to an interlocutor overturned, and a concluding position, not simply determined by one speaker, arrived at; what are the implications of treating this as the primary locus of illusion or unfreedom?

The fear expressed is of totalization: all negotiation moves inexorably towards identity, all exchange presupposes an attainable sameness or equivalence. The otherness of negotiation is, *ex professo*, temporary. What this anxiety underrates, however, is the degree to which the identity towards which negotiation or dialect moves is a construction not simply determined by either of the identities present at the start; it can only be described as '*returning* otherness to same' by a violent abstraction from the fact that this otherness is constituted substantially by the passage of (irreversible) time. Time and understanding do indeed belong together. The suspicion proper to understanding is not directed against the communicative/negotiating process itself but against *specific* distortions and evasions that show themselves in the conduct of the process. The liberation sought for or required is not from a global illusion about linguistic exchange, but from whatever conditions hinder the movement to a jointly accepted mode of continuing. Fear of totality, of the tyranny of identity, would be appropriate if such an accepted 'mode of continuing' were regarded as an end of all negotiation, rather than being itself in turn a negotiable position – i.e. if it were absolutized against possible criticism; it might also be appropriate if each phase of dialectic, each act of negotiating, systematically ignored its location in a history of exchange, believed its positions to have no past, no process of construction. Indeed, such a prior commitment to ahistorical truth would be precisely one of those claims to power that dialectic's business is to dismantle, or at least to put to the test.

II

Which brings me – at last – to Hegel. It is of course true that Hegel believes there to be only one story to tell of the life of the mind (or of followable speech, to give it a less self-condemning designation); but it is emphatically not a story of *return* to the same. His disagreement with Fichte is normally held to turn on this point, and it is what decisively marks him off from Neoplationist thought. Absolute spirit is characterizable as ultimate self-presence, but (despite all the disastrously misleading trails laid by Hegel's philosophy of history) it is at least debatable whether, in the Hegelian system, it could actually make any sense to claim that Absolute Spirit was realizable as the term of any specific historical process.[10] It is possible in Hegel's terms to talk about the term towards which all acts of understanding (all negotiations) intrinsically move – the 'actuality' (as the *Logic* has it)[11] in which concrete presence and intelligible structure are no longer separate in the subject's engagement in the world; in this sense, there is and must be a teleology in reflection. But the *telos* is not *representable* (not present) in the structure of any given historical consciousness or set of consciousnesses, not *a* meaning which a speaker or writer could articulate as a piece of communicable information (no one would need to know it; no one could learn it by being told it as an external state of affairs). Therefore all that is *said* about this *telos* has a necessarily quasi-fictional character: it has the negative force of insisting that we don't take for granted *any* level of dualism between self and world, the perceived and the real, the concept and the 'brute fact', and so on. Derrida complains that the negative moment in Hegel is simply 'contradiction'; the cancelling of what is there, to be cancelled in its turn by the negation of the negation which (re-)establishes identity. But – as Deborah Chaffin has shown in a remarkable essay on Derrida's Hegel[12] – the structure of Hegel's dialectic is meant to challenge the allsufficiency of the polarity of simple identity and simple difference. Reflection does not work with such symmetries, it requires the plain opposition of positive and negative (presence and absence) to be left behind. What is thinkable is so precisely because thinking is not content with the abstraction of mutual exclusivities, but struggles to conceive

29

a structured wholeness nuanced enough to contain what appeared to be contradictories. Once again: time and understanding belong together; language constantly remakes itself in the fact of what is not yet understood, criticizes itself unceasingly. Its problem (if that's the right word) is not a timeless shadow of pure alterity, but the otherness engendered in a temporally shifting situation. To talk here in Derridean fashion of *différance* as such is to say something with only tangential relation to the processes of concept formation as they show themselves in language. What is strange to reason moves around in the field of cognition: we can indeed abstract to the trace of a perpetual shadow (though in so far as this supposes a fundamental contingency in language it misses Hegel's central concerns), but this shadow *can only 'appear'* in the historical process of making (communicable, communal) sense, in the 'following' of discourse.

I am genuinely not sure how far this would represent a model acceptable to Derrida himself; that is, as Chaffin intimates, a very large question.[13] My present interest is to return to the question of God and the sacred in Derrida's theological commentators. Hegel does not use 'the sacred' as a category; but it is perfectly plain that the meaning of 'God' for Hegel is bound up with the making of sense. God is – ultimately – the actuality in which concreteness and intelligibility coincide; the life of God is therefore, in temporal terms, the movement towards that coincidence, the movement towards a kind of action that is the proper consummation, the bringing to sense, of the world's process, the movement towards non-dualistic understanding, the movement towards 'rational' (just and natural) communality, and so on. Grace (not a particularly Hegelian word, I know) is in the making of rational connections, the overcoming of otherness not by reduction to identity but by the labour of discovering what understanding might be adequate to a conflictual and mobile reality without excising or devaluing its detail. Liberation here is liberation from a sterile and reductive adhesion to a fixed perception of fixed states of affairs. The holy, the graceful, is not interruption, the timeless overthrowing of process and purpose, but is inseparable from the labour of making – which is necessarily, for Hegel, the labour of finding: hence its innate and massive *difficulty*, its distance from voluntarist play.

A Hegelian version of negative theology would thus be neither Taylor's a/theology nor a merely conceptual moment in the clarification of ideas about God – 'dialectical' in a rather cheap or trivial sense. It would be a move away from the hope of 'merely conceptual' clarification as such, towards an actuality in which the dualisms of self and world, thought and deed, were sublated. It would be, in more conventional terms, a moral and spiritual dispossession and recreation, inseparable from the process of a corporate making of sense. Seen in these terms, it actually stands rather closer to the negative way of John of the Cross and others (notably also to the definitions of apophatic theology in modern Eastern Christian writers like Lossky[14] and Yannaras[15]) than to the negative graces of art celebrated by Taylor. It seems that both radical and fairly orthodox theological readers of Derrida have too hastily assumed that the 'anachronism' of the Derridean trace is the proper mode of a Christian apophaticism, and that what has to be done to reconcile Derrida with the negative theology he is both fascinated and alienated by is a sharpening of the anti-metaphysical thrust of apophaticism – whether in the direction of a conscious retrieval of Eckhart and Aquinas (as in Caputo) or in the direction of the nameless space of holiness, as in Taylor. But the question remains of whether the negative strain in Christianity – or, indeed, other faiths, including Buddhism – can be read so exclusively as an anti-metaphysical strategy, as opposed to a discipline interwoven with others in a general project of what Hodgson calls 'transfigurative praxis'.

The risk of a negative theology in abstraction, the identification of the sacred with the void, is the purchase it gives to a depoliticized – or even anti-political – aesthetic, in which there is a subtle but unmistakable suggestion that social and linguistic order (as opposed to this or that particular and questionable order) is what we need to be delivered from, and that a particular kind of artistic praxis can so deliver. The 'meaning' which our unillusioning about language offers is the anti-meaning of timelessness, the empty and endless space of pure difference. To revive a question posed many years ago by Gerald Graff,[16] how is this to avoid a basically dishonest rhetoric of risk or cost, 'redescribing resignation as heroism'? Is there a *labour* of the negative here? To turn to Hegel for help in formulating this challenge is not to endorse the Hegelian system in all its ambition and complexity, but only to ask whether certain Hegelian themes may help to undermine a sacralizing of absence and inception at the expense of the work of social meaning. Gillian Rose's comment on the antinomies of sociology has pertinence here: 'If actuality is not thought, then thinking has no social import.'[17] Translated into our present context, this implies that to look for liberation to what is not thought is to misconceive the entire project of human reflection and to bar the way to an authentically critical philosophy.

Hegel's structuring narrative is, of course, that of incarnation – more specifically of incarnation as understood in the Lutheran framework in which the humanity of God incarnate is not a 'picture' of the divine power, but the enacting of divine resource in the poverty, pain and negativity of a life and death which could not by any stretch of the imagination be held up as natural symbols of divine identity. The point, for our purposes, is threefold. Hegel assumes that what we might call the 'interests' of God and the reasoning subject are not alien or in competition: the sacred is our fruition not our annihilation. *But*: the merging of human and divine interest in any kind of static pantheism can only have the effect of dehistoricizing (derationalizing) the human project; there is no identity *yet to be found* in the endless exchanges of speech and understanding. *Thus*: the union of divine and human interest must be affirmed and understood at just that point where the sheer historical vulnerability of the human is most starkly shown, where unfinishedness, tension, the rejection of meaning and community are displayed in the figure of a man simultaneously denied voice and identity by the religious and the political rationalities of his day.[18] To understand the (historical) cross as God's is to understand the negative 'speculatively' – the negative not as absence or mystery but as the denial of human spirituality in oppression, suffering and death. And it is the *concrete* character of the negative here that makes the Hegelian sublation something quite other than a return to the same: we are discussing the historical denials of spirit, the lack of meaning or closure not as a verbal/conceptual aporia but as the denial and death of persons; so that the 'identity' lying beyond can only be a new set of conditions for thought in which the concrete denial of spirit is overcome. Hence, for Hegel, the nexus linking the cross with the 'spiritual community'.

Whatever is at issue here, it is not the negative as a detour on the road from simple identity to simple identity. The negative, as it appears in the cross, is the destruction of human valuation, and so the collapse of communicative practice itself;[19] more than a formal polarity set against affirmations of presence, etc. In a sense, it is just as much a breach in language, an interruption of exchange, as the 'trace' in Taylor's aesthetic; what is different is that it cannot, in Hegel, stand as a timeless space for the holy. Because it is the negation of the human itself, it demands to be *thought* if the project of communication is to continue. If it is *not* to continue, then, in Hegelian terms, there is no liberation from that partial or pre-reflective or fetishistic practice that turns violently on spirit itself in the negation which the cross represents (and this, incidentally, is why Hegel would not be able to see the Shoah as a *unique* interruption of the project of spirit, or as a kind of ontological barrier to the possibility of communicative practice; what would have to be said here is, of course, authoritatively opened up in Edith Wyschogrod's *Spirit in ashes*).[20]

So I am reluctant to settle too rapidly for a theological retrieval of negative theology along Derridean lines. I am suspicious of the sacred as the void. In so far as the Derridean critique of dialectical negation warns us of the dangers of a glib historicism – such as Hegel's rhetoric does not always avoid – and a reduction of the apophatic dimension to a play of concepts, it is of crucial significance. If we are steered away from a metaphysics of anthropomorphic divine subjectivity and recalled to the recognition that the God of Christian theology is not *an* agent among agents, well and good. If we learn to look warily at systematic claims to overcome the plural and conflictual character of our speech and world, we shall have profited. But I am left with my questions: does the Derridean construal of the arbitrariness or contingency of communication actually do justice to the linguistic essence of the human and so to the bodily constraints on what is sayable? And does such a construal remove from language its critical and liberative possibilities? Is 'exchange' profane? Postmodern theological receptions of this problematic seem to suggest so; but my aim has been to invoke Hegel's shade to help put the question of whether this in fact dissolves the complex differentiations of a religious tradition committed to both divine liberty and divine 'commitment' to a historical life and a social practice, whose mark of godliness is self-critical vigilance (what used to be called repentance, I think).

Notes

1. J. D. Crossan, 'Difference and divinity', *Semeia* 23 (1982), 29–40. Crossan distinguishes negative theology, 'conceived as a simple alternative strategy within ontotheology', from an apophaticism genuinely marginal to the mainstream of theological metaphysics – a refusal of the questions, not only of the answers, of that tradition, which is properly comparable to Derridean *différance* (38–9).

2. John Caputo, 'Mysticism and transgression: Derrida and Meister Eckhart', in Hugh J. Silverman (ed.), *Derrida and deconstruction* (London: Routledge,

1989), 24–39, suggesting that Eckhart's apparent 'metaphysics of the one' is not an ontological claim but 'just a way of making the prevailing onto-theo-logic tremble' (38). The aim is the mind's dispossession, not a new *theory*. Cf. Caputo's earlier studies, *The mystical element in Heidegger's thought* (New York: Fordham University Press, 1986) and *Radical hermeneutics* (Bloomington: Indiana University Press, 1987).

3. Kevin Hart, *The trespass of the sign* (Cambridge: Cambridge University Press, 1989), esp. §III.

4. Joseph O'Leary, *Questioning back* (Minneapolis: Winstan, 1985), a very important attempt to bring Augustine into the discussion.

5. Especially in Don Cupitt, *The long-legged fly* (London: SCM Press, 1987) and *The new Christian ethics* (London: SCM Press, 1988), where the intense insistence on the *creation* of values seems still to slip towards the idea of a voluntary imposing (individual or corporate) of meaning on the Void which is at least as much post-Kantian as postmodern.

6. Mark C. Taylor, *Tears* (Albany: SUNY, 1990).

7. Ibid., 119.

8. Ibid., 182.

9. Peter Hodgson, *God in history* (Nashville: Abingdon Press, 1989), 88.

10. See, e.g., Charles Taylor, *Hegel* (Cambridge: Cambridge University Press, 1975), ch. 15, esp. 419–21, 426–7.

11. 'Actuality is the unity, become immediate, of essence with existence, or of inward with outward' – *Hegel's Logic* (Oxford: Clarendon Press, 1975), no. 142.

12. Deborah Chaffin, 'Hegel, Derrida and the sign', in Silverman (ed.), *Derrida and deconstruction*, 77–91.

13. Ibid., 83–4, 90–1.

14. Vladimir Lossky, *The mystical theology of the Eastern Church* (London: James Clarke, 1957); see also Tomasz Weclawski, *Zwischen Sprache und Schweigen* (Munich: Minerva, 1985).

15. Christos Yannaras, *De l'absence et de l'inconnaissance de Dieu* (Paris: Cerf, 1971).

16. Gerald Graff, *Literature against itself* (Chicago: University of Chicago Press, 1979), esp. chs 2–3, and p. 62 on learning to 'redescribe resignation as a form of heroism'.

17. Gillian Rose, *Hegel contra sociology* (Cambridge: Cambridge University Press, 1981), 214.

18. Hegel, *Lectures on the philosophy of religion III: The consummate religion* (Berkeley: University of California Press, 1985), 124–31.

19. Ibid., 130: 'Since the dishonoring of existence has been elevated to a position of highest honor, all the bonds of human corporate life are fundamentally assaulted, shaken and dissolved'; 131: 'everything ethical, everything commonly viewed as having authority was destroyed'.

20. Edith Wyschogrod, *Spirit in ashes* (New Haven: Yale University Press, 1985), esp. 205–11 on the tension between language and violence.

3

Logic and spirit in Hegel

What is difficult in reading Hegel is understanding what (for him) it is to *think*. He will not countenance a splitting of the world into active mind and passive matter, insides and outsides:[1] thought as a process, and thought as something that 'falls upon' a reality otherwise undiscovered. Thinking is what we do; we can't think ourselves not thinking. And if we can't think ourselves not thinking, we can't think ourselves speechless and alone, engaged in or with or by nothing. In Hegelian terms, to think what is nothing but 'identity' is to think nothing – though if we grasp *that*, we shall see that thinking nothing is importantly different from not thinking. This is where Hegel's logic takes off:[2] if, in trying to think what it-is-to-be, we recognise that we are thinking sheer emptiness, we encounter the most primitive of all contradictions, because we cannot think *away* what-it-is-to-be without thinking pure nonsense, yet we cannot think it as such. Shifting out of the purely Hegelian vocabulary, we should have to say that we can't *begin* to think, decide to take up a 'thinking' stance towards something called The World, analysing it into primitive components like essence and predicates. If 'thinking is what we do', thinking is contemporary with our being around in the first place. Yet we cannot think that bare fact of 'being around' without thinking a context for it – which means we cannot think what it is to think *in the abstract*; we think our being and our thinking in their concrete, time-taking actuality. We think in relation to particulars; but we cannot, quite strictly cannot, think particulars simply as particulars, because we can't concretely think a pure self-identity. To think a particular is to think 'this, not that; here, not there; now, not then': to map it on to a conceptual surface by way of exclusions or negations, yet in that act to affirm also its relatedness, its involvement; to move from empty identity, thinkable only as a kind of absence and indeterminacy, to the specific position, this not that, and by way of that 'contradictory' state to arrive at thinking the 'individual' as convergence of the universal and the particular.[3] Thus to think is, ultimately, to step beyond all local determinations of reality, to enter into an infinite relatedness – not to *reflect* or *register* or *acknowledge* an infinite relatedness, but to act as we cannot but act, if our reality truly is what we think it is, if thinking is what we (just) do.

Two of the themes that surface here (and without which we cannot begin to understand Hegel) are, first, that there is no concrete identity that is not 'mediated', i.e. realised and maintained by something other than itself alone, and, second, that really to think what is other is to discover its otherness as implicated in the act of thinking and the thinking implicated in the otherness: more briefly, that to think otherness is to be 'reconciled', to stop seeing what is other as a rival, a competitor with the thinker's reality and so a menace. These two theses are, of course, at heart the same point approached from different perspectives. And their implication, which consistently disturbs Hegel's readers, is that no otherness is unthinkable, that an unthinkable otherness would leave us incapable of thinking ourselves, and so of thinking about thinking – and so of thinking itself. If there is what is not and could not be thought, there would be some sort of life or reality with which consciousness could not be in relation. But what could it *mean* to say this? We should have no word or idea for such a 'reality' (we could not even call a reality what we could not in any way engage with). The idea of an absolute otherness is fundamentally confused.[4] Before we too rapidly conclude that Hegel offers a total and implicitly totalitarian scheme for which nothing is *in principle* inaccessible or indigestible, we need to reflect on what else we could possibly say that isn't nonsense. For Hegel, an otherness that couldn't be thought would not even be a negation, because it would not negate anything that *could* be thought (if it did, it would not be absolutely other; part of its definition would be given, as 'not *x*'). To say that there was thinking *and* . . . whatever, that there was no identity between nature, action, history, law, society or religion and thinking, would be to conclude that thinking is not what we do, and that therefore we cannot think what we are. And, once again, what could that actually mean?[5] We should, of course, note in passing that, within Hegel's framework, thinking and knowing are not opposed to sensation or emotion or love[6] in the crude way that a late twentieth-century reader might suppose; we are talking about the awareness of relation, and the awareness of relatedness as constituting identity. As we shall see, quite a bit can be said about love in this connection.

The comprehensive power of thinking is not a power exercised *on* something *by* something else. In the *Logic*, Hegel, having begun by discussing the nature of 'understanding' (*Verstand*),[7] proceeds to give an account of 'dialectic' in terms of power, which makes it clear that the power in question is essentially the irresistibility of the motion of thought.[8] Because there is no moment of pure, unmediated identity in the actual world, there are no discrete and simple objects for thought to rest in. No perceived reality is stable and self-contained for thinking: Hegel offers some rather weak analogies from physics and (anecdotal) psychology, but his argument is stronger than these might suggest. As the fuller statements of his long treatment of identity and difference in both versions of the *Logic*[9] make clear, the point is that thought is bound to dissolve the finite perception, the isolated object, as such, moving from the level of diversity (a contingent multiplicity of things) to that of complementary opposition: each 'thing' is defined by not being another, lives in and only in the absence of another, and so 'passes over' from being a discrete object to being a moment in a complex movement. Everything is what it is because of what it is not; it is what it is by *excluding* what it is not; being what it is entails exclusion of what is in fact intrinsic to it. Contradiction and collapse: the whole scheme has to be shifted to another level, since the self-identity/exclusion-of-the-other model can't be sustained. Thinking passes through this process as action that realises itself in 'emptying' itself: and its continuity is secured in and by its challenging or denying of itself. And this is why dialectic can be conceived as power, as that which outlives and 'defeats' stable, commonsense perception, not by abolishing it from outside, but by the penetration of its own logic and process.

What is interesting for our purpose is how this analysis of dialectic and power is given by Hegel a clear theological point of reference. Dialectic is what theology means by the power of *God*, just as *Verstand* is what theology means by the goodness of God.[10] *Verstand* says 'Everything can be thought', 'nothing is beyond reconciliation', every percept makes sense in a distinctness, a uniqueness, that is in harmony with an overall environment. It is, as you might say, a doctrine of providence, in that it claims that there can be no such thing as unthinkable contingency. But, as we have seen, thinking the particular in its harmonies, thinking how the particular makes sense, breaks the frame of reference in which we think the particular. God's goodness has to give way to God's power – but to a power which acts only in a kind of self-devastation.

And, says Hegel, the 'speculative' stage to which dialectic finally leads us is what religion has meant by the mystical, which is not, he insists, the fusion of subject and object but the concrete (historical?) unity or continuity or followability of what *Verstand* alone can only think fragmentarily or episodically.[11]

The theology underlying the *Logic* has not perhaps been given its full weight. Hegel here anticipates some of what is said in the *Lectures on the philosophy of religion* about divine predicates:[12] considered as describing different 'qualities' of the divine life, they fall short of actually bringing God into speech because they deal with what look like multiple determinations; and since God is not (as all classical theology agrees) a determinate object, a member of a class, these predicates collapse upon themselves. And if they are interpreted as relating to God's action upon the world, they fall short once again of speaking of God *as God*. The divine predicates cannot express the concrete life of God when they are taken as denoting discrete properties subsisting alongside each other. In the light of this later discussion, what is said in the *Logic* acquires added depth and interest. The *Logic* addresses the fundamental question of what the process of thinking concretely is; and it is Hegel's contention all along – as we have seen – that to think about thinking is to think about, or rather to think *within*, an infinite relatedness, a comprehensive intelligibility. To say, as Hegel effectively does in the *Logic*, that this is to think God and to participate in God, is to acknowledge that a comprehensive and unitary metaphysic is unlikely to be able to dispense (certainly in the Western intellectual tradition) with the term that has historically grounded a trust in the thinkable (and thus reconcilable) character of reality. But when this slightly banal observation has been made, do we simply conclude that the explicit theological reference is window-dressing, concealing an underlying secularism?[13] No; because it is precisely the grammar (including the paradoxes) of classical pre-Cartesian theology that shapes the actual structure of thinking about thinking. To think about thinking must, for Hegel, bring us finally to the point to which theology directs us, to a reality that is determined solely as self-relatedness: the grammar of the God of Augustine, Anselm and Aquinas is the grammar of thought, and without the former the scope of the latter could not be apprehended. The *un*thinkability of God in the tradition, the recognition that discrete predicates are a clumsy vehicle for indicating divine simplicity, is skilfully transmuted by Hegel into the conviction that to think is to think ultimate simplicity, indivisibility and self-relation.

But the way this transmutation is achieved is first, by rethinking the divine predicates dialectically – as in the *Logic* – and second, by rethinking the divine simplicity and self-relatedness in terms of another crucial aspect of the classical Christian tradition, the doctrine of the Trinity, understood (importantly and surprisingly, given some textbook accounts of Hegel) as the elaboration of belief in God as love. To think what is real, in the *Logic*, which is, of course, to think a reconciled totality, is to affirm the thinkable character of contingent particulars, and, precisely in so doing, to think what is not any particular but that which 'holds' the flow of one particular into another. And if the intelligibility of the particular cannot be thought without the transition to 'dialectic' and speculative reconciliation, what we have is a transcription of the doctrine of divine simplicity into the terms of a process – a temporal movement, in one sense, but not anything that could usefully be described as a sequence of happenings; it is, rather, a structure that could only be talked about in the language of temporal sequence, yet *could not be* 'a' series in the world's history, and which certainly could not be talked of as 'happening' in the sense of 'happening to occur'. The time in question is the time of thinking, which is not a series of contingent occurrences. Thus we are pushed at last to say that this structure exists only as self-sufficient, self-related, independent or absolute; that its grammar is that of the word 'God'; but also that this traditional grammar is flawed to the extent that it thinks divine simplicity as the pure negation of complexity and thus thinks the divine predicates in static, discrete or world-dependent ways. What the *Logic* hints at is that, if the divine predicates are thought as they should be, they 'yield' the divine simplicity as a dialectical unity. To think God's goodness only in terms of the orderliness and intelligibility of an endless series of objects is to bind God to a shapeless or contingent multiplicity; yet theology cannot rest in a picture of divine life moulded by an alien, unreconcilable otherness – prime matter, raw indeterminacy. So to think the goodness of God must pass into thinking the independence of God from particular determination, the power of God as Hegel understands it; and that power must in turn be rescued from a mythological, dualist construction (God imposing the divine will on what is alien) and brought to speculative unity. In other words, God's 'Godness', God's difference from the world, is too radical to be expressed by any formulation that rests content with some version of 'God *and* the world', whether it is the world that determines God or God who defeats or overcomes the world. To think the divine self-sufficiency, *aseitas*, is to think away any boundary between God and the world as between two entities; and this, Hegel might argue, is no more than an exegesis of the strict sense of classical theology, God as the *non aliud*.[14]

This, however, cannot be the resting point for Hegel's philosophical transcription of the divine aseity. The inchoate remarks in the *Logic* about theological equivalences are unfinished business insofar as they still speak of God in relation to the world by way of goodness and of power: the 'mystical' resolution remains sketchy. While it is clear that, in terms of the logic expounded,[15] God's relation to the world is nothing other than God's relation to God, the perfect self-relatedness of what Hegel calls 'the Idea', we have not yet fully seen how the attempt to talk of God as God, rather than God in relation to the world, prescribes this conclusion. We can begin, as in the *Logic*, with one kind of talk about God, the interweaving of the grammar of *aseitas* with the classical predicates, but we shall have done no more than establish that, given the traditional language of God (autonomous and self-sufficient) and the world (contingent but intelligible) we cannot think through what we are saying without collapsing the distinction between the two terms in its conventional and unreflective form. However, there is a more basic question to be addressed: is thinking *God-as-such* necessarily to think the form of the dialectic? If not, if the analogies of the *Logic* are all that can be said, there remains an unclarity in the conception of God, a something not reconciled: we are not shown how God and the world must be thought together from the beginning. We have to start again, and show that the end to which the *Logic* has brought us is also the primitive condition for thinking. In short, we cannot be content with starting from 'God and the world': the reconciliation arrived at means that we must think 'back' to the grammar of God, so that God is no longer given as a discrete entity or identity.

God cannot be unmediated self-identity because thinking cannot recognise unmediated identity: and if God cannot be thought, nothing in our thinking holds or anchors trust in unconditional or comprehensive reconciliation. But a God whose identity is mediated *simply* through the world won't do. We have first to think what it is in talking about God and the world that makes God's self-relation and God's relation to the world inseparable: otherwise we remain at the level of master–slave relationship, in which one discrete subject uses another to secure its peace with itself.[16] Nor is God thought if God appears as merely identical with the world's process: this would leave the world with an unmediated identity, and God as non-subjective or pre-subjective reality, and therefore not in the strictest sense thinkable[17] – i.e. God becomes inferior to the thinking mind, something that has to be connected with and reconciled with mind so as to be thought; and the idea of a *universal* 'substance' that is pre-subjective is a nonsense in Hegel's terms, since what is pre-subjective cannot be universal. Hegel's repudiation of charges of pantheism is profoundly serious.

II

And so to the doctrine of the Trinity. It is quite specifically the Christian doctrine of God's triune being that here resolves our aporia in thinking God. The most summary statement of why this is so is to be found in the *Philosophy of nature*,[18] where God is defined as 'the living process of positing His Other, the world, which, comprehended in its divine form is His Son'. But for its elaboration we have, of course, to turn to the *Lectures on the philosophy of religion*. The section on the 'consummate religion'[19] – that is, the religion that is properly related to itself, the religion that is transparent to itself, thinks itself – spells out the inseparability of thinking God and thinking the reconciled consciousness; it also, very importantly, explains why such a religion can only be a historically determined ('positive' or 'revealed') faith. Consciousness is necessarily the recognition of self in the other, and so no individual or timeless subjectivity could be actual, could think itself, the world, or God. To think myself is to discover my identity in the alien givenness of the past, and to think history is to find it in my consciousness (thereby discovering that there is no such reality as a consciousness that is 'privately' mine). Thus the supreme awareness of thinking, thinking reconciliation, God, must be a *historical* discovery or recognition. Yet the recognition issues in something more than mere historical narrative – or rather it must dispossess itself of the positive so as to recover it as the content of thinking. And in terms of the actual process of exposition in the *Philosophy of religion*, this means dealing with the doctrine of the Trinity before proceeding to reflection on the positivity of Jesus Christ, and indeed on the whole realm of createdness: which leads to the full and mature thinking of God, as spirit in community.[20]

We have been led to begin to think what thinking is, and so we are able to say that the condition for thinkable reality is the fundamental 'process, movement, life' of self-differentiation and self-recovery.[21] To speak of this condition 'in itself', to speak of spirit beyond time, God before creation, is in one sense an impossibility, since it is apparently to try to think being without otherness; but in fact the structure of trinitarian doctrine enables us to avoid talking plain nonsense here, because it speaks of an eternal, irreducible being-in-the-other. To try and think the condition for thinkable reality would be a contradiction if God were envisaged as an unmediated identity; but the Christian vision is of a God who is quintessentially and necessarily mediated in a divine selfhood that is simultaneously its own absolute other. And, Hegel concludes,[22] the complete transparency of self in the other that is God's act of being (as 'Father' and 'Son') is what constitutes God as 'Spirit', as living consciousness proceeding into the determinate otherness of the world. 'That this is so is the Holy Spirit itself, or, expressed in the mode of sensibility, it is eternal love.'[23]

The introduction of *love* at this point is likely to be a surprise to the casual reader of Hegel, or, more globally, to a readership disposed to assume that a philosophy of thinking is bound to devalue love. But Hegel's elaboration of how he understands what it is to define God as love makes it clear that his thinking here converges startlingly with an older tradition, represented, for example, by Aquinas' assertion that love is a reciprocal *inhaesio* and *ecstasis*:[24] in the background is Pseudo-Dionysius' account of divine love as ecstasy, being-in-the-other, and Aquinas stresses that this is the love to which the believer must be assimilated. Compare Hegel's words:

> I have my self-consciousness not in myself but in the other. I am satisfied and have peace with myself only in this other – and I am only because I have peace with myself; if I did not have it, then I would be a contradiction that falls to pieces. This other, because it likewise exists outside itself, has its self-consciousness only in me, and both the other and I are only this consciousness of being-outside-ourselves and of our identity; we are only this intuition, feeling, and knowledge of our unity. This is love, and without knowing that love is both a distinguishing and the sublation of the distinction, one speaks emptily of it. This is the simple, eternal idea.[25]

Our thinking, then, is ultimately radical loving: ecstasy, being-outside-ourselves. And it is manifest as such because of the way in which the specific Christian tradition instructs us to think God: prior to any *contingent* otherness in the world, beyond a supposed determinate otherness between 'God' and 'the world' (which, as we have seen, is

42

not really thinkable) God as such, *in se*, is the positing and sublating of 'ideal' otherness. Traditionally,[26] all that can be predicated of the Father can be predicated of the Son, except that the Father stands to the Son in an irreversible relation of origination; yet that origination is necessarily and eternally what it is to be 'Father', and there is no 'remainder' in this relation; *nothing* of the source that is not real and actual in the utterance or positing of the issue, and nothing of that issue that is not the life of the source lived in reflection or response. In scriptural and classical terms, this is what it means to say that God is substantively and necessarily love; and the much misunderstood notion[27] that the Spirit is the mutual love of Father and Son as a subsisting reality functions, among other things, as an affirmation that the relation of Father and Son is not all that is true of the divine life; the 'ecstatic' nature of the divine love exceeds the symmetry of the mutual self-dispossession of Father and Son, in constituting a life productive of infinite otherness and reconciliation. Theologically, the Spirit is what makes possible the extension or repetition of the Father–Son relation for persons within the created order. So, for Hegel, if the pattern of identity-in-the-other constitutes a unity that is living, active, historical, productive, concrete, this establishes a necessary third term in the movement of thinking and of thinkable reality. Thought thinks itself, 'abstractly', thinks the concrete other, its alien but inseparable and necessary partner, and thinks itself ultimately as the productive historical life that issues from living-in-the-other – as the life of the subject in community. And insofar as the community is truly *thought*, it is a life in which reconciliation and freedom are actual:[28] it is 'ethical' life, in which sacred and secular are indistinguishable. What is more, thinking the life of the community in this sense is passing beyond the Enlightenment,[29] which conceives only of an abstract and non-historical reconciliation. The Enlightenment becomes aware of the power of thought *over against* externality, heteronomy, tradition or authority, so that its ideal of freedom remains fundamentally negative. It also is incapable of thinking God except as a determinate other (which is, of course, not *thinking* God at all): its God will either become the abstract and unknown deity of Kantianism or – as a twentieth-century reader is bound to conclude – disappear entirely. Enlightenment thought leaves the gulf open between two possible destinies for the spirit: an 'absolute' freedom that is in fact bondage because it is incapable of enactment in the concrete world, and a subjectivity without content, legislating for itself according to 'private' sensibility.[30] Concrete freedom is the development of selfhood in the otherness of what is given – at every level; and the concluding message of the *Philosophy of religion* lectures is that concrete freedom is unimaginable, unrealisable, if thinking revolts against the triune God, against thought as self-love and self-recovery in the other, against thought as *ecstasis*.

The conclusion to which this points is, in effect, that politics is not thinkable apart from the trinitarian dogma as thought by Hegel. 'Concrete freedom' is the condition in which human selves have understood that they have no unmediated identity, and so (of course) no legitimate interests that are purely private or individual: they recognise the identity of their interests with the 'law' of the community (not necessarily the *de facto* law of a presently existing state).[31] Thought as *ecstasis* dictates the dissolution of any conception of rights as competitive assertion or safeguards against the claims of an alien collectivity, though the perception of rights in such terms is the necessary step away from the tyranny of an illegitimate collective power, the force of a corporate political entity that has not yet been thought or understood. The concrete freedom that lies beyond the Enlightenment assertion of rights 'against' authority is the action that follows on grasping that my welfare or fruition is attainable only in the welfare or fruition of all: I lose my conception of private right so as to negotiate with the otherness of other persons a good neither mine nor theirs. And to do this with understanding, not slipping back into the forms of primitive consciousness in which the otherness of the other is eroded, is the business of free political life – which is the life pointed to by the Christian Church, but conspicuously not realised in its history, since it has been historically guilty of reverting to pre-conscious patterns of power.[32] The Church itself has failed in its trinitarian witness, remaining at the historical point of Jesus' collision with the power of his day: it treats freedom as interior and spiritual, and so offers no reconciliation with the political; it does not understand its own belief in the resurrection and the Holy Spirit.

In the 1831 lectures on the philosophy of religion,[33] Hegel asserts that 'the reversal of consciousness begins' at Calvary. The beginnings of the Church have to do with the discovery of reconciliation, the discovery that freedom is realised on the far side of a dispossession so total that it is now impossible to think of a God who claims the 'right' to be separate from humanity. God repudiates an identity as God-over-against-us, in the fact of creation itself and then, with deepening intensity, in the history of Jesus, who proclaims the kingdom, the presence of God – but does so by proclaiming an absolute interiority; God-with-us can only be thought first as the negation of all external, politico-legal forms as they are historically constituted. This negative proclamation is appropriately consummated (the 1831 lectures add) in a death at the violent hands of external religious and political authority, a death entailing curse and humiliation.[34] The kingdom, in other words, can only appear initially as that which has no place in the 'normally' constituted world: it is first interiority, then death, death without any sanctioning glow of heroism or any consoling sense of resignation to natural mortality. The significance of this is twofold for Hegel. It means both that the life of God comes to its fullness in the world solely by the death, the stripping, of the human – the human, that is, conceived as something solid in itself, as the finite negation or contradiction of the divine, and that human fragility and mortal weakness are not 'outside' God, in the sense that they do not prevent union with God.[35] After Calvary, then, human self-awareness, the human knowledge of humanity as vulnerable and finite, becomes inseparable from awareness of God. If we affirm the human in its frailty as senseless or Godless, as unthinkable, as a reality in and for itself alone, we cannot think God; if we put to death that affirmation of our vulnerable and mortal being as a something-in-itself, we can understand that this weakness is a moment in the life of God. And on this basis the new community is established.

It needs to be emphasised that Hegel sees the possibility of the community of freedom as rooted in a highly specific historical transaction – the violent death of Jesus and the perception of Jesus as the agent or locus of the divine life.[36] Unless it is a tangible historical sequence it cannot be a reality in the world of spirit (since this is not 'another' world to that of history). For thought to lay hold of its own nature, it must think its own dispossession,[37] its emptying-out – otherwise we never get beyond the primitive stage of thinking about two different sorts of *thing*, things that understand and things that are understood. But how is thinking to be 'dispossessed'? For Hegel, the answer is 'Only through a *history* of the emptying-out or bringing to nothing of the fullness of Spirit'; so, only beyond such a history can thinking establish itself, because only in such an event can we definitively lose the pretensions of the individual consciousness. By knowing that the power of the individual consciousness, the mind at home in and with itself over a passive externality, is a fiction, we 'come to ourselves', recognise what life, mind, spirit, speech, reality actually are. In Jesus, the substance of this reality is realised – and it is recognisable as such precisely because it is realised as interiority: it is something at last independent of anything external, anything that is not Spirit. But equally, it is precisely *as interiority* (over against the 'external' order) that it must disappear. The absolute difference between Spirit's reality and what is humanly constructed must be shown not only in the retreat of Spirit into the inner life (as in the preaching of Jesus) but also in the violent repudiation of this interiority by positive, *de facto* authority. In this violence, positive authority displays itself as groundless, as unthinkable: it is what destroys thought. But the thought it destroys is thought isolated (privatised?), thought that cannot think the public sphere, the shared territory of social acts. And thus it is that, in the mutual subversion of positive, unthought externality and the divine as a purely interior or individual reconciliation, the way is cleared for the unillusioned consciousness of 'concrete freedom', and for the *community* of Spirit, the community that lives from the recognition not only that God is 'at hand' in human intellectuality, but that this being-at-hand is manifest in the historical order as a concrete possibility for all humanity, and thus manifest as a community without exclusion or faction in which the negotiation and bonds of social life are given a transfigured valuation.[38]

I said earlier that, for Hegel, an authentic politics was unimaginable without the doctrine of the Trinity, since the doctrine affirmed the impossibility of unmediated identity. What the concluding sections of the *Lectures on the philosophy of religion* further affirm is that the doctrine is not thinkable except through the narrative of incarnation, crucifixion, resurrection and Pentecost. This is not to identify the fundamental structure of thinking with what history happens to throw up, but to understand (as noted above) what it is to *think* history at all – to recognise it as the enactment of the basic human reality, the dispossession and recovery that is mental life. But history would not make this recognition possible if it did not contain the narrative of divine dispossession: the idea of God as ultimate reconciliation is not established

through speculative thinking. This presupposition [of the certainty of real reconciliation] implies the certainty that reconciliation has been accomplished, i.e., it must be represented as something historical, as something that has been accomplished on earth, in [the sphere of] appearance.[39]

So, from the fundamental analysis of mental life as relatedness, we are led first to understand what 'God' means, as the guarantor of the thinkable (reconcilable) nature of our world, and thence to the understanding of divine identity as complete and *inclusive* relation to self (thus dissolving the idea of an 'essential', relationless selfhood or mental/spiritual identity), as Trinity; and finally to the acknowledgment that our history has *already* told us all this, though in ways that have yet to reach full self-consciousness. Scripture and doctrine must be unveiled for what they truly are, and this is the destiny of philosophy.[40]

III

It is not my task here to discuss the 'compatibility' of Hegel's scheme with the traditional self-understanding of Christian doctrine – though it is important to register how very misleading some accounts of the areas of incompatibility can be. To say, for example, that Hegel neglects the tradition of God's perfect self-sufficiency and asserts a simple interdependence of God and the world (perhaps in the style of modern 'process' thought) is a bad misunderstanding. The basic structure of spirit is not dependent on, or a fact in, 'the world': it is what it is, identity, otherness, reconciliation. Because this is what mental life is, we can't think it apart from thinking ourselves; to think it as separate is to fail in thinking-as-such. 'But', we ask impatiently, 'would there be a God if there were not a world?' And Hegel simply refuses us the vocabulary and conceptuality to put such a question intelligibly. Insofar as God is the ungrounded or self-grounded reality without which there is nothing thinkable (and therefore *nothing*, if we seriously understand who and what we are), we can indeed deploy the traditional language of *aseitas*. Yet that reality is such that it refuses to be an object for thought, a life lived 'beyond' us that we can yet talk about. God's 'exceeding' of thought cannot itself be thought or spoken, and, in this regard, Hegel's convergence with Wittgenstein on religion is worth teasing out further.

Similarly, the idea that Hegel reduces the specificity of Christ to a speculative deduction[41] is fundamentally wrong. Necessity, for Hegel, is what history teaches if we think history, not an imposed or intruding destiny leading history by the nose. That the Christ *must* suffer before entering his glory, that this and this alone is the intelligible form that could reveal the kenotic quality of thought and set us free, is precisely

47

what the record of cross and resurrection tells us, and it is what we could not think or structure in advance, because we can't think necessity *forwards* without falling into fantasy. While Hegel's reading of Christ's 'interiority' is quite unsustainable in the light of a more historically acute exegesis, this does not mean that his reading of the gospels was, by the standards of his day, fanciful or irresponsible; and it is a provoking question to wonder how much of his argument could be recast in the light of more recent versions of the original Jesus tradition, whether in terms of apocalyptic national regeneration or of popularised Cynic philosophy.[42]

My chief aim here has been to suggest two substantial points that should make us wary of any once-fashionable minimising of the theological impetus in Hegel. The first is connected to my caveats in the preceding paragraph. To say that Hegel is serious about history is a bit of an epic understatement: for him, history cannot ever be an *adjunct* to thinking. What we understand is what history has made it possible for us to understand; and what we understand is history, the story of mental life – which, for speaking and understanding subjects, is life or reality *tout court*. If Hegel's thought is dominated, as it unmistakably is, by the scriptural narrative, read through the Catholic doctrinal tradition in general and the specifically Lutheran emphasis on the revelatory significance of Christ's dereliction on the cross, it is no use saying that these things are a ladder he simply kicks away, let alone a bit of apologetic window-dressing. Hegel's thinking about thinking is, inexorably, a thinking of a narrative (incarnation and dereliction) and also, as we have seen, of a traditional theological grammar framing the narrative, of power and providence and simplicity. Again and again, his philosophical energy is roused by the unfinished business of both this narrative (the primitive self-consciousness of the Church impeding the freedom it portends) and this grammar (the need to think the divine simplicity in uncompromisingly trinitarian terms).

Second, I want to underline Hegel's commitment to the vision of thought as 'ecstatic' and 'kenotic'. Not enough is normally granted to Hegel's (admittedly tentative and undeveloped) assimilation of the process of thinking to love, understood as the self's being-in-the-other, but it must be allowed to modify any hasty judgments about the privileging of identity or the 'return to sameness' in his philosophy. It is precisely the model of thinking as a form of love that secures the real *otherness* of what is thought and thus the real voiding or negating of the self-identical subject and the final vision of thought as communal, its identity established only in the mediation of a shared language and in the recognition by each of the identity of the mental process in all (which means 'in history', and 'in the collaborative life of the community now', rather than being a recognition of parallel exemplifications of a process in separate individuals). That this puts in question any reading of Hegel as straightforwardly totalitarian should not need saying, but probably does:[43] 'concrete freedom' is not present if there is any coercion or any inauthenticity in the recognition of unity of interest. More serious is the tension in Hegel's thought between what the *Philosophy of right* seems to say[44] about the empirical limits of community and the necessity of war as confirming a community's *Selbstgefühl*, and what is clearly laid out in the *Philosophy of religion* as the optimal form of reflective human sociality, the form adumbrated but not realised by the Church: what is said here has to do with the life of *humanity* as such, and it is wholly unclear how, in the light of this, local loyalties (to this state as opposed to that state, instead of loyalty to *the* state as social form) could be said to be intelligible. We can grant that the discussion in the *Philosophy of right* remains at the level of what is actually negotiable in the political world; we do not pass beyond the 'maelstrom of external contingency'[45] in considering international relations, and international reconciliation remains an 'ought', external to the concrete life of real societies.[46] That the individual nation-state has in some sense to lose its being-in-itself by finding (at least) its legitimation in the recognition of such other entities[47] does suggest that there is no unreflective positivism about Hegel's view (let alone a glorification of military struggle as such); his concern is explicitly to think the identity of the state in a world of uncontrollable contingencies. Yet we are left with an uneasy tension which prompts some questioning of Hegel's account of the optimal relation of Church and state (insofar as *neither* realises what it portends or promises as possible). An 'ecstatic' politics remains as a teasing *marginale*, a convergence of Church and state that we cannot satisfactorily formulate.

Whatever needs saying about this, however, the theological force of Hegel's agenda and the theological idiom in which he thinks the nature of thinking are obstinate presences in the *oeuvre*. Certainly they challenge the theologian to be more consistently theological – oddly enough: to think God in more uncompromisingly trinitarian and incarnational terms. But at the same time they invite the theologian to abandon a theology-in-itself, a theology that refuses to be a way of thinking the nature of human sociality. They invite theology to enact what it talks about and so (*only* so) to become authentic thinking. To the cultured despiser of theology, Hegel's challenge is simpler and more radical: is a universally shareable, self-cognisant freedom possible for human beings? If not, we had better abandon all pretence to be thinking subjects or political subjects. This latter option has, apparently, found a good deal of favour in the twentieth century, by way of the cultural and political totalitarianisms of fascism, nationalism, enforced collectivism and the 'free' market; but that doesn't make it truthful.[48]

Notes

1. See particularly David Kolb, *The critique of pure modernity* (Chicago: University of Chicago Press, 1986), 87.

2. See, e.g., §24 of the Encyclopedia Logic – *Hegel's Logic* (Oxford: Clarendon Press, 1975), 39ff. To think the nature of thought is to think a process that depends on nothing, in the sense that any formative contribution from my own contingent position or standpoint has to be denied. Cf. the discussion of 'beginnings' in the *Science of logic* (London: Allen and Unwin, 1969), 67–78; and §§86–8 of the Encyclopedia Logic.

3. §§163–5 of the *Logic* explain the concept of a concrete notion, the particular as the object of thought in the strict sense, as opposed to mere abstract representation (generalities, class predications).

4. This is an area where the tensions between Hegel and 'postmodern thinking' come most clearly into focus – not because Hegel allows a timeless grasp of total presence (on the contrary) but because *pure* absence or difference cannot be spoken.

5. We should have to *think* that our thinking was systematically frustrated or distorted, to think away the possibility of thinking; this would have to be the ground for a Hegelian challenge to behaviourism of any kind, and it relates back to the point from §24 of the *Logic* – thinking has to think a process that is not dependent in *essence* upon contingencies, otherwise every possible mental operation is marked by unfreedom and alienation.

6. Such a misunderstanding is bizarrely in evidence in Hans Küng, *The incarnation of God* (Edinburgh: T&T Clark, 1987), 235–7.

7. *Logic*, §80, 113–15.

8. Ibid., §81, 115–19.

9. Conveniently digested in Charles Taylor, *Hegel* (Cambridge: Cambridge University Press, 1975), ch. 10.

10. *Logic*, 114–15, 118–19.

11. Ibid., 121. There is something here in common with the early Wittgenstein's definition of the mystical, in the sense that the *Tractatus* assimilates *das Mystiche* to the sensation of the world as a (determinate) whole – *Tractatus logico-philosophicus* (London: Routledge and Kegan Paul, 1963), 6.45 – the debate

between them would be, I suspect, about the meaning of 'determinate'. Hegel would certainly repudiate any suggestion that the world could be thought of as a very large 'individual'; but it is not clear whether this is anywhere near what Wittgenstein means.

12. Hegel, *Lectures on the philosophy of religion: the lectures of 1827* (Berkeley: University of California, 1988), 419.

13. Not, unfortunately, an uncommon view. For an interesting recent study redressing the balance and offering a good account of the theological agenda of the work on logic, see J. W. Burbidge, *Hegel on logic and religion* (New York: SUNY, 1992) – though its conclusion fails, I think, to weigh the abiding importance in Hegel of the specificity of the narrative of divine self-negation in the incarnation.

14. The expression is associated with Nicholas of Cusa in the fifteenth century, but crystallises the doctrine of earlier medieval theologians: God is never an item numerable with others, and therefore is never *an* entity additional to the sum of entities in the universe.

15. §§213–15, 236–44 of Hegel, *Logic*; cf. the *Lectures on the philosophy of religion*, 170–1.

16. Cf. Hegel, *Phenomenology of spirit* (Oxford: Clarendon Press, 1977), IV.A.

17. Hegel, *Lectures on the philosophy of religion*, 260–3.

18. From the second *Zusatz* of the Introduction: *Hegel: the essential writings* (New York: Harper and Row, 1974), 209.

19. As Peter Hodgson notes in his introduction to the *Lectures on the philosophy of religion* (17–18), Hegel uses *vollendete* for the supreme form of religion, not *absolute*, the title imposed by his editors.

20. Ibid., 413–16, 460ff.

21. Ibid., 418.

22. Ibid.

23. Without this moment, consciousness remains alienated and contradictory; God would be 'frozen' in the contradictory position of externalizing what he is without there being a recognition of the *identity* between himself and himself in the other. Thus there could be no *real* identity, since the lack of recognition would introduce a moment of unthought differentiation.

24. Aquinas, *Summa theologiae* I.IIae.28.ii and iii.

25. Hegel, *Lectures on the philosophy of religion*, 418.

26. E.g., Aquinas, *Summa theologiae* I.31.ii and 29.iv on persons and relations.

27. Strongly criticized by some Eastern Christian thinkers on the grounds that it makes the Spirit less 'personal' than the Father and the Son. A closer reading of what, say, Augustine understands by this suggests a more nuanced picture; see his *De trinitate* 15.17–19.

28. Hegel, *Lectures on the philosophy of religion*, 475–9.

29. Ibid., 484ff.

30. Cf. Hegel's *Philosophy of right* (Oxford: Oxford University Press, 1952), Introduction, 144–9, 185, etc.

31. Ibid., 189–208, 217, 260ff.

32. Cf. Gillian Rose, *Hegel contra sociology* (Cambridge: Cambridge University Press, 1981), 112ff.

33. Hegel, *Lectures on the philosophy of religion*, 463, n. 196, which gives the 1831 text.

34. Ibid., 465, n. 199.

35. Ibid., 468: 'finitude, negativity, otherness are not outside of God and do not, as otherness, hinder unity with God'.

36. Ibid., 270: 'it had to be a sensible certainty, which, however, at the same time passes over into spiritual consciousness, and likewise is converted into the immediately sensible – in such a way that the movement and history of God is seen in it, the life that God himself is'.

37. Here above all is the point at which Hegel's thought converges with the Kierkegaard of the *Philosophical fragments* – reason passionate for its own disabling; except that Hegel would insist that the equivalent of the Absolute Paradox of the *Fragments* is not something that reason meets as an external barrier. Reason's passion effects its own disempowerment through the thinking of the concrete and historical death of God – Søren Kierkegaard, *Philosophical fragments and Johannes Climacus* (Cambridge, MA: Princeton University Press, 1985).

38. Hegel, *Lectures on the philosophy of religion*, 473–84.

39. Ibid., 471–2.

40. See, e.g., ibid., 399–404.

41. John Milbank's discussion of this point in his magnificent *Theology and social theory* (Oxford: Blackwell, 1990), 163, does not completely avoid such a suggestion.

42. For the former, see N. T. Wright, *The New Testament and the people of God* (London: SPCK, 1992); for the latter, J. D. Crossan, *The historical Jesus* (Edinburgh: T&T Clark, 1991).

43. And is said by Rose, *Hegel contra sociology*, esp. chs 2 and 7, and Taylor, *Hegel*, ch. 16.

44. Hegel, *Lectures on the philosophy of right*, §§209, 321–9.

45. Ibid., §340.

46. Ibid., §333.

47. Ibid., §331, *Zusatz*.

48. The challenge is articulated in Taylor, *Hegel*; also, with a better appreciation of the centrality for Hegel of the incarnational narrative, by Andrew Shanks, *Hegel's political theology* (Cambridge: Cambridge University Press, 1991).

4

Between politics and metaphysics: reflections in the wake of Gillian Rose

I

Can we find a way of talking about metaphysics that doesn't immediately descend into the quagmires of fantasy, the sort of thing Nietzsche excoriated in the context of religious discourse as talking about unreal objects and causes? But why should we want to find any way at all of talking about metaphysics? In what we are constantly told to regard as a post-realist age (told by whom, though?), the project of speaking with generality about the real or actual has become marginal; we are frightened of generating a discourse that seems to aim at rivalling our talk about talk itself, to aim at the grasp of structures or 'conditions' or 'transcendentals' in a way that sidesteps the fundamental contemporary axiom in so much of our speaking about reflection and method – the axiom that language cannot, ultimately, have any 'matter' but itself. Violating this axiom raises the spectre of claims to presence, to privilege or to totalising vision; and we (who?) know that these are the claims that we must resist on pain of losing what language is, and thus losing the only thing we can now find to say of our human essence – that it is constructed and enacted in speech, which is 'essentially' without privilege, in the sense that it is not amenable to closure or stasis. No position is or could be available that would have the right to arrest the process of exchange. And, if we are to find room here for the sacred, it will be only in absences, blanks and pauses in the exchange, unthematisable and alien to will and reflection.

This will do only if we fail to read 'reality' or 'actuality' as *difficult*. My parenthetical questions in the last paragraph were not frivolous asides: there are issues of power wherever there are questions of proscription, and an intellectual style that declines to engage with matters of legitimacy, or even truthfulness, if we want to be primitive, is making

53

a strong *political* bid. It rules out the question of judgement (in various senses of the word); and in so doing rules out what we could call the question of recognition and thus of internal critique. That is to say, there is an inescapable issue in the speech that is actually employed by material and temporal subjects that has to do with how what is said is appropriated, how it sustains intelligibility in the exchanges and negotiations that constitute our actuality. This is where difficulty lies. Another material speaker is someone whose deployment of conceptual and rhetorical strategies will be in some ways parallel and in some ways divergent in relation to mine: I recognise a strategy that is faced with what I am faced with, yet one that operates out of a distinct accumulation of past negotiation and from a different material location, whose perspectives are accessible to me *only* in the exchanges of language. But the material of my own negotiation in and with my environment is nothing other than these other perspectives and histories: it is in fact impossible for me to have as the matter of my thought and speech only what I generate for myself. And to speak here of negotiation with an environment is already to say that I must *labour* here, that I must determine and maintain a position from which to communicate. Hence what I say is questionable to myself (as well as to others); whence does it come, how does it connect in the processes of exchange, at what points does it fatally ignore another perspective, so rendering itself without effect or actual presence, at what point does it so absorb another perspective as to disempower itself in another way, by failing to own its peculiar locus in the map of exchange? These are the questions that arise in the processes of discovering what it might be to exercise a *historical* freedom, a determination within constraints of how my and our life is to be shaped. They are the issues where politics and epistemology are entwined, and they are notoriously resistant to general resolutions.

The aspirations of post-realism seem to be aspirations not only after a solitary career of self-determination, but aspirations to what can only be called a non-historical freedom; they look to a situation in which there are few or no issues about power arising in the context of discourse: the exchanges envisaged are not what I have called negotiations, but simply the co-existence of (at best) mutually tangential projects – what Roy Bhaskar has called 'a succession of poems, all marginally different; and a succession of paradigm shifts, for which no overarching or commensurating criteria can be given'. As he says, this is an intelligible ideology (just) for 'a leisured elite, in conditions of plenty.'[1]

Indeed, I suspect that it isn't only a matter of 'conditions of plenty'; the situation envisaged seems to be rather one of *un*conditioned access to goods, since there is no pressing or significant negotiation over ownership and distribution. The tensions and *aporiai* of power arise, I suggest, because of primitive scarcity, in the sense that human agents are aware of operating in an environment where desire can be and is frustrated by the access of others to goods. To find our way around in such an environment is inevitably to be brought up against exchange and labour in respect of the desire of others; so that an account of speech that ignores scarcity and the consequent problem of mutual limitation is one that has no purchase on material agency.

For all the fascination in postmodernity with difference (however spelled), and the criticisms of strategies, metaphysical or religious, that appear to privilege a return to the same, the perspective here in fact sidesteps the practical constructions of difference with some elegance. By absolutising *the* other, otherness becomes un-thinkable; the laborious process of evolving a practice in which my desire, my project, redefines or rethinks itself in symbiosis with others, a practice in which the presence of scarcity ceases to be simply an occasion of 'war', is avoided. The other becomes an area of something like sacred terror, not the occasion for a developing and often deeply ironic self-articulation, and the discovery of a way of transcending scarcity. For if the access of others to desired goods is, with my own and like my own, negotiable, revisable, it may be possible to recognise the environment as one of potential abundance. Difference, in this kind of politics, is an occasion of work, the work by which human beings constantly query what they have assumed is their interest as individuals or definite groups; as that work is carried forward, two distinct errors or misperceptions are uncovered, the illusion that any specific (individual or group) subject has unlimited access to the use of the goods of an environment, and the illusion that any (individual or group) subject can intelligibly define its good as the possession of such use in exclusion of all others. The environment is one of scarcity in the sense that goods and their use have to be the object of *thought*, of planning; but it is one of potential abundance insofar as it is possible for goods in an environment to be 'underwritten' by the intelligence of others – insofar as the work of others can secure my or our interest as the object of their thought and labour (and vice versa).

The question of how we are to construe difference is in the long run a metaphysical one; that is, it is not a question that can be settled by appeal to a tangible state of affairs or set of facts, yet at the same time not a question that can be relegated to a matter of taste or private judgement, since the matter is one that, as we have just seen, shapes decisively the way in which political options are understood. Is this, then, simply a plea for philosophy to produce a transcendental ground for political options already determined? a functionalising of that area of philosophy once regarded as dealing essentially with what is to be contemplated rather than used? an illegitimate attempt to give political commitments a supra-human guarantee that no human commitment can possibly have? The answer to such a challenge is not a short one. At this preliminary stage, all I shall say is this. There *is* a sense in which, classically, metaphysical reflection arises from the impulse to look for a ground in the discussion of justice and injustice in political affairs: Plato's *Republic*, after all, begins here. The *Republic*'s reflection on the conditions of judgement (mathematical, moral, aesthetic) is an inalienable part of the project described by Socrates[2] as constructing a city in speech or discourse. We might say that here the question of how we spell out the conditions of coherent thought arises with urgency only as we unscramble what it is to speak at all about an interest that is more than local; how we make sense of common life as opposed to seeing it as simply the battleground of competing bids for the use of goods. If we grasp what it is to relate in language itself, to be capable of challenging or recognising the uses of words, asking about legitimacy, defensibility and consistency in relation to what we habitually say, we are, in Plato's eyes, committed to uttering and exploring statements about what does *not* just 'happen' to be the case in the world of objects. Once we start creating a city in discourse, working at and testing the bonds that language requires and presupposes so as to rule out the arbitrary and the partial, the 'passionate' in isolation, the task before us is finally 'metaphysical'. We may be puzzled by the question of what status we are to assign to the structures Plato believes he has uncovered, but what matters is *not* some discovery of a parallel world of occult objects exercising an eccentric variation of ordinary worldly causality, but simply the articulation of a discourse that is confidently about something other than casual states of affairs. If this is properly describable as the realm of the metaphysical, it looks as if, on one account at least of what intelligible political discourse demands (discourse about how we make sense of human bondedness and exchange), metaphysics is not extrinsic to the task. It is not an extra hurriedly brought in to provide justifications for commitments; it might better be called the underlying intelligible structure of the commitments themselves, what constitutes them as more than arbitrarily willed options. And thus the political location of metaphysical discourse is not the reduction of metaphysics to functional subordination within an alien setting, but something more like the laying bare of a contemplative or non-functional dimension to the political, the element of 'seeing' that is contained in any idea of intelligible action in a world of diverse agents.

By 'intelligible action' here, I mean action that can be recognised by other agents as analogous to their own; and thus action capable of being talked about, action that is not the assertion of blind will, but is bound up with the exchanges and negotiations that constitute a pattern of language. 'Intelligible action' is action that can be criticised and defended, understood or misunderstood. To borrow an idiom of Wittgenstein's, it is action that can be 'followed'.[3] Just as in speech, we know how to continue when certain things are said, certain signals given, we recognise the conventions at work and can contribute to the enterprise, so in patterns of agency, we know or do not know how to respond or contribute. 'Intelligible action' can thus vary from the hackneyed example of moves in a game to matters of ritual or etiquette to any shared labour of planning and executing a human task. And, insofar as problems of communication in this context have to be dealt with by asking something like 'What do you see?' the dimension I have been calling contemplative inevitably enters in. If you are doing *that*, I can't understand what you're seeing, because I can't make a sensible analogy with what I'm doing or might do, seeing what *I* do. And, in turn, if there is a solution to such problems of communication, it may lie in the critique of both prior standpoints. Intelligible action is action significantly dispossessed of the control of a 'private' will: the sense I make is not under my control. Thus to speak at all about action as open to critique, to understanding and misunderstanding, to the possibility or impossibility of its being 'followed', is at least to raise the question of what is 'seen' in respect of the environment, especially the human environment. In the first place, this requires certain explanatory strategies, above all strategies that will make it possible to give an account of how error arises.[4] But this explanatory exercise takes us only so far if it seeks only to identify the distortions arising from external conditions, significant as these are. For if external conditions are in fact capable of producing distortions of consciousness, the recognition of this still entails the need for a general account of understanding and misunderstanding. To refer once again to Bhaskar, a theory of the genesis of

57

false consciousness must be also a theory of communication and intelligibility, a theory of how meanings are constructed and negotiated in a wide variety of relations – including our relation to the 'unmotivated conditions for our substantive motivated productions' which prohibits a theory dealing only with actors' accounts of their meanings.[5]

The point is that an understanding of human action that puts at its centre the character of human existence as work or production demands not only (as any Marxist would agree) a 'realist' epistemology, but, more controversially, a 'metaphysic' – an overall proposal concerning the character of reality as known by agents. The classical and fairly crude materialist realism of mainline Marxist epistemology is not, of course, free from metaphysical commitments in the wide sense. But the point at which this tradition joins hands (surprisingly) with some very different styles of philosophising over against a postmodernist discourse is in their common, though diversely articulated, stress on the involvement of work/production in the essence of the human. To the extent that 'production' implies the formation for some other of something that is either required or receivable or both, something whose identity is not internal to the agent's definition, it applies to the entire range of communicative activity extending from cookery to philosophy or mysticism. What is here being affirmed against the general idiom of postmodernity is that what human beings do is characterised by the kind of difficulty that arises when the effects of action or decision are open to the judgment and interpretation not only of other finite agents as individuals or clusters of individuals, but of what is discerned as the order or structure of a reality not determined by anyone's decision. To 'produce' or to engage in work that issues in the changing of the environment, material or conceptual or imaginative, is to accept conventions or standards, communicative and evaluative conventions, outside the power of the producing agent, if what is produced is to 'count' as a recognisable production, an entity capable of being described and discussed with reference to more than the producer's will in itself.

Isn't this exactly what postmodernist criticism itself insists upon, though, the radical ability to challenge authorial intention and the hermeneutical privilege of the producer? I suspect that this takes us back to the earlier question of how *difference* is construed. If the product is intelligible in entire abstraction from the conditions of its production (including the motivation of the producer), it ceases to be either risky for the producer or difficult for the interpreter; it is poised between producer and interpreter, or rather not *between* at all, since its place is not in any hermeneutical territory common to the two. Interpretation prescinds from the question of recognition (and so of misrecognition); it does not need the labour of analogy, the seeking of some sort of convergence in processes of production. Thus the 'otherness' of the work offered to interpretation hovers between the ineffability of the (quasi-) sacred and the reflexivity of something that can be conscripted into the projects of the interpreter. Two models are at work of the way in which the producer is dispossessed by production or labour. On the postmodernist account, the producer is effectively wholly alienated from the work; any claim to the contrary would be to reinstate a 'metaphysics of presence', author and authority. On the account I have sketched, locating itself in the passage between politics and metaphysics, the producer's dispossession is a move in a collaborative (at least potentially collaborative) project, the construction of a meaning, a set of signifiers systematically organised, not determined by any individual decision or project, challenging agents to reconceive their goal and interest *in* what is other.

And so to come at last to Gillian Rose, and to why I elect to discuss her work as a vehicle for thinking about the genesis of metaphysical concern, and even, specifically, of metaphysical concern in a religious context. In an unusually direct passage, part of the introduction to her collection of essays on *Judaism and modernity*, she identifies in the postmodern ethics she is attacking a failure to engage with the 'Other' as enacting concrete intentions within a limited cultural and institutional space, so that

> 'The Other' is misrepresented as sheer alterity, for 'the Other' is equally the distraught subject searching for its substance, its ethical life ... *New ethics* would *transcend* the autonomy of the subject by commanding that I substitute myself for 'the Other' (heteronomy) or by commending attention to 'the Other'. Yet it is the inveterate but occluded *immanence* of one subject to itself and to other *subjects* that needs further exposition. Simply to command me to sacrifice myself, or to commend that I pay attention to others makes me intolerant, naive and miserable ... [T]he immanence of the self-relation of 'the Other' to my own self-relation will always be disowned.[6]

Central to Rose's concern is the philosophical importance of error and the recognisability of error. To recognise misperception is to learn;

to learn is to reimagine or reconceive the self; and this in turn is to encounter the 'violence' – a crucially significant and difficult word in Rose's recent *oeuvre* – that is inescapably involved in our position towards others and towards ourselves. It is because this violence is always presupposed by our particular positions in any network of relations that law is required in our sociality. And the insistence on a sociality never 'mended' in a final way (another recurrent theme) is precisely what raises, obliquely but inexorably, a religious question; not the facile and tempting question of law's relation to grace, but the harder one of how the very experience of learning and of negotiation can be read as something to do with God. As Rose herself is pretty clear, this is, of course, a repristination of the Hegelian project in something like its full ambition. But to see how this is so, we need to look at what Rose actually says about that project.

II

According to Rose, the most spectacular misunderstanding we could have of Hegel's *Phenomenology* is to suppose that it is an account of how consciousness absorbs its objects, overcomes the duality of knower and known so that consciousness is left with no 'outside'.[7] To read the *Phenomenology* adequately we have to enter upon a process that will show us that we have not yet understood the nature of thinking; thinking the thoughts of the *Phenomenology* is discovering the ways in which 'natural consciousness' repeatedly undermines itself and by so doing advances – not towards a conclusive theoretical reconciliation, but towards a practice of scepticism that, so far from inducing despair or withdrawal or apathy, empowers us to attempt transformative action in the clear recognition that any liberation from the distortions of 'natural' thinking is a necessary step to the removal of those social relations that reflect and intensify untruthful consciousness. This is not a process that can necessarily of itself deliver a social ideal, a programme for concrete improvement; it is simply a project that, by insistently showing us that the model of consciousness as a kind of property owner, accumulating known objects, is a myth incapable of coherent statement, keeps us uneasy about patterns of both speech and relation (the two, of course, not separable) that continue to take as axiomatic the model of contending 'proprietors'.

The proper implication of this is that any scheme of thought that proposes to eliminate the difficulties of 'natural consciousness' is going to be an obstacle to emancipatory thinking and practice. Contrary to some textbook accounts, Hegel (especially in the *Phenomenology*) does not offer to dissolve natural consciousness, with its specific objects of knowledge; how could he? For it is in the continual renewal of the 'natural' errors of pre-speculative thinking that speculation (self-aware thinking, thinking that thinks the nature of thinking) is itself renewed. Of course we go on having determinate experiences of objects that we think of as other to the natural consciousness; it is in a continued re-engagement with these experiences that we move constantly and afresh into the properly speculative mode in which we 'unmake' the natural consciousness.[8] The question we must then raise in respect of any conceptual scheme is that of how far it proposes or threatens to remove the direct otherness of the natural consciousness's objects *at the outset* of the thinking process. That we misrecognise the character of thinking by entertaining the deliverances of natural consciousness is all-important: entertain the particular in its strangeness, and out of that will, properly, come the speculative recognition of the unsustainable character of the 'natural'. The thinking subject over against the object thought succumbs to the contradictions of this opposition. Yet – and here Rose is boldest in her reading of Hegel – every moment of recognition is also a new moment of salutary error to the extent that it is the taking of a *position*. The truth lies in the 'system', which is *not* the theory that the mind can possess at one moment, but the entirety of the path, the project, of critical dissolution of the positional and partial definition. 'This idea of a whole which cannot be grasped in one moment or one statement for it must be experienced is the idea of the system.'[9]

If we turn from Rose's Hegel to Rose's presentation of the various thinkers dealt with in her most hermetic and taxing work, *The broken middle*, we may be able to make better sense not only of the three declared themes of the book ('anxiety of beginning, equivocation of the ethical and agon of authorship'), but also of the recurrent and at first sight teasing discussion of 'violence' here. The ideal of 'love without violence' is characterised as lacking in faith:[10] in reality, love is always found to be involved in violence, and the attempted reversions to a beginning or an end free from violence found in writers like Thomas Mann or René Girard[11] in fact condemn the human agent to the alternatives of an *agape* beyond structures and negotiations or a conflict without containment. Love and violence are both involved in *law* – that is to say, in strategy and social form. The underlying *riskiness* of strategy cannot be circumvented: all strategy is 'agonistic', involved in a struggle of the will against the resistance of an environment, and it becomes impossible to disentangle this from some account of violence.[12] The difficulty arises when violence is given a wholly negative definition; in which case (as in Girard), it is given a solidity and identity that cloud our reflective possibilities. Violence negatively constructed suggests a primordial situation of equal or 'parallel' subjects, each in possession of itself, a situation that violence proceeds to disarrange (Girard again);[13] but in fact there is no such situation. Subjects are always already unequal, and the processes of negotiation work with a fiction of equality as a critical tool for thinking and changing the relations actually subsisting. The abstract universalism and egalitarianism of enlightened social philosophy must be simultaneously *exposed* as fiction, shown to fail in respect of specific human groups, and still used obliquely: this is the task Rose sees being variously performed in the authorships of Rahel Varnhagen, Rosa Luxemburg and Hannah Arendt – all of them, as women and as Jews, excluded from the universalist fictions of the Enlightenment and the rhetoric of universal Christian *agape*.[14] In very diverse ways, each witnesses to the temptations of the reflective consciousness in the modern age – the withdrawal into the private cultivation of a 'beautiful soul', the revolutionary divorce of means and ends that lures socialist transformations away from their properly *political* task, and the isolation of a kind of timeless culture of friendship and civility, alien to the labour of public construction.[15] In varying degrees, all three writers return us to risk: to 'the anxiety of beginning, the equivocation of the ethical and the agon of authorship'.

What do these reiterated and gnomic expressions mean? The detailed discussion of Kierkegaard as well as of the three Jewish women already mentioned clarifies this a little. Thinking is afraid to begin; or rather, it looks for a beginning that is not a risk, a beginning that already controls or contains its goal. It is therefore constantly in flight from the recognition of the 'already' that locates all our putative beginnings in an unsought and uncontrolled middle. The only honest beginning is with difficulty; that is to say, we cannot 'start thinking', but 'begin' only with the acknowledgment that what we say is already put in question, already involved in the fertile error or misperception that Hegel and Kierkegaard alike[16] identify as, in the most ironic sense, natural to thinking. But why do we look in this way for a beginning that gives mastery? Because the involved, the 'middle' situation where we are in fact located, is an ambiguous place. We do not occupy a place in which we can *originate*, make what is new, where our desire or our intelligence can make terms with the environment unconstrained by prior determinations of action and possibility and speech. It is the constraining 'already' of such determination, the whole of what Rose conceives as 'law', that in fact defines what power we really possess; the failure to acknowledge this imprisons us. But this liberating awareness of an imperative actuality prior to, and powerful in respect of, our specific desire is also a 'beginning of anxiety', the moral and conceptual source of how we understand what it is to *fail*. When a culture effectively loses the sense of what it is to fail (which is what Kierkegaard believed to be true of his Christendom), the ethical is broken: that is, the agent is left poised unhappily between an external order which, because it has forgotten what failure is, ceases to be a source of power, and an internal critical self-perception, an anxious self-perception, that likewise has no access to power, no resolution of its own impotence. What Kierkegaard called the suspension of the ethical has its place in this context. There is a necessary moment in which we must simultaneously know and not know the ethical, the presence of empowering constraint; what we know is a universal condition, a definition beyond our power and choice, but one that cannot here and now compel or create 'witness'. In order to recover the possibility of an act that will have the character of 'witness', the character of powerfully setting in being a state of affairs other than the existing uncritical order, we must 'suspend' the existing order *understood as a system that has forgotten how to fail*, a system that guarantees successful performance. But it is suspense, not abolition, that we are talking about here. Any proposal to abolish the ethical, the givenness of constraint, the already that grounds any present act of will, is an attempt to take us out of time, and thus to seal our powerlessness once and for all.[17]

The extremely dense argument on this point in *The broken middle* is an effort to lay hold of a paradox in intelligible acting. Without the awareness of what constrains us, which is not only the given material environment but the history of negotiation with other agents that surrounds our projects before they are articulated or formed, we cannot act so as to initiate or change; yet the act itself that changes or introduces the critical, the possibility of failure, requires that we stand over against the ethical as *order*, recognising that the action we inaugurate is not in advance specified as successful, well-formed or orderly. It is involved with 'violence'. But, in turn, that violence is rendered recognisable, capable of being criticised, by the fact that the ethical is not abolished; the act of inauguration does not establish an anti-order of arbitrary free-for-all.[18] The action taken in the moment of suspending the ethical is an act not of self-assertion but of self-dispossession or even self-*gift*.[19] It is a renunciation of the self-possession that is content with never failing; because (and here we have to look back to earlier and more fundamental discussions of the nature of thinking) such putative self-possession, invulnerable to the judgment of the other and the prior, issues in the contradictions from which speculative thinking is meant to free us. To act in the equivocation of the ethical is to renounce the finality of my judgment on myself – which is, of course, what I do when I initiate any kind of communication, any speech.

This argument can be read as a protest against the essentialising of violence: against the isolation of violence (quâ struggle or strategy) as a factor amongst others, or rather a 'lowest common denominator'[20] in action, an element either always present (which induces cynicism) or capable of being totally extruded (utopianism or 'totalist' politics, claiming an order that is peaceful and timeless). Instead, violence is only to be thought of as the risk entailed in power, the presence of the possibility that my action, by *inevitably* in some measure misrecognising the nature of the interest of others, establishes a new imbalance of power and justice. Yet there is no way of being actively and historically within the ethical without such risk, since the ethical without risk is powerless – that is, it is incapable of truthfully negotiating the otherness, the differences, that it always contains (in both senses of the word). The issue can be put in another way, in terms of the unresolvable tension between attention to the particular and commitment to the universal. Since the abstract universal is present in our history only as a disempowering and would-be timeless sameness, and since the purely arbitrary assertion of the particular can never found a social practice, with its necessary temporal involvement, truthful action is inescapably shadowed, but destined to achieve only by confronting its shadow. Not to confront this means – in fact – the kind of society we inhabit, in which properly political life is made functional to the economic exchanges in civil society, but civil society is constantly being eroded in favour of collective interest, defined in terms of whatever group currently possesses hegemony. The modern pattern is the steady removal of intermediate institutions, local corporations, in such a way that the fundamental conflicts of interest are between two abstractions, the state and the individual.[21]

'The agon of authorship is to remain with anxiety of beginning and equivocation of the ethical'.[22] That is to say, thinking the tensions of truthfulness in action and about action must resist an unsupportable and menacing pull towards false reconciliations, towards what Rose calls the 'holy' – peace beyond time. Any imaginable claim for such a state will in practice be a commendation of some sort of political totalism. Authorship is the staking of the intelligent self, a risky act, once again like any act of communication: an invitation of judgment; thus, too, a declaration of *faith*. The author has to refuse divinity, or rather the pretence of divinity, not by refusing to *make* judgments but by knowing the risky and 'violent' nature of the judgments s/he cannot but make, staking a position that necessarily involves claiming something over against an other, while remembering that the other still imperiously requires to be understood, to be *thought*. This is why it is (or should be) difficult to do philosophy, especially political philosophy.

One of the things that is striking about the conclusions of *The broken middle* is the way in which the basic problem identified is that of the relation of universal and particular: one problem that pervades Aristotle's metaphysical discussion is whether the individual or the generic sense of 'substance' is basic,[23] and this echo brings into sharp focus the way in which Rose's agenda, like Hegel's, insists on the interconnection of the political and the metaphysical. In an essay on Derrida,[24] Rose interestingly dubs Derrida's evocation of 'spirit' 'meta-metaphysical',[25] after noting how Derrida's genealogy of Nazism involves a huge and vague range of mediating institutions in such a way that the *life* of social institutions (their actual determinations in history) is effectively rejected. Meta-metaphysics is meta-politics; the seduction of the one is practically identical with the seduction of the other. The discourse of metaphysics and politics is one that is faithful to 'the difficulty of actuality';[26] both registers of reflection, when they are doing their job, properly leave us stranded in history, which is where we ought to be. Both, by insisting on a universality of perspective, hope, or communicative intent *and* upon the inalienable capacity for the empowering of specific action that is contained in the thinking of thinking itself, reacquaint us with our situation in time. It must of course immediately be added that both the metaphysics and the politics in question belong to 'modernity' to the extent that they are aware of their own processes; we are not talking about the importation of orders from elsewhere, known as given structures in an unproblematic way. What metaphysics faces now is the challenge to reconceive Aristotle's *aporia* in terms of consciousness and social/communicative action, since this is the place where we now engage with what does not just happen to be the case, that which is *not* negotiable in our environment, not subject to will.

There of course is the intrusive 'we' again; to define the political/metaphysical task in terms of what 'we' can and cannot do 'now' is surely to be bound in the same paradoxical historicism that postmodernity's rhetoric (as I indicated at the opening of this essay) constantly slips into. The defence that Rose – or anyone who had digested Hegel anywhere near adequately – would offer is that the thinking of thinking inescapably involves a 'staking' (to use one of Rose's favourite terms, especially in her later work) a claim on what it is that human agents, or subjects as such, are answerable to and engaged in; without this there is no conversation and so no change. Yet, as we have seen, the staking in turn involves the possibility of error and critique. There is, in other words, an irony in the 'we' here that is arguably absent from the ahistorical historicism of the postmodernist understanding, with indifference to the conditions of the production of meaning.

'Irony' is an important word in this connection. In an essay on Adorno, Rose notes the way in which Adorno misses the ironic dimension in Hegel's system and accordingly remains at the level of a dialectic that fails to think itself consistently. Adorno appears as the apostle of irreconcilable non-identity, the renunciation of comprehensive theory; but to arrest the dialectic *as* dialectic is to leave the terms of the contradictions of dialectic untouched. By contrast, Hegel's thinking insists not on a return to identity but on the 'speculative' projection of a continually self-adjusting, self-criticising corporate practice – which can, from another point of view, be described as a politics. 'Pure' dialectics becomes another strategy for avoiding strategy, violence, time and error.[27] The same point is approached in a piece on Benjamin,[28] a particularly dense and significant reflection. Benjamin plays dangerously with the notion of Messianic time, the interruption that forces or 'shocks' history into unity or intelligibility; for history is the history of irredeemable loss (fascism is always already victorious), and only a divine violence can save. But when saving violence is construed as divine, what disappears is the crucial self-understanding and self-critique of the 'violence in love' that features in *The broken middle*. In Benjamin's perspective, 'Only the violence of God or the general strike, which is invisible because total, can counter the partial and bloody violences of the law. This divine or sovereign violence abolishes law by destroying boundaries without making new ones. It is bound-lessly expiatory; without demanding sacrifices, it accepts them.'[29] Over against the world of loss and concrete violence stands the divine in its purity; and because it is pure, it is accessible not through mediation but only in reproduction, correspondence.[30] Thus the inauguration of change comes about not through thinking, critique, strategy and risk, but by the undiscussable, unfollowable irruption of lawless unification. Benjamin's famous image of the *Angelus novus*, looking back on a history of catastrophe, effectively impotent in horror as the paradisal wind blows him towards the future,[31] captures the sense of history as a record of what is lost, abandoned and beyond reclamation: memory serves only to keep alive the truth that oppression is victorious, so that we do not cease to mourn.[32]

One thing that this interrogation of Benjamin implies is that the common ground of politics and metaphysics is a particular kind of reclamation of history, history as a 'coming to learn'.[33] The danger of turning this into a totalising and falsely reconciling theory of historical unity is real only when the thinker forgets that the act of interpreting, expressing 'learning', is itself historical, strategic and without guaran-tee. But the nature of thinking about thinking requires precisely a thinking of the past as empowerment (which is vitally different from thinking the past as 'justified', as inevitable, as simply convergent). Talking about history is talking about the record or deposit of speech, in every possible sense, including very obviously the paradoxical speech of those silenced in history by the voices of others; the enterprise of reading history as intelligible, as generative of understanding and strategy now, is, it seems, the unavoidable form of thinking about thinking, once we have understood that what we can say and think is empowered by what has been said and thought. This is ultimately to return us to Hegel's fundamental insight: history is how we do our metaphysics, how we reflect on what we non-negotiably are and what are the conditions of our concept-formation. Not that history as record delivers to us a map of the constructions of the universe, or a compre-hensive account of natural kinds or a compelling thesis about the nature of reference; but engagement with history lays bare for us the character of thinking *as* engagement, as converse, conflict, negotiation, judgment and self-judgment. What we discover in the attempt to think the past is our nature, and so the possibilities that present dispositions of power and administration may obscure. What we discover is a steady formal presence in this process, the form of what I have called dispossession:

at each stage of reflection, we are made aware, if we do not run away from the contradictions and difficulties, of the impossibility of *thinking* reality in terms of individuals 'owning' selves, ideas, property in a fixed and uncontended way. We are always redistributing, never timelessly sure of our 'interest'. Thought unsettles any definition of my interest or our (specific group) interest, and it does so largely through the tracing of the changes of consciousness in history. This does not seek to provide a teleological or evolutionary story in a simple sense; but it does or should lay bare to us the character of thought as sensing its own misrecognitions and non-communications, as dissatisfied with its self-positioning even though it never avoids self-positioning. And this appears constantly as also a story of power and its distribution, since the possibility or otherwise of recognition or intelligibility is a profoundly political issue (one could define injustice radically as the situation where recognition of common or convergent interest fails; but that is only to paraphrase Hegel again).

Rose's reading of Hegel and her subsidiary readings of numerous other figures leave us, then, with an apprehension of how the metaphysical task might (should) be conceived. The price of post-realism is 'post-political' withdrawal, itself an unquestionably political strategy refusing to know itself. The authentically political, the project of continually challenging localised and incommunicable discourses about human interest, arises out of a commitment to thought in a certain mode, thought aware of its own production, its own vulnerability and its own commitment to risk. This carries an account of reality-as-such, not in the sense of talk of unreal objects or invisible but discussable entities, but in the sense that it uncovers what we cannot but do if we are concerned with truthfulness. A negative metaphysic, comparable to a negative theology? Perhaps; this needs more unpacking. But a metaphysic undoubtedly, and so too an ethic for both thinking and acting.

III

Gillian Rose's work has had far less discussion than it merits; but one quite searching essay on her earlier writing about Hegel and Marxism is that by Peter Osborne in 1982, a strongly worded contention that the re-worked Hegelianism Rose commends is incapable of understanding the *specific* determinations that shape consciousness. Hegelianism deliberately settles for a phenomenological critique of consciousness, consciousness dismantled and reconceived 'immanently' through the examination of its innate stresses or contradictions, its ineluctable movement of self-subversion. But, Osborne claims,[34] this effectively prohibits a social theory, and, in so doing, prohibits also a genuinely transformative practice. All Rose allows, on this showing, is a recognition of how consciousness is always already distorted; transformation can only be seen here as a bare negation – 'not *this*'. As the last paragraph of his essay makes clear, Osborne assimilates Rose's argument, at the end of the day, to Adorno's, a dialecticism that is 'impotent in the face of contemporary reality'.[35]

Clearly such a critique would be harder to sustain in the light of Rose's later work; we have already noted the way in which she distances herself from Adorno and the pathos of the perpetual negation. But is Osborne right in seeing in the phenomenological method itself an incapacity to think the concrete and so to think its transformation? Much of what I have so far written might serve to answer this. And Rose would, I think, justifiably object that Osborne simply repeats the fundamental misunderstanding of Hegel by Marx, the 'Fichtean' reading that reverts to a mythology of spirit diffusing itself in nature and fails to break through the opposition between thinking and the given, between the active Inside and the passive Outside. 'Immanent' critique is not an analysis of objectless thought; to talk about thinking itself is always to talk about thought thinking its concrete determinations. All immanent critique, in this sense, is 'social theory'; and a social theory that is not ultimately a thinking of thinking is still stuck at a prespeculative and so (strictly) pre-political stage. Rose's fundamental Hegelian insight is, I have suggested, that it is the understanding of the basic character of deformed consciousness as the myth of the subject in possession that grounds not simply a 'negative dialectic' but a clear speculative recognition of the inevitable need for negotiation of goods. Without the speculative, the understanding of what invariably goes wrong with consciousness, social reconstruction, transformative practice or anything else will not advance beyond a rearrangement of existing power relations.

Speculative thinking, in the Hegelian sense, is in fact nothing if it is not the thinking of specific determinations, specific deformations of consciousness; if it tries to be other than historical and concrete in its proceedings, it thinks something other than its own real processes. And it is at this point that we might venture a tentative theological comment.

Thinking is itself a learning of some sort of dispossession, the constant rediscovery and critique of the myth of the self as owner of its perceptions and positions; thinking unsettles all claims to a final resolution of how we define and speak of our interest. This much has emerged from our earlier discussion. Insofar as this is always critical thinking about particular historical varieties of unfreedom or inequality, it is in fact always suggesting specific kinds of historical liberation, directions in which we can look for change, even if the speculative alone doesn't and could never deliver a 'programme' for political action, since this (*ex hypothesi*) could emerge only through the particular negotiations that are necessary and possible in a particular setting; to think otherwise would be to surrender to the temptation to apocalyptic resolutions, ends of history, final solutions. But the constant is this: that truth requires loss. Or to put it slightly differently, the constant is that existence as a subject is recognised or re-learned all the time as a process of self-displacement, a never-ending 'adjustment' in search of the situation where there is real mutual recognition and thus effective common action, because we have moved away from the illusions of rivalry. This is not something that can be avoided by a short cut enjoining total self-cancellation before the sacredness of the Other: this would be to flee the claims of understanding, the painful job of discovering my moral substance in relation and so honouring the other's moral substance in the process of uncovering and understanding my own. The other is not honoured by my undialectical abnegation, because the other is configured, in such an encounter, as itself beyond negotiation and so beyond understanding; and there is a hairsbreadth between this and the violent denial or repudiation of the other as beyond understanding.

But what does it mean to speak here about a 'constant'? It is one way of restoring a language for the 'absolute' in less alarming terms, I suppose, to look for ways of articulating what is non-negotiable in being a thinking subject. And if the understanding of what it is to be a thinking subject in fact tells us how we are to construe the real, if the phenomenology of consciousness is also an ontology, the patterns of thought are 'the sinews of substance', to adapt Knowles's phrase about Aristotle. Within the Hegelian perspective, to *deny* that phenomenology of consciousness is ontology would be to reinstate the lethal confusion about thinking represented by the idea that there is a clear difference between active mind and passive stuff, between the mind and its intellectual property or acquisitions, between language and 'objects', those mysteriously self-contained or self-defined things lying around waiting to be noticed and collected.

The metaphysical tradition we have been discussing and working with here would indeed agree that, if thinking is ineluctably a pattern of self-displacement, the fundamental category that operates in speaking about the final constraints of reality, the constants in language, is self-displacement. We cannot think a reality in which substances exist as atomised systems whose goals (or interests) can be specified in mutual isolation; the being of things is on the one hand marked by authentic difference, and hence difficulty in conceiving and reconciling, but on the other hand by the everlasting 'slippage' of definition away from the model of labelling discrete lumps of stuff. To return to observations made at the beginning of this essay, we are pressed towards a metaphysic in which difference is *neither* (at any moment) final, a matter of mutual exclusion, *nor* simply reducible, a matter of misperception to be resolved by either a return to the same or a cancellation of one term before the Other.

Hegel's question – not one raised in these terms by Rose, yet insistently in the background of what she writes – is how, historically, we come to think of thinking in the framework of dispossession; and his answer is, of course, that this requires a history that can be told as the narrative of the absolute's self-loss and self-recovery. Hegel's genius is to read the Judeao-Christian narrative as precisely this. His reading requires a fair bit of strain at a number of points, and it takes wholly for granted a version of Jewish identity circumscribed by the Christian, and more particularly Lutheran, account of Judaism as primarily and simply that Other that Christianity overturns. Both historically and theologically, we cannot repeat that reading with a clear conscience now; but is there a way of re-reading the underlying point? We might start from the other, or another, end: thinking about thinking as dispossession and negotiation is made possible not by an abstract analysis of the processes of thought removed from temporal contingency; what then conditions or makes possible such an account in the material histories of social units? The theologian could say that the answer to this lay in the history that claims to be a history of God-in-relation to a historical community. The Jewish and Christian narrative is one in which the absolute is bound: by covenant for the Jew, by covenant and incarnation for the Christian. That is to say: the concrete articulation of divine (founding, creating) action is *in* what is other to the divine, in the life of the covenantal nation, in the life of the human agent who carries the divine meaning. The supreme disinterestedness of the divine, which, by definition, has no 'positional' corner to defend, articulates itself in the interest of a human community – a profoundly dangerous moment, since the interest of the community can then easily be elevated into a pseudo-independence of history. But the paradoxical reality of a community believing itself to stand for the 'interest' of a God without interest or favouritism is somewhere near the centre of how reflective Judaism and reflective Christianity have tried to imagine themselves. As Gillian Rose sees so clearly, the temptation for both is to lose the paradox – and so to lose the *political* vocation implicit in the paradox, the task of realising a corporate life whose critical practice constantly challenges sectional interest and proprietorial models of power or knowledge. In the language of both traditions, though in dramatically different ways, the people of God are a specific and vulnerable human group whose perception of their interest is as flawed and liable to violence as any other's, but who understand their fundamental task as embodying the 'non-interest' of God, the universal saving generosity of divine action. God is spoken of here as (mythologically) surrendering the no-place of an abstract absolute being, enacting the indiscriminate love or inclusive compassion that eventuates from divine life in a historical process (Israel, Jesus, the Church). And the contingent reality in which this enactment takes place is itself dispossessed of its own self-definition, as an 'interested' or sectional presence in the world: Israel's identity becomes bound up with exile, Jesus' identity with the cross, the Church (in some of its more primitive self-reflection) with the imagery of the 'resident alien'.

The point is that in this narrative and reflective tradition, the most fundamental reality that is (in some sense) thinkable requires to be spoken of in terms of dispossession or, to use the overtly theological word, *kenosis*. This is not an emptying of God without remainder into the otherness of history or contingency: what is enacted in history *is* the divine life, but living in its other, realising its 'interest' in its other. If, in simple terms, this is how God is, this is how God's creation also is, its very otherness to God the occasion of something like *work*, in the transformation of the contingent not out of its contingency but into the quest for a convergence always 'real' and always elusive. And for Christianity in particular, there is the further twist to the argument represented by the doctrine of the Trinity, which seeks to give some reflective substance to the 'always real' of that last formulation. In some sense, the existence of identity in otherness, neither term sacrificed, is not something that has to be thought as an ideal to be worked towards, but is timelessly actual. For the Christian theologian, this can be spelled out in connection with the history of the community of God's people – though it would be important to say that the reality in question was not the *product* of this or any history.[36]

We had better try to clarify what all this does and does not claim. It does not claim that there is a given metaphysical structure to which religious or doctrinal talk must conform. It does not claim that Christian doctrine either specifies a metaphysical structure or gives 'information' about invisible states of affairs. It does claim that certain models of thinking come to be available because of the presence of certain narratives about God and God's people, narratives that insist on speaking of divine displacement in one sense or another. It also claims, implicitly, that to reflect on these narratives pushes inexorably towards a particular vision of what the constants must be in human reflection and negotiation; that is to say, it is difficult to reflect here without simultaneously generating a discourse about fundamental ontology and a discourse about politics.[37] As to why the narratives are to be entertained in the first place, there can be no tidy or systematic answer; but it might be worth observing (to return to the starting point of this paper) that what stories we entertain as authoritative or revelatory has something to do with how or whether we do in fact construe actuality as difficult. And this in turn has to do with a certain leaning towards intellect rather than will as telling us basic things about ourselves-in-the-world. It may sound odd to associate what is, in effect, a theology of the cross with 'intellectualism'. But it is an important corrective to a version of the *theologia crucis* that resolves itself into an ethic of sacrifice that 'leaves me with no way to understand my mistakes by attempting to recover the interference of meaning or mediation',[38] or into an anti-metaphysical rhetoric of sacrificial faith that is ultimately sentimental because it refuses to *labour* at its own substance. Hegel explicitly, and Rose more ironically and guardedly, both locate the theology of the cross (in something other than a strictly dogmatic sense, certainly) between politics and metaphysics. Thinking what is difficult, thinking in dispossession, is essential to a politics that is anything other than a programme for the alternation of tyrannies and the unthought conflict of unreflective interest; thinking what is difficult, thinking in dispossession, insists on an ontology of some sort, capable of holding together the reality of difference and the imperative of work (i.e. reconciliation).

But how is a story of the death and resurrection of meaning, God in dispossession, generated? The theologian's proposal is that there is a narrative lens through which the political and the metaphysical can be synoptically envisioned, a human narrative about divine (constant or absolute or creative) action. It is not so much that we have to look for a borderland between theology and metaphysics, as if there were two territories in need of identifying a common frontier and perhaps concluding a non-aggression pact. But we have for too long been sheepish about the theology in metaphysics and the metaphysics in theology – the narrative echoes and underpinnings of what is said about general ontology, especially in an intellectual context in which we are better attuned than we once were to the materiality of our knowing; and the pressure of our narratives towards a practice of self-understanding, which in turn obliges us to think the conditions of our thinking. To be interested in thinking how we learn about learning is a condition for politics (including ethics), theology and metaphysics alike: and learning to see each of these in and through the others leaves us with plenty of labour to get on with. At least it will free us from the eccentric tribalisms that isolate these discourses and so fix and institutionalise an error that needs to be exposed if our intellectual health is to flourish and if our unthought modern repressions are to be challenged.

Notes

1. Roy Bhaskar, *Philosophy and the idea of freedom* (Oxford: Blackwell, 1991), 135.

2. Plato, *Republic* 369.A–C.

3. In the sense of 'continued' in the same frame of meaning, as in the *Lectures on aesthetics*, but also with allusion to the question of knowing how to go on, 'following a rule', etc., in the *Investigations*.

4. Bhaskar, *Philosophy and the idea of freedom*, 148, 155–6; see also Bhaskar, *The possibility of naturalism* (Brighton: Harvester, 1979), 69–82.

5. Bhaskar, *The possibility of naturalism*, Appendix I, esp. 145–51.

6. Gillian Rose, *Judaism and modernity* (Oxford: Blackwell, 1993), 8; see my own review of Edith Wyschogrod, *Saints and postmodernism* (Chicago: University of Chicago Press, 1990) in *Modern Theology* 8.3 (1992), 305–7, esp. 306 on the ambiguity of a 'saintly' desire wholly immersed in the unconditional demand of the Other in a way that allows little if any space to the element of reflection or discernment.

7. See David Kolb, *The critique of pure modernity* (Chicago: University of Chicago Press, 1986), 87: '[Hegel] is elevating our awareness of our own existence

to an awareness of our full necessary conditions and context. There is no move from inside to outside ... For Hegel we are involved in a whole we can come to reognize; we cannot get outside.'

8. Gillian Rose, *Hegel contra sociology* (Cambridge: Cambridge University Press, 1981), 150.

9. Ibid., 182.

10. Gillian Rose, *The broken middle* (Oxford: Blackwell, 1992), 147.

11. Ibid., ch. 4.

12. Ibid., 150–1.

13. Ibid., 155–6; I think that Rose's criticism, while weighty, does less than justice to Girard's association of the roots of violence with the anxiety of mimesis. It could be said that Girard, at least by the time of *Things hidden since the foundation of the world* (London: Athlone, 1987), is proposing an understanding of violence as itself the product of a mimetic process of *equalisation* between primitively *un*equal agents.

14. Arendt is judged most severely of these three as failing to conserve the tension between public and private, i.e. allowing a morally unambiguous place to the self-contained 'private' in certain spheres; see Rose, *The broken middle*, 223–36.

15. Ibid., ch. 5.

16. Ibid., 29–30 for a suggestive set of juxtapositions.

17. Ibid., 153ff., 258–64.

18. Ibid., 147–52.

19. Ibid., 148.

20. One could read this as parallel to Augustine's argument on the nature of evil in Book VII of the *Confessions*: if evil is a kind of substance, it is either present or absent in a situation, and there is no such thing as moral risk; we are either doomed or safe.

21. Rose, *The broken middle*, 303, 287–307.

22. Ibid., 296.

23. See, e.g., the well-known article of Donald MacKinnon on 'Aristotle's Conception of Substance', in Renford Bambrogh (ed.), *New essays on Plato and Aristotle* (London: Routledge and Kegan Paul, 1965), 97–119.

24. Rose, 'Of Derrida's spirit', in *Judaism and modernity*, 65–87.

25. Ibid., 75–6.

26. Ibid., 5.

27. Ibid., 60–3.

28. Rose, 'Walter Benjamin – out of the sources of modern Judaism', in *Judaism and modernity*, 175–210.

29. Ibid., 188.

30. Ibid., 182.

31. Ibid., 209.

32. The essay on Benjamin sketches the distinction between 'aberrated' and 'inaugurated' mourning (186–7, 209–10). The former is associated with desertion and catastrophic loss; the latter with the sense of being the object of knowing, being known or named by what we do not know or cannot speak of. Rose's conclusion is that only the latter leaves open the way to *forgiveness*, because it

issues in silence – words give way to a speechlessness that may signify dependence or grace. Benjamin, says Rose, is trapped in 'aberrated' mourning, where existence is itself construed as a kind of loss and fall, with grace located in an impossible historical or metaphysical elsewhere.

33. Ibid., 8.

34. Peter Osborne, 'Hegelian phenomenology and the critique of reason and society', *Radical philosophy* 32 (1982), 8–15, esp. 14–15.

35. Ibid., 15.

36. Against what seems to be the argument of Jürgen Moltmann in *The Trinity and the kingdom of God* (London: SCM Press, 1981) and other works.

37. See my article 'Trinity and ontology', in *On Christian theology* (Oxford: Blackwell, 2000), 148–66 – though I now demur from some of my remarks there about Hegel.

38. Rose, *Judaism and modernity*, 8.

5

Balthasar and difference

Difference preoccupies the postmodern consciousness. That portion of the intellectual world that can be called 'postmodernist' is in systematic revolt against the dominance of identity and the erosion of the reality of what is not said in any act of saying. Put more prosaically, the postmodern consciousness rejects the possibility of a representation of the world that harmonizes and includes any and every act, phenomenon or dictum, a representation that does not have to acknowledge its own locatedness and thus its own 'failure'. And so far from being a malign assault upon 'ordinary' human discourse, this contemporary insistence – certainly in the hands of Derrida, at least – claims to be the only adequate way (yes, of course that is a paradoxical claim in this context) of articulating what language actually is; for a searching after presence, identity and totality is a searching for the end of language. As if language were the imperfect means of knowing with which we have to struggle for the time being until something greater than language is here: which is no way to go about constructing theories of speech.

Hegel has often been the target of such revolt. He is understood (not necessarily rightly understood) as canonizing the search for the end of language under the guise of what looks like a dialogical structure. Hegel's spiritual subject posits itself and *then* negates itself; the negation is *conditioned* by the first affirmation, it is always and necessarily and exclusively the other *of* the thesis. In such an otherness, there is no real difference expressed; the semantic lack acknowledged in the thesis is the gap that the antithesis articulates, and there is no excess of what is unspoken that will, so to speak, free the second moment from the conditions fixed by the first. Even if we say that the negation of the negation means that there is some kind of excess in the second moment (its denial does not simply reinstate the first term), it remains, like the original negation, a moment of denial *of* the specificity of the foregoing moment. The Hegelian dialectic, in other words, is always bound to the model of otherness as conditioned by a *prior* sameness: at every juncture, sameness is what is primordially present and active, otherness is what reacts.

Yet what might it be to speak of a simultaneous or equipollent otherness? The characteristic seduction of literary and philosophical postmodernity is to look towards a rhetoric of unconditional difference, an unspeakable otherness that is the inevitable shadow of speech or thought; what is known, said, represented is present in its mode only because of the unrepresented and unrepresentable, which is not some substantive mystery 'behind' the speaking world but the sheer fluidity and contingency of speech itself, knotting itself around the emptiness of duration. Derrida's *différance* is still paradoxically infused with something like (almost) the numinous: the thereness of language itself, so necessarily mobile that it cannot embody 'real presence' and cannot be understood as a system of static representation, evokes something of the awe of the last propositions of the *Tractatus*. If there is speech, there is the unsayable, simply because speech cannot be everything, cannot escape its mobile, anarchic temporality, cannot do other than reflect itself and rework itself. But what is unsayable is strictly unsayable, not to be gestured towards in a timidly religious way. There is no relation between the same and the other, the said and the unsayable. The one is not even the 'opposite' of the other, as it cannot belong in one frame with it at any point.

But what makes this a seduction is precisely this refusal of a relation between same and other. If this is strictly maintained, the result, ironically, is another kind of reduction to the same. What is is speech, which finds its own otherness in its own life, responding to and reflecting on itself. Its temporality is curiously discarnate, as the passage of time is markable only by the play of linguistic events with one another. It is as if what is crudely understood as time, the time of the body's trans-actions, retreats, to be replaced by the variegated times of textual transaction and interaction, diverse, often reversible. If otherness is the always unsayable, what can be said about the prosaic and diurnal otherness of the processes of dialogue, the relations of concrete social power, the specific rather than general moments where speech is arrested (terror, passion, doubt; the awful fragmentations of sense we hear in Shakespeare's virtuosos of sexual jealousy, Othello and Leontes; the violent abruptness of the techniques with which Herbert ends so many of his poems; the nightmare fluency of the diabolical voices in Dostoevsky, showing by their uninterrupted movement the gulf between diabolical and human speech, with its hesitation, backtracking and marks of struggle)? If the interruptions of discourse are always the sacred unsayable other of some postmodernist theory, what becomes of the temporal conflicts and resistances of 'ordinary' interpersonal exchange? The absolutizing of the other, whether in the hermeneutic vein of Derrida or the ethical vein of Levinas, can work to reinforce a sameness more enclosed than Hegel's (or Hegel's, at least, as understood by so much of modernity and postmodernity).

Two poles, then: a model that suggests first identity or presence, next difference (resolving again into identity); and a model that suggests always an identity shadowed by a wholly unrepresentable otherness. Neither model, it could be said, allows easily for a difference that is both simultaneous and interactive, a difference that allows temporal change, reciprocity of action, and thus avoids the two different but depressingly similar varieties of totalization that might be implied by the polar models we began with. And this is where theology stakes a claim to be heard within the cultural debate. The themes of Christian theology, above all its reflections on otherness within the divine life and the peculiar otherness between the divine and the human in the identity of the Saviour, demand, in our present context, to be read afresh, as attempts to think through otherness so as to avoid totalization. In the 1998 book, *Balthasar at the end of modernity*,[1] Fergus Kerr, Graham Ward, Lucy Gardner, David Moss and Ben Quash examine the thought of a twentieth-century theologian who has devoted more energy than most theologians to pursuing the logic of the trinitarian and christological traditions of the Church, and has outlined a metaphysical idiom that could shed much light on the threatened stand-off between a philosophy of unproblematic identity and an anti-metaphysics of speech and the void. All the contributors to the book share a central conviction that it is in his treatment of difference that Balthasar has most to say to the present intellectual scene; and this is worked out in several different ways (which permeate all the essays in varying degrees).

To start with there is the fundamental importance of understanding analogy itself as a tool and a principle in Balthasar's corpus. The theme has been the subject matter of quite a bit of study in recent years, and these remarks will be woefully superficial to those more familiar with the material. But briefly, the important points made about Balthasar's approach to analogy have much to do with two features of his discussions. There is, in the first place, his repeated reference to the dictum of the Fourth Lateran Council: whatever the likeness between God and creatures, it is outweighed by a greater unlikeness (*maior dissimilitudo*). Balthasar connects this with the principle classically formulated by Nicholas of Cusa that God is *non aliud* in respect of creation – not *an* other, an item enumerable in a list along with the contents of the universe. Analogy is thus emphatically *not* a correspondence between two or more things exhibiting in varying degrees the same features, as if God had a very great deal of good and creatures steadily diminishing quantities of the same. There is no system of which God and creatures are both part (so much can be granted to a rhetoric of unqualified *différance*). But what then *is* analogy? It is the active presence of the divine liberty, love and beauty precisely within the various and finite reality of material/temporal reality. 'The divine' is not present in creation in the form of 'hints of transcendence', points in the created order where finitude and creatureliness appear to thin out or open up to a mysterious infinity, but in creation being itself – which includes, paradigmatically, creation being itself in unfinishedness, time-taking, pain and death. The crucified Jesus is, in this context, the ground and manifestation of what analogy means.

The implications of this are many and complex. God and the created order do not and cannot stand together as prototype and image in any straightforward sense – which means that the relation between them is not that of primordial identity and derivative response, even though it is a relation of unqualified dependence. They cannot be moments in one story. But the dependence of creation upon God is the free bestowal of God's life *in* the forms of finitude, with all their historical and conditioned diversity. The otherness of God and creation is to be conceived at once in two ways that are deeply in tension, yet equally grounded in the *non aliud* principle. On the one hand, the otherness between God and the world is inexhaustible and irreducible; nothing can bring these realities into co-ordination or – in the ordinary sense – subordination and superordination. There is always an 'unlikeness' that defies (by definition) measure and category. On the other hand, the life of creation is not an independent subject alongside the divine life, but that life itself freely 'alienated' from itself in a gift so absolute that it establishes the possibility of a free response, of an authentic love. God truly loves God; yet God truly loves God in and through what is, without qualification, *not* God – the realm of time and vulnerability, in which loving subjects are formed. Thus God is neither an identity into which otherness must be assumed, nor a nameless and abstract sacredness around the corners of speech. The representation of God is always starkly paradoxical within the contingent Godlessness of a vulnerable and corrupted world. And because the variousness of that contingent world is so grounded and affirmed or allowed in this strange relatedness, the hierarchies of the world are unsettled: we cannot simply assent to the vulgarized Platonism that would order the creation according to whether this or that reality was 'closer' to the divine and the spiritual. The otherness of the contingent world to itself, the dualities of body and spirit, male and female, and so on, can no longer be thought of as higher and lower, first and second, pure and compromised. The analogical presence of divine love in the form of the worldly other makes differences in the world in some sense simultaneous and reciprocal, not to be read in terms of a fall from pure presence or transparency, or a descending *scala naturae*.

But this reading of the analogical relationship makes sense only in the context of what Christians say of God-as-such. The Catholic faith is that God is not *a* subject, nor even a plurality of subjects in intimate connection. God is intrinsically that life which exists only and necessarily in the act of 'bestowal', in a self-alienation that makes possible the freedom and love of an other that is at the same time itself *in* otherness. The extremity of the relation between God and the God-forsaken Jesus is our way in to this claim for the life of God-as-such: the divine life is what sustains itself as unqualified unity across the greatest completeness of alienation that can be imagined; and so appears as unqualified gift or (as I have been calling it) bestowal. The gulf between Father and crucified Son, between Father in heaven and Son in hell, now appears as the immeasurable measure of the way divine love 'leaves' itself, travels infinitely from itself (from self-possession, self-presence). Here there can be no identity prior to differentiation: the only identity in question is precisely the total and eternal self-bestowal that constitutes the other. The generative or originary moment in the divine life, the Father, has no reality except in the act of generating the otherness of the Son and sustaining the unity of divine life across this gulf of immeasurable otherness by the issuing of 'spirit': the life bestowed in its wholeness upon the Son is both returned to the Father and opened up beyond the duality of Father and Son as the Holy Spirit. Or, in other words, the self-alienating of divine life in the Father's self-gift to the Son itself 'alienates' itself, posits itself as *more* than a symmetry of self-sacrifice, becomes that which the Son gives, realizes, liberates, from the depth of his distance from the Father.

These dense theological insights, by no means easy to trace clearly

or formulate economically in the terms of Balthasar's work, yet fundamental to practically all of his immense output, return us to the starting
point of these remarks. Here is a theological language which can make
some claim to have gone beyond the sterile opposition of undifferentiated presence/identity on the one hand and unthinkable *différance* on
the other. How far Balthasar realizes the promise of his own insight is
a question that invites a reflection at least as extensive as his own
writing, and is therefore not a question that a single book is going to
answer. But a highly significant area noted here, in which Balthasar
tantalizingly both opens up revolutionary perspectives and intimates
some very firm and traditional closures, is that of sexual differentiation.
It is theologically important that humanity itself is not thinkable as a
monistic identity; to be human is to be gendered. And if the unity of
the divine life and love is analogically active in the differentiation
of the material and contingent world, theology is bound to take the
genderedness of human existence with complete seriousness. Balthasar
undoubtedly does so. But what makes his analysis tantalizing is a
central unclarity about how far sexual differentiation really can be said
to partake of the differentiation of the trinitarian persons, a differentiation in which there is no unilateral and fixed pattern of priority or
derivation but a simultaneous, reciprocal conditioning, a pattern of
identity *in* the other without remainder. To engage with this *aporia* in
Balthasar, we need more than an enlightened outrage at a rhetoric of
sexual differentiation apparently in thrall to unexamined patriarchy.
Balthasar is not so easily written off. What is needed, rather, is a
response within his own rhetoric, within the terms of the extraordinary
affirmation of simultaneous and reciprocal difference that his account
of the trinitarian relations and the relation of God to creation insists
upon (and I say 'insists upon' rather than simply 'allows', because it is
so clear that his entire theological enterprise falls if these relational
distinctions can in any way be reduced to a system of co-ordination
and subordination).

But this inevitably brings into sharp focus the extreme difficulty of
realizing in our theological speech the 'simultaneity and reciprocity'
required by the formative patterns at work here. Inevitably – because
our speech is temporal, like the rest of our human being – we say one
thing, then another; in speaking of the trinitarian relations, theologians
have always found it difficult to avoid various kinds of virtual subordinationism (how do you speak of dependence without at once speaking
of some kind of 'coming after'?). It is not too surprising if the same

issue arises in connection with speaking theologically about gender. Hence the provocative idea, central to the essay by Lucy Gardner and David Moss,[2] that 'something like the sexes' is part of what is involved in speaking of God. And if all accounts of difference in the world other than static oppositions of competing atomic subjects are constructed narratively and dramatically, if the way we speak of self-dispossession and gift is unavoidably the telling of a sequential process, do we not also have to say, boldly, that 'something like time' is involved in speaking of God? That is: however hard we insist upon the simultaneity of the divine subsistents, we can say nothing of this simultaneity that is not abstract and formal unless we take the necessary (not to say canonical) risk of *evoking* simultaneity by telling a cluster of 'stories' that configure in different and reciprocal ways the relations of the trinitarian persons. In short, it is not by denying undialectically the realities of time and gender that we arrive at an apt rhetoric for the divine, but by so working with the modalities of talk about time and gender that the timeless (that is, in concretely theological terms, the faithful, always active) reality of the reciprocal differentiations of trinitarian life is brought to view.

And this returns us yet again to our starting point: all this discussion has about it something of the character of a Moebius strip. God is not to be spoken of by denying contingency. The mysterious difference of God is never an abstract otherness defined simply by the negation of the predicates of contingent being. Balthasar is always ambivalent about much of the apophatic tradition in Christian theology (and sometimes, as perhaps in his pages on John of the Cross, does some of its representatives less than complete justice), precisely because it insufficiently observes the true and radical sense of divine difference that his cruciform understanding of analogy intimates. God is not different *like that*: if divine difference were the negation of all finite predicates, God would be the other belonging to a discourse about the finite world. God's life would be subsumed under that of the world, the antithesis of the world's thesis; and out of such a discourse, no possible language for divine freedom or love could be generated. Balthasar's form of negative theology is close to the fierce Lutheran conviction that it is only in that concrete otherness to God embodied in the abandonment of the crucified Messiah to death and hell that the divine difference, both within God and between God and the finite order, can be seen. Here and here alone can we begin to think the freedom of God that is entailed in the power to bestow the divine life without reserve and without limit, unconstrained by any imaginable distance, threat or absence.

Here and there in *Balthasar at the end of modernity*, some unease or at least interrogation is expressed as to Balthasar's capacity to allow in specifics what his theological vision enjoins in general. It is not only a question about his handling of gender issues; there is the teasing and challenging abstraction from the actual history of this century, the abstraction from the specific calls to 'stake' an identity in dialogue and action (to borrow a familiar idiom of Gillian Rose); there is the sense that at times the spiralling inwards towards the 'marian' moment in the Church's reality, the unqualified contemplative self-abnegation that allows God's act to *be* in the world, slips towards a reinstatement of certain kinds of hierarchies within creation, hierarchies of transparency to the divine, and a concomitant impatience with the realities of conflict within the Church. This is expressed neatly in the charge that Balthasar's espousal of the 'dramatic' in his theology is persistently over-taken by reversion to the 'epic', understood as a narrative of unfolding and final containment.[3] What I earlier called the temporal conflicts and resistances of 'ordinary' interpersonal exchange, what might equally be called the sense of the tragic – always a significantly difficult area for the theologian to handle – are often felt as absences in Balthasar's *œuvre*, despite the often stunningly powerful focus on the unconsoled dereliction of the crucified.

But if the overall perspective here outlined is correct, if Balthasar does indeed open up a path beyond the twin threats of an eternal return to the same and an eternal alienation between thought or speech and the void, he is proposing a programme so searching and radical that even a theologian of his stature is unlikely to realize it with uniform fidelity. Part of the hinterland of this book is a strong dissatisfaction with a good deal of the reception of Balthasar in the theological community, a reception that has become increasingly politicized. He has not been adequately located within a continuing European cultural and intellectual debate (granted that his *awareness* of the debate is at best uneven); he has been adopted as a canonical authority for certain disciplinary and doctrinal options among Catholics (Roman and Anglican), most notably in just that area where his thought is (as the foregoing pages have illustrated) most contestable and complex, his reflections on matters of gender; he has been stigmatized as a simplistic purveyor of unreformed certainties, appealing to corrupt or oppressive models of authority and obedience in the Church; or merely ignored as one of those eccentrics who assume that the whole breadth of human reality can be illuminated by the Nicene and Chalcedonian faith.

The essayists in *Balthasar at the end of modernity* are happy to be counted themselves among such eccentrics; but they are for that very reason concerned to pursue Balthasar's own method of tracing a path towards the 'formless' form of the beauty of God's Word through the cultural agon of the end of the twentieth century. Theology is fragmented now as never before, at precisely the moment when certain of its traditional patterns and resources have extraordinary pertinence to the cultural culs-de-sac and standoffs amongst which we live or try to live or fail to live. Balthasar is one of a very small number of contemporary theologians to articulate this pertinence in a way other than simple reiteration of a sealed and finished tradition. (As one or two scholars have observed, Michel de Certeau is another, whose convergences with Balthasar – as well as some dramatic divergences – badly need more discussion.) Balthasar is too important for a renewal of Christian ontology to be left to the politics of the Catholic institutions; he undoubtedly needs to be 'politicized', but in the widest possible theatre of politics, the muddled, struggling debate, so often stifled or abandoned, as to the character of human difference – the debate in which the Christian theologian obstinately battles to understand why it might be that the concrete plurality of human life, from conception to death, demands an unqualified, attentive and hopeful contemplation and a response of nurture and of love.

Notes

1. Lucy Gardner, David Moss, Ben Quash and Graham Ward, *Balthasar at the end of modernity* (Edinburgh: T&T Clark, 1998).

2. Lucy Gardner and David Moss, 'Something like time; something like the sexes – an essay in reception', in ibid., 69–138.

3. See Ben Quash, 'Drama and the ends of modernity', in ibid., 139–70.

6

Balthasar, Rahner and the
apprehension of being

Most people who are at all alert to the situation of Catholic theology over the last two or three decades will be aware that there is a certain tension between these two most seminal figures in that world. Cornelius Ernst notes, in 1970,[1] the rumour that Balthasar, le Guillou and others of like mind are about to start a periodical designed to counter the influence of *Concilium* – a journal very much associated with Rahner's style and approach; and to the present day, *Communio*, otherwise the *International Catholic review*,[2] continues to represent, if not entirely an opposite pole, at the very least a significantly different set of concerns from those of *Concilium*. It is marginally more European in its focus, rather more suspicious of 'political theologies', rather more interested in spirituality and in the world of the imagination and the arts. These are only the loosest characterisations; but they probably express for many people something of the felt difference in tone between Balthasar himself and the majority of Catholic theologians associated with *Concilium*. It would be misleading to see this simply as a conservative–radical split: the solidarity of *Communio* and of Balthasar himself with ecclesiastical tradition is a highly critical one, and the characteristic stance of *Communio* contributors was at least for its first few years quite sharply distinct from that of favoured curial theologians (Galot, for instance). Where, then, is the heart of the conflict? And how real a collision is it? Do we have to do here with a difference of temper only, or with a more fundamental disagreement? In this essay I hope to explore the nature of these differences, linking them to some of the basic philosophical options of the writers in question, rather than attempting to plot them on a graph of contemporary Catholic politics. Of course there are pretty obvious political and institutional aspects to, and consequences of, such options; but I think it is worth while to step back from a definition of conflict primarily in such terms, if only to avoid journalistic banalities.[3]

The publication in 1966 of *Cordula oder der Ernstfall*[4] made it abundantly clear that Balthasar and Rahner had arrived at a serious parting of the ways. This fiercely worded tract reproached Rahner and his school on several counts – the reduction of the love of God to mere philanthropy, the ideas of a systematic 'hiddenness' of grace, of the natural aptitude of human beings for a 'transcendental' revelation in and through the structures of their own spiritual dynamism: everything, in short, summed up in the Rahnerian picture of the 'anonymous Christian' outside the visible Church, the person who, even if a theoretical atheist, lives by faith, hope and love. A good deal of Balthasar's work in the sixties and early seventies is marked by a similar animus: even where Rahner is not named, we find a sharp polemical insistence on the *particularity* of revealed love[5] and thus on the particularity of Christian response, nourished by a concrete image, characterised by specific and unique marks.[6] Balthasar is not, he assures us,[7] attempting to force theology back into a narrow ecclesiasticism, denying the existence of God's grace beyond the frontiers of the Church: 'the Christian may have the new and rather confusing experience of discovering that most of what he brings with him to the world has in some way or another already reached the world, not in its entirety of course, but only in fragments'.[8] But he is insistent that in so far as Christian action is *significant* action, action demanding interpretation and enriched and stimulated by interpretation, it requires a normative and generative focus. It is not enough to say that the Christian image or language gives shape to existing forms of action; distinctive forms of action arise in response to a fundamental event of address or call, and are constantly interwoven with speech and image in a single process of interpretation – a process which is best understood as the testimony *of* love *to* love. And to speak of Christ as 'image' is not to reduce him to a hermeneutical projection on our part, a vehicle of understanding; he is image *as* Word, the projection to us of a 'free self-expression', an absolute initiative.[9] The beauty of God incarnate can never be determined in advance by a theological *a priori*.[10] It appears as a phenomenon whose necessity is internal to itself, and thus as a manifestation of freedom.[11] No outer condition or plastic force dictates the form of beauty: it cannot be other than it is, simply because of the logic of its own inner balance and inner adequacy, even 'comprehensiveness'.

I

Such a view will inevitably challenge a transcendentalism which takes as axiomatic the need to establish an epistemology primarily on the basis of *Vorgriff* – formal 'pre-understanding', determining in advance the possibility of specific (categorial) knowledge. In his immensely important early work, *Spirit in the world*,[12] Rahner develops the concept of *Vorgriff* in detail. 'Agent intellect', the power of making differentiations between perceived things, objectifying them and so rendering possible linguistic reference, is the condition for knowing any particular object *as* a particular object ('something actually intelligible'). However, this capacity can only operate if it has at its root the sense of difference between the concrete formal object, the object which is this-rather-than-that, and the unlimited existential possibility 'underlying' it. Or, in other words: to understand *contingency*, the truth that things are as they are but might have been otherwise, is in the same moment to understand the entirely open-ended potential of being itself. Nothing *need* be as it is; thus everything specific we grasp, we understand as *one* possible limitation or determination of an infinite range of possibilities.[13]

If this is so, we can say that 'agent intellect' is a pre-apprehension, *Vorgriff*, of unlimited possibility,[14] and ultimately of being-as-such, *esse*, the very act of existing, which is the universal ground of each and every specific possibility. It is affirmed as an entirely formal and simple concept, but not in such a way as to make it empty; rather it is the ultimate and total 'overplus of meaning', 'absolute fullness in unity'. It can only be thought in and through particulars, as we grasp at once their particularity and limitedness and the unlimited possibility out of which they come; it cannot be conceived abstractly (in independence of particulars), although it is conceived in the *act* of abstraction (thinking away specific limits and determinations, to reach an ideal fullness of potential). In so far as this *esse* is presupposed (or pre-apprehended) as absolute and real, the *Vorgriff* of *esse* is a pre-apprehension of God – not as an object, but as the condition for grasping all objects.[15]

The act of abstraction, by which the transcendental condition of any and every particular is grasped, is not, Rahner insists, separable from what Aquinas called *conversio ad phantasmata*, turning to the particular in its concrete manifestation.[16] Abstraction and conversion are two aspects of a single act or process, and neither is unilaterally prior to the other. Knowledge does indeed begin in space and time, with sense data; yet, as we have seen, the knowledge of sense data as intelligible, as having form, includes and presupposes the priority of abstraction, though that abstraction would be logically unthinkable without concrete *sensibilia* to abstract *from*. So in knowing the particular as intelligible, knowing it 'spiritually', spirit becomes conscious of its own structures; and it would not become self-aware in this way without the *conversio*, the apprehension of the particular object as *object*, as *other*. And if spirit is fundamentally constituted by desire for absolute and unconditional being, by a pull towards the infinite, it requires sense knowledge as a mediation of itself to itself – something which enables it to act in the way necessary to reach absolute being; i.e., to abstract. Thus we must see spirit as in some sense 'producing' sensibility 'as a condition of its own fulfilment'.[17]

Spirit in the world concludes with some general reflections on revelation, distinguishing 'the revelation of being-as-such which places man before God' from the revealing act of God in the particularities of history. Abstraction 'reveals' a real but unknown God; but in doing so it provides a basis for the question of whether God has acted or spoken in the world, because it points dumbly to an absolute freedom and opens itself to the possibility of encountering it and *recognising* it in wordly events. Abstraction reveals the human subject to itself as a potential 'hearer' of communication from absolute freedom; and again, in affirming the possibility of free, gratuitous self-communication, it affirms the possibility of love, which can be grasped fully only in a response of love.[18] So to be 'placed before God' in the transcendental self-awareness by which the spirit comes to itself establishes the spirit as capable of love, hope, faith; and there are all sorts of human activity in which these capacities are realised, when men and women act as authentically spiritual, self-transcending subjects, responding to the inner pressure of unconditional claims. When the possibility of love has been opened up, there is a call to love unconditionally and radically, and the refusal of such a call is the spirit's denial of its own nature.[19] And when the spirit does freely and consciously respond to its pre-conceptual grasp of a transcendent and infinite horizon not only for its knowledge but for its love and desire, it is receiving and responding to saving grace, living in obedience to a God who may not yet be named but is none the less actively present.

There is therefore a universal *praeparatio evangelica*, a tacit expectation of hearing loving self-communication, in the radical openness of the human spirit's love and searching. This means that we possess in advance a framework within which to understand Jesus Christ: a person who lives out unreservedly and wholeheartedly the response to an 'infinite' vocation to love and trust, who 'hears the Word' with no resistance or doubt, will be the complete realisation of human potential, and will thus express humanly the unconditional love of God himself, God's total commitment to the world.[20] This realisation depends upon God's initiative, God's freedom; but it is an answer to the quest for fulfilment implied *a priori* in the structures of the human spirit. We cannot 'deduce' Jesus of Nazareth from our anthropology, although we can demonstrate from the transcendental analysis of spirit that he does in fact fulfil the conditions there apprehended for a concrete manifestation of the absolute.[21] In fact, Christology illustrates precisely the unity between transcendental *Vorgriff* and particular apprehension that we have seen to be fundamental to the whole of human knowledge. Without the particular ('categorial') revelation of Jesus, we should not be able fully to articulate the range and significance of the already existing transcendental apprehension of love and absolute trust;[22] without that precondition, we should not be able to recognise the event of Jesus as decisive and revelatory. We must in some degree know our own hearts before we can recognise the heart's desire which is the Incarnate God.

So, just as knowledge is one,[23] revelation is one. 'Transcendental' and 'categorial' revelation have the same content and the same purpose, God's gracious giving of himself.[24] When a human being accepts the gracious invitation to self-transcendence, he or she receives the grace of revelation, even when the mind's object in this process is purely formal and not consciously grasped in relation to the events of 'categorial revelation'. Here, though, there is something of an unclarity. Given that the transcendental *Vorgriff* cannot operate without some categorial occasion, how are we to understand the categorial element in revelation to non-Christians? Rahner himself is not all that helpful here (he has written comparatively little *explicitly* dealing with non-Christian religions, as opposed to European secularism):[25] he suggests that, as in the Old Covenant there is a concrete institutional religious structure which both expresses God's saving will and incorporates ambivalent and even corrupt elements, so, in religions in general, the institutional form may mediate, though not in an uncriticisable way, 'the legitimate and concrete form of the divine law',[26] until the advent of a faith in which the relation of institution and moral or spiritual form of life is an intrinsic one, the institution becoming 'an element of this form itself'.[27] This is in effect to say that the transcendental revelation outside the Church has an inadequate but never wholly invalid categorial form. The *conversio* of the spirit to concrete forms is not controlled by the particular categorial and historical event willed by God as the uniquely adequate and comprehensive manifestation of the human destiny. Though Rahner does not develop the argument in precisely these terms, various of his followers and pupils have done so.[28]

Thus Rahner's thesis about 'anonymous Christianity' has its roots firmly in a philosophical grounding which also determines the shape of his Christology. The foundations laid in *Spirit in the world* represent a bold attempt to interpret St Thomas's insistence on the epistemological primacy of sense experience from a post-Kantian standpoint, reckoning with the irreversible shift in philosophy towards the critical analysis of subjectivity as the starting point for discussion. If metaphysics is to be done again after Kant, it can only begin by observing the Kantian prohibition against the speculative deduction of non-apparent states of affairs: metaphysics must be shown to be demanded precisely by and in the analysis of the knowing subject.

II

It is just this philosophical starting point which Balthasar consistently queries. His debate with Rahner goes back to the very early days of their careers, and it is a great error to represent it as merely a part of Balthasar's alleged 'conservative evaluations and negative criticism of contemporary tendencies within the Church'.[29] In discussing the later and post-conciliar Rahner, Balthasar several times[30] refers back to his review of the first edition of *Geist im Welt*.[31] Here, at the end of a very careful and sympathetic summary of the book (and of an earlier paper by Rahner),[32] he sets out his questions and reservations. Rahner's mentor and precursor Maréchal seems, in Balthasar's eyes, to have transformed what should be only the starting point of metaphysics into metaphysics itself – i.e., (presumably) he has so concentrated on the analysis of subjectivity as to make the metaphysical pre-apprehension of *esse* excessively formal and abstract, and virtually empty. Rahner corrects this – to some extent: his concluding section on metaphysics and imagination[33] repeatedly stresses the necessity of the objective other, imaginatively and sensibly grasped, for any self-understanding and any openness to 'the absolute breadth of *esse*'. However, Balthasar is concerned that the experience of intersubjectivity is not much developed in this discussion, and also that the 'agent intellect' of Rahner threatens to become more and more an inaccessible inner capacity, so abstractive in its mode of operation that it is hard to see how it can really deliver an affirmation of *esse* as *plenitude* rather than merely as a void of pure negative indeterminacy. In other words: can the *Vorgriff* of *esse* actually do a useful theological job, pointing to a source of creative freedom – quite the opposite of sheer indeterminacy, as Rahner is well aware? Might it not be preferable to begin from the basic experience of the *Gestalthaftigkeit des Wesens*, the potential orientation of being towards concrete form, rather than a pre-apprehension of limitlessness? This at least permits us to distinguish satisfactorily between negative infinitude and positive capacity.[34]

What Balthasar seems to mean is this: 'being' is apprehended primarily in the endless variety of particular forms, and it is only by attending to the fact of this *variety* that being may be grasped as gratuitously creative – and thus as concrete fullness. The formal *Vorgriff* of unlimited possibility is not enough: if we attain to the affirmation of *esse* only through the rich plurality of worldly experience, that *esse* must be affirmed as containing not simply unspecified potentiality but the potentiality for existing in and as the world's particularities. Behind this is not only Balthasar's fundamental Platonism (the One is not simply *innominabile* but *omninominabile*) but also the specific Christian Platonism of a writer like Maximus the Confessor,[35] with his theory of the *logoi* of all things pre-existing in God as *particular* creative intentions, dependent upon the eternal *Logos* who is the divine ground of the possibility of all otherness, all differentiation.

Balthasar elaborates this in a densely written conclusion to his survey of Western metaphysics.[36] Conscious experience is experience of being in a world, being part of a whole; and to experience another entity is to experience it likewise as a part of a whole. Thus the fundamental cognitive moment is the apprehension of *participation*, the participation of beings in being; and this affirmation of being is not the grasp of a formal limitlessness, since there is no possibility of expressing or thinking being without beings. Being depends upon the existence of particulars – in the Heideggerian language Balthasar employs here, *Sein* is dependent upon *Dasein* – and so is non-existent in itself. So being cannot itself be the source of beings, of concrete forms; and if (with Heidegger) we regard the *Sein–Dasein* distinction as ultimate, we risk the nihilistic and tragic conclusion that being overall, instead of offering illumination and significance to the world of *Dasein*, is an organic, impersonal and alien process of fate or necessity. But if I am genuinely aware of the world as contingent, a different consequence suggests itself. I participate in the world, but I am not a *function* of the whole; I am aware of my unique, non-necessary concrete being as distinct from the 'necessity' of the world around. Yet *all* particular subsistents have the same characteristic of participation in the whole in a unique, non-functional manner. If this is so, it is impossible to conceive being-as-a-whole in a mechanical, supra-personal mode: it is a system of contingent and flexible interdependence, in which novelty and gratuity are possible – and in which therefore beauty is intelligible. It is not to be understood as necessity, and therefore points to a deeper ground and context which equally cannot be conceived as necessity. It is 'ultimate freedom', such as neither *Sein* nor *Dasein* can possess, a freedom which is both total concrete fullness (limitless possibility, if you like, though conceived in strictly personal, therefore non-abstract, terms) *and* utter 'poverty' since it wills to keep nothing back, but is entirely gift and love. From this freedom flows the liberty of created *esse*, capable of endless particular transformation, and 'seeking' ever greater variety because – as an image of the divine freedom – it can hold nothing back for itself. And, finally, from the freedom of *esse* flows the freedom of particular being, which is again fullness and poverty together: the fullness of having received the act of being in all its richness as a gift, the poverty of 'shepherding' it (Heidegger again) in chance and limited circumstances, and also the poverty of knowing that only in 'ekstasis', in letting go of the particular as something to be possessed, clung to, privatised or hoarded, is the fullness of the act of being realised in the world of particulars, in its own infinite poverty and 'ekstatic' self-gift.[37]

This, for Balthasar, is the abidingly valuable aspect of the notion of an *analogia entis*[38] – the *analogia libertatis*, which affirms that created freedom is the more fully realised the more deeply it gives itself up to uncreated freedom.[39] And this analogy depends upon that basic sense of belonging in a world, of radical contingency, which Balthasar makes his metaphysical foundation. Thus his objection to Rahner is in fact an objection not so much to one contemporary theologian (for whom, in fact, he has enormous respect)[40] as a protest against the whole tradition of European 'mainstream' philosophy between Kant and Heidegger – what he refers to in *Cordula* as 'the system' – a tradition which he sees as negating the 'sense of belonging in a world' by its obsession with subjectivity and the self-constitution of the subject. Kant himself, Balthasar is careful to point out, is very much a frontier figure, whose thought cannot simply be collapsed into the idealism that came in his wake. His ethic is anything but an individualistic eudæmonism: the experience in which I become aware of myself in the summons to *Achtung*, attention to the imperative of the Good, reveals a self called to belonging in the world, a self to which the world is prior. *I* become authentic and significant only because I have been touched and called by the demand made on me by *another* whom I recognise as an 'end in himself' and thus as possessing value and significance independently of my will and my prior consciousness. My autonomy as an ethical being depends upon my obedience, my humility.[41] Clearly, this is not far from Balthasar's formulation about created and uncreated freedom – at least from the human side. But this is the point where Kant is fatally ambiguous, since the deduction of the postulates of practical reason leaves little room for the affirmation of a free, infinite subjectivity.[42] He is poised between the *reflexio* of an earlier philosophical style, reflection establishing the possibility of knowing supra-empirical reality, and the idealist model of reflective rationality as itself constituting objective being;[43] his strong sense of the essential receptivity of consciousness prevents his taking the final step towards the latter option.

Yet, once again, the mode of deduction of the transcendental postulates illustrates a deep cleavage between the 'pure' ego which is merely 'the unity of apperception, the thinking subject, pure spontaneity', and the empirical ego which is the object of self-reflection, in its manifold experiences; the latter, the human person as *Naturwesen*, has nothing to do with metaphysics.[44] And so the ground is cleared for the separation in Kant's aesthetics between beauty and objectivity, between beauty and the realms of truth and goodness:[45] we are already on the road to Fichte, for whom the starting point of metaphysics is solely the ego in its autonomy. The material world is, for Fichte, instrumental in the realisation of the ego; it is without significance independently of the ego; thus it is incapable of manifesting God. Spirit swallows up nature, and the non-human world is wholly subordinated to human self-fulfilment (and in this sense, says Balthasar, there is a paradoxical convergence in practical consequences between idealism and materialism).[46]

What has been disastrously lost in this metaphysical rake's progress is the possibility of *wonder*, of contemplative receptivity in the face of the world's richness, the overthrowing of a contemplative (and thus potentially God-directed) mode of knowledge by a model of *Bewältigung* – thought as mastery, domination, even exploitation, Bacon's nature on the rack.[47] This is the anthropocentric distortion to which Balthasar takes such exception; and when, in *Cordula* and elsewhere, he so sharply questions the redefinition of salvation as 'hominisation', it is not in any anti-humanist sense. He is posing a profoundly important question about our understanding of the human *vis-à-vis* the world as a whole, echoing Heidegger's polemic against the technocratic distortion of human relations with the natural order.[48] It is a point worth pondering by those who regard Balthasar's theology as reactionary or uncritical in the socio-political as well as in the ecclesiastical sphere, or as psychologically regressive[49] (since his protest against the anthropocentric approach could be fruitfully read as a critique of the mentality of 'infantile omnipotence' in our attitudes to nature and matter).

Now it is precisely the Fichtean development of Kant's transcendentalism which Balthasar identifies in Rahner (and in Maréchal).[50] The transcendental *Vorgriff* of *esse* establishes the priority of spirit to sensibility, even though the former cannot realise itself without the latter; and, as we have seen, Rahner does speak explicitly of the 'production' of *Sinnlichkeit* by spirit, without giving any very satisfactory account of this ambiguous expression. He can also, of course, stress that sense and spirit stand in a position of 'mutual' origination,[51] and even describes sensibility as 'the *receptive* origin of spirit';[52] so that there is no suggestion that there exists a real prior positive intuition on the part of spirit to which sensibility is 'later' added (Rahner is rightly dismissive of this kind of two-storey epistemology, whichever way up it is erected). Yet there is a good deal in *Spirit in the world* which lends colour to a suspicion that the concrete and historical world is in some degree seen as instrumental in furthering the fulfilment of spirit, and has no significance apart from that. The tight connection forged between *abstractio* and *conversio* is one of the most impressive intellectual achievements of Rahner's study, but it does not in itself provide a wholly satisfactory account of the experience of the *Wunder des Seins* as Balthasar understands it – the apprehension of being as a system of interdependent contingencies, the response to which can never be *abstractio*, but only the yielding of a privatised, self-enclosed perception to an 'ekstatic' participation – a self-forgetful lived involvement, both active and receptive, in the world as a whole.

This may help to explain the importance to Balthasar of the category of *drama* in explicating his theology. If knowledge is essentially participatory (not in the sense of a transcendental pre-conscious union of subject and object, but as recognition of a place within a network of relations), it is inseparable from history and *praxis*: there is 'no neutral "teachable" truth'.[53] Knowledge occurs and develops as reflection on the process of interaction between God and the world, a drama in which we are actors and not spectators.[54] Without this 'dramatic' dimension theology runs aground in various rationalistic abstractions. Paraphrasing (fairly freely) Balthasar's programme at the beginning of his second *magnum opus*, *Theodramatik*, we might say that theology requires not only the exegesis of its foundational deposits but also their 'performance' – as if the text of Scripture were a 'libretto', says Balthasar.[55] This means a call to human subjects to enter into the dialogue of God with 'the other', which is grounded in his own trinitarian life,[56] and enacted in the drama of Jesus and his Father, and Jesus and the human world. 'Drama' involves the active-and-receptive encounter with 'the stranger', the contingencies of relationship and reaction; it is truth manifest in dialogue, in a narratively structured interaction which resists theoretical reduction and premature or facile resolution – in current literary terms, resists 'closure'. The drama is at one level determined by the form of revelation, which is the reflection of an eternal form, a final source of meaning, yet is also indeterminate in so far as it can only be realised and re-presented in the world of historical contingency, diversity and liberty. The form of the paschal mystery is not a theoretical programme, not a total structure of functional relations. Thus in the 'dramatic' perspective, with its inbuilt tension between rôle and plot, the creation of meaning and the imposition of meaning, Christian theology offers a deliverance from the menace of pure (structuralist) functionalism, without simply taking refuge in a static essentialist dogma or a privatised existentialism. By means of the trinitarian doctrine and the controlling symbol of Good Friday and Easter, it enables an affirmation of both subject and structure without 'freezing' or absolutising either term.[57]

This is a most imperfect summary of one of Balthasar's most brilliant and condensed bits of writing, unsystematic and aphoristic in many places, but showing a remarkable range of awareness of the contemporary intellectual scene. And not the least point of interest here is the implicit community of interest between Balthasar and the whole post-Heidegger approach to philosophical hermeneutics, insisting as it does on the 'historicity of understanding', the inseparability of the knowing subject's mental history from the encompassing structures of language and culture.

> Self-reflection and autobiography – Dilthey's starting-points – are not primary and are not an adequate basis for the hermeneutical problem, because through them history is made private once more. In fact history does not belong to us, but we belong to it.

'Understanding begins ... when something addresses us.' These remarks, from Gadamer's classic treatment of the foundations of hermeneutics,[58] present the act of understanding as wholly bound to the sense of belonging in a world: what is 'transcendental' here is the hope or expectation of the discovery of meaning in the givenness of the past, the trust involved in any interpretative enterprise that participation in 'linguistic being', in communities and continuities of speech, is also participation in meaning, in a community of vision of how the world is. Truth is disclosed in so far as this trust proves to be sustainable.

If we follow Ricoeur[59] in widening the notion of the 'text' which interpretation encounters to include all systems of significant human action, capable of interpretation through present responses of significant action, we have a very clear convergence with Balthasar's *Dramatik*. It is curious that Balthasar so seldom refers to Ricoeur, though he is evidently familiar with at least the major early essays of *Le conflit des interprétations*[60] and with *Le symbolisme du mal*;[61] but the parallels have been noted.[62] A. Moda, in his excellent discussion of Balthasar, speaks of his 'ontology of language', worked out in *Das Ganze im Fragment*,[63] but implicit elsewhere. Language, for Balthasar, is the means of opening the human subject to 'being', it is the sacrament, we might say, of the totality to which we belong; and for Ricoeur likewise, the fact of language testifies to the truth that consciousness is not self-originated, and is called to response – in the Christian case, not 'merely' linguistic (if there is such a thing) but, because of the character of the speech and symbol involved – the Cross of God's love – a language of loving action and relation.[64]

Rahner's relation to this hermeneutical development is less easy to assess. Certainly the Heidegger of *Sein und Zeit* is a considerable (if muted) presence in *Spirit in the world*; but whether the later Heidegger has left any serious impression on Rahner's mature work is doubtful. In so far as Rahner remains firmly within the limits of a transcendentalist analysis of subjectivity, he belongs in that world of 'onto-theology' and

Cartesian introspection on which Heidegger so firmly turned his back. Attempts have been made[65] to present Rahner as the author of a historical hermeneutics comparable to Gadamer's, chiefly on the ground of Rahner's repeated insistence upon the historical mediation of all consciousness; but the question remains of whether, if this historical mediation is taken with complete seriousness, the whole transcendentalist apparatus will not need radical revision, such as Rahner has not in fact chosen to undertake. L. Malevez, in an early attempt to confront Rahner with Balthasar,[66] tentatively suggested that Rahner's *Vorgriff* needed transposition into the terms of the historical pre-understanding of the hermeneutical philosophers if it was finally to avoid being elevated into a prescriptive norm against which tradition could be measured (so that elements of dogmatic development not conforming to the demands of transcendental anthropology could be jettisoned); and a more sustained critique has come from J.-P. Resweber,[67] who stresses the ambiguity and inconclusiveness of a supposed apprehension of *esse*, and demands closer attention to the question of whether the fact of language as such can provide a starting point for speaking about God – precisely the question which, in their diverse ways, Ricoeur and Balthasar are struggling with.

III

We have come some distance from the deceptively straightforward problem of 'anonymous Christianity', to which the Rahner–Balthasar disagreement is so often reduced. Balthasar has granted (with slightly ill grace) that there *might* be a defensible interpretation of 'anonymous' faith – largely thanks to the conciliatory formulae of de Lubac, distinguishing 'anonymous Christians' from 'anonymous Christendom';[68] and so he has made it fairly clear that the disagreement runs deeper than a mere division over how best to speak of the 'natural' ground upon which faith builds. This paper has sought to show how the debate may be seen as one to do with the problem in contemporary philosophy about the status of the 'autonomous' subject or consciousness. Of course Rahner is anything but an uncritical idealist; and of course Balthasar does not ignore the discussion of 'transcendental conditions' for religious and Christian meanings. But Rahner does not engage directly with recent hermeneutical thought, and Balthasar makes little attempt at stating a sustained and coherent account of the 'ontology of language' he regularly presupposes;[69] and so it is proportionately difficult to assess whether the disagreement is comprehensive and radical. I suspect it is more so than some of Rahner's sympathisers have made out (if less so than Balthasar himself, in his more bitterly polemical moments, implies). Balthasar's challenge to the residual hints in Rahner of a 'self-constituted' consciousness remains a serious and profound question, both philosophical and theological, to any incautious uses of 'transcendental deduction' in Christian thought; and it has yet to generate a comprehensive response from the Rahnerian school.

And behind all of this lies the one decisive issue of Christology. Balthasar accuses Rahner of avoiding a *theologia crucis* in his vision of Christ as the (undialectical?) fulfilment of human potentialities.[70] Faith in Christ is not straightforwardly a recognition of the satisfaction of my needs; the form of Christ is always a revelation of our untruth (and thus unreality and unloveliness) and so a demand to follow Christ into the abyss of Holy Saturday, into *silence*, before the Holy Spirit is capable of bringing forth a new language in Easter and Pentecost, the Word restored to the Father's throne, yet simultaneously given to the community of believers as their heart and their life. From first to last, Christ is *gift*. Even if a Rahnerian transcendentalist insists that it is *practically* only *a posteriori* that we can say that the form of Christ fulfils our needs, such a statement still diminishes the depth of gratuity in the paschal event, and still implies that it is abstractly possible for us to know our needs truly independently of Christ.

This is less than fair to Rahner on many counts: he is by no means insensitive to the need for a theology of the Cross,[71] though it is true that his system as a whole could not be so described. The heart of the difference here seems to be that Rahner thinks of human frustration in terms of incompletion, Balthasar in terms of tragedy. Freedom is not simply a smooth trajectory of finite towards infinite; it is, more importantly, the possibility of self-deceit, self-destruction, refusal. And the 'question' to which God's incarnation is the 'answer' (the terms are hopelessly imperfect) is of how

God can gather back into himself the whole freedom of his creatures including all the consequences of such freedom, including, that is, rebellion and self-damnation, can gather it up and bear it up. And still remain God.[72]

99

The resolution of this can only be in terms of drama, dialogue, enacted in the singularities and risks of our own history, speaking to us of a God who is dialogue in his very being, who can be 'other than himself' and yet restore himself to himself, who because he can 'lose' and 'retrieve' himself can lose and retrieve the world, can lay down his life and take it again. Fulfilment alone leaves the tragic problem of self-loss untouched, and so fails, in the long run, to take freedom sufficiently seriously. And this also helps in understanding why, for Balthasar, dialogue with 'the world' is so much more complex a matter than it sometimes seems to be for Rahner; because the world is *not* a world of well-meaning agnostics but of totalitarian nightmares, of nuclear arsenals, labour camps and torture chambers. *Cordula* contains a savagely satirical little dialogue (the word is deliberately ironic) between a Christian and an – anonymously Christian? – commissar.[73] Unjust, perhaps; but Balthasar's harsh clear-sightedness is an important disturbance of any assumptions about easy 'humanist' convergences in our world.

That particular dialogue is, in effect, a trial scene. Deliberately or not, it echoes other such scenes, as a shameful parody of the *Acta* of the martyrs, and perhaps of the single great trial of Christ himself by human power. Dostoyevsky's Inquisitor claimed to know better than Christ what human needs were, and to love humanity more than he did; and George Steiner, in his brilliant essay, *Tolstoy or Dostoyevsky*,[74] hears in Tolstoy's confident and impatient humanism more than a trace of the Inquisitor's voice.

> If Christ had not existed it would have been easier for men to arrive at rational, Tolstoyan principles of conduct and thus to realise God's Kingdom. Through his humble ambiguity ... Christ had made human affairs infinitely more difficult.[75]

Christ's mediation of human meaning interferes with the rational recognition of God in direct human self-understanding. But 'The Dostoyevskian position is gathered into the silence of Christ; it is realised not in language, but in a single gesture – the kiss which Christ bestows on the Inquisitor.'[76] Steiner rightly notes that this is a *dramatic* resolution which may equally be read as a philosophical evasion. Whether there is a way of stating such a resolution without evasion, whether there is – so to speak – a metaphysics of the Cross, is precisely the issue to which Balthasar's monumental *oeuvre* addresses itself. It has been said that to understand a philosopher you must understand what he is afraid of. Balthasar's dread is the Inquisitorial claim to love humanity more than its maker does – the most comprehensible and sympathetic of all blasphemies – and that is why, for him, revelation is a radical assault on what we know of love, or of liberty, or of hope. If Rahner's Christ is an answer to the human question, a faintly but distinctly Tolstoyan figure, Balthasar's Christ remains a question to all human answers, and to all attempts at metaphysical or theological closure.

Notes

I have to acknowledge a great debt in the composition of this paper to my former student Christopher Seville (Fr Thomas Seville), CR, who has studied Balthasar's understanding of analogy and his use of Przywara. Seville's exceptionally detailed knowledge of Balthasar's work has illuminated and clarified many areas for me.

1. Cornelius Ernst, 'The *Concilium* World Congress: impressions and reflections', *New Blackfriars* 52 (1970); reprinted in *Multiple echo* (London: Darton, Longman & Todd, 1979), 42.

2. *Communio* first appeared as a bi-monthly in 1972. Its first issue contains, in addition to a densely written 'Programme' by Balthasar, contributions by de Lubac and Ratzinger, and – equally characteristically – a review article on Heinrich Böll's *Gruppenbild mit Dame*.

3. Jeffrey Kay contributes an interesting piece on 'Hans Urs von Balthasar: a post-critical theologian?' to *Concilium* 141 (1981), 84–9, attempting to go beyond facile characterisations in terms of 'reactionary' and 'progressive' strategies; but it is a little ironic that the issue should be one on *Neo-conservatism: social and religious phenomenon*. Editorial policy, at least, seems to be sure where Balthasar is to be located.

4. Hans Urs von Balthasar, *Cordula oder der Ernstfall* (Einsiedeln: Johannes Verlag, 1966); ET *The moment of Christian witness* (Glen Rock, NJ: Newman Press, 1969).

5. E.g., Balthasar, *Love alone* (London: Sheed and Ward, 1968), 48–50, 62, 66; *Who is a Christian?* (Westminster: Newman Press, 1968), 51ff. etc.

6. E.g., Balthasar, *Love alone*, ch. 8; *Engagement with God* (London: SPCK, 1975), 47–8, 56–60, 63, and chs 5 and 6. 'Christian involvement . . . has always been initiated with a persistent and sometimes almost stubborn preference for places where, humanly speaking and from the point of view of this world, no further hope remains . . . for the dying, for life grown old and worn out, for the incurably sick, for the mentally ill, for the handicapped' (63).

7. E.g., Balthasar, *Engagement with God*, 17–18.

8. Ibid., 97–8. L. Malvarez, SJ, reviewing the French translation of *Cordula* in *Nouvelle revue théologique* 89 (1967), 1106–7, picks out a similar admission in this book, and regrets that it is confined to a footnote. *Engagement with God*

is obviously in part an attempt to respond to such comments by giving far more prominence to the acknowledgement of extra-ecclesial grace.

9. E.g., Balthasar, *Love alone*, 66–7; also several of the essays in *Word and revelation* (New York: Herder and Herder, 1964), esp. 'The Word and history' (31–55) and 'The implications of the word' (57–86).

10. See Jeffrey Kay, *Theological aesthetics* (Berne and Frankfurt: Herbert Lang, 1975), 41–5, for a useful account of what Balthasar understands by 'apriorism' in contemporary theology.

11. E.g., Balthasar, *Love alone*, 44–5; *The glory of the Lord* I: *Seeing the form* (Edinburgh: T&T Clark, 1982), part III, esp. 481–90 (the form of Christ is described on p. 488 as 'a mystery of the divine freedom, which, as in the work of art, coincides with supreme necessity'); and cf. vol. II: *Studies in theological style: clerical styles* (Edinburgh: T&T Clark, 1984), 27.

12. Karl Rahner, *Spirit in the world* (London: Sheed and Ward, 1968).

13. Ibid., 135–42.

14. Ibid., 142–5.

15. Ibid., 169–83.

16. Ibid., 226.

17. Ibid., 284; cf. 280–6.

18. Ibid., 408. See also Rahner's earlier essay, 'Religionsphilosophie und Theologie', in G. Baumgartner (ed.), *Die siebenten Salzburger Hochschulwochen* (Salzburg: Pustet, 1937), and the longer treatment in *Hearers of the Word* (New York: Herder and Herder, 1968).

19. See, e.g., Karl Rahner, 'Reflections on the unity of the love of neighbour and the love of God', in *Theological investigations* 6 (London: Darton, Longman & Todd, 1969), 231–49.

20. E.g., Karl Rahner, 'I believe in Jesus Christ', in *Theological investigations* 9 (London: Darton, Longman & Todd, 1972), 165–8; more fully in, e.g., 'On the theology of the Incarnation', in *Theological investigations* 4 (London: Darton, Longman & Todd, 1966), 105–20.

21. Karl-Heinz Weger, in his *Karl Rahner: an introduction to his theology* (London: Burns and Oates, 1980), confuses the question considerably by speaking of a 'transcendentally deduced Christology' (154) and a deduction of the 'idea of Christ' from human self-understanding, and then proceeding to *deny* the possibility of a deduction of the 'idea of Christ' (156). Clearly, for Rahner, the deduction involved in the enterprise of Christology cannot be a prescription in advance of what the *event* of revelation will involve, yet Christology involves a deduction of the idea of an absolute fulfilment of human potential. What Weger does not make clear is the exact range of the vague expression 'idea of Christ' – despite a promise to expound this (157).

22. See esp. Karl Rahner, 'Anonymous and explicit faith', in *Theological investigations* 16 (London: Darton, Longman & Todd, 1979), 52–9, in particular 58–9.

23. Rahner, *Spirit in the world*, 237–9.

24. E.g., Rahner, *Theological investigations* 9, 162–3 (in a paper on 'Atheism and implicit Christianity'); cf. Weger, *Karl Rahner*, 128–34.

25. The main essay in this area is Karl Rahner, 'Christianity and the non-

Christian religions', in *Theological investigations* 5 (London: Darton, Longman & Todd, 1966), 115–34.

26. Ibid., 129.

27. Ibid.

28. See esp. J. Heislbetz, *Theologische Gründe der nichtchristlichen Religionen*, Quaestiones disputatae 33 (Freiburg: Herder, 1967).

29. Francis Fiorenza, 'Karl Rahner and the Kantian problematic', in Rahner, *Spirit in the world*, xxxii.

30. E.g., Balthasar, *Cordula*, 3rd edn (Einsiedeln: Johannes Verlag, 1968), 123, n. 5.

31. Balthasar, Review of Karl Rahner, *Geist im Welt*, and J. Lotz, *Sein und Weit*, in *Zeitschrift für katholische Theologie* 63 (1939), 371–9.

32. Rahner, 'Religionsphilosophie und Theologie'.

33. Rahner, *Spirit in the world*, 387–408.

34. Balthasar, Review of Rahner and Lotz, 378–9.

35. See Balthasar's major monograph on this great Byzantine thinker, *Kosmische Liturgie* (Freiburg: Herder, 1941); rev. edn (Einsiedeln: Johannes Verlag, 1961).

36. Hans Urs von Balthasar, *Herrlichkeit* III/1: *Im Raum der Metaphysik: Altertum* (Einsiedeln: Johannes Verlag, 1965), 943–57; ET *The glory of the Lord* 4: *The realm of metaphysics in antiquity* (Edinburgh: T&T Clark, 1989).

37. On this last point, see once again Balthasar's *Kosmische Liturgie*. For the encounter of creative with created 'ekstasis', cf. the writings of Vladimir Lossky. Balthasar's work on Maximus was clearly influential for Lossky, and his own researches in patristic thought were familiar to Balthasar. Cf. ch. 1 above.

38. Balthasar, *Herrlichkeit* III/1, 956.

39. E.g., Balthasar, *Cordula*, 67.

40. Ibid., 124.

41. Balthasar, *Herrlichkeit* III/1, 831–5.

42. Balthasar, *Love alone*, 29.

43. Balthasar, *Herrlichkeit* III/1, 827.

44. Ibid., 831.

45. Ibid., 840–1.

46. Ibid., 883–4.

47. E.g., Balthasar, *Cordula*, 68–9.

48. On which, see Heidegger's essays in *Poetry, language, thought* (New York: Harper and Row, 1971), esp. 165–71, and in *The question concerning technology* (New York: Harper and Row, 1977); see also George Steiner, *Heidegger* (London: Fontana, 1978), 131–2, 140–1, and H. Alderman, 'Heidegger's critique of science and technology', in M. Murray (ed.), *Heidegger and modern philosophy* (New Haven: Yale University Press, 1978), 35–51.

49. See, e.g., the extraordinary remarks of Jeffrey Kay, *Theological aesthetics*, 94–5: 'Balthasar's implicit rejection of this "selfish", "egotistical" stage [the "middle stage" of human development as seen by, e.g., Erikson] and his exaltation of the innocence of past childhood and future sainthood are typical of apocalyptic religions. Christianity must come to an honest affirmation of the indispensable value of the self-centred feelings and passions that seek expression

during this middle stage. It must encourage people in the straightforward expression of anger, aggression, sexual desire and pride as well as receptivity and self-sacrifice.' The scale of the misunderstandings implied here, not only of Balthasar but of neo-Freudianism as well, defies summary in a footnote.

50. Balthasar, Review of Rahner and Lotz, 375. Rahner reproduces Fichte's 'radikale Bindung des Geistes an die [als Material der Selbstverwirklichung, als die Ebene des Nicht-Ich, des anderen als solchen, der "materia" erfahrene] Sinnlichkeit'. On Maréchal, there are some scattered pertinent remarks in *Love alone*, 34; *The glory of the Lord* I, 149; *Herrlichkeit* III/1, 799, 881, 884, 904, etc., and a rather longer treatment in *Karl Barth: Darstellung und Deutung seiner Theologie* (Cologne/Olten: Kohlhammer, 1962), 303ff.; ET *The theology of Karl Barth* (San Francisco: Communio, 1992).

51. Rahner, *Spirit in the world*, 266.

52. Ibid., 285 (my italics).

53. Balthasar, *Theodramatik* I: *Prolegomena* (Einsiedeln: Johannes Verlag, 1973), 16; ET *Theo-drama* I: *Prolegomena* (San Francisco: Ignatius, 1989).

54. Ibid., 17.

55. Ibid., 22; I am indebted here to some reflections by Nicholas Lash in his paper 'Performing the Scriptures: interpretation through living', in Ronan Drury (ed.), *The New Testament as personal reading* (Springfield, IL: Veritas, 1983), 7–18.

56. For the idea of the trinitarian relation as the ultimate ground and norm for all otherness or object-relatedness, cf. Balthasar, *Cordula*, 68: 'Gott ist nicht die Welt, es herrscht deshalb zwischen beiden ein Urphänomen von *Gegenständigkeit* analog wie zwischen Ich und Du, und analog zum innergöttlichen Mysterium der Gegenständigkeit zwischen den Drei Personen, das die letzte Wurzel aller andern Gegenständigkeit ist.'

57. Balthasar, *Theodramatik* I, 23–46.

58. Hans-Georg Gadamer, *Truth and method* (London: Sheed and Ward, 1975), 245, 266.

59. See his extremely important essay, 'The model of the text: meaningful action considered as text', in J. B. Thompson (ed.), *Hermeneutics and the human sciences* (Cambridge: Cambridge University Press, 1981), 197–221.

60. Referred to in Balthasar, *Theodramatik* I, 41 n. 7.

61. Apparently referred to in Balthasar, *Theodramatik* II/2: *Die Personen des Spiels: Die Personen in Christus* (Einsiedeln: Johannes Verlag, 1978), 430, n. 10; ET *Theo-drama* III: *Dramatis personae: persons in Christ* (Edinburgh: T&T Clark, 1993). Balthasar, *Theodramatik* II/1: *Die Personnen in Spiels: Der Mensch in Gott* (Einsiedeln: Johannes Verlag, 1976), 177, n. 4; ET *Theodrama* II: *Dramatis personae: man in God* (Edinburgh: T&T Clark, 1990) also mentions Ricoeur's *Philosophie de la volonté: le volontaire et l'involontaire* (Paris: Aubier, 1949); ET *Freedom and nature: the voluntary and the involuntary* (Evanston: Northwestern University Press, 1966).

62. L. O'Donovan, 'God's glory in time', *Communio* 2 (1975), 268; Aldo Moda, *Hans Urs von Balthasar, un' esposizione critica del suo pensiero* (Bari: Ecumenica Editrice, 1976), 510–14; Jeffrey Kay, 'Hans Urs von Balthasar: a post-critical theologian?' Moda's book is one of the finest critical monographs on Balthasar.

63. Von Balthasar, *Das Ganze im Fragment* (Einsiedeln: Johannes Verlag, 1963); ET *Man in history* (London: Sheed and Ward, 1968). See esp. ch. 7, 'The word and history'.

64. Moda, *Hans Urs von Balthasar*, 512–13, referring particularly to Ricoeur's 'Contribution d'une reflexion sur le langage à une théologie de la parole', in Roland Barthes et al., *Exégèse et herméneutique* (Paris: Editions du Seuil, 1971). Compare also 'Toward a hermeneutic of the idea of revelation' and 'The hermeneutics of testimony', in Ricoeur's *Essays on biblical interpretation*, ed. Lewis S. Mudge (London: SPCK, 1981).

65. E.g., V. P. Branick, *An ontology of understanding* (Saint Louis: Marianist Communications Center, 1974).

66. L. Malevez, 'Présence de la théologie à Dieu et à l'homme', *Nouvelle revue théologique* 90 (1968), 785–800, esp. 799–800.

67. J. P. Resweber, 'La relation de l'homme à Dieu selon K. Rahner et M. Blondel', *Recherches des sciences religieuses* 46 (1972), 20–37, esp. 37; also his monograph, *La théologie face au défi herméneutique* (Paris and Brussels: Vander, 1975), discussed in a review article by M. Sachot in *Recherches des sciences religieuses* 50 (1976), 168–73.

68. Balthasar, *Cordula*, 129. For a development of what such a distinction might involve, see the very interesting discussion of non-Christian faiths in *Theodramatik* II/2, 376–88.

69. Though it is *very* misleading to suggest that he is unaware of or unconcerned with the 'question of theological meaning in its last implications', as Peter Mann does in 'The transcendental or the political kingdom, II', *New Blackfriars* 51 (1970), 4–16, esp. 15–16.

70. Balthasar, *Cordula*, 89–92.

71. See, e.g., the short piece on 'Self-realisation and taking up one's cross', *Theological investigations* 9, 253–57, and Rahner's various pieces on the 'theology of death'.

72. Hans Urs von Balthasar, *Elucidations* (London: SPCK, 1975), 50–1.

73. Balthasar, *Cordula*, 110–12.

74. George Steiner, *Tolstoy or Dostoyevsky?* 2nd edn (Harmondsworth: Penguin, 1967).

75. Ibid., 239.

76. Ibid., 308–9.

7

Barth on the triune God

She caught the crying of those Three,
The Immortals of the eternal ring,
The Utterer, Utteréd, Uttering.
    (Gerard Manley Hopkins, *Margaret Clitheroe*)

I

That man should hear the Word of God is an impossibility; but it is an impossibility revealed to man by that very Word. It is this essential *strangeness* in the event of man's hearing the Word to which Barth's discussions of revelation again and again return; and this sense of strangeness is of major importance in the whole of Barth's analysis of the nature of man's encounter with his Lord, since it at once raises the question of how the impossibility of revelation is compatible with the *fact* that the Word is heard. It raises the question, that is to say, of where the possibility of revelation is grounded. How is it that God can abrogate the principle *homo peccator non capax verbi divini*?[1] There is no ground of possibility in man; that is axiomatic for Barth, not as an abstract principle but as a consequence of what in fact the Word itself reveals about man's God-less condition.

> The insight that 'I have sinned . . . and am no more worthy to be called thy son' (Lk. 15:18) is not an insight of abstract anthropology. Only the son who is already recalling his father's house knows that he is a lost son. We know that we are God's enemies first and solely from the fact that God has actually established that intercourse with us.[2]

The abstract statement that man is incapable of hearing the Word is a nonsense, in that it presupposes that we know in some way what this Word is from which we are alienated. In pretending to affirm an impossibility, it really affirms a possibility, the anthropological 'condition', the human capacity for hearing so vehemently rejected by Barth in his long discussion of 'The knowability of the Word of God'.[3] And, on the other hand, the revelation of an impossibility is the creation of a possibility: 'If we ascribe to man this aptness [for the Word, in faith] which is not his own but is loaned to him by God . . . then we cannot shrink from speaking of a conformity to God proper to him in faith.'[4] Conformity in faith, the *analogia fidei*: this is the ground of the possibility of hearing the Word, and it is a 'retroactively' established possibility.[5] That is, it depends entirely upon God's creative address to man, the Word spoken out of his freedom, his decision; so that when we speak of the possibility of hearing the Word, we are ultimately speaking of the possibility for *God* of uttering the Word which is constitutive of man-as-hearer.[6] To ask, 'How can God abrogate the principle *homo peccator non capax verbi divini?*' is to ask 'What kind of God is it with whom we have to do?' Or, more strongly and more accurately, '*Who* is our God?'[7]

'In scientific theology we begin with the actual knowledge of God and seek to test and clarify this knowledge by inquiring carefully into the relation between our knowing of God and God himself in his being and nature.'[8] This, from one of Barth's foremost disciples in the English-speaking world, neatly states the heart of Barth's intention in his theological method. And, as Eberhard Jüngel has insisted,[9] Barth considers that to think *theologically* is above all to take seriously the fact that God's being is prior to the enterprise of human theological questioning, that God's being in its character as 'in motion' (*gehende*) establishes theology upon its path. The structures and inner relations of the event or events which constitute the uttering of the Word to men determine absolutely what theology is to say about the being of the Lord who speaks and reveals. Theology is regarded by Barth as an essay in *Nachdenken*, following out in thought the 'order' of revelation.[10] The nature of God is uncovered to the theological inquiry by undeviating fidelity to the 'story' of God's movement towards men, that which makes man a knower of God in the first place; which, it might be said, decisively introduces the name of God into the language of the world.

The structure of this man-ward movement is, as Barth sets out in Section 4 of his first half-volume ('The Word of God in its threefold form'), manifold. There is a primary revelatory occurrence, the determinative speaking of the Word in the Word-made-flesh. There is the 'recollection' of this in Scripture; 'The prophetic and apostolic word is the word, witness, proclamation and preaching of Jesus Christ',[11] and it 'imposes itself' upon the Church in virtue of (and *only* in virtue of) its reference to and dependence upon the primary event, upon God's free utterance. And finally there is the Church's preaching, 'man's talk about God on the basis of God's own direction', 'on the basis of the self-objectification of God ... which is really only in the freedom of His grace';[12] preaching can become the Word in and only in obedience to God's free self-determination in Christ, and the re-presentation of this in the scriptural witness. The primary event alone *is* the Word. Scripture *becomes* the Word in fidelity to Christ, preaching *becomes* the Word in fidelity to Scripture, but Christ is 'the divine act itself and as such'.[13] 'If "written" and "preached" denote the twofold concrete relation in which the Word of God is spoken to us, revelation denotes the Word of God itself in the act of its being spoken in time.'[14] The concrete and particular event of God's utterance to this man at this moment occurs in the prophetic and apostolic experience recorded in Scripture, and in the convicting and converting proclamation of the Church; but it occurs 'derivatively and indirectly', dependently upon the one direct speech-act of God in Christ. And it is the unity of that act which guarantees the unity and self-identity of Scripture and preaching. At the heart stands the one event, the *Deus dixit*, the fulfilment of time; when Scripture and preaching become the Word, they are 'filled with the fulness of this time'.[15]

The unity of the Word of God in revelation is, then, a unity-in-plurality.[16] The structure of revelation is the structure of a complex unity in which three terms are defined entirely by their mutual relations: each is known only through and in the other two. And the three terms are constituted as *identical* with each other because they enact the same free action of God towards men. 'There is', Barth concludes,

> only one analogy to this doctrine of the Word of God. Or, more accurately, the doctrine of the Word of God is itself the only analogy to the doctrine which will be our fundamental concern as we develop the concept of revelation. This is the doctrine of the trinity of God.[17]

If the Word of revelation has a pluriform identity, this is something which is of substantive importance for our answer to the question, '*Who* is the God Who speaks in revelation?'

This particular line of reasoning is not wholly clear, and Barth does not trouble to spell it out at any length; but it is a point which is made at a significant stage in the whole argument of the first half-volume, and it is therefore perhaps worth while to try to elucidate it a little. Barth is not, I think, simply suggesting that the triplicity of the Word is an 'external' analogy to the postulated triplicity of God, that one 'gives us the idea' for the other. Rather is he pointing to a basic principle necessary to our understanding alike of the revealing Word and of its speaker; and that is the concept of the divine freedom. The pluriformity of the Word's revealing activity is an index of God's capacity to be free *for men* in their particular and concrete circumstances. In no sense is he imprisoned in a past revelatory event which can be the subject only of human recollection: he is free to speak the same Word in oblique, 'wordly' mediating realities.[18] 'The direct Word of God meets us only in this twofold mediacy';[19] and there is no general concept under which the Word can be subsumed, since 'The Word of God is an act of God which takes place *specialissime*, in this way and not another, to this or that particular man.'[20]

The freedom of the Word is God's capacity to speak not 'publicly' or 'generally', in a single form (*Gestalt*) which is then once and for all accessible to all men without mediation, but in hiddenness which requires his own free decision in every particular instance in order to become manifest. 'Where the Word of God is known and therefore can be known, it must have been spoken and it must have come as a divine call to specific men.'[21] 'The Word of God ... is to be understood primarily and basically as decision and then and as such as history too.'[22] God is not trapped in the historical or secular form under which he speaks; his Word is identical with the form of Jesus (substantially), and of Scripture and of preaching (derivatively) because he elects that it be so. And the pluriformity of the Word is precisely a witness to the fact that he is not so 'trapped', but can actualize his revelation in any and every circumstance, in the utter absence of any human 'condition'. God 'can not only come to man but also be in man ... and thus achieve His revelation in Him'.[23]

God speaks; he speaks one Word; but he speaks it and realizes it at once obliquely, concretely, fully, and in manifold particularities. And it is from this analysis of what is involved in the act of revelation that we can proceed to the construction of a Trinitarian theology.

God reveals Himself. He reveals Himself *through Himself*. He reveals *Himself*. If we really want to understand revelation in terms of its subject, i.e. God, then the first thing we have to realise is that this subject, God, the Revealer, is identical with His act in revelation and also identical with its effect.[24]

The doctrine is an interpretation, and a necessary interpretation, of the basic *Deus dixit* of faith; though, having suggested in the earlier *Christliche Dogmatik*[25] that Trinitarian doctrine dealt with the subject, predicate, and object of *Deus dixit*, God has spoken, Barth felt obliged in this section of the *Church dogmatics*[26] to qualify this in the face of criticism which maintained that he was constructing a 'grammatical and rationalistic proof of the Trinity'. He explains later that the reference to a *Deus dixit* is not to a general or abstract concept of the revelatory speech of God; for we have no such concept.[27] We have only the speech which God has elected to utter in the event underlying the scriptural witness, and it is this which compels us to answer the question, 'Who is the self-revealing God?' in Trinitarian terms.[28]

II

If, then, we say (as is commonly said) that Barth's Trinitarian doctrine is an explanation of what is entailed for him by the idea of revelation, we shall need to tread circumspectly. For Barth does not consider that he is interpreting an *idea* of revelation, but the concrete structure of revelation as it has in fact occurred and is in fact occurring. To interpret an idea of revelation would be to revert to the 'anthropological condition' for revelation, a prior human model against which events can be measured, a category into which they must fit. And when Barth says so gnomically that '*Revelation is not a predicate of history, but history is a predicate of revelation*',[29] he is affirming that 'revelation' is not one of the categories under which history can be spoken of (if it is, we simply have some kind of Hegelian notion of history *as* in itself revelation).[30] 'History', on the contrary, is one of the categories under which revelation can be – indeed, *demands* to be – spoken of. And this implies that God demands historical predicates, and cannot be spoken of except historically.[31]

To discuss this adequately would require a full treatment of Barth's concept of 'The Time of Revelation', as set out in the *Church dogmatics* 1/2, § 14; but in this context I can treat it only briefly. Whether the implication of this insistence that revelation is (in theological discourse) subject, not predicate, of the historical, 'worldly' events with which dogmatics has to do, amounts to such a radical devaluation of the created order as Richard Roberts argues,[32] I am by no means sure. But we may note (at least) the awkwardness of a scheme which so divorces the substance of revelation from its historical form, in making the latter's relation to the former basically external. Revelation demands, we are told, historical predicates, yet there is nothing *in* these predicates which in any sense makes them 'appropriate' to their content. Despite Barth's vehement disavowals, it is hard not to conclude that this does indeed make the revealing Word's secularity and historicity 'accidental' to its nature.[33]

Barth in effect admits this in speaking of the impossibility of removing the distinction in our thinking between 'secular form' and 'divine content'.[34] This impossibility he (predictably) considers a mark of man's distance from God, who alone achieves the miraculous synthesis of the two terms. Faith does not look for synthesis but for the unity which God's act establishes. Now this is a difficult and rhetorically overloaded passage. While it continues to stress the inseparability of form and content in revelation, it allows no possibility at all of any *unity* between them. The power of God and the freedom of God can make form and content one in effect or operation; but there is nothing here (or, indeed, in the discussion in 1/2) to suggest that, even *ex parte Dei*, any more internal or substantial union can ever be envisaged. History, and the *world* as such, are wholly foreign to God: he can act through, but not in, the historical *qua* historical. 'Fulfilled time [sc. the time of revelation] in our midst is the enemy who has forced himself in.'[35]

Barth is evidently working with a sharply defined model of revelation, whether or not we conclude that it is ultimately determined purely by the revelatory event. It is germane to his whole exposition that revelation is a unitary event, a divinely actuated event, and therefore an *effective* event (*God* responds to God in the human occurrence of faith). In a sense, therefore, for Barth as much as for Bultmann, faith must be preserved from the dubieties associated with strictly historical knowledge, since (for both) revelation and faith are one event, and for Barth they have one primary agent. It is precisely the rigorous definition of this model which raises questions about Barth's protestations that he is interpreting the simple fact of revelation. Robert C. Roberts, in a provocative recent study of Bultmann,[36] has complained at Bultmann's thoroughgoing 'homogenization' of what the New Testament has to say about faith and assurance, the reduction of a family of images and ideas to one clear principle. Barth does not expose himself to quite the same charge; but we may properly ask whether some such homogenizing process is not going on in his treatment of the events of revelation. David Ford questions whether Barth's scheme of Christocentric typology can do justice to the 'complexity of reality'[37] and this query is exactly the one which I wish to enter against his account of revelation. Did the Hebrews conceive of the Exodus and Sinai experiences as both veilings and unveilings of God? For that matter, did the Twelve so understand the resurrection?

Hardly; but of course, it could be said in reply that it is the Cross which ought to provide the paradigm of revelation, since the resurrection is never other than the resurrection of the one who has been crucified, and that the cross most sharply poses the problem of revelation in hiddenness. Barth refers us to Luther for this, and to W. von Loewenich's superb study of Luther's understanding of the Cross.[38] Yet this does not in fact resolve the issue. It is one thing to speak of 'revelation in hiddenness': as von Loewenich makes clear,[39] Luther is concerned to maintain a sharp distinction between the 'naked God', God in se, and the revealed God, God on the cross, 'under the appearance of the opposite', in order to guard against any notion that there can be a showing of God apart from manger and cross. God is, simply and absolutely, in these forms, in the contradiction, the doubt, and the pain. This is, indeed, the essential feature of Lutheran Christology, its almost monophysite understanding of the communicatio idiomatum.

At first sight it looks as if Barth is saying precisely the same. The difference, however, is that signalized in the Reformation debates by the concept of the extra calvinisticum: God is present mit und unter, with and under, the contingent and historical, but he cannot be said to be in it, identified with it in the way Luther envisages. For the Lutheran, what is involved in the revelation of God in suffering and darkness is a real communication of God; the worldly circumstances of cross and dereliction themselves say something about God.[40] They are not simply a concealing exterior vehicle: the mercy of God is such that the divine opus proprium 'translated' into worldly form is necessarily and properly the cross. And this, I suggest, is not the same as saying that we can only hear the Word in its secular form, as this says nothing (as it stands) about the Word's relation to its form.

In Barth's eyes, such an understanding of a relation between Word and form would be 'trying to do God's miraculous act ourselves'.[41] The revelatory event is God's miracle from beginning to end, and its unity, continuity, and *trustworthiness* depend upon God alone. The act of God cannot be uncertain or inconclusive in effect; when God speaks, he 'achieves His revelation', 'He makes himself sure of us . . . establishes and executes His claim to lordship over us by His immediate presence.'[42] To say that God's Word becomes fully identical with the ambiguous circumstances in which it is spoken is to prejudice the sovereign freedom of the speaker. 'God is his own interpreter/And he will make it plain.' As his own interpreter, God lifts for the believer the veil of ambiguous fact. Through the medium of uncertain secularity, the clear witness of God to himself establishes the certainty of faith, which is a standing in this royal road from God to God, by God's grace. Only in face of this 'uncertain secularity' can such faith occur; but it does not occur by a grasping of any inner unity between Word and form. That would be too perilously near to putting the Word at our disposal; and God does not so give himself into our hands, but keeps us in his.[43] 'Man must be set aside and God Himself presented as the original subject, as the primary power, as the creator of the possibility of knowledge of God's Word.'[44] Revelation is a unitary act, and its God-grounded unity in diversity secures for the faith it effects an absolute and stable character, God's guarantee.[45]

The reason for engaging in what may seem a laboured and disproportionately long digression on Barth's view of revelation and its *Gestalt* is simply this: that the defensibility or otherwise of his claim to be interpreting the fact, not the idea of revelation is of material importance in assessing the viability of his Trinitarian theology. If it can be shown that Barth is actually operating (even unconsciously) with a concept of revelation defined in advance of his exegesis of the records of revelation, substantial questions are raised about not merely the ground but also the *shape* of his articulation of the doctrine. It will be liable (to say no more) to be seen as a capitulation to precisely the anthropological determination which Barth wishes at all costs to avoid; it will be open to evaluation not, as he would wish, purely on the grounds of its adequacy as exegesis of saving history, but in terms of the validity or acceptability of an anthropological premiss. Now what has emerged from our argument in the foregoing paragraphs constitutes, I believe, a strong case for regarding Barth's view of revelation as *not* determined exclusively by the structure of saving events. Revelation must be such as to be characteristic of a God who is sovereign and free; and therefore its relation to any historical circumstance, whether of triumph (like the Exodus) or of humiliation (as on Calvary) is bound to be arbitrary –

or, if that word seems too pejorative, freely elected. Thus what can be said about the pattern of events reported in Scripture as being of saving effect is determined by a prior consideration of the sovereign effectiveness of the acts of God. All saving events are alike in containing the dialectic of veiling and unveiling; and this might well be called (using a term proposed earlier) a 'homogenization' of these events.

A defender of Barth could respond that, since the revelatory event reproduces the *Urgeschichte*, the 'primal history', *historia praeveniens*, of God's act, or the 'event' of God's being, it cannot simply be 'arbitrarily' related to this divine act.[46] But this argument is frustratingly circular; for the *revelatory* event, properly so called, is not simply identical with its historical form. It is the event of God uttering himself and witnessing to himself; and of course this is not arbitrarily related to the primal act of utterance. What remains as unrelated as ever is the circumstantial historical event 'with and under' which revelation occurs. This applies even to Barth's reworking of the doctrine of election in the *Church dogmatics* II/1 (to which Jüngel devotes much attention), in which the eternal election of the man Jesus is so emphasized. Jesus of Nazareth is the form under which God eternally chooses to determine himself in giving himself to man;[47] yet, even as presented by Jüngel, this does not justify anything like the Lutheran view of the *communicatio idiomatum*. Nor, it seems, does it cope fully with the problems raised by the fact that the existence of Jesus of Nazareth is historically contingent, a point in the interrelated, interdependent system of worldly events, from which it can in no way be abstracted. It is an existence of a certain character, with its own historical singleness, because of its occupation of a certain point of convergence for innumerable systems of worldly causality. The election of Jesus logically entails the election of his 'world' – not in the sense in which Barth speaks of the predestination of all in Jesus, but in a rather more mundane way. And if God does so elect the world of Jesus – which means, finally, the world, *simpliciter* – it is hard to maintain a Barthian insistence upon revelation as highly particularized interruptions of the worldly story. But this raises issues of large generality of which I do not propose to treat here.

To sum up this discussion: I believe there are grounds for caution in accepting at face value Barth's claim that his Trinitarian scheme is simply exegesis of the facts of revelation. We have seen his understanding of revelation to be a highly defined and specific view, a prescriptive programme. In spite of all, Barth is, it seems, determining in advance what can and what cannot be admitted under the heading of 'revelatory events', finally refining the concept so as to make it clear that it really comprises only the witness of God to the speech of God. The revelatory event and experience is not only unitary but infallible, God guaranteeing the divinity of his Word, miraculously grasping man through the uncertain medium of worldly happening and bringing him into the single true event of the divine being. It is Calvin's irresistible grace rendered into epistemological terms.

It remains true, then, that Barth's Trinitarian theology and his doctrine of revelation are intimately connected; and in the next section I shall endeavour to set out this relationship, as Barth conceives it, in more detail. However, it is important to remember constantly that Barth's account of revelation is by no means as 'neutral' as it purports to be. A powerful ideological motive – the need to assert the infallibility and irresistibility of God's self-communication – underlies all that is said about the revealing event. This is not to prejudge the validity of Barth's treatment of the Trinity, not to take for granted that this 'ideological' root is simply to be deplored or dismissed; but no understanding of Barth (or any other writer, for that matter) can begin to be adequate if it simply relies upon his own description, however sincere, of his method and intention.

III

Theodore W. Jennings, Jr, in a recent and very valuable essay in theological method,[48] complains that 'Barth's reliance upon a doctrine of the Trinity and Incarnation as the starting-point of his reflection subordinates reflection to ecclesiastical formulations whose appropriateness and intelligibility it has yet to evaluate.' This is an unfortunate and rather unperceptive comment, though it represents fairly enough a widespread view of Barth; unperceptive, because for Barth the starting point for dogmatics is not a dogma or dogmas (not even 'all of them together', a further formulation dismissed by Jennings), but revelation, the pure fact that God speaks to man. Jennings allows that theology does involve a 'hermeneutical circle', that it begins in *Vorverständnis*, 'pre-understanding', but fails to see that Barth's is no more grounded in dogma as such, than is his own. Barth's starting point is the actuality of God's speaking and being heard. The appropriateness of the Trinitarian confession is precisely what is under consideration in Barth's basic question in the *Church dogmatics* I/1: what *must* be said of God in himself if he reveals himself in such-and-such ways? if this is the actuality of revelation, what is it in God that makes it possible? Thus the doctrine of the Trinity is not for Barth a 'centre of theology' (as Stephen Sykes argues,[49] no doctrinal articulation explicitly holds such a place in the *Church dogmatics*; though we may well conclude that the level of conceptual control is much higher than Barth admits, whether, with Sykes, we consider this to be exercised by Christological dogma, or whether, as I have proposed above, we find it in an all-pervading epistemological premiss about the nature of revelatory event). Its position in the *Church dogmatics* is not a matter of its being the most important out of an ensemble of dogmatic formulations. It is placed at the beginning of the dogmatic investigation because its subject-matter is what makes the whole of dogmatics possible: the grounds of the confession that 'God reveals Himself as the Lord'.[50] Thus it contains the question: 'Who is our God?' What (as we might rephrase it) is God's subjectivity like?

'God reveals Himself as the Lord' amounts to saying that God is free; he is free over against man, so that to reveal himself *is* to reveal himself as man's God and Lord. 'Lordship is present in revelation because its reality and truth are so fully self-grounded, because it does not need any other actualisation or validation than that of its actual occurrence, because it is revelation *through itself* and not in relation to something else.'[51] Revelation is the statement of God's autonomy, that he is a self-subsistent 'I', addressing man as 'thou', and in so doing displaying his absolute independence of us, and thus his lordship, ἐξουσία, over us.[52] This is what is meant by speaking of revelation as God's 'self-interpretation'.[53] He explains to us what and who he is; and he does so by being himself a second time, becoming his own *alter ego*. By nature he cannot be unveiled to men;[54] but he transcends his own hiddenness and becomes 'God a second time in a very different way, namely, in manifestation, i.e., in the form of something He is not'.[55]

Revelation thus establishes two things concurrently. Just as it reveals to man at once the impossibility and the actuality of human knowledge of God, so it reveals God as the Lord, the utterly autonomous, free subject of whom men can have no *concept*, no analogical or connatural knowledge, in revealing him as *our* Lord, the one who is free to be for us. 'He is not tied to His secret eternity and external secrecy but can and will and does take temporal form as well.'[56] And in revealing himself under an alien form, 'something He is not', he shows himself to be capable of self-differentiation. He is thus Lord as 'Word' or 'Son', in the differentiated form of revelation;[57] he remains by nature hidden and free, and so is Lord as 'Father';[58] and he causes men to see the identity of his veiling and his unveiling, which otherwise no man would see, and thus is Lord as 'Spirit'.[59] God is identity-in-distinction. This is the direct implication of the fact that revelation occurs, it is no 'arbitrarily contrived speculation'.[60] The doctrine of the Trinity is implicit (and sometimes, Barth ventures, explicit) in what Scripture reports of revelation, and as such is 'exegesis' of the biblical record; but it is better seen as the Church's response to the question which Scripture poses about the divine identity.[61]

To speak of 'identity-in-distinction' obliges us to do full justice to both terms in the expression. If we fail to see that the Trinitarian dogma is an 'explanatory confirmation' of the single divine name of biblical revelation, we should be postulating three objects of faith, and so three gods.[62] We must, rather, say that the unity of God's essence 'consists in the threeness of the "persons"'.[63] God's unity is such that it must be threefold; we cannot conceive it on the model of any other kind of unity. 'Singularity and isolation are limitations necessarily connected with the concept of numerical unity in general. The numerical unity of the revealed God does not have these limitations.'[64] God is one in being three, and this is what makes Christian monotheism Christian.[65]

This a point of importance for the understanding of Barth's characteristic doctrinal concerns. As he has already insisted (in the section on 'The place of the doctrine of the Trinity in dogmatics'),[66] there is properly no preliminary treatise *de Deo uno* as a 'neutral' prelude to a statement of what is specifically Christian. We do not hold the confession of God's unity in common with other monotheistic religions. Without revelation there would be no understanding of the unity of God, and any conception of that unity independently of revelation is vacuous. And what revelation shows as the structure of God's unity is the threefold *repetitio aeternitatis in aeternitate*, 'repetition of eternity for eternity'. 'The doctrine of the Trinity confirms the knowledge of the unity of God, but not any knowledge of any unity of any God.'[67] Trinitarian doctrine is therefore not 'answerable' to or measurable by any non-revealed system of monotheism.

Leaving aside for the moment Barth's discussion of the notions of 'person' and *Seinsweise* ('mode of being') in trinitarian terminology, let us pass on to examine the way in which, according to Barth, the structure of the revelatory event specifies the distinctive characters of

Father, Son, and Holy Spirit respectively. The event itself Barth considers as the story of 'Easter, Good Friday and Pentecost':[68] and it is noteworthy that this ordering of the three terms of the event is meant to correspond to the order of '*Son*, Father and Spirit' (not, as we might perhaps expect, 'Father, Son and Spirit'). Good Friday is the revelation of the Father: 'The One whom Jesus reveals as the Father is known absolutely on the death of man, at the end of his existence.'[69] The will of the Father is death to man, it stands in utter opposition to man's 'will to live'.[70] And this revelation of God as dealing death to men establishes his character as Lord over human existence, as a God whose power is not coterminous with our limited nature and aspirations. He is not only the death of man, however: this would deny his Lordship over our existence as such, and reduce him to the status of a mere boundary, a 'limit concept' (and therefore, once again, a datum of anthropology). He deals death to men so as to create the new man to whom he can speak, whom he can encounter. *As* dealer of death, he is giver of life. In human death, he shows that he rules and overrules man's life, since man's life is a constant essay in reckoning with, coming to terms with, his death; and God is the promise of that which human life of itself knows nothing of. He is outside it, a power absolutely unlimited by it, and so Lord of life and death alike. Thus it is he who sustains our existence and is its source, its free and self-sufficient Author, its Creator.[71]

The man Jesus, in all that he does, turns in obedience towards his Father; and his obedience issues in death, so the Father of Jesus is revealed as Lord of life and death, as Creator. This is a difficult and compressed piece of reasoning; but, as I have tried to show, it is closely bound up with the entire structure of Barth's understanding of God and man. God's absolute 'otherness' can only impinge upon human awareness, human will, human self-reliance as negation. This may seem to involve a contradiction: God is experienced as the negation of a life of human self-reliance, yet he is equally experienced as the negation of a life directed towards himself, as he is revealed in the death of a righteous man. Here, however, we must remember the peculiar character of Barth's view of revelation. Without the Word, man does not know the negating judgement of God upon his whole existence; in hearing the Word, he is at the same time judged by it and (because of its divine effectiveness) re-created by it. God 'wills death in order to lead our life through it to eternal life'.[72] Christ is not a hearer of the Word; but *as man* he places himself in the situation to which the Word is addressed. He knows and does the Father's will in the place where fallen man stands; that is, he does God's will as God's enemy, as a sinner, and so dies of it. This is not made explicit in I/1, and has to be worked out from the general structure of the argument.

If, however, we turn to Barth's major treatment of 'The doctrine of reconciliation' in the enormous fourth volume of the *Church dogmatics*, we find in the section on 'The judge judged in our place'[73] a full state-ment of the Son's identification with sinful men. This long, and often very moving, presentation makes it clear that Jesus' obedience, Jesus' righteousness, *consists in* the willing assumption of the limitations of sinful creatureliness. Alone among men, he declines the temptation to 'impenitence', to rebellion against these limitations. 'In (men's) place and for their sake, instead of committing fresh sin, He returned to the place from which they had fallen into sin.' His 'free penitence', wholly accepting the condition and consequence of sin, begins with his baptism and culminates in the Cross, and in it 'there took place the positive act concealed in His passion as the negative form of the divine action of reconciliation'.[74] And later, in a long exegesis of the New Testament evidence,[75] Barth puts it still more clearly: for God's will to be done, the old man must die, must be totally immolated; Jesus alone can, as God's man, perfect this offering, shedding 'our wicked blood in His own precious blood'.[76]

These clarifications and refinements are absent from I/1, and it may be argued that their working out in detail implies some substantial modification of the over-all argument of I/1. I shall return to the point; enough for the present to note how significantly Barth's view of the Father is related to the dereliction of the incarnate Son. The Easter Sunday revelation of 'God as Reconciler' leads us on – as we might expect – to what is beyond wrath and death, the unqualified miracle that God overcomes the enmity of man and *speaks* to him, establishes fellowship with him. Here is the new life created by the Father freely offered to the world, yet not offered by the Father, purely and simply. We are not dealing with a natural law of life-through-death,[77] a 'con-tinuation of creation,[78] but with utter novelty. Here is a second divine act, the possibility behind the impossibility, the Word heard and received by the enemies of God. So, says Barth, we have to do with a second, and in *some* sense 'subordinate', way-of-being-God (*Seins-weise*), God the Reconciler following on God the Creator: an 'irrevers-ible relation', but one in which each term is wholly necessary to the apprehension of the other.[79] In creation and reconciliation we see two miracles, two modes of transcendent strangeness. At the beginning of this essay, it was suggested that the sense of *strangeness* in man's hearing of the Word was one key to understanding Barth's view of revelation; here we see how it functions in establishing the dialectic of Fatherhood and Sonship in God, the tension between the lordship which rules and overrules, and the lordship which restores and re-creates. Only God can rule as Creator; only God can renew and reshape the world he has made. Each mode is divine, and equally divine,[80] yet their order is irreversible. But again, God is known as Creator only in the act of reconciliation: the Father is always the Father of Our Lord Jesus Christ.[81]

The final term of the triad is (as we have already noted) that mode of being in which God 'makes Himself sure of us'. The doctrine of the Holy Spirit is the answer to the question of how men can confess the lordship of the God revealed in Jesus 'as the beginning and not the end of their thinking about [Jesus]'.[82] The Holy Spirit is to be distinguished from Christ, because he (the Spirit) is found only after the Good Friday and Easter event, 'in the form of knowledge of the crucified and risen Lord, i.e., on the assumption that objective revelation has been con-cluded and completed'.[83] In the Spirit we have to do with the 'subjective' side of revelation: not that the Spirit is in any sense at all a human capacity,[84] but that it is he who gives to each human subject the miracu-lous possibility of hearing the Word. The Spirit is emphatically not the bearer of a new revelation (Barth has some harsh things to say later in *CD* I/1 about speculative Russian Orthodox thinkers whose systems cut loose from the givenness of revelation in Christ and appeal to the revealing Spirit for justification),[85] but the realizer of the one revelation in Christ. Once more the theme of the absolute unity of the revelatory act governs what can be said. 'The Holy Spirit is the authorisation to speak *about Christ*'.[86] The freedom of man to hear the Word and so to become God's child is the gift of the Spirit, whose miracle it is to *make* men responsive to the lordship of Jesus and the Father. Man does not become *capax verbi divini* and then hear the Word; hearing and capacity to hear are given in one act by the Spirit.[87] And the gift of the Spirit remains irreducibly gift, miracle; it does not become a possession. We can understand only, as it were, from God's point of view, 'as it is posited by God'.[88] All that can be said of man's relation to God in the Spirit has to do with *promise*: it is eschatological. If this were not so, God would not remain the Lord; our security would be in ourselves, not in him.[89] The deity of the Spirit, as that of Father and Son, is always to be understood as radical freedom – in this case, the freedom of 'God's future'.

All this seeks to establish the threefold nature of the act of God as exhibited in the event of revelation. But there is more: as we have noted, Barth's pressing concern is to establish the foundation *in* God for these structures, and each section on the manifestation of a person in revelation is followed by a treatment of the eternal aspect of that person's distinctness. The method of these sections is relatively simple, consisting basically in a further application of the principle of the divine autonomy. Thus, God is not Father in virtue of being *our* father and creator: 'He already is that which corresponds thereto antecedently and in Himself.'[90] He *can* reveal himself as Creator and lord of our existence because he *is* 'antecedently and in Himself' Father, originator, one who is capable of setting himself in relation to what is other than himself.[91] 'Father', designating as it does, inter-creaturely relations, may seem an improper word to describe the divine originator; but its impropriety is removed when we consider that our use of terms involving origination is properly dependent upon the divine act of origination.[92] God's sovereign will to be himself a second time (*repetitio aeternitatis . . .*) is the ground of his fatherhood and of all fatherhood. However, it is essential to remember that he is *himself* a second time. It is not as though God the Father alone is Creator: God as Creator is revealed inalienably under the form of Jesus' relation to his Father, but his is precisely a revelation of *God*, the three-personed God as Creator. 'Not the Father alone, then, is God the Creator, but also the Son and the Spirit with Him. And the Father is not only God the Creator, but with the Son and the Spirit He is also God the Reconciler and God the Redeemer.'[93] The knowledge given in revelation is thus 'relativized', but in no way devalued. Revelation remains our only access to the truth of the triune God, and the language which revelation makes possible is only 'improper' in not being exhaustive. The 'appropriation' of the work of creation to the Father is not wrong; but we must understand it from the proper perspective of God's unique unity-in-distinction, the *perichoresis* of the three modes of being. The 'particularity' of knowing God the Father as Creator is essential, so long as we remain sensitive to what God's unity involves. We cannot be modalists (dissolving the Trinity in a 'neutral fourth'): there is 'order' in the Godhead. But it is the order of a 'repetition' of *one* divine subject.[94]

As to 'The Eternal Son', the same general principles apply in the discussion. Without the 'antecendently in Himself', it is impossible to say that in Christ God reveals himself as himself, reveals himself in the mode in which 'He posits and knows Himself from and to all eternity'.[95] The mode in which God is God as Jesus Christ is not something accidental to God's simply *being God*: if it were so, it would not in fact be a mode-of-being-God at all. And, at the same time, if we say that God's relation *to man* in Jesus Christ is constitutive of his simply being God, we introduce an anthropologically conditioned necessity into God, and destroy the gratuity of grace.[96] And furthermore, if we simply refuse to ask the question about the nature of Christ, appealing in characteristic liberal fashion to Melanchthon's *beneficia Christi cognoscere*, we fall back upon Christological language as 'evaluative', and such evaluation can only be on the basis of some human standard brought to bear by the theologian. The anthropological condition rears its head, and a theology of revelation becomes impossible.[97] God is eternally Son because he is eternally himself; that is the burden of Barth's argument. If he is not eternally Son – if he is Son only in relation to us, or if his revelation in Christ begs no ontological questions – he is not eternally himself, and cannot reveal *himself* to us. Either what is revealed is not God; or else God is not truly God and Lord, but is ontologically bound up with and conditioned by the world of men, and so cannot reveal himself as the Lord. The basic statement, 'God reveals *himself* as the *Lord*' demands the 'antecedently in himself' of eternal sonship, the eternal self-reiteration of God. He gives himself to be known by us on the grounds of his eternal knowing of himself: 'The Word of God in which He gives Himself'.[98] That God reveals himself, becomes knowable in the form of an 'other', Word and Son. For God to be God (as Barth has clearly said at an earlier stage in the same volume) he must be an object to himself,[99] he must not need creation as a means of self-realization or self-interpretation.

Barth is, of course, tacitly rebutting anything like a Hegelian notion of the world as the divine self-objectification or 'noetic realization'. It is illuminating to turn briefly from the *Dogmatics* to Barth's discussion of Hegel in his *Protestant theology in the nineteenth century*,[100] where he deals particularly with the Hegelian identification of self, mind, and God, as an enormous theoretical justification for Romanticism,[101] the identification of ego with non-ego. Barth proposes that the key to Hegelianism is its treatment of 'reason, truth, concept, idea, mind, God himself' as *event*, 'life, movement, process'.[102] Misunderstanding arises in thought when this life is conceived in terms of a state. Reality – including God – is historical, and so true understanding is inevitably historical;[103] because historical understanding alone can grasp the movement of truth, the resolution of contradictions in ceaseless process. Truth *is* method, in effect, as far as thinking is concerned, for true thinking is the entry into the world's processes.[104] Thus God's truth must be apprehensible by the dialectical flow of thought and as *being itself* the dialectical flow of thought at its most fundamental level. 'The truth is God, God, however, is God only *in actu*. This means for Hegel, only as the God who is three in one, the eternal process which consists in something distinguishing its parts, separating them, and absorbing them into itself again.'[105] Reality is one; knowledge is established as secure upon this basis, since the unity of all things rests upon the unity of God, with whom begins and ends the noetic process. We know the world rightly in that the world is God's medium for the knowing of himself.

Barth expounds all this with great sympathy and perceptiveness (and we shall return later to the question of the points at which his own presentation is marked by Hegelian epistemology), but his major disagreement comes over the matter of sin. For Hegel (says Barth), sin is finitude and fate, and its overcoming is as necessary a part of the cosmic process as is its occurrence in the first place.[106] There is no *fall*, no radical, mutilating breakage of man from God; indeed, how could there be, since divine and human nature are one, as Hegel makes quite plain in his *Philosophy of religion*? In such a scheme, the basis of Christian knowledge cannot be revelation, and so cannot be God's freedom. If God is the universal noetic process, all that is is necessary to him. If he is to speak his word, he requires a world with which to utter it. The Word is concrete being, creation is the Word of God.[107] 'Hegel, in making the dialectical method of logic the essential nature of God, made impossible the knowledge of the actual dialectic of grace, which has its foundation in the freedom of God.'[108]

Once more, therefore, it is evident that, for Barth, the trinitarian dogma is the only ultimate safeguard for belief in the divine freedom. Without the 'antecedently' of the doctrine of the Son's eternal generation, God is caught in the Hegelian trap, subjected to a necessity which is both his and the world's. He is *obliged* to reveal himself, since 'A mind which is not manifest is not a mind.'[109] And, theologically, this is not and cannot be revelation in the proper sense. There can be no dialectic of hiddenness and revealedness, only the one organically evolving 'manifestation'. So to insist that God is God *in-und-für-sich-selbst* ('in and for himself'), whether or not there is a world, is necessarily involved in any confession of 'revealed religion' (to use an un-Barthian expression); and any faith which does not rest upon revelation cannot be faith in a free God, faith in God as Lord.

Barth begins his discussion of 'the Eternal Spirit', with the usual programmatic statement: 'What [God] is in revelation He is antecedently in Himself.'[110] Scripture clearly testifies that the work of the Spirit in revelation is God's work. If 'man's own presence at revelation' were *not* God's work, man would confront the Word as an object.[111] Thus the Spirit is God, and God in another mode than that revealed in the incarnate Word. Barth proceeds to a complex exegesis of the final section of the Niceno-Constantinopolitan Creed to establish what may be said of the eternal Spirit; and here it is clear that the exposition is halting a little. What emerges from the discussion of the credal statements is a curious and uncharacteristic uncertainty about the person of the Spirit in the 'immanent' Trinity. Κύριον, says Barth, is used 'adjectivally' of the Spirit in the Creed: it is neuter (τὸ κύριον not τὸν κύριον), like the word πνεῦμα itself. And this suggests to Barth that the Spirit's mode of being is – so to speak – 'neutral'; it is not involved in the reciprocal relatedness which characterizes the other two modes. The Spirit is the common factor in the mode of being of God the Father and that of God the Son. He is what is common to them, not in so far as they are the one God, but in so far as they are the Father and the Son.[112] The Spirit *is* the communion of the Father and the Son (the *vinculum*, *nexus*, *donum*, bond and gift and so forth, in Augustinian terminology), their common intra-divine 'act' or 'work'.[113] Thus as the intra-divine act of communion, he can be in revelation the act of communion between God and men.[114]

What is curious here is, first of all, the rapidity with which Barth moves into a consideration of the credal text, laying what may seem a disproportionate weight upon a grammatical point. Here – as happens very seldom in the *Church dogmatics* I/1 – he gives the impression of hurrying the argument forward towards a conclusion determined in advance (evidently with a lot of help from Augustine and the rest of the Latin tradition). The notion of the Spirit as *vinculum* provides a good basis for connecting the Spirit's role *ad intra* with his work *ad extra*; yet this can only be satisfactorily stated if the Spirit's work in revelation as *witness* to the Word (elsewhere so much emphasized by Barth) is allowed to drop into the background. Indeed, the whole structure of περιχώρησις (reciprocal movement and communication) in the Trinity, as set out earlier in the volume,[115] becomes problematic if one *Seinsweise* is seen primarily as a function of the other two. If the Spirit is a common *act* of Father and Son, why is it necessary to postulate him as a third hypostasis to account for the divine origin of human response to revelation? As an 'act', the Spirit cannot be a subject of predication in any way analogous to that in which Father and Son are such subjects. Barth, in his treatment of the concept of 'person' *in divinis*, has firmly rejected[116] any identification of 'person' with 'personality' or 'centre of consciousness' in Trinitarian discourse, and the point is repeated in the section on the Spirit. 'Even if the Father and the Son might be called "person" (in the modern sense of the term), the Holy Spirit could not possibly be regarded as the third "person".'[117] This is confusing: Barth seems to be saying that, although no 'person' of the Trinity is an independent centre of consciousness in the modern sense, yet the Father and the Son more nearly approximate to it than does the Spirit. And the whole tenor of the argument about the Spirit as *donum* supports such a conclusion. If the Spirit is the communion or love between Father and Son, the implication is that there are two subjects and one 'operation' or, perhaps, 'quality' involved. In the words of a very different theologian, 'The revealed parable of the Godhead is a story about two characters, Father and Son ... The Trinity is not (in human terms) a society of three, but a society of two.'[118]

This does not seem satisfactory. Barth is, in his introductory sections on 'Trinity', deeply concerned to avoid any appearance of imbalance between the three modes of God's being; all that he says about the need to see God's unity as *consisting in* his trinity reflects such a concern.[119] Yet, when he comes to discuss the Spirit, a curious kind of Trinitarianism seems to appear. It is noteworthy that he devotes fourteen pages[120] to the *Filioque* clause, and is implacably opposed to the Eastern *ex Patre solo*: without the *Filioque*, he maintains, the internal nature of God as 'fellowship', which is the basis of the redemptive act of God, is not conceivable.[121] 'The love which meets us in reconciliation, and then retrospectively in creation, is real love, supreme law and ultimate reality, because God is antecedently love in Himself.'[122] Unless the Holy Spirit constitutes, as we might say, the 'lovingness' of God, there can be no ground for God's loving movement towards the world. Something has impelled Barth to qualify his earlier model in a direction which is both more explicitly pluralistic and less precisely triadic, and the oddity of this qualification prompts some further questioning about Barth's systematic assumptions, which we shall attempt to pursue in the next section of this essay. The relative clarity of the treatment of

Father and Son is itself put in question by the apparent failure of the same method to produce an adequate theology of the Spirit.[123]

That God is, in himself, Father and Son is a matter which can be firmly established, in Barth's terms, by the simple demonstration that, for revelation to *be* revelation, God must be what he shows himself to be, and must be 'capable' of self-showing. But for God to be in himself what he shows himself to be as Spirit is an idea which immediately raises difficulties; for God as Spirit is his own witness in the event of revelation, God 'making sure' of us, and it is not easy to see how God in himself can 'make sure' of himself. He may perhaps 'utter' himself to himself; but it is distinctly odd to say that he *reveals* himself to himself, and assures himself of his self-revelation. That has unhappy echoes of the Fichtean self-positing *Ich*, which does not know itself until it has set itself against the *nicht-Ich*, and then establishes a balance of mutual limitation within the over-all *absolute-Ich* ('absolute I'), so that the ego's self-knowing is not, so to speak, annihilated by an all-pervading otherness, but is secured by an abiding complementarity between ego and non-ego. Now the whole point of Barth's theology of revelation is that revelation is a miraculous act of God towards what is radically apart from himself: it has nothing to do with some kind of interior divine self-clarification. Thus the Spirit's role in the Godhead cannot be the *Offenbarsein* (the 'revealedness') of revelation; and the emphasis has to be moved from revelation as such to communion, the fellowship of the Holy Spirit which God bestows on believers, as a mirror of his own life. But this suggests a problem of a very fundamental nature in Barth's Trinitarian scheme: is the all-important model of revelation or divine self-interpretation really capable of bearing the weight it is given in the argument if it breaks down at this point? It is to a consideration of this that we must turn in our next section.

IV

I have already indicated at various points in the course of this essay that I believe Barth's understanding of revelation and its place as a governing point of reference in theology is, although powerful, fruitful, and attractive, attended by grave difficulties, and not without its own inner tensions. And such doubts about the all-sufficiency of the revelation model have been raised by others. Gustaf Wingren, in a vigorous and provocative study of Barth,[124] has argued that the *Dogmatics* is pervaded by the 'modern' question about knowledge of God rather than the authentically Protestant question about righteousness before God. It is a situation not without its ludicrous aspect to find Barth being attacked for anthropocentrism; but Wingren makes a very serious point, although the compression and polemical intensity of his writing may make it difficult to grasp. Barth's frame of reference, Wingren claims, is a model of two 'beings', a higher (God) and a lower (man), separated by an epistemological gulf: God sends a message to man across the gulf, which both 'itself indicates the difference between God and man, and . . . discloses God's will to fellowship with men'.[125] The fundamental situation is the antithesis of God and man; if the biblical imagery of conflict is to be used, it must refer to the conflict between God and man. The Devil, or the active power of evil, or the force of sin which keeps man in slavery, all these are absent from Barth's theology: there is no *Christus Victor* story to be told.[126] The human predicament is ignorance. And Barth, by taking this as axiomatic, aligns himself with precisely that liberal theology which he is concerned to attack; what he and the liberals have in common is a lack of any sense of human bondage. Thus Barth's efforts in the *Church dogmatics* IV/1 to give some weight to the idea of God liberating or rescuing man are largely vitiated by the unreformed structure of epistemological assumptions still underlying them. The Incarnation is still seen as essentially *manifestation*.[127] ' "Revelation" stands in the place where "justification" or "forgiveness of sins," i.e., the gospel in the essential meaning of that word, ought to stand.'[128] The Pauline (and, we might add, the Lutheran) understanding of law can have no place here. Fallen man's situation, in Barth's eyes, is catastrophic, but not, as for Paul, strictly *tragic*. Barth allows no true knowledge of God in the creation or the law, and so is unable to utter the Pauline cry of despair at man's inability to obey the God he knows as Creator and Lawgiver (Rom. 7:7–25).

Similarly, 'The statement, "the word became flesh", ought to be rendered "the word assumed flesh".'[129] Not even in Christ can the gulf between God and man cease to exist, because God can never act *as* man or *in* man, only through man.[130] And the paradoxical issue of all this is that we are left with a system in which human knowledge, not the activity of God, is central. If we do place the activity of God at the heart of theology, we do not have to ask the obsessive question, 'How do we know?', 'Where is all this revealed to us?' Faith implies a readiness to speak of such activity in the world precisely in the *absence* of clear and secure 'revealed' evidence.[131] Salvation is not simply a being delivered from 'false thinking': God has acted to deliver us and make us righteous. There is, indeed, a focal *event* here, but it is an eschatological victory over the power of the Devil, not simply the uncovering of a timeless truth.[132] To remove the centre of theological gravity from the liberating act of God in the death of Christ is to jeopardize the very notion of God as living and as free to act.[133] Man with his epistemic capacities or incapacities occupies the centre of the stage, and the theological question is about the sources of his knowledge of ultimate truth. The Barthian *Nein* denies that nature can be such a source, and indicates that Christ is so – that is, that Christ answers *the same question*.[134] The burden of Wingren's critique is the refusal to accept this question as self-evidently the correct starting point for theology.

This is a penetrating and damaging criticism. Even if it is thought that Wingren does less than justice to the Barth of the *Church dogmatics* IV/1, he has drawn attention to a presupposition in Barth's system which has not, on the whole, been sufficiently examined. In a discussion of Barth's hermeneutics later on in the same work,[135] Wingren explains how the anthropological presupposition of man without knowledge of God dictates a reading of Scripture almost entirely in terms of 'communication' from God to man; whereas in fact the scriptural record points far more consistently to the struggle between God and evil, to a dramatic picture of God engaging in the tragic situation of man. It is a picture at the centre of which is not *Das Wunder der Weihnacht*, the Christmas miracle, which Barth so much emphasizes in the *Church dogmatics* I/2, but the defeat and victory of Good Friday and Easter Sunday. Wingren notes[136] the way in which the story of the virginal conception of Jesus provides Barth with a vehicle for stressing yet again the utter passivity of man before and in the event of revelation. Christmas is centrally important because it shows so clearly the nature of revelation in Christ, the divine Word present in the negation of human act and ability. Yet, as Wingren remarks,[137] the birth of Jesus is not, *in itself*, of any significance in New Testament preaching, and Christmas is not celebrated by the Church until a fairly late date. Properly speaking, it cannot be more than an introduction to the human life in which the incarnate Word works our salvation. Wingren implies, without ever stating it in so many words, that Barth has no doctrine of the humanity of Christ.[138]

It is true that the long and subtle treatment of Christ's obedience in the *Church dogmatics* IV/1 weighs against any such conclusion, and

Wingren, as we have seen, is not unaware of Barth's efforts to state a more authentically incarnational scheme of the work of redemption. Indeed Barth's understanding of Christ bearing our condemnation in the same act as that in which he perfects our failed obedience is very close indeed to Wingren's own Christology. Yet here again Barth presses back towards talking about revelation. The obedience of Christ is the way in which the love of God is made *known*: 'space' is made for God's communication in the world by the self-abnegation of Christ. We may refer back here to our earlier discussion of the revelation of God the Father in the Cross. Christ's obedience, says Barth 'proves Him to be the Mediator between God and man'.[139] In his obedience is revealed his lordship. This, of course, raises the issue of how the obedience of Christ reveals (as on Barth's presuppositions it must do) some aspect of the divine life *ad intra*; and we are given a very long and tortuous treatment of this, proposing the existence of 'above' and 'below', *prius* and *posterius*, command and obedience, in the life of God, while still insisting that the divine hypostases are modes of being, and not centres of volition.[140] 'In His mode of being as the Son He fulfils the divine subordination, just as the Father in His mode of being as the Father fulfils the divine superiority.'[141] What, if anything, this can possibly mean, neither Barth nor his interpreters have succeeded in telling us. The whole movement of IV/1 is towards a very much more 'pluralist' conception of the Trinity than is allowed for in I/1; the attempt to harmonize the two models – or rather, to bring the former into line with the latter – produces one of the most unhelpful bits of hermetic mystification in the whole of the *Dogmatics*. Wingren is right at least in saying that Barth has failed to carry through any major reformulation of his assumptions in IV/1.

The conclusion suggested by all this is that as soon as the *history* of Jesus, in a fairly simple sense, the detail of a human life and death, is allowed a place of genuine salvific import, the unity, clarity, and security of a scheme based upon a single and compelling act or event of revelation is put in question. It has more than once been remarked (by Hastings Rashdall, for example)[142] that a 'substitutionary' theory of the Atonement – any theory, in effect, which lays emphasis upon Christ's bearing the consequences for human nature of the Father's 'wrath' – implies a strongly, perhaps insupportably, pluralist conception of the Trinity. God must confront God across the gulf of fallenness, from the place of Godless man. Barth puts this eloquently in IV/1:

> It therefore pleased [God] ... for the redemption of the world, not to alter Himself, but to deny the immutability of His being ... to be in discontinuity with Himself, to be against Himself ... His identity with Himself consisted strictly in His determination to be God, our God, the reconciler of the world, in this inner and outer antithesis to Himself.[143]

In the act of reconciliation, God, for our sakes, 'risks' his very identity, his continuity with himself.[144] And if we are to take this at all seriously, the kinds of assumption about the freedom and lordship of God with which Barth is working in I/1 will need radical revision. The pluralism to which the logic of Barth's argument in IV/1 points not only demands a modification of any exclusively revelatory or 'interpretative' reading of Trinitarian doctrine; it also demands a rethinking of the *kind* of revelation with which Christian theology has to deal, and so of the kind of divine subjectivity from which revelation emerges.

Such issues as these have been discussed, with an insight shown by few other contemporary theologians, in the work of Hans Urs von Balthasar. Donald MacKinnon[145] has indicated the importance, in von Balthasar's treatment of the death of Christ, of the theme of a 'coincidence of opposites' grounded in the eternal Trinity – the *kenosis* of Christ in his manhood and mortality revealing an eternal self-determination of God which in some manner includes this manhood and mortality, and so includes the whole created order. The place of Christ before the Father, as elect and beloved of the Father, is not an afterthought in the being of God, but eternally in the identity (*Eigentlichkeit*) of God.[146] Our distance from God is itself taken into God, finds place in God; by the Spirit of adoption we enter the relation between Father and Son, the relation of exchange and mutuality.[147] In the Incarnation, God distances himself from himself: the divine, intra-Trinitarian love is enacted and realized in the world by the descent of Christ into Hell. And the separation between Father and Son is bridged by the Spirit, who is the common will and love of Father and Son. The inconceivable self-emptying of God in the events of Good Friday and Holy Saturday is no arbitrary expression of the nature of God: this is what the life of the Trinity is, translated into the world.[148]

> God causes God to go into abandonment by God while accompanying him on the way with his Spirit. The Son can go into the estrangement from God of hell, because he understands his way as

an expression of his love for the Father and he can give to his love the character of obedience to such a degree that in it he experiences the complete godlessness of lost man.[149]

Von Balthasar fully acknowledges, in his *magnum opus, Herrlichkeit*, as elsewhere, his great debt to Barth's presentation of some of these themes in IV/1. And perhaps it requires a theology like von Balthasar's to show us just how far from the schema of I/1 we are led by the implications of IV/1. The Trinitarian scheme which can be developed out of the doctrine of the Son of God in a far country is one which must allow not only for a plurality of agency within the Trinity but also for the inclusion of the history of man in the being of God. Such a formulation may instantly suggest the kind of Hegelian blurring of boundaries against which Barth so violently reacts. Yet it is Barth himself who struggles to formulate this in II/2 of the *Church dogmatics* in a celebrated discussion of the predestination of Christ to which Jüngel draws our particular attention.[150] God's *Urentscheidung*, his primary determination, is also the *Urgeschichte*, the primary history, of the act of grace. 'Originally God's election of man is a pre-destination not merely of man but of Himself.'[151] Once more, the ground of what God does in redemption and revelation must be his self-determination: he elects, before all ages, to be the God of grace.

The difficult implication – and Barth does not shrink from it – is that the elected Christ, Jesus of Nazareth, is 'in the beginning with God'.[152] 'If that primal history is real *history* between God and man, then the Son of God cannot be thought of in this history without the man Jesus ... God's prevenient being is being *imparting* itself as grace. In the sense of such prevenient imparting, the man Jesus *has* already a part in God's eternal being.'[153] The Logos, the Son, is the holder of Jesus' place (*Platzhalter*) before God.[154] From all eternity, God's self-differentiation as Son or Word is directed towards the human and worldly object of election, Jesus of Nazareth.

Does this then imply the eternal existence of *a man*? Not precisely: Jüngel appeals[155] to the late patristic terminology of *anhypostasia* and *enhypostasia* to explain how the presence of Jesus with God is not simply 'a projection of a temporal existence into eternity'. The temporal, historical existence of Jesus of Nazareth would not exist, would not be a temporal existence at all, without the primal determination of God as Word; without the Word it is 'anhypostatic', it has no basis or centre of subsistence. It is thus 'enhypostatised' in the Word, it subsists as itself because of the Word. It seems, however, as though Barth's position is stronger in statement than Jüngel's paraphrase. Jüngel in effect proposes a solution whereby God eternally 'foresees' the man Jesus, and, although he denies that the pre-existent being of Jesus is 'gnoseological' or 'ideal' (i.e. presumably, only 'in the mind of God'), it is hard to see what else such a 'foreseen' existence could be.

The point becomes clearer if we return to the discussions in the *Church dogmatics* IV/2 about the sufferings of God in Christ,[156] and about the fellow-suffering of the Father with the Son.[157] It seems as though, in this connexion, we have to do with more than a foreseen contingency, more even than the holding of a 'place'. It is a matter of the suffering and the death of a particular human being at a particular time being true for and in God in his eternity. Because Jesus of Nazareth suffers and dies, the eternal God suffers and endures his own negation in the world; and by enduring transforms death into life, *human* death into renewed human life.[158] The divine verdict on the world, the verdict of negation, is affirmed in the Cross; but the world is saved on the Cross because it is God himself who has borne his own judgement and surrounded and penetrated this negation with his unlimited life. God's being is his act; if he acts in and through a man's death, that death is involved in what he *is*.

Does this represent a capitulation on Barth's part to the Hegelianism he so desired to avoid and combat, or to Schleiermacher's understanding of the Trinity as 'the doctrine of the union of the Divine Essence with human nature, both in the personality of Christ and in the common Spirit of the Church'?[159] So long as Barth insists, as he does, upon speaking of God's *free* self-determination in the Word, he remains in a different framework from that of Hegel; and so long as he insists upon the divine self-determination as true of God *in se*, he distinguishes his position from Schleiermacher's. For Schleiermacher, the projection of God's differentiated forms in revelation into the divine essence itself is the construction of useless, and indeed un-Christian, 'philosophemes', idle speculative constructions.[160] Barth's doctrine of election is precisely a projection into God of the form of his revelation; and, as a doctrine of *election*, it remains bound to his primary doctrine of the freedom of God. God wills to be himself in such a way (as Son or Word) as to make place for the man Jesus. He does not have to be thus. Yet, God 'reveals His very essence in this streaming forth of grace. There is no higher divine being than that of the gracious God.'[161] He wills freely to elect Jesus; but this is no arbitrary act, accidental to his nature. He is eternally – how might it be said? – 'liable' to elect, 'tending' or 'intending' to elect, and so, in some sense, eternally exposed to the suffering of his creature Jesus, to the 'negation' involved in his own judgement upon the fallen creation. Eternally and in himself he meets and contains and overcomes the possibility of negation.

This is therefore a picture in which the revelatory event incorporates in itself the extremest possible risk of its own failure and deficiency. The radical hiddenness of Luther's incarnate God is far closer here than in the *Church dogmatics* I/1. Revelation includes, at least, tension, perhaps even conflict, between 'Utterer' and 'Uttered', so that the hearing of the Word cannot be conceived simply as the reception of a clear and unambiguous utterance, revealed in what might be called a 'linear' fashion. To put it metaphorically: it is not that we are simply addressed by a speaker; we are drawn into a conversation. In I/1, Barth proposed that the event of revelation, although in a sense pluriform, is most simply and basically the utterance of a subject (the Father) about himself: in Christ, this utterance is projected outwards to men as a true predication about the Father. It is a pattern which corresponds (almost disquietingly) to what von Balthasar characterizes[162] as the Old Testament's view of the God–man relation: God the Lord addresses man the servant across the immense chasm of separation between creator and creature. But, by IV/1, it has become far more difficult to employ so simple a pattern. God's utterance about himself has now to include his utterance of a contradiction; indeed, his utterance *is* the contradiction, a divine other which (or who) does not simply 'express', but responds and questions. Merely to put the matter in terms like these shows the difficulty of holding two such models together. It seems that revelation is itself to be discerned *in* the event or transaction between Father and Son on the cross, the dialogue of Father and Son. Borrowing Hopkins's imagery (from the poem quoted at the beginning of this essay), 'the crying of those Three' is, like that of the seraphim, *alter ad alterum* ('one to another'). And the believer, apprehending the event of revelation, is called upon not simply or even primarily to hear a word, miraculously imported into his consciousness, but to 'catch' that crying, to learn a language and so to join a society, to take seriously the 'strangeness' of revelation in a very different way from that indicated in Barth's earlier proposals, as the manifestation of a life and a system of relations which men are invited to enter and share.

Let us attempt at last to sum up this discussion. Problems begin to appear in Barth's Trinitarian scheme when the controlling model of revelation or self-interpretation proves difficult to apply to a theology of the Holy Spirit. What I have called the 'linear' view of revelation (God – the Word – the hearing of the Word) is no help at all in thinking about God's 'immanent' being *(in-und-für-sich)*, and the idea of the Spirit as *donum* (gift) and *communio* or *nexus amoris* (bond of love) has to be developed. This has the result of intensifying the sense of plurality in God: not very much sense can be made of 'modes' relating to each other in love. And this becomes still clearer when Barth turns to a serious consideration of the cross, of God the Son existing at the extreme point of distance from the Father. If this is rightly understood, there is in God, eternally, the capacity for this 'distance' or 'displacement', union with another even across the greatest gulf of contradiction and opposition. God's otherness to himself in his Word is the existence in him of *response*, mutuality, not simply a 'self-expression' of some sort. He is not, in short, *a* self. The basic weakness of a self-interpretative model is its implied conviction that we are dealing with something comparable to an individual human subjectivity, rather than a unity consisting in a system of relations. Barth (as we have seen) insists that the Trinity of God is indeed a special kind of unity; yet his view of revelation in I/1 necessarily dictates that God be thought of as a single self analogous to human selves. If there is one speaker, there can be only one subject; hence the *aporia* of I/1.

The role of the Spirit even in the later parts of the *Dogmatics* remains a difficulty. Barth never wrote a 'Doctrine of Redemption' to crown the threefold structure of the *Dogmatics*, so that we cannot tell how far his excursions into pluralism might have carried him. Von Balthasar's conception of the Spirit as 'going with the Son' into his exile and holding Father and Son together across the gulf of dereliction and death suggests one way in which such a development might be pursued; though this does not, at first sight, go very far towards resolving the question raised earlier, of whether we are not thus left with a model of two subsistents linked by a quality – a very asymmetrical Trinity indeed. However, it may yet provide the ground for a resolution. The cross is not the end of the Gospel, and this means that what is shown on the cross as the relation between Father and Son does not 'exhaust' what can be said of the Godhead. If we restrict what we say about God to what we say about Father and Son, we are left with only a relation of potentially radical difference, and *that* relation in itself cannot (by definition) constitute for us a third term independent of Father and Son.

But to confess the Holy Spirit is to affirm that beyond Calvary the life of God is still life. Christ is raised and exalted 'in the Spirit'. And so Barth, writing on 'The verdict of the Father' in the resurrection,[163] can speak of how very near the cross comes to a totally alienating, annihilating judgement on the world, to be salvaged only by God's freedom to be Spirit, to resurrect Jesus, and to renew the face of the earth.[164] The resurrection, indeed, is not simply the verdict of the Father, but the verdict of the *Spirit*,[165] the new divine judgement on the whole creaturely and human situation, which is imparted to men in the miracle of faith. The Spirit *does* present to us the relation of Father and Son, he does not witness to himself; but presents it precisely as a relation which is not closed or fixed, but one into which the human world may be brought. God's being is, in one sense, the act manifested on Calvary; but it is also the act whereby *we* are brought into Calvary, Hell, and newness of life, the inexhaustible resource of God's life. If this is so, God can 'send' his Son into the far country in the Spirit, the Son can offer himself wholly, even in death and dereliction, to the Father in or through the Spirit (Hebrews 9:14), and we are made partakers of the Spirit by baptism into Calvary, whereby we stand before God as Christ did, as sons of one father.

The Spirit, then, is the relation of Father and Son, but is not to be thought of as some kind of common possession which the Father takes from himself and bestows upon the Son for the Son to return to him. He is not the same as the Father or the Son, *or* the two together. Against Barth's vigorous defence of the *Filioque*, we may set 'the verdict of the Spirit' of IV/1, the divine freedom to be Spirit 'beyond' the Father–Son relationship. Vladimir Lossky, whose attack on the *Filioque*[166] is the most penetrating and systematic statement in this century of the Eastern view of the Holy Spirit, has argued that the *Filioque* presupposes an abstract monotheism for which distinctions in the Godhead can be stated only in terms of internal 'relations of opposition'. God postulates himself as Father, knows himself as Son, and returns into himself in love as Spirit; the Spirit turns the 'dyad' of Father and Son into a primal 'monad' again. Proper Trinitarian theology, on the other hand, sees the procession of the Spirit as 'an infinite passage beyond the dyad, which consecrates the absolute (as opposed to relative) diversity of the persons. This passage beyond the dyad is not an infinite series of persons but the infinity of the procession of the Third Person.'[167] We may compare with this some words from Raimundo Panikkar's obscure but profoundly suggestive essay on *The Trinity and the religious experience of man*:[168] 'Could one not say that in spite of every *effort* of the Father to "empty himself" in the generation of the Son, to pass entirely into his Son, to give him everything that he *has*, everything that he *is*, even then there remains in this first procession, like an irreducible factor, the Spirit, the non-exhaustion of the source in the generation of the Logos?'

Barth's Trinitarian scheme seems, finally, to be moving towards a pluralism of this kind; and, although we can have no certain knowledge of what might have been said in a 'Doctrine of redemption', there is material enough for the construction of a revised model of the Trinity. Jüngel goes some way towards this, but the boldest and most systematic attempt at such a construction so far is Jürgen Moltmann's *The cruci-fied God*.[169] In Moltmann's conception of the Father whose love 'aban-dons' the Son to death and dereliction, the Son whose love takes his and all men's 'abandonment' into himself, and the Spirit who is the inexhaustible future opened and offered in the love of the cross, we have perhaps the fullest indication yet of the potential of the later Barth's Trinitarian thinking. If future Trinitarian systems are to make use (as I believe they must if they are to be humanly – as well as theologically – serious) of the 'dereliction theologies' of Moltmann and von Balthasar, they must engage at some point with Barth's seminal discussions. Theology after Barth is also (as Moltmann never lets us forget) theology after Auschwitz; it cannot now operate without a condemned God, a dying God – 'the judge judged in our place'.

V

In this brief final section, it remains to consider some of the possible impulses behind the epistemological position of the *Church dogmatics* I/1, since it is this position which seems chiefly responsible for the unsatisfactory nature of the Trinitarian scheme there proposed. And, before going any further, it is worth noting that Barth is operating with a particular model of language in I/1, which is never directly expressed but is everywhere present. The nearest thing we have to a clear state-ment is the section on 'The Word of God as the speech of God'.[170] Barth here begins by denying Tillich's idea of speech as symbol – understanding 'symbol' as a designation chosen by men to substitute for a different kind of reality. Speech is an intellectual activity capable of corresponding to reality: *God's* speech, given for our use in his Word, corresponds to God's reality. It is, as Barth explains in his next section ('The speech of God as the act of God'), the act of God's lordship. And, if God's Word is speech, it is 'spiritual', 'personal', and 'purposive'. 'Speech, including God's speech, is the form in which reason communicates with reason and person with person';[171] it may happen physically, corporeally, but it is by nature spiritual, and cannot be reduced to the 'naturalism' of concrete images.[172] In God's Word alone, truth and reality perfectly coincide: 'Typical of every other word is an uncertain oscillation between a spasmodic idealism and an equally spasmodic realism',[173] but in God's Word it is truth which comes first and governs reality (the concrete and particular). The Word is also personal, *Dei loquentis persona*, God-in-the-act-of-speech. It is the utterance of the one entirely free subject.[174] And thirdly, it is 'purposive', it is 'address': 'We know it only as a Word that is directed to us and applies to us.'[175] God is already object to himself in his eternity, but he freely creates us as objects of address and of love. 'God did not need to speak to us. What He says by Himself and to Himself from eternity to eternity would really be said just as well and even better without our being there.'[176] His positing of himself as his object is the eternal ground of his positing of the world as object.

What picture of language emerges from a discussion like this? Language here is seen, I would argue, as before all else self-expressive utterance. It is the articulation of inner ('spiritual') structures, the ultimate truth or truths underlying 'reality' (perceived empirical structures). Speech is an externalizing of the *verbum intellectus*, the internal form of thought, which in God is the thinking of himself.[177] Thus the Word, the language, of God is his expressing as object what he knows in knowing himself. In the Word, God literally *utters* himself, makes himself 'outer', external, *sich äussert*. And so his speaking to man is also primarily self-expressive utterance, this time *directed* towards man (the 'purposive' Word), and it is truth because it is the externalization of God's infallible knowledge of himself. Furthermore, since it is a part of God's self-knowledge to know himself as Lord and creator, his truth is the truth of all created things. Man has no word with which to reply, because he has no subsistence of his own, no truth of his own: all he can do is hear and obey the Word, allow himself to be brought into the single divine act of the expression of divine truth, by the power of the Holy Spirit, and the miracle of faith.

If language is first and foremost self-expression, then God's Word is first and foremost the expression of God's truth; so that to hear the Word is to enter into the infallibility of God's truth. This concern with the appropriation or impartation of infallible truth is, I believe, quite basic to the argument of I/1. At the very beginning of I/1, Barth says that 'All sciences might ultimately be theology', if they so chose:[178] science in general works with concepts of truth and certainty which are foreign to the dogmatic inquiry because they stop short of obedience to the one authentic truth; if the scientist bows to this truth, he becomes a theologian. Theology cannot therefore be among the sciences; yet she claims the name and dignity of a science, if only to register 'a necessary protest against a general concept of science which is admittedly pagan', to remind the secular scientists 'that the quasi-religious certainty of their interpretation of the term is not in fact undisputed, that the tradition which commences with the name of Aristotle is only one among others'.[179] Theology in fact claims the name of science to witness to the lordship of the Word over true science, and to call the perverted secular sciences to obedience, and so to 'the theological task'. 'Dogmatics', Barth goes on to say, 'is a part of the work of human knowledge';[180] but it is more also, it is the fruit of *acknowledgement*, of faith. It is not and cannot be divorced from the free act of grace which establishes faith on the secure foundation of God's truth. 'It always rests with God . . . whether our dogmatics is blessed and sanctified as *knowledge of the true content of Christian utterance* or whether it is idle speculation.'[181]

The implication of this argument is plain. Knowledge properly so called, certain knowledge, is the prerogative of dogmatics in obedience to the Word. Dogmatics is the sole authentic science, because it alone conforms (necessarily conforms) to the truth of its object. It does not thereby deny absolutely the legitimacy of the 'special sciences', but it calls in question any and every claim to finality or ultimate certainty in these sciences.[182] When secular science claims such certainty in its own right, it has become crypto-theology – or rather *ersatz* theology. When it consciously abides within its own limits, looking beyond them for final truth, it is pre-theology. And when it passes over into obedient reflection upon and receptivity to the Word, it is true theology, know-ledge of God's truth, 'acknowledgement'. It is shaped by the 'noetic necessity' of *Fides quaerens intellectum*. The *Dogmatics* begin with the question of how the *security* of faith and talk about faith is to be grounded, how the nature of dogmatics as pure science can be demon-strated. The predominant concern in the argument is the search for certainty; not, indeed, a certainty which can be tied up in dogmatic propositions, but one which *participates* in the absolute dependability of its object, which is unified with its object, so that 'in the Object of dogmatic statements there is already included human subjectivity'.[183]

God is subject as well as object of faith and of theology; his stability in himself, *in-und-für-sich*, is the same stability which holds for propositions about him made in conformity with his self disclosure.

We come full circle. Truth exists, dogmatics exists, the Word is heard. Man is seized by the Word and brought under its lordship, into the event of its eternal utterance. So, first among the tasks of dogmatic science is the attempt to understand how it is itself possible: not merely 'possible' in general, however, but possible as *science*, as certainty, 'acknowledgement'. The particular work which a doctrine of the Trinity therefore has to do is to provide an account of how God can communicate his truth to men; it must describe the divine capacity for perfect self-expression and the perfect communication of that self-expression. The need to assure the 'noetic necessity' of faith and dogmatics demands just such an 'expressive' view of language as we have seen to be at work in I/1, and so dictates what I have termed the 'linear' model of God's Trinitarian utterance. And the consequence of this is Barth's pervasive interest, in the earlier volumes of the *Dogmatics*, in the unity of the revelatory event: an event in which disclosure and apprehension or appropriation are the single act of God in a duality of modes. To allow any positive place of human freedom of response (in the usual sense of those words) is at once to abandon certainty, to say that the eternal unity of God's utterance is, as it were, adulterated by the plurality and confusion of human minds and hearts.

It is surely here that Barth's kinship with Hegel is most evident. The Idealist obsession with what has been called the 'concrete universal' arose from the desire to ground knowledge securely in an ontology of participation: *das absolute Wissen*, Hegel's final synthesis of consciousness and self-consciousness, is the level at which the divisions and contradictions of prior levels are overcome by the finite subject's identification with, recognition of itself in, Absolute Spirit, the one and universal self-thinking thought. It is the finite self's participation in the One. Barth substitutes the Word for the Hegelian pan-unity, and so, by beginning from the total strangeness of God and man to each other, turns the Hegelian system on its head. Yet there is a recognizable similarity of pattern, something of a mirror-image. We may recall Wingren's strictures on Barth's anthropological-epistemological starting point. The question is still one about certain knowledge, and for Barth it is answered by the possibility of man's 'inclusion' in the one divine speech-act, his participation in the Trinitarian event of God's self-differentiation and self-unification as Word and Spirit.

Perhaps the most fundamental trouble is that Barth (at least in this context) has as little of a doctrine of creation as has Hegel. For Hegel, God and the world are entirely continuous, for Barth, entirely discontinuous. The Fall has, it seems, obliterated any theological significance in the created order as such in the Barthian picture; and Wingren is surely right to complain that this (whether accurate or not as a theologoumenon) is not the biblical or traditionally Christian, or even traditionally Protestant view. An emphasis upon the compelling, irresistible character of revealed truth leaves almost no room for a conception of free, creative, and *distinctive* human response. Man is free *for* God, free to respond in the Spirit, as Barth explains at length in I/2 §16, free to know the Word as his master;[184] but it is a freedom which can only be 'theologised' from *within* faith, *within* the relation of obedience. There is, in the earlier volumes of the *Dogmatics*, little sense of that to which Bonhoeffer was so uniquely sensitive, God's self-abnegation in the face of created freedom, God's 'deference' to the will, even the evil will, of his creatures. God's relation to the fallen world is (as revealed in the cross) an all but annihilating negation, in Barth's view; yet it may well be asked how this related to the Isaianic Servant, who will not break the broken reed, or to the tempted Christ in the wilderness, refusing (as Dostoyevsky put it) the lures of 'miracle, mystery and authority' as means of imposing the divine truth, or to the Lord who stands at the door and knocks. Even in IV/1, the emphasis is far less on the Son of Man given up into the hands of sinners, God at man's mercy, than on the judgement of *God* upon *man*. Barth will write eloquently of the suffering and dereliction of Jesus bearing the wrath of God; but not of Jesus as 'God bearing the wrath of man', Bonhoeffer's God 'pushed out of the world on to the cross'. We have already noted Barth's denial[185] that God gives himself into our hands; yet the incarnational paradox is that this is precisely what he does. Having created free men, he submits to man's judgement, man's freedom to reject. 'Man's religiosity makes him look in his distress to the power of God in the world ... The Bible directs man to God's powerlessness and suffering.'[186]

To suggest that Barth is in fact a theologian of 'man's religiosity' is too neat an inversion, too facile and eye-catching a point: Barth is evidently not making a naïve appeal to 'the power of God in the world'. Yet power, lordship, the master–slave relationship, all play an uncomfortably large part in Barth's system. No doubt the so-called 'social' analogy for the life of the Trinity has its grave deficiencies, but at least it insists that the divine life into which the believer is baptized is a relational pattern in which 'none is afore or after another', where the predominant model is not address and obedience (significant though that remains), but mutual sharing. Christian Duquoc, in the second part of his magnificent essay in Christology,[187] has given serious consideration to the Freudian charge that Christianity is an inflation of infantile beliefs about the omnipotent father who can solve all problems and heal all wounds. Referring to a celebrated paper by Paul Ricoeur on this subject, Duquoc argues that this is an accurate account only when 'God the Father' is the phantasm projected by 'la toute-puissance du désir': the omnipotent father, that is to say, is the substitute for the failed omnipotence of the self. If, however, the Father is 'symbol', not 'phantasm', a term integrated into a symbolic unity of understanding, self-understanding, and world-understanding, not simply projected over against self and world, it may be less ambiguous, more creative. And Duquoc goes on to explain how the realization of Jesus' divine sonship *in* a human life sets the Father–Son relationship on a new footing for us. 'Elle souligne que la paternité de Dieu n'évoque pas seulement l'origine radicale, créatrice, mais qualifie nouvellement le souci que Dieu porte aux hommes.'[188] Furthermore, since Father and Son are one, in will, act, and substance, the Son has no 'desire' to be what the Father is, since he *is* what the Father is (the Christological hymn of Philippians 2 springs to mind here); and his refusal to 'desire' omnipotence is what makes him human and finite without ceasing to be divine. Free of self-directed desire, he can live authentically as Son and as man at the same time; and from this man learns that *he* may live as Son by accepting his finitude and renouncing the infantilism of desire. 'Le sujet humain, en effet, n'est susceptible d'une relation filiale adulte que dans la mesure ou il est libre à l'égard de la mégalomanie du désir.'[189]

This is an original and impressive proposal. Like Bonhoeffer, Duquoc is profoundly concerned to answer the question, 'What constitutes an *adult* human relationship to God?' and this is a question which no theologian can afford to ignore. Whatever one's final judgement of Duquoc's suggestions, they at least remind us that our talk about man and God and their relations to one another is being conducted under the cold eye of the behavioural sciences. And, while this fact need not induce in the theologian the paralysing anxiety which seems to afflict much contemporary theological debate, it is clear that what theology has to say about man will inevitably be worked out in some degree of engagement with other contemporary models of man, whether consciously or not. What the nature of human flourishing may be is a weighty and complex issue. For the theologian, it will be defined more or less clearly in relation to the will of God or the purpose of God; but considerations of will and purpose push constantly towards the deeper question of the nature of God. The anthropological question leads into the theological, and what is said about God is of more than peripheral relevance to what may be said about man. And if this is true, Trinitarian theology, in so far as it is concerned with what 'kind' of God Christians worship, is far from being a luxury indulged in solely by remote and ineffectual dons; it is of cardinal importance for spirituality and liturgy, for ethics, for the whole of Christian self-understanding.

This was clear enough to Barth; and if a study of Barth's Trinitarian theology brings us round again to insisting on the point, it will have been a worthwhile enterprise. Barth, almost alone among twentieth-century dogmaticians, undertook to present Trinitarian doctrine as foundational for theology as a whole;[190] and I have attempted to show in this essay that Barth's Trinitarian scheme is indeed tightly interwoven with his whole conception of the life of faith. What is said about the Trinity is initially conditioned (though perhaps in ways which Barth did not fully recognize) by certain questions and assumptions about the nature of religious language and religious knowledge; and it in turn conditions the understanding of man's response to God, reflecting back upon the issues of language and knowledge. If, then, the student of Barth becomes aware of weaknesses in the structure of argument and, more importantly, of problematic consequences if the argument is strictly followed out, it is not easy for him to point to any one stage in the discussion and say, '*Here* is the flaw.' He is condemned to the uncomfortable and potentially unfair expedient of suggesting that somewhere in the background a wrong question is being asked. I have indicated in these pages that I consider Barth's failure to be a certain lack of concern with human growth, human diversity, and human freedom of response – with the possibility and character of adult relationship with God; and in reply to the glib 'Barthian' defence, that these matters are not the primary interest of theology, I can only appeal to the orthodox conviction that they *are* of interest to a God who is made known to us in a human life and death.

On what this failure rests, I am not sure: it is possible to attribute it to the kind of preoccupation with 'ontologically' secure knowledge discernible in the early Barth, to a residually Nestorian (or too radically

Calvinist) Christology, to covert idealism or covert gnosticism. Most centrally, it may be (as I have proposed) the absence of a doctrine of *creation*, as opposed to a doctrine of the infinite gulf between the created and the uncreated. None of these, however, constitutes an explanation of 'what is wrong with Barth'. The non-Barthian's attitude to Barth has about it something of Barth's own attitude to Catholicism – a fascinated exasperation at a system which is at once compelling and alienating in its range and seriousness, which constantly provokes one to attempt a counter-statement which will be no less serious. Barth's counter-statement to the doctrine of the *analogia entis* is the whole of the *Church dogmatics*; and, while one may not think that a counter-statement to Barth can or should be another *Dogmatics* (and many would say that, for various reasons, such an enterprise is no longer possible for the theologian), Barth's great work still sets a standard of engagement and comprehensiveness not easy to satisfy. If we object to a Barthian Trinitarian or Christological model and its implications for doctrines of man and grace, we are obliged to examine the roots and the norms of our own understanding, to find out whether we are asking the same questions and, if we are not, at least to explore our own questions with the same committed passion as Barth does. Barth reminds the systematic theologian of his obligation to be not only systematic but theological – in the patristic sense in which Θεολογία designated the whole self's growth into understanding of the threefold God who saves. It is a humbling and a salutary reminder.

Notes

1. Karl Barth, *Church dogmatics* (*CD*) I/1 (Edinburgh: T&T Clark, 1975), 407.
2. Ibid.; cf. 161, 199.
3. Ibid., §6; 187–247, esp. 190–8.
4. Ibid., 238.
5. See esp. ibid., 243–4.
6. Ibid., 156–62.
7. Ibid., 298–304.
8. T. F. Torrance, *Theological science* (London: Oxford University Press, 1969), 9.
9. Eberhard Jüngel, *Gottes Sein ist im Werden* (Tübingen: Mohr, 1965), 9–10; ET, *The doctrine of the Trinity: God's being is in becoming* (Grand Rapids: Eerdmans, 1976), xix–xx.
10. This is fully and painstakingly argued in David Ford's essay, 'Barth's

interpretation of the Bible', in S. W. Sykes (ed.), *Karl Barth: studies of his theological method* (Oxford: Clarendon Press, 1979), 55–87.

11. *CD* I/1, 107.

12. Ibid., 90, 92.

13. Ibid., 117.

14. Ibid., 118.

15. Ibid., 119. The pivotal importance of Barth's system of fulfilled time (*erfüllte Zeit*), and a proper indication of its relation to the *Moment* of the *Romans* commentary, is the burden of Richard Roberts's article, 'Barth's doctrine of time: its nature and implications', in Sykes (ed.), *Karl Barth*, 88–146.

16. *CD* I/1, 120–1.

17. Ibid., 121.

18. Ibid., 156–7; cf. 117, 138–9, etc.

19. *CD* I/2 (Edinburgh: T&T Clark, 1956), 121.

20. *CD* I/1, 159.

21. Ibid., 189.

22. Ibid., 156.

23. Ibid., 450; cf. the long section in *CD* I/2 on 'The Holy Spirit as the subjective reality of revelation', esp. 206–8 and 223–4.

24. *CD* I/1, 296.

25. Barth, *Die Christliche Dogmatik im Entwurf* I (Munich: Chr. Kaiser Verlag, 1927), 127.

26. *CD* I/1, 296–7.

27. Ibid., 299–300.

28. Ibid., 303.

29. *CD* I/2, 58, italics in original.

30. See *CD* I/1, 146–7.

31. Jüngel's treatment of the question (*Gottes Sein ist im Werden*, 76–7, 106–8; *The doctrine of the Trinity*, 64–5, 94–6), although compressed and difficult, makes this particular point very clear.

32. See the essay cited in n. 15 above.

33. *CD* I/1, 168–74.

34. Ibid., 175–6.

35. *CD* I/2, 61.

36. Robert C. Roberts, *Rudolf Bultmann's theology: a critical interpretation* (Grand Rapids: Eerdmans, 1976); esp. pt I, ch. 2 ('Existence, world and the New Testament') and pt III, ch. 9 ('Faith').

37. See the essay cited in n. 10 above.

38. W. von Loewenich, *Luthers theologia crucis* (Munich, Chr. Kaiser Verlag, 1929); ET of 5th (1967) German edn, *Luther's theology of the cross* (Belfast: Christian Journals, 1976).

39. Von Loewenich, *Luther's theology of the cross*, ch. 1, esp. 38–49.

40. Ibid., 47: 'Is the form of revelation perhaps accidental, or is it not to the highest degree characteristic for the content of revelation?'

41. *CD* I/2, 175.

42. *CD* I/1, 454.

43. Ibid., 176.

44. Ibid., 247.

45. Stephen Sykes, in his essay 'Barth on the centre of theology', in *Karl Barth*, adverts to Barth's expression (as used in *Fides quaerens intellectum*) 'noetic necessity', and Richard Roberts (in the essay cited in n. 15) touches on the implications of Barth's model of knowledge as 'acknowledgement' (see, for instance, *CD* I/1, 205–6 for this). The points which they make shed much illumination on Barth's understanding of the stable and 'guaranteed' character of faith and of theological reflection from, in, and upon faith.

46. See Jüngel, *Gottes Sein ist im Werden*, 87–90; *The doctrine of the Trinity*, 74–8.

47. *CD* II/2 (Edinburgh: T&T Clark, 1957), 161ff.

48. Theodore W. Jennings, Jr, *Introduction to theology: an invitation to reflection upon the Christian mythos* (Philadelphia: Fortress Press, 1976), 81.

49. See the essay cited in n. 45 above.

50. *CD* I/1, 295–6, 306–7.

51. Ibid., 306, my emphasis.

52. Ibid., 307.

53. Ibid., 311.

54. Ibid., 315.

55. Ibid., 316.

56. Ibid., 320.

57. Ibid.

58. Ibid., 324.

59. Ibid., 331–2.

60. Ibid., 333.

61. Ibid.

62. Ibid., 348–9.

63. Ibid., 349–50.

64. Ibid., 354.

65. Ibid.

66. Ibid., 295–304.

67. Ibid., 353.

68. Ibid., 332.

69. Ibid., 387.

70. Ibid., 388.

71. Ibid., 388–9.

72. Ibid., 388.

73. *CD* IV/1 (Edinburgh: T&T Clark, 1956), 211–83.

74. Ibid., 259.

75. Ibid., 273–83.

76. Ibid., 280.

77. *CD* I/1, 391.

78. Ibid., 410.

79. Ibid., 412–13.

80. Ibid., 414.

81. Ibid., 412.

82. Ibid., 448.

83. Ibid., 451.

84. See, for instance, ibid., 46off. See also a rather neglected essay of Barth's, 'Der heilige Geist und das christliche Leben', in K. and H. Barth, *Zur Lehre vom heiligen Geist* (Munich: Chr. Kaiser Verlag, 1930), 39–105, esp. 54–5, 92.

85. CD I/1, 481.

86. Ibid., 455, my italics.

87. Ibid., 457; cf. *Zur Lehre vom heiligen Geist*, 94–100.

88. CD I/1, 462.

89. Ibid., 464–5.

90. Ibid., 391.

91. Ibid., 394.

92. Ibid., 392–3; there is a reference to Eph. 3.15.

93. Ibid., 394–5.

94. Ibid., 395–8.

95. Ibid., 416.

96. Ibid., 420–1.

97. Ibid., 421–2.

98. Ibid., 435.

99. Ibid., 140.

100. Barth, *Protestant theology in the nineteenth century* (London: SCM Press, 1972), 384–421.

101. Ibid., 392ff.

102. Ibid., 398–9.

103. Ibid., 400.

104. Ibid., 405–6.

105. Ibid., 413.

106. Ibid., 418.

107. For a useful, if uncritical, summary see James E. Griffiss, 'Hegel's logos Christology', in R. W. Norris (ed.), *Lux in lumine* (New York: Seabury Press, 1966), 80–92.

108. Barth, *Protestant theology in the nineteenth century*, 420.

109. Hegel, *Philosophy of Religion* III, 35; quoted by Barth in *Protestant theology in the nineteenth century*, 420.

110. CD I/1, 466.

111. Ibid., 468.

112. Ibid., 469.

113. Ibid., 470.

114. Ibid., 471.

115. See esp. ibid., 348–75.

116. Ibid., 355ff.

117. Ibid., 469.

118. Austin Farrer, *Saving belief* (London: Hodder and Stoughton, 1964), 128–9.

119. See, e.g., CD I/1, 349–50.

120. Ibid., 473–87.

121. Ibid., 480–1.

122. Ibid., 483–4; cf. CD II/1 (Edinburgh: T&T Clark, 1957), 275, 279.

123. The near total lack of reference to the Spirit in Jüngel's book is interesting in this connection.

124. Gustaf Wingren, *Theology in conflict* (Edinburgh and London: Oliver and Boyd, 1958).

125. Ibid., 24.

126. Ibid., 24–5.

127. Ibid., 27–8.

128. Ibid., 28–9.

129. Ibid., 30–1.

130. Cf. ibid., 123–4.

131. Ibid., 35–6.

132. Ibid., 37–8.

133. Ibid., 38, 40–1.

134. Ibid., 42.

135. Ibid., 108–28.

136. Ibid., 111–12.

137. Ibid., 120–2.

138. The importance of this in Wingren's own dogmatic theology is plain from his early work on Irenaeus, *Man and the Incarnation* (Edinburgh and London: Oliver and Boyd, 1959).

139. *CD* IV/1, 208.

140. Ibid., 192–210.

141. Ibid., 209.

142. Hastings Radshall, *The idea of atonement in Christian theology* (London: Macmillan, 1919), 444–6. I am indebted to Stephen Sykes for drawing my attention to this passage.

143. *CD* IV/1, 184.

144. For a uniquely sensitive treatment of this theme and its implications, the reader is referred to D. M. MacKinnon's article, 'The relations of the doctrines of the Incarnation and the Trinity', in R. W. A. McKinney (ed.), *Creation, Christ and culture* (Edinburgh: T&T Clark, 1976), 92–107.

145. Donald MacKinnon, 'Introductory Essay', in Balthasar, *Engagement with God* (London: SPCK, 1975), 7.

146. Hans Urs von Balthasar, *Herrlichkeit: eine theologische Ästhetik*, III.2.2 (Einselden: Johannes Verlag, 1975), 367–8.

147. Ibid., 369.

148. Ibid., 196–200. For a fuller exposition, the whole of this section (196–211) on *Kenose* should be consulted, as should the long essay 'Mysterium Paschale' 1969; translated by Aidan Nichols, OP as *Mysterium Paschale: Mystery of Easter* (Edinburgh: T. & T. Clark, 1990; second corrected edn, Grand Rapids: Eerdmans, 1993).

149. Hans Urs von Balthasar, *Elucidations* (London: SPCK, 1975), 51.

150. Jüngel, *Gottes Sein ist im Werden*, 81–95; *The doctrine of the Trinity*, 68–83.

151. *CD* II/2 (Edinburgh: T&T Clark, 1957), 3.

152. Ibid., 96ff.

153. Jüngel, *Gottes Sein ist im Werden*, 93; *The doctrine of the Trinity*, 80.

154. CD II/2, 96.

155. Jüngel, *Gottes Sein ist im Werden*, 94; *The doctrine of the Trinity*, 81–2.

156. E.g., *CD* IV/2 (Edinburgh: T&T Clark, 1958), 186–8.

157. Ibid., 357.

158. *CD* IV/1, 304–9.

159. Friedrich Schleiermacher, *The Christian faith* (Edinburgh: T&T Clark, 1928), 738.

160. Ibid., 741–2.

161. *CD* II/1, 356.

162. Balthasar, *Herrlichkeit* III.2.2, 365–6.

163. *CD* IV/1, 283–357.

164. Ibid., 306–9.

165. Ibid., 919ff.

166. See Lossky's long article, 'The procession of the Holy Spirit in Orthodox Trinitarian doctrine', in the posthumous collection of essays, *In the image and likeness of God* (London: Mowbrays, 1975), 71–96.

167. Ibid., 84–5.

168. Raimundo Pannikar, *The Trinity and the religious experience of man* (London: Darton, Longman & Todd, 1973), 60.

169. Jürgen Moltmann, *The crucified God* (London: SCM Press, 1974); esp. ch. 6.

170. *CD* I/1, 132–43.

171. Ibid., 135.

172. Ibid., 136.

173. Ibid.

174. Ibid., 138–9.

175. Ibid., 139.

176. Ibid., 140.

177. The section 'Language and verbum', in Hans-Georg Gadamer's *Truth and method* (London: Sheed and Ward, 1975), 378–87, has a very valuable treatment of the concepts of *verbum* and *logos* in this connection.

178. *CD* I/1, 7.

179. Ibid., 11.

180. Ibid., 17.

181. Ibid., 18, my italics.

182. See T. F. Torrance, *Theological science*, ch. 6, 'Theological science among the special sciences'.

183. Ibid., 351.

184. *CD* I/2, 265–79.

185. *CD* I/1, 176.

186. Dietrich Bonhoeffer, *Letters and papers from prison*, enlarged edn (London: SCM Press, 1971), 361.

187. Christian Duquoc, *Christologie: essai dogmatique*, II: *Le messie* (Paris: Editions du Cerf, 1972), 327–48.

188. Ibid., 341. 'It emphasises that God's "fatherhood" should evoke not simply the ideas of radical or creative origin, but is something which suggests a new characterisation of the loving care which God has for men.'

189. Ibid., 344. 'The human subject is, indeed, open to an adult relation of sonship only in the measure in which it is free from the megalomania of desire.'

190. Perhaps the closest comparison is with the Russian émigré theologian, Sergii Bulgakov, whose trilogy, *The Lamb of God* (1933), *The comforter* (1936), *The bride of the Lamb* (1945), represents a vast systematic integration of Trinitarian theology with anthropology. Although the first two volumes were translated into French, and the third now into English (Grand Rapids: Eerdmans, 2002), they have yet to receive the serious discussion they deserve.

8

Barth, war and the state

I

During the later 1950s, German-speaking theology made its first sustained attempt to engage with the problems posed for the Church by the development of atomic armaments. The years 1957 and 1958 in particular saw a flurry of ecclesiastical activity and theological discussion, in which perhaps the most significant episode was the presentation to the German Evangelical Church (EKD) Synod in April 1958 of ten theses on the question of atomic warfare and the possession of atomic weapons.[1] The theses had been adopted by a number of the 'Church brotherhoods' in West Germany, study-circles whose origins lay in the theological fellowship groups of the Church struggle days of the 1930s, and which established a formal network in 1957. The document presented to the Synod aroused spirited controversy, not least by its suggestion[2] that the atomic issue should be recognized as one on which the Church should adopt a *status confessionis*; the brotherhoods insisted[3] that they were simply drawing out the implications of the fifth article of the Barmen Declaration (on the function of the state), and, in October 1958, at a convention of the brotherhood groups in Frankfurt, a further declaration[4] was adopted by over 200 delegates, a declaration modelled on that of Barmen, and explicitly appealing not only to Barmen but to the post-war statements of Stuttgart (1945), on the need for repentance and acknowledgment of guilt in the German churches, and Darmstadt (1947), on the need to forswear ideological commitment to German reunification and anti-Communist militancy.[5] The Frankfurt declaration was in part a response to the Synod's reception of the ten theses. No official acknowledgment had been made, but a statement had been issued,[6] calling for agreed restraints on military research and the deployment of warheads; although the Synod supported the 1957 condemnation of total war issued by the WCC, it also acknowledged the wide difference of opinion that existed within the

EKD on the question of whether *all* use (including defensive use) of atomic weapons was absolutely ruled out. The brotherhoods, understandably, were not prepared to let the matter rest with this splendidly synodical evasion, and the Frankfurt declaration was a challenge to the opposition to put forward a case equally grounded in the Christian gospel, rather than in any considerations of expediency.[7] A would-be neutral stance, leaving the question open as the Synod had sought to do, was 'incompatible with the confession of Jesus Christ'. 'Any attempt at a theological justification of any such employment [of atomic weaponry] or any such neutrality becomes false doctrine, seduces people from the truth and sets the will of the triune God aside as of no worth.'[8]

It may be useful, at this point, to reproduce the ten theses of spring, 1958 (they do not seem ever to have been seriously discussed in the English-speaking world). They form the third part of the *Anfrage* addressed by the brotherhoods to the Synod: the first section notes the theological unsatisfactoriness of preceding discussions of the question and outlines the considerations that make traditional categories for the theological justification of armed conflict useless in the new context of the atomic age. The second insists that, if the Synod declines to adopt the theses, it should reply with a defence of its refusal from Scripture, confession and reason. The third puts the question directly:

> Therefore we ask the Synod whether they are able to join with us in pronouncing the following ten propositions for the informing of consciences, as a response to the question of how the Christian should behave in respect of atomic weaponry:
>
> 1. *War* is the ultimate means of political confrontation between peoples and states, a means that is in all its forms questionable and ambiguous.
> 2. *Churches* of all lands and ages up to the present day have maintained that preparation for and employment of this means, for particular good or less good reasons, are not inadmissible.
> 3. The prospect of a future war waged with the use of modern means of annihilation has created a new situation, in the face of which the Church *cannot remain neutral*.
> 4. War in the form of *atomic* war means the mutual annihilation of the peoples involved as well as of innocent people of other nations not involved in the conflict between the two parties.
> 5. War in the form of atomic war is therefore manifestly *useless*

as a means of political confrontation, because it destroys the preconditions for such engagement.

6. The Church and the individual Christian can therefore only say *No* in advance to any war waged as an atomic war.

7. Even the preparation for such a war is in all circumstances *a sin against God and neighbour*, and no Church, no Christian can share in the guilt of this.

8. Thus we demand, in the name of the gospel, *that there be an immediate end* to all preparations for such warfare in our country and state, with no regard for any other considerations.

9. We call on all those who are serious in their wish to be Christians to *refuse* to co-operate in preparation for atomic warfare, unconditionally and in all circumstances.

10. An opposite viewpoint or a neutral stance on this question is *indefensible in Christian terms*. Both would mean the denial of all three articles of Christian faith.

Barth had been invited to speak at the convention of October 1958, but was obliged to withdraw because of ill-health and fatigue.[9] Since there had already been rumours that he disagreed with the ten theses, he was urged by Helmut Simon, one of the two moderators of the brotherhood network, to make a clear statement of his support for the *Anfrage* of March; and in an open letter, written in September 1958, Barth told Simon to proclaim loud and clear 'to each and all, that I fully concur with these theses . . . as if I had written them myself.'[10]

That is, of course, exactly what he *had* done, as Busch's biography reveals,[11] and as his correspondence of January 1958 makes clear![12] Why anyone should have thought him likely *not* to approve of the theses is a puzzle: he had already, in 1957, made clear public statements[13] in condemnation of the arms race and the already rapid burgeoning of military research. His views were sufficiently well known for representatives of the brotherhoods to approach him for help at the beginning of 1958; and the consistency of his opposition to atomic armaments up to the time of his death is easily documented from his letters. Yet as late as 1963 his name was still being invoked by supporters of the nuclear deterrent – on the basis, it seems, of his discussion of the ethics of war in the *Church dogmatics* (CD) III/4.[14] He admitted more than once that this discussion (dating from 1951) was flawed by its failure to give serious consideration to the new problems raised in the era after Hiroshima; but unfortunately he was never able to present the kind of extended discussion that would be needed to do justice to these problems. What I shall propose in this essay is that it is possible to see the lines along which such a discussion would proceed if we trace the evolution of Barth's doctrine of the *state*, and not only what he has to say about war; and if we read the ten theses against this background, it is easier to see why Barth believed the nuclear issue to be a 'confessional' matter. At the same time, I believe, we must recognize the shifting and unfinished character of his reflections on the state, the need to develop some of his arguments more thoroughly and consistently, and some of the weaknesses still evident in his thinking in this area. But to recognize this is not at all to question the accuracy – and present pertinence – of his perceptions as they took shape in the later 1950s. As usual with Barth, the powerful underlying consistency of his thought can best be seen as the consistency of a lifelong process of reworking and purifying what was last said, and it is no tribute to him to exploit only one 'moment' of his exploration. Since it is manifestly important that we think far more deeply than before about the theology of the state in an age when concepts of state sovereignty and security bring forth monsters on all sides, it should be an enterprise worth pursuing to follow through one of the most integrally *theological* discussions of the question in this century, in the hope that we be enabled in some degree to continue the process of 'reworking and purifying'.[15]

II

The second *Römerbrief*[16] lays the foundations for a great deal of what is to follow in its discussion of Romans 13: here already are the main themes of Barth's view of the state – the the emphasis upon its *soteriological* (and thus Christological and eschatological) foundation, the notion that the state is primarily to be seen as *limit* by the believer, and the consequent refusal to make Romans 13 (or any other NT passage) the basis for a positive theology of 'citizenship' or a doctrine of the 'essence' of the state.[17] Commenting on Romans 12, Barth has been considering the significance of the 'negative possibilities' opened to faith, the varieties of not-doing that bear witness to the presence of transforming judgement;[18] and the culmination of this line of thought is that obedience to the state is described as 'the Great Negative Possibility'.[19] If Romans 13.1–7 is meant to be a gloss on 12.21 ('Be not overcome of evil . . .'), then Paul's commendation of obedience to 'the powers' is an exhortation to the resignation of our supposed 'right' to overthrow the evil of worldly order. That it *is* an evil should not be in doubt: all *de facto* order rests more or less remotely upon violence and deceit, and we must not suppose that there exists any natural right whereby one human being rules another – even in the most seductive form of a democratically represented majority. The more a state can point to its own legitimacy and justice, the more it embodies 'the supreme wrong-doing': *summum jus, summa injuria*. The claim is implicitly made to establish final peace and resolution in a self-consciously 'just' society; and that claim is blasphemous.[20]

But what makes each and every system of state authority evil is exactly what makes revolutionary *resistance* to the state equally evil; one form of legitimist idolatry is simply replaced by another.[21] This is not designed to give comfort to the conservative, for the Christian's refusal of worldly revolution has nothing to do with a 'principled' support of the existing order; and Barth very plainly says that if an existing order collapses, there is little justification for counter-revolution as for revolution ('there is also a conservative insubordination!').[22] Both conservative and revolutionary must be stripped of 'pathos' and romanticism, of the illusion of occupying a 'high place', a *locus standi* from which the radically (sinlessly) new can be devised and initiated, or the status quo sacralized.[23] Worldly order in its full ambiguity must remain, seen for what it is, so that God's order remains visible in and as the world's negation. The only authentic revolution is that of God in Jesus Christ; no other *act* in judgement of the world's order is possible. *We* can utter that judgement only in our non-action, dying in the place where we were born, in Barth's phrase.[24] The present order is under God and answerable to God and works for God in the sense that its evil, and the 'terror' involved in it for the rebel, bring human action as such under judgement – human action as self-assertion and self-justification. The state condemns us as agents, as architects of our own salvation; but it has no terror for the good, since 'the good work is the "not-doing" by which all action is related to its Prime Origin'.[25] In a wholly ironic sense, the believer becomes a good citizen because he is 'invisible' to the powers, not an agent over against the organized agency of the state (which is in fact organized disorder, evil).

The extraordinary *prima facie* quietism of this analysis is a little qualified by Barth's observation that the demands of the state have a certain 'parabolic' significance for the believer.[26] The state is a limit to the *eros* of the individual and represents the claims of fellowship and peace, and so it has a remote likeness to God's claim on our obedience, the offering of our bodies. Social efforts towards greater harmony or justice are not therefore worthless, and it is possible to imagine a 'political career' for the believer – but only if it is regarded as a 'game', as something which renounces absolutist commitment and trust in human possibilities.[27] The good, the absolute good of God's righteousness, is the enemy of the (socially or politically) 'better', insofar as, and only insofar as, the latter is confused with the true end and work of human beings, as if action were what we are made for. Absolute good, righteousness, remains invisible and atemporal: our laying-hold of it in faith, in the non-action of obedience to the Word, is beyond time, *i.e.* it does not compete for a place in time with the multitudinous succession of our acts, it is not an *episode* in a biography. However, at another level, it is *as* temporal beings that we are aware of having no place to stand, no right to act; and so it is that our knowledge of our importance also appears to us as a kind of temporal future, as hope – 'the hope of the Coming World where Revolution and Order are one'.[28] From this point, Barth can go on, commenting on Romans 13.8–14, to describe the 'Great Positive Possibility' of love: when we abandon our rights, negating the negations of worldly order, we are at once involved in love – the 'active' subversion (in a very paradoxical sense of 'active', the act worked by God in our emptiness) of the existing order,[29] and the miraculous presence of God's eternal freedom in time, the eschaton anticipated.[30] Love lies in the full appropriation of my own limitedness and mortality as this appears in encounter with the human other who is a mystery, a challenge and a summons to me, through whom I discover my self as a self eternally already called and loved of God, and lost and meaningless outside that relation.[31] 'It is the fact of the existence of our fellow men – the ethical problem – by which we are brought face to face with the great disturbance'.[32]

Active love in community is thus central for faith, and constitutive of what it concretely is; but we can only know what this means when we have first grasped that this love is essentially *non*-action. Here Barth most radically corrects the perspective of the first *Römerbrief*,[33] with its far more explicit and 'undialectical' summons to political engagement[34] – and its direct confrontation with Leninism;[35] the second commentary sweeps all this away with its eschatological critique of human organization as such, and establishes once and for all the impropriety in Barth's eyes of a theological legitimation of any specific social order *in itself* – *i.e.* as anything other than a reality dialectically caught up in the saving work of God. Here too, then, is the foundation of Barth's consistent repudiation of any variety of 'Two Kingdoms' doctrine: the state is answerable to and bound to the gospel in a direct if still preliminary way (as bringing us under judgement); and so it can equally obstruct the gospel, when its organization claims absolute legitimacy and justice, *summa jus*. The price paid for this in the second *Römerbrief*, however, is high: Dannemann, in his lucid and sympathetic account of Barth as political theologian remarks[36] on the *Statik und Geschichtslosigkeit* that overshadows what the work has to say about political action and observes that 'since there is in the second *Römerbrief* no real teleology and history for the reconciling and redeeming action of God, no corresponding teleology and history for human action in the world can appear'. This is a perceptive judgement. And the 'timelessness' of encounter with the Word is dramatically reflected in what is said in the second *Römerbrief* about Jesus: 'The particularity of the years A.D. 1–30 is dissolved by this divine definition, because it makes every epoch a potential field of revelation and disclosure';[37] '[Jesus] sacrifices to the incomparably Greater . . . every claim to genius and every human heroic or aesthetic or psychic possibility, because there is no conceivable human possibility of which He did not rid Himself'.[38] Jesus is the paradigm, in fact, of timeless non-action; but the nature of his *continuity* with the world of human agents (and of human limit) becomes dangerously obscure.

It is not surprising, then, that Barth's reconstruction of a theological perspective on the state should advance in step with the maturation of his Christology and of his understanding of *time* as a category of God's action. He himself rapidly realized that 'abstract eschatological waiting',[39] an eschatology that failed to work transformingly on the painful realities of an increasingly nightmarish present, was a betrayal of the Church's call to 'political service'. In and after the period of the Church struggle, he attempted to make better sense of the state's inclusion in the *saving* work of God – at a time when it was of first importance to give no ground to another and more poisonous abstraction, that of an *Ordnungstheologie* abstracted from the decisive 'limit' of Christ.

III

The classical statement from the 1930s of Barth's rethinking of 'political theology' is the 1938 lecture, 'Rechtfertigung und Recht'.[40] There are clear indications here of his unease with the positions outlined in *Römerbrief*, an awareness of the risk that these positions could weaken the Church's 'discernment of spirits',[41] and justify a purely abstract or general critique of political reality. The Barth of this lecture is perceptibly post-Barmen: the insistence of Barmen that the state exists by God's dispensation for the sake of peace and justice is the kernel around which the argument is built up. But the decisively new element is the location of political power, as now constituted, in the period between resurrection and parousia: the state as it now is exists *after* the manifestation of Christ's victory, and so, along with all the other potentially ambiguous 'powers' in the cosmos, it is led captive, it does not belong to itself. There can be no ultimate and successful rebellion by the powers. The state cannot help manifesting Christ's glory at the end of time, and so, in time, it cannot help participating in the salvation of sinners, in God's *Rechtfertigung*.[42] Romans 13 must be read in this Christological light: the state is to be obeyed because it is an (admittedly secondary) sphere of the work of justification. Its *Recht* allows the freedom necessary for the proclaiming and hearing of the gospel,[43] and so is evidently something that shares in that divine authority which is *wholly* directed to our salvation. If the Church prays and gives thanks for the state as guarantor of its peace, this does not imply a longing for bourgeois ease: peace and liberty are given for preaching, not – in this aeon – as ends in themselves.[44]

Barth boldly claims that the 'demonization' of the state has nothing to do with its autonomy or secularity; on the contrary (and here the essential question of the 1930s appears), the problem is that the state is unwilling to be faithful to its proper *independence* – *i.e.* its *distinct* reality, over against the Church. The state as such 'knows nothing of the Spirit, nothing of love, nothing of forgiveness',[45] nor is it gathered together by free decision; it exists in and only in coercion, and as such is essentially other than the Church[46] – a kind of reverse image. If the Church comes to be seen as an uncomfortable, disturbing or alien presence in the state, this means that the state is failing to be itself, regarding the Church as a *rival* – because it (the state) is implicitly or explicitly laying claim to do what only the Church can do – to pronounce a word of ultimate release and promise, to bestow meaning. And if the state then attempts to limit what is permitted to the Church, the time has come for resistance, non-cooperation, the refusal of participation (*e.g.* by conscientious objection). The Church cannot challenge the legal authority of the state as such, it cannot adopt an anarchist critique; it must and will become a victim of the state apparatus, bearing the punishment for its disobedience. In such active but not strictly revolutionary disobedience, it performs its proper service to the state by reminding the state of its *difference* from the Church and so recalling it to the foundation of its claim to obedience in the first place.[47] *Only* this kind of critical activity offers the state what it needs, the assurance of legitimacy: 'Apart from the Church, there is nowhere any fundamental knowledge of the reasons which make the State legitimate and necessary'.[48] The Church critique announces to the state that its order and its *Recht* exist on the firmest base possible – God's eternal will for *Rechtfertigung*; beyond this, the state has no reality, no coherence, no legitimate claim, no *Recht* in any sense. When the state seeks to do God's work as that work is committed to the Church, it subverts its own foundation.[49]

The advance from *Römerbrief* is remarkable. No longer is the state seen as evil; the rather tortuous exegesis connecting Romans 13.1–7 with 'be not overcome of evil' has yielded to a related but more nuanced antithesis between the community of freedom and the community in which the *possibility* of freedom is secured by coercion. Participation in the work of the state is far more positively enjoined,[50] because that work is related to the justification of the sinner – not in the highly paradoxical way sketched in *Römerbrief*, but comparatively directly, as what enables concrete proclamation.

But this can only be affirmed because of the gradual shift towards commitment to the essential *temporality* of God's work. To quote Richard Roberts, 'The dialectic of antithesis in *The Epistle to the Romans* has given way to a dialectic informed by a new conjunction of transcendence and immanence, that is a creative "inclusion" of time by eternity.'[51] Already in *CD* I/1 the notion of the 'time of revelation' is sketched out,[52] and in *CD* I/2 it forms the subject of a lengthy discussion (§14): God's revelation cannot but be spoken of historically, temporally, though this does not and cannot mean that history is a category prior to revelation and intelligible apart from it for the theologian. The result is the Christology of *CD* I, in which, although history is the 'predicate' of revelation,[53] the specific temporal relations, the particularity of the history of Jesus can still *become* revelatory only according to the divine decision. History cannot be given a self-subsistent significance. The fleshliness of incarnation is necessarily both veiling and unveiling at once. It is clear that this relates on the whole quite neatly to 'Rechtfertigung und Recht', insofar as historical-political reality, the concrete 'time' of the state, is indeed caught up in the history of God's work from resurrection to parousia and works, willy-nilly, the righteousness of God, yet remains in itself something fundamentally opposite to the community of faith, without autonomous meaning, knowing nothing of love, a reverse image. As in the incarnation itself, God works in what he is not. In short, although the timelessness of *Römerbrief* has been set aside, the essentially *negative* character of the state's relation to the gospel is still insisted on. However, this is not a covert 'Two Kingdoms' theology; the relentlessly antithetical presentation of the 'communities' of state and Church preserves some echo of Lutheran dualism, but it is a dualism brilliantly and triumphantly deployed against the extraordinary muddles of Lutheran political theology in the 1930s.

Furthermore, at the time of the composition of 'Rechfertigung und Recht', Barth was already considering the questions that were to dominate *CD* II, and these concerns seem to cast some shadow before them. The notion of a time *given* to the Church, between resurrection and parousia, for promise, hope, proclamation, already requires – on Barth's presuppositions – a theology of God's eternal choice to give this time (because he always *is* what he *shows* himself to be): we are on the frontier of the great discussion of election that pervades all of *CD* II. God's being is free act, self-determination, and that act is the life, death and resurrection of Christ: before all ages, God elects to be Christ for us, and so elects and ordains the consequence in our world of the event of Christ – including the time given us for proclamation.[54] It is clear, in this light, how, in *CD* II/2, Barth can move from the theology of election to his first major essay in ethics; and when we turn to the account of the state offered in *CD* II/2,[55] brief as it is, we can see something of the effect of this newly dominant theme of election. A very small step further is taken towards qualifying the negativity of the political order.

For the most part, *CD* II/2 recapitulates the conclusion of 'Rechtfertigung und Recht'; but, turning once again to Romans 13, Barth links it in a new way with the passage that precedes the injunctions to obedience. Romans 12 speaks of the imperatives of non-resistance, of a reconciliation that arises directly from our reconciliation with God: what the state then assures is that reconciliation does not lead to chaos.[56] Human life together is held in security by the powers that be. The shift from the 1938 lecture is in the idea that the state not only preserves social peace for the sake of the preaching of the gospel, but safeguards the possibility of active and creative reconciliation within ordered bounds. The severity of the state, its expression of God's 'wrath', is seen (in the light of Romans 1.24–28) as the limiting of human powers of self-destruction: God defers the natural consequences of our competitive, mutually cannibalistic social behaviour to make time for faith – in the work of Church and state alike.[57] Thus the state's unavoidable violence and 'gracelessness' is understood as a function of its eschatological orientation, the 'not yet' because of which it exists. It cannot be in itself the order of grace. But that order is already real in God and in faith; and the presence in the state of the Christian community reveals the grace that is actually within the superficially 'graceless order' of political life.[58] As in 'Rechtfertigung und Recht', only the Church can manifest the true rationale of the state; but here it is the Christian's willing share in the preservation of order precisely *as* a believer that uncovers grace. Coercion is shown, by the believer's engagement, to be the indefinite postponement of disaster and mutual slaughter and social dissolution, for the sake of the universalizing of a reconciliation already secretly present. And the believer is free for political commitment because he knows that everything except reconciliation in community is provisional;[59] such a person has the detachment which makes proper and truthful political action possible. The member of the Church, after all, knows that the Church itself as such is *provisional* – as Barth says in 'Rechtfertigung und Recht',[60] the final goal of God's redeeming work is a *polis*, a *basileia*, not an *ekklēsia* – so that the experience of being in the Church generates an unavoidable solidarity with the provisional experience of the state. The one illuminates and uncovers the other.[61]

The negative or antithetical note is still present, but significantly qualified both by the eschatological orientation of the state's coercive power, and by the recognition of the active presence of the other, reconciled, mode of existence within the historical and political order. Time is transformed as well as judged – or transformed *in* being judged; there is, *solely* by the gracious act of God, of course, positive achievement in the political world, and some hint of a positive or creative vocation within the political order. This is stated still more strongly in the post-war (1946) essay, 'Christengemeinde und Bürgergemeinde'.[62] Here we find the notion of *Recht* as a provisional image of *Recht-fertigung*,[63] *Recht* as the gift of God, its gift-character brought out by the Church's witness,[64] the Church's active responsibility for political freedom,[65] and, very significantly for our present enquiry, a firm denunciation of the positivist view of sovereignty: the Church, in committing itself to support for the *Rechtstaat*, commits itself to supporting political *potestas*, not *potentia*, power defined in terms of the purposive capacity to serve and effect law so as to realize harmony, as opposed to pure might, defining its own ends.[66] This is a necessary clarification of the earlier stress on the state as essentially coercive: the means and the limits of political coercion are, for the first time, brought within the horizon of this discussion. Also significant is the idea of the Church as actively resisting 'all abstract local, regional and national interests', and treating all *de facto* sovereign boundaries as relative and provisional[67] – a working-out, it seems, of the emphasis in *CD* II/2[68] upon the unlimited character of the Church's fellowship (also noted in 'Rechtfertigung'), its witness to God's decision to be *for* all his creation. The whole of this essay is, in fact, a further gloss on the theology of the election of Jesus Christ: 'the eternal history, encounter and decision between God and man', the primordial self-determination of God as saviour, is 'the presupposition of all the movement of creaturely life'.[69] If this were not so, God's decision would be supplemented or superseded by other events, and could not be eternal. But in fact all things move in accordance with God's will to fellowship with his creatures; Israel and the new Israel manifest the core of authentic history (the story of God's salvation) within what the world thinks of as its own 'neutral' duration.[70] And in this light, it becomes harder to draw an absolutely clear line between the pre-evangelical 'time' of politics and the true time of the Church – not least because (as we have seen) the Church itself is in one aspect still pre-evangelical. The 1946 essay shows just how fluid the boundary can be; yet this fluidity can only be spoken of from the vantage-point of the Church. There can be no setting side by side of Church and state as empirically comparable types of community, no absorption of Church into state, no reduction of the gospel to a social programme – not least because no social goal has meaning without the gospel.

IV

The period from Barmen to 1946 represents Barth's most sustained and creative exploration of political theology; and I have suggested that it is no accident that this corresponds broadly to the period in which the still residually ahistorical Christology of *CD* I/1 is slowly remoulded in the direction of the magnificent synthesis of *CD* IV/1,[71] where the highest possible evaluation is given to the historical specificity of Jesus Christ. *Römerbrief* could be taken as giving far too much ground to positivist politics because of its reiterated stress on the timelessness of the saving encounter; but by 1946, the commitment to a doctrine of God's election of historical predicates has produced a very thorough repudiation of positivism. The state remains other than the Church, and essentially involved in coercion (it is not *chosen* as a context by its members), but the means as well as the goals of its coercion are increasingly brought under the gospel's discernment, and it is held to have some responsibility in *creating* equity and harmony, not only sustaining security. When Barth returns to ethics in *CD* III/4, these insights are applied directly to the state's means of self-defence.

The political theology of *CD* III/4 is pursued under the general rubric of 'The protection of life'.[72] Barth gives what at first seems a startling amount of ground to the Tolstoyan and Gandhian prescription of non-violence in all circumstances, insists that no human being has authority over another's life, denies any 'natural' right of self-defence, and generally demolishes any notion that the state's coerciveness is grounded in some order of unredeemed nature.[73] If there is ever an imperative (not a right) to self-defence, it can only be seen in the light of our fundamental defencelessness before God, and is to be obeyed as part of *God's* assault, not ours, upon disorder.[74] Thus the state has no natural right to inflict capital punishment, and usurps the place of God if it thinks otherwise;[75] only in extreme circumstances where the very *esse* of the state is in question may the possibility be raised, because the state's *esse* is willed by God.[76]

The same principle applies to defensive war. The exercise of force is *not*, says Barth, part of the *opus proprium* of the state, and there can be no general legitimation of the right to wage war in such terms.[77] The *opus proprium* is the nurture of life and the fashioning of peace.[78] What makes war inevitable is an inadequate peace in the political order: 'It is when the power of the state is insufficient to meet the inner needs of the country that it will seek an outer safety-valve for the consequent unrest and think it is found in war'.[79] And Barth is keenly aware too of the economic factors making for war, not only the energy generated by the quest for new material acquisitions but the manipulative influence of what we have learned to call the interests of the military-industrial complex.[80] There are or may be circumstances in which, once again, the state is commanded to defend itself, insofar as its continuance is necessary to the fostering of the standing of its people before God. The *responsibility* (not the right) of the state in such a situation is to undertake defensive action – 'independent of the success or failure of the enterprise'[81] – and the responsibility of the Christian is to support this. But even then, the question of each individual's responsibility remains open, because the state is not a 'hypostasis' over the individual, making his or her decisions.[82] Although *general* opposition to war is inadmissible, each individual in each particular case is obliged to decide for or against involvement – and this is one aspect of the Church's service of the state, sustaining it by setting limits for it, and reserving the right to object, as a body, or through an individual decision by believers, to any particular decision by the state.[83]

This argument is the furthest Barth goes towards a positive evaluation of the active struggle for justice in the political order, and a radical qualification of an identification of the essence of the state with *Gewalt* and coercion. Despite the challenge to absolute pacifism – the one aspect of the discussion in III/4 seized upon in the 1950s and '60s by those arguing for every possible level of rearmament[84] – Barth is entirely clear that the means the state uses to secure its continuance, both in its internal and external relations, are open to Christian discernment and judgement. The possibility of self-defence cannot be turned into a self-evident legitimation for military policy – not least because, when defensive violence is undertaken, it may well be in circumstances that will in practice make the state *more* not less vulnerable. It is witness not success that is at issue in self-defence, witness to and obedience to the God who ordains the ministry of the state, but does not guarantee its invulnerability.

Barth notes in passing that modern (atomic) warfare makes any residual romanticism or idealism about war unthinkable:[85] it reveals the real face of war. Despite this, as he admitted in 1963,[86] he did not regard the events of 1945 as having made a permanent difference to what could be said about war. By the 1960s, however, it is quite clear that he had become convinced that a 'just war' in the atomic age was impossible: war can no longer have any meaning as the defence of a state. As the 1958 theses put it, atomic war is 'useless as a means of political confrontation'. In the light of our tracing of Barth's development as a political theologian, it should now be possible to see why this conclusion imposes itself, and why the issue becomes a confessional one. The final section of this essay will attempt briefly to set out the implicit argument here – and to suggest some further questions for theology in our time arising from all this.

V

The state exists, not as a thing in itself, but as a means of getting things done. A political unit can look for no metaphysical, trans-historical ground: it *happens* to be there, and certain people *happen* to be born into it; it may or may not coincide with a 'nation', and it does not in the least matter whether it does or not (Barth in *CD* III/4, §54.3 effectively and decisively dismisses the idea that the nation in itself has any positive significance in God's dispensation). Its 'vocation' or 'destiny' is simply to contribute to the new creation, the reconciled and reconciling humanity willed and chosen by God in his decision to be our God in Christ; and it fulfils this vocation by resisting disorder, restraining, by compulsion where necessary, the mutual destructiveness of sinful human beings, creating equity and harmony. Because it is a way of preserving the world of human intercourse – even to the extent of not slaughtering the evildoer – it is not simply a negative limit, but a positive sign of hope. In a shadowy but still quite discernible way, it echoes the Church's promise of 'time for amendment of life and the grace and comfort of the Holy Spirit'. It is enabled to be and to do all this because, in electing Jesus, God elects to make the time from resurrection to parousia a gift to us. To the state, the Church announces the good news that it has a right to exist because God is God, and is God as Jesus Christ, and that therefore it has a legitimate task to perform. The Church unites itself with the state in what Barth at the end of his career called the 'revolt against disorder', against the self-destruction of sin;[87] and its service to the state lies in this proclamation of a *determinate* task for it. No political unit has any finality (in both senses of the word) independently of this determination by God in Christ.

So the Church cannot allow that the state can have different goals from itself – the goal of all human action is set by the will of the *one* God, who is never other than saviour. The Church judges, resists and disobeys the state as and when the state, by refusing to accept (implicitly or explicitly) its determination by the gospel, forgets its provisional nature, the specific integrity of its task, its proper *functional* autonomy. When this happens, the state ceases to be properly a state, a means of doing certain specific things, and lays claim to being the form of human existence as such; so it turns itself into a 'lordless power' and becomes itself an agent of disorder.[88] The Church's response is to declare itself over against such a pseudo-state, to announce how precisely the gospel should judge and limit the specific infidelities and disorders of this pseudo-state; in short, to declare a *status confessionis* and prepare for costly struggle.

The nuclear state, by the mere possession of the means of mass annihilation, pronounces its belief that it must survive at all costs; it identifies its own *Recht* with eternal value and legitimacy, and regards itself as having *in principle* the authority to exterminate what threatens it – not to resist, control, or discipline, but to exterminate. This is the meaning of the crucial fifth of the 1958 theses: the nuclear state has ceased to be a *political* (a determinately functional) reality. And it sets itself up in opposition to the goal of human fellowship, by exalting local right to unconditional status. Further – extrapolating from Barth's most important insight in this area – such a 'state' rejects the notion of time as promise. By conducting its policy under the sign of an *ersatz* eschatological menace, it denies that it lives between resurrection and parousia, and so turns its back on Christ. In so doing (as thesis 10 of 1958 states) it rejects 'all three articles of Christian faith'. The Church is summoned to confession, and to non-cooperation (Barth's open letter of 1959 to the European Disarmament Conference in London[89] goes some way towards recommending civil disobedience) – though not to revolutionary anarchy. The state never becomes *wholly* demonic,[90] utterly incapable of fulfilling its calling (even against its will), and so the Church cannot ever attack the idea of a state, by, for example, offering to do the state's job itself, or by preaching a utopian ideal of non-institutional forms of human community.

I do not propose to argue that this is in every respect a political theology we are bound to adopt today; but I believe it goes far towards setting an agenda for such a theology. Many issues are left disturbingly in mid-air: notoriously, Barth gives only limited guidance as to how the state's definition of its *specific* priorities is to be informed by the

Church – how the Church as such can participate in the formation of policy. If the state is a mechanism for getting things done, Christians are bound to be involved in the laborious job of political persuasion, the tactics of mapping out acceptable shared social goals (what *needs* getting done?) with those who work with different concepts of legitimacy, different accounts of history – though it is clear enough, on Barth's presuppositions, that the Christian is bound to be closer to any political outlook that maintains some ideal of social creativity or teleology than to a 'neutral' or static account of social order as something whose content as well as form is basically a 'given'. And, at the same time, the creative or teleological outlook has the possibility of being the Church's major enemy. The Church cannot but look for allies in more or less radical ideologies (*i.e.* among those who believe that states are *for* something), yet must do so in the fully ironic awareness that it thus courts profound conflict. I suspect that Barth's response to theologies of liberation would be to ask if they had fully grasped the latter point: if only the Christian can operate a properly 'secular' (non-utopian, non-messianic) polity, the Christian is therefore *ex professo* committed to resist all utopianism insofar as it becomes embodied in the structure of a state.

Thus questions of tactical priorities, and of the ultimately tragic and paradoxical implications of Barth's thinking, remain unexplored in Barth's own work. But we could do worse than begin from his axiom that it is essential to have a theology of the state in *functional* terms – or, to quote Ernst Wolf,[91] that we have a theology of 'political virtue' rather than a *Staatsmetaphysik*; and that, consequently, we have a theological critique of positivist views of sovereignty. This requires us to turn back to Christological fundamentals, to the question of God's will towards us as historically embodied in Jesus and historically proclaimed in the believing community. *Of course*, all this is the wrong way round: our political critique does not generate our Christology, but vice versa. Yet Barth's own evolution – if my presentation of it in this essay is correct – shows that the interaction of political exigency and Christological exploration is close and subtle. Without Christology simply becoming an ideological tool to legitimate political resistance, it is clear enough that certain centrally serious theological issues – for us as for the first Christians – emerge only in and through fundamental conflicts over the nature and future of humanity. We may yet look to the programmatic and comprehensive political conflicts of our time to teach us something of how to do our theology; and Barth, at the very least, leaves us with the question of how we shall find anything interesting or hopeful to say in the political realm without some commitment to the proposition that what is said of Jesus in his living, dying and rising is said of the unchanging nature-in-act of God.

Notes

1. Text in Werner Schmauch and Ernst Wolf, *Königsherrschaft Christi*, Theologische Existenz Heute 64 (Munich: Chr. Kaiser Verlag, 1958), 70, and – with a very comprehensive selection of other documents relevant to this issue from the period – Ernst Wolf with Heinz Kloppenburg and Helmut Simon, *Christusbekenntnis in Atomzeitalter?*, Theologische Existenz Heute 70 (Munich: Chr. Kaiser Verlag, 1959), 70.

2. Schmauch and Wolf, *Königsherrschaft*, 68–9; Wolf, Kloppenburg and Simon, *Christusbekenntnis*, 102–3.

3. Wolf, Kloppenburg and Simon, *Christusbekenntnis*, 104–5.

4. Ibid., 15–16.

5. Ibid., 26–9.

6. Ibid., 107–8.

7. Ibid., 6.

8. Ibid., 16.

9. See the note with information from Helmut Simon in Barth's *Gesamtausgabe* 5: *Offene Briefe 1945–1968* (Zürich: Theologische Verlag, 1984), 440–2.

10. Ibid., 444.

11. Eberhard Busch, *Karl Barth: his life from letters and autobiographical texts* (London: SCM Press, 1976), 431.

12. Barth, *Gesamtausgabe* 5, 440–1.

13. Ibid., nos 56 and 57; for later statements, see nos 59, 67 and 72.

14. Barth, *Fragments grave and gay* (London: Collins, 1971), 81–3.

15. Barth's doctrine of the state is discussed especially in R. E. Willis, *The ethics of Karl Barth* (Leiden: E. J. Brill, 1971), 391–427; F.-W. Marquardt, *Theologie und Sozialismus* (Munich: Chr. Kaiser Verlag, 1972); Robert E. Hood, *Contemporary political orders and Christ* (Allison Park, PA: Pickwick, 1984), esp. 63–90, 137–66; and Eberhard Jüngel, 'Zum Verhältnis von Kirche und Staat nach Karl Barth', *Zeitschrift für Theologie und Kirche*, Beiheft 6: *Zur Theologie Karl Barths* (1986), 76–135 – a magisterial exposition, responding to Lutheran criticism of Barth (Ebeling's in particular) for 'ethicizing' the gospel. A number of important essays on Barth's political thought are translated in George Hunsinger (ed.), *Karl Barth and radical politics* (Philadelphia: Westminster Press, 1976), and an overview of earlier controversies in this area may be found in Markus Barth, 'Current discussions of the political character of Karl Barth's theology', in H.-M. Rumscheidt (ed.), *Footnotes to a theology* (Waterloo, Ont.: Corporation for the Publication of Academic Studies of Religion in Canada, 1974), 77–94. Barth's stance on the nuclear issue is barely mentioned in any of

these – nor even substantially in J. H. Yoder, *Karl Barth and the problem of war* (Nashville: Abingdon Press, 1970); for a fleeting reference, see Jüngel, 'Zum Verhältnis von Kirche und Staat', 117 n. 158.

16. Karl Barth, *The epistle to the Romans* (Oxford: Oxford University Press, 1933).

17. Ibid., 477.

18. Ibid., 461.

19. Ibid., 477.

20. Ibid., 478–80.

21. Ibid., 480–4.

22. Ibid., 486.

23. Ibid., 483, 485.

24. Ibid., 481.

25. Ibid., 487.

26. Ibid., 488.

27. Ibid., 489.

28. Ibid., 491.

29. Ibid., 493.

30. Ibid., 498–502.

31. Ibid., 494–5.

32. Ibid., 505.

33. Karl Barth, *Römerbrief: unveränderter Nachdruck der 1. Auflage von 1919* (Zürich: EVZ, 1963). See U. Dannemann, *Theologie und Politik im Denken Karl Barths* (Münich: Chr. Kaiser Verlag, 1977), 354–92 on the political themes and priorities of this work, and the shifts of emphasis in the second edition.

34. Barth, *Römerbrief* (1919), 367, 390.

35. Ibid., 354–92.

36. Dannemann, *Theologie und Politik*, 118.

37. Barth, *The epistle to the Romans*, 29.

38. Ibid., 97.

39. Busch, *Karl Barth*, 290.

40. Karl Barth, *Rechtfertigung und Recht*, Theologische Studien hft. 1 (Zollikon: Evangelischen Buchhandlung, 1938). References are to the English translation, *Church and State* (London: SCM Press, 1939). A fuller discussion would need to relate this to Barth's 1935 lecture, *Evangelium und Gesetz*, Theologische Existenz Heute 32 (Munich: Chr. Kaiser Verlag, 1935); see Jüngel, 'Zum Verhältnis von Kirche und Staat', 96–108, and the same author's 'Gospel and law', in *Karl Barth: a theological legacy* (Philadelphia: Westminster Press, 1986), 105–26.

41. Barth, *Church and State*, 31–2.

42. Ibid., 27–9.

43. Ibid., 32–4, 50–1.

44. Ibid., 50–1.

45. Ibid., 29–30.

46. Ibid., 54–5.

47. Ibid., 67–9.

48. Ibid., 70.

49. Ibid., 85–6.

50. Ibid., 78–9.
51. Richard Roberts, 'Barth's doctrine of time: its nature and implications', in S. W. Sykes (ed.), *Karl Barth: studies of his theological method* (Oxford: Oxford University Press, 1979), 109.
52. Karl Barth, *Church dogmatics* (CD) I/1 (Edinburgh: T&T Clark, 1975), 116, 426.
53. *CD* I/2 (Edinburgh: T&T Clark, 1956), 58.
54. *CD* II/1 (Edinburgh: T&T Clark, 1957), 411ff.
55. *CD* II/2 (Edinburgh: T&T Clark, 1957), §38.3, 721–6.
56. Ibid., 721.
57. Ibid., 721–2.
58. Ibid., 722–3.
59. Ibid., 723–4.
60. Barth, *Church and State*, 40–1.
61. *CD* II/2, 724.
62. Karl Barth, *Christengemeinde und Bürgergemeinde*, Theologische Studien 20 (Zollikon–Zürich: Evangelischer Verlag, 1946); references are to the English translation, 'The Christian community and the civil community', in Barth, *Against the stream: shorter post-war writings 1946–1952*, ed. R. Gregor Smith (London: SCM Press, 1954), 13–50. Jüngel, 'Zum Verhältnis von Kirche und Staat', 122, rightly stresses the controlling importance of the notion of *analogy* in this essay, and relates it to the growing significance of the theme in Barth's work overall. §§14 to 26 of this piece (*Against the stream*, 32–42) illustrate how this is worked out in specific instances to do with 'the external, relative and provisional problems of the civil community' (42). For the Church as the *provisional* image of what the true state must become eschatologically, see 29–30, 48, echoing and elaborating some of the most significant themes of *Church and State*.
63. Barth, 'The Christian community and the civil community', 19–20.
64. Ibid., 22.
65. Ibid., 36–8.
66. Ibid., 40.
67. Ibid., 40–1.
68. *CD* II/2, 719–20.
69. Ibid., 184.
70. Ibid., §34.
71. *CD* IV/1 (Edinburgh: T&T Clark, 1956).
72. *CD* III/4 (Edinburgh: T&T Clark, 1961), §55.
73. Ibid., 430–4.
74. Ibid., 434–5.
75. Ibid., 445.
76. Ibid., 446–7.
77. Ibid., 456ff.
78. Ibid., 458–9.
79. Ibid., 459.
80. Ibid., 450–1, 459.
81. Ibid., 462–3.

82. Ibid., 464.

83. Ibid., 468.

84. Barth, *Fragments grave and gay*, 82: 'and if people actually get up in the German Bundestag with the *Dogmatics* in their hand and quote it to justify war, that is of course sheer wickedness . . . sheer dishonesty'.

85. CD III/4, 453.

86. Barth, *Fragments grave and gay*, 83: 'I should have realized and said that the appearance of atomic weapons had so changed the situation that one must say: This is enough.'

87. Karl Barth, *The Christian life* (Grand Rapids: Eerdmans, 1981), §78.1.

88. Ibid., §78.2.

89. No. 67 in Barth, *Gesamtausgabe* 5.

90. Barth, 'The Christian community in the midst of political change', *Against the stream*, 81. This Hungarian dossier, *Die Christliche Gemeinde im Wechsel der Staatsordnungen* (Munich: Chr. Kaiser Verlag, 1948), contains some of Barth's seminal reflections on the Christian in a Marxist society, and pp. 80–2 provide an excellent summary of his theology of the state.

91. Ernst Wolf, 'Die Königsherrschaft Christi und der Staat', in Schmauch and Wolf, *Königsherrschaft*, 53–4 – a fine statement of the Christological approach to theologizing about the state. For resistance to the idea that we need a 'metaphysic' of the state, cf. also 'The Christian community and the civil community', *Against the stream*, 25.

9

Girard on violence, society and the sacred

Studying peace obviously involves us in studying what stands in its way; no programme of 'peace studies' can do without a serious engagement with the phenomenology of violence. It is rather surprising that we have only a relatively small number of serious essays in this field. Jacques Ellul's *Violence*[1] is more of a brilliant polemic than a sustained analysis, though Rollo May's *Power and innocence: a search for the sources of violence*[2] goes rather further towards a serious theoretical discussion. By means of the distinctive marriage of psycho-analytic theory with sociology which flourished in the USA in the late '6os and '7os, May connects violence with powerlessness: it is aggression directed in the first instance against a self that is felt to be without worth because it is without power. It is, paradoxically, both an assault on the self and an affirmation of the self, 'a uniting of the self in action'.[3] Violence is irrational assertion, a *creation* of power out of nothing; it may be an authentic overcoming of powerlessness, the opening of a door to a higher self-evaluation, or else it may be an intensifying of real long-term powerlessness. Which it is to be depends on whether the act of assertion harnesses the processes of reality, whether it is in some significant way a breakthrough into a participation in the way things work, or whether it remains at the level of pure *protest* against reality. If the latter is the case, the way is open to the schizoid, 'affectless' violence against self and others characteristic of the mass murderer and the terrorist. The degree to which the world is seen as open or closed to participation is the degree to which violence is determined as self-affirming or self-and-other-destroying: hence, in May's terms, the role of symbolic mediation in defining the conditions for violence.[4]

This is a persuasive and flexible account, and elements of it have become part of the enlightened folk-wisdom of our culture. The violence of oppressed communities in affluent countries (in Handsworth, Detroit or Soweto) is regularly turned against the community itself, or against welfare agencies and workers – against those close at hand rather than against 'enemies';[5] and on May's account this is precisely what we should expect from those whose image of the world is 'non-participatory'. There is no possibility of finding a world that can confirm any individual self-valuing: so what is destroyed is the immediate sources of relative value (locality, welfare) which are seen to be either inadequate or deceptive or both. If the world at large is hostile, why delude oneself with fantasies of localised friendliness? Work on gang culture in Los Angeles, with its complex interweaving with drug abuse, a classic form of self-directed violence, brings these themes sharply into focus:[6] gang membership is both a source of violent self-assertive power 'out of nothing' and itself a form of depotentiating the individual, whose membership is acquired and kept by threat. May's analysis is as resourceful as ever in trying to come to grips with this kind of tragedy.

However, there are areas of the question which May touches upon at best only in passing, and which require fuller consideration. What precisely makes whole societies violent? One can certainly answer this, as May does by describing how the threat of impotence leads to the build-up of ritualised threats of violence; one can account for pogroms and persecution by ascribing to the dominant culture a dramatic decrease in its sense of moral confidence or security.[7] But these issues press us further back towards a consideration of what is fundamental for that moral confidence. In what follows, I want to present and discuss the view of violence and society developed by the French critic and anthropologist, René Girard, a view which could be said to offer a context for May's theses, anchoring them in a deeper grasp of the tragic in human community, and pointing towards a resolution of this tragedy in a perspective far wider than that of the immanent 'economics' of power May is concerned with.

I

Girard begins from a fundamental observation of ethology: biological individuals are assimilated or inducted into common life by means of *imitation*. 'There is nothing, or next to nothing, in human behaviour that is not learned, and all learning is based on imitation'.[8] Imitation, however, is deeply ambivalent: learning to do the same thing, reach out for the same object, suggests potential conflict, rivalry. The double-bind of imitation is that only by it do we sustain interaction with other individuals while at the same time it threatens the profoundest division. Primitive societies prohibit certain forms of imitation, often kill twins, fear the revelation (and thus repetition) of a person's name, associate magical power with the possession of hair or nail clippings by another (who thus possesses a potential 'double' of the self). Such societies recognise that imitation is both necessary and disastrous: uncontrolled, it threatens social dissolution, unrestrained rivalry. Thus the stability of the community depends upon the limiting of the threat of imitation.

It is in this need that Girard sees the roots of ritual: 'rituals consist in the paradox of transforming the conflictual disintegration of the community into social collaboration'.[9] Ritual lifts ordinary prohibitions and dramatises the fact of social conflict to a point of crisis; and the crisis is resolved by *sacrifice*. A victim is identified as the 'true' source of the crisis, the paradigm rival for the good which the community is agreed in seeking. This needs a little further interpretation: basic 'mimetic' conflict is rivalry about an object; but the more it is pursued, the more interest centres not upon the object but upon the rival, the one who, actually or potentially, possesses the object I desire. The rival becomes a model, and desire is focused on this model more than on the object. Rivalry itself creates community of a sort, and its culmination comes at the point where a whole ensemble of rivals comes to agree that *all* are being denied possession of what they desire by *one* paradigm possessor. To eliminate that one person secures, *de facto*, access to what is desired by all the others. So, since ritual dramatises the process of rivalry, it necessarily culminates in sacrifice, the killing of a victim.[10]

This, for Girard, is the essence of 'the sacred' – '*The sacred is violence*'.[11] That is to say, the unique and privileged transactions which are held to preserve and empower an ordered community, to relate it to what is more than contingent, temporal and vulnerable, are to do with the 'double transference' of ritual sacrifice,[12] the identification of a victim who is both supremely menacing and supremely blessed. This is made plain in the rituals of kingship,[13] in which power is deliberately concentrated in the hands of a designated victim for a limited period, at the end of which he is slaughtered. *Actual* political power of a centralised kind results from the gradual prolongation of the interval before slaughter: the power ritual resigned into the hands of the sacred victim is retained, and a substitute victim identified. Girard thus effectively turns on its head the textbook view of the relation between religion and social order:[14] social power is a transformation of the sacred, of the status of the privileged victim, the paradigm possessor of desired goods, rather than the sacred being an ideological transformation of social relations.

Ritual, then, points to a 'founding murder' as the origin of social unity and, ultimately, of centralised social power; myth is the attempt to eradicate the explicit memory of this event. Girard argues that myth makes the victim/saviour a *stranger* to the community in certain circumstances, a bestower of benefits from above; and in other circumstances it sees the victim as a *native* who is somehow taken into another order of reality.[15] In either case, the end-result, the 'saving and refounding of the community', obliterates the arbitrary violence required to bring this about. Society learns, through myth, to 'forget' the *essentially* arbitrary character of its foundational ritual and the 'occasional and passive' character of the victim.[16] There can have been no real death, no real murder, if the victim is the living source of social good. Girard here manages to retrieve some aspects of Freud's notorious account in *Totem and taboo* of the origins of religion and myth; but, by severing it from the Oedipal theme, he is able to unite it with Lévi-Strauss's discussion of myth as describing the elimination of certain elements in a complex situation in order to secure a proper 'space' for the differentiation, the secure co-existence of the elements that remain.[17]

Because the 'victimage mechanism' is essentially arbitrary, it cannot be acknowledged and affirmed *as such* in a society in which there are differentiated concepts of guilt and responsibility. These concepts are the building bricks of secularisation[18] and they are also (and *therefore*) menacing. The history of Western culture is a history of the halts and advances of this kind of secularisation, and of the attempts to return to sacred violence. Our own century offers dramatic instances of such attempts – of the project to found or re-found social unity by means of the cataclysmic slaughter of particular categories of humanity, whose extinction will bring blessings.[19] This is the characteristic hidden agenda of modern ideology, which has the capacity to generate real myth and so produces quasi-scientific rationalisation for the saving murder – the economic threat of international Jewry, the inexorable road of history towards the dictatorship of the proletariat, and so on. But it is equally the case that we now have the conceptual apparatus that enables us to identify the persecution *as* persecution, i.e. as irrational victimisation. We are able to demystify or 'demythologise' persecution, because we have to hand the notion of 'innocent' victims, and are aware of the needs that persecution meets in society. Sacred violence thus becomes increasingly inaccessible – which, for Girard, explains the extraordinary *scale* of victimage when it does recur, as in the Shoah, or, one might add, Kampuchea under the Khmer Rouge.[20] If saving victimage is no longer possible, enormous anxiety is going to be generated as to the defensibility of the social order: we are in an impasse between the residual forms of victimage and the secular space where there is no remaining means of founding social order. Girard does not elaborate, but we can recognise resurgent victimage in a whole range of phenomena above all in populist racism and homophobia in our culture, in the quasi-sacral role of hostages for terrorist activity (it is instructive to read accounts by hostages in Lebanon of their treatment, with Girard in mind), in the genocidal violence of parts of India and Africa, in the obsessive interest of certain forces in the USA with the extinction of radicals in Central America, and so on. And on the other hand, at the level of the most sophisticated global diplomacy, we see the impotence of the secular to resolve rivalry in the sclerosis of arms negotiations between the 'superpowers'.

It is worth pausing on this. As already noted, Girard insists that, as rivalry intensifies, attention is concentrated on the rival rather than the desired object: 'Desire becomes detached from the object, bit by bit, and attaches itself to the model'.[21] This leads to the psychosis of violent forms of reciprocal exchange (duels, vendettas), which are conflicts about no concrete object but about mutual perception of status or power.[22] The resistance of, the frustration generated by the rival becomes the essential motivation of desire: the rival as model is there to be destroyed, yet in that destruction the desiring self destroys itself. Unresolvable rivalry is a commitment to death.[23]

'This tendency', Girard writes, 'is at work in some of the main aspects of contemporary culture . . . It is concretised in a particularly spectacular manner in nuclear rivalry'.[24] It is extraordinary (though perhaps not untypical of the more depressing features of French intellectual priorities) that there has been so little serious discussion of Girard's theory as a framework for understanding our nuclear paralysis. Yet both Girard's account of 'objectless' rivalry and his analysis of violence as simultaneously destruction and creation provide exceptionally resourceful tools for reflecting on this. In a powerful rhetorical passage, Girard describes how we are living through a genuine 'apocalypse', a revelation of the nature and function of violence.[25] The nuclear arsenal is the product of a secularised world: it is unambiguously a human fabrication, and cannot be understood as an external or transcendent source of threat or promise. Yet it is hypostatised ('*the* bomb') and treated as a power in its own right.

> The bomb does indeed seem like the prince of this world, enthroned above a host of priests and worshippers, who exist, so it would seem, only to do it service. Some of them bury the poisoned eggs of the idol beneath the earth; others deposit them at the bottom of the seas; yet others sprinkle the heavens with them, causing the stars of death to revolve endlessly above the teeming antheap. No slightest section of nature – now that science has cleansed it of all the ancient projections of the supernatural – has not been reinvested with the truth of violence . . . Never has violence so insolently asserted its dual role of 'poison' and 'remedy'.

There is in global terms, then, a high pitch of 'conflictual mimesis', of rivalry without a readily identifiable object. What, after all, is the conflict between the superpowers actually *about*, stripped of rationalising rhetoric about 'world domination' which has little clear concrete content? Of course there are conflicts about the prevalence of this or that ideology (though it is often unclear enough what this *means*), and more prosaic conflicts about what markets are open to trade; but military rivalry has become a world to itself. Each side compulsively insists upon the threat posed by the other's greater or potentially greater resources, and so upon the need for constant vigilance and expansion; just as each side must also insist upon its triumphant possession of superior force, the capacity to launch one more missile when the other side is exhausted. This competition, as we all know, has long extended far beyond what would be needed to destroy the enemy once over. We have a fetishised rivalry in the acquisition of intrinsically meaningless objects; a reciprocal psychosis.

We know now that we cannot consciously resolve this by the classical mechanism of victimage. What then 'founds' our social order, our 'peace'? What once was done by the identification of a saving victim has now to be done by an enforced immobilising of rivalry – enforced by the unprecedentedly total character of the violence threatened. Thus the total threat involved in nuclear rivalry steps into the void where sacred violence once was; and it is not surprising that it then takes on so much of the colouring of sacred violence itself. We are caught in an absurd – though not, for Girard, a hopeless – situation. The threat of annihilation acts as a strong dissuasive to uncontrolled 'conflictual mimesis': there are circumstances in which a certain loss of face is preferable to the defence of status because the latter is unacceptably risky.[26] There is a *pragmatic* commitment to non-violence. But at the same time this commitment is the direct result of a continuing commitment to the threat of violence, with all the sacred resonances violence has traditionally possessed. 'The bomb' has become a foundational myth for us. 'The nations are not wise enough to abandon the power of creating mutual terror, nor are they mad enough to unleash irreversible destruction': this form of sacred violence *must* remain only potential because it is – unlike all other forms of violence – incapable of being absorbed by a continuing historical environment; and so it seems to promise an unprecedently secure social order.[27] It is a parodic Kingdom of God,[28] but at least involves a level of secularised self-awareness that keeps the door (just) open for a critique of violence.

This is a subtle account of our situation; but I think it may be an over-optimistic one. If the nuclear standoff did indeed have the exact reciprocal character Girard describes, his analysis would be more plausible. But the contradiction he rightly identifies in our situation is not merely an internal one: it is a contradiction in the actual policies of nuclear rivalry. As I have argued in a paper on SDI,[29] the nature of technology compounds the reciprocal threat: modernisation of weaponry will always be necessary, and refinement and improvement always possible. Because there is no immediate (or long-range) possibility of agreed limitations on modernising weaponry, since such limitations would weaken the deterrent force of armaments, deterrence is a necessarily escalating process. In Girardian terms, there is something inherently uncontrollable in the 'conflictual mimesis' of the nuclear powers: each continually stimulates the mimetic desire of the other, so that the process retains the element of 'commitment to death', and continues to presuppose the possible annihilation of – at least – the power and status of the other. The SDI project, which implies the possibility of an impregnable *aggressive* force guaranteeing lasting security, is the ultimate stage in the development of a foundational myth of 'the bomb' – the ultimate security and the ultimate destabiliser at the same time. Mutual terror remains bound to an acquisitive spiral, and the tensions of conflictual mimesis remain uncontrolled.

II

There is still a good deal to be said, I suspect, about the application of Girard's scheme to our present situation. Girard himself is evidently feeling his way here: the discussion of these matters in *Things hidden since the foundation of the world* is sketchy and needs tightening, but suggests a good many fruitful avenues for further thought – for instance, the idea of the weapon as fetish, as a pseudo-object, in nuclear rivalry (especially the theory of 'overkill'), and the nature of the relation between technological refinement as, in principle, an endless advance in mastery over the human environment, and the problems of endless conflictual mimesis. The brief remarks on the 'ecological field' that can normally be relied on to absorb the upheavals of violence, and the absence of such a field where global violence is in question, could also do with expansion.[30] These questions apart, however, there remains one central aspect of Girard's system which remains to be examined: the connection between our secularised understanding of violence and the radical reworking of the whole understanding of violence which occurs in and through the foundational story of Christianity.

Why are we capable of distinguishing between innocent and guilty suffering? What makes it possible to re-identify victimage as persecution? 'During the course of Western history representations of persecution from the persecutor's perspective gradually weaken and disappear. There are not necessarily fewer or less intense acts of violence; but it does mean that the persecutors could no longer permanently impose their own perspective on those around them. Centuries were needed to demystify mediaeval persecutions; a few years suffice to discredit contemporary persecutors.'[31] This is because, Girard claims, 'Our own ability to detect the scapegoat mechanism is wholly determined by the detection that has already taken place within the gospel text.'[32] The secularising of violence, the exposure of its arbitrary nature, is decisively achieved in the Christian story, which represents the final and unanswerable critique of sacrificial religion. As we shall see, this is not a piece of glib apologetic, nor a commendation of ecclesiastical Christianity, nor a recovery of simplistic Tolstoyan rhetoric about Jesus' non-violence; it is an invitation to read with attention the specific *shape* of the gospel story as a story of sacral violence exposing its own absurdity. It is not, I think, particularly relevant to complain (with Lucien Scubla)[33] that there are other, perhaps contrary, themes in the

Gospels, or that what Girard regards as sacrificial distortions of Christianity are the necessary conditions for its propagation. Girard's reading of the gospel narrative is certainly selective, even cavalier at times; but all he needs to establish is that one novel and subversive theme is *present*, as the distinctive change wrought by Christ. As for the issue of how Christianity preserves or fails to preserve this *novum*, once again Girard needs only to demonstrate that Christianity possesses the transforming critical principle he identifies: even if this may not be the prevailing voice in historical Christianity, it is certainly arguable that Girard's view of what is centrally and distinctively Christian corresponds to one of the elements that has given to historical Christianity a certain quality of restlessness and self-criticism. Christianity is a tradition constantly in search of its own centre. Nor do I read Girard as suggesting a programmatic 'overcoming' of ritual as such. The ritual which is, *de facto*, almost universal, the ritual of victimage, needs unmasking; and – as we have just seen – even when this unmasking occurs, displaced forms of victimage and sacral violence continue. But Girard seems to leave open the question of how the knowledge of Christ's undermining of sacred violence is communicated. Nothing in his account seems to prohibit an analysis of Christian ritual – the mass in particular, of course – as itself a demystifying mystery, an anti-sacrificial sacrifice. Girard is oddly silent about the history of eucharistic doctrine, which could provide some far-reaching confirmations of his thesis. Nor does he raise the question of how a community founded on the *overthrow* of sacral violence actually develops and works, except in rather large and bland terms ('The Kingdom is perfect reciprocity').[34] These are questions of theology, in one sense (I should say that they require a consideration of *resurrection* such as Girard does not offer) but they are also issues about the *practical* intelligibility of his project. I think that some of his critics have missed his point as regards Christianity; but there is still some refinement and clarification to be done.

This is not the place for that exercise. We must turn to look in more detail at what he actually says about the secularisation involved in the Christian story, and how precisely the life and death of Jesus function as a critique or exposure of the nature of sacral violence. Jesus' first priority in his ministry is the preaching of the Kingdom; and the Kingdom appears as 'the complete and definitive elimination of every form of vengeance and every form of reprisal in relations between men'.[35] Because violence is rooted in mimesis, it can only be overcome by a renunciation of rights – desire's claim on the object of gratification, desire's identification of the other as rival aggressor, source of violence. And because mimetic violence is threatening an unprecedented cataclysm, the apocalyptic end of God's people and their sacrificial system, the 'hour' of Christ is a moment of unprecedented crisis: the inability of sacrifice to secure its goals is about to be made plain, since 'the community is on the brink of dissolution'.[36] The 'word' Jesus speaks, the word which will not pass away, is a word subversive of the world of violence: 'For this word brings the world the only truth that it cannot hear without vanishing – its own truth'.[37]

But we are not dealing only with the word of Jesus: his person is identical with this word. 'Jesus continues to see himself as being bound by the promise of the Kingdom.'[38] Thus the rejection of the word will entail, sooner or later, the rejection of his person. The 'logic of sacrifice'[39] identifies Jesus as a victim – rightly so, in its own terms, since he is the ultimate threat to an order based upon violence. Yet this selection of Jesus as victim also exposes the real nature of the whole mechanism: Jesus is 'innocent' – in the sense that he *is* nothing but the proclamation of a possible going beyond violence – so that his murder by the social and sacred authorities shows the irrationality of victimage. Violence is seen to be a path arbitrarily chosen: the destruction of violence by violence in sacrifice is after all a cementing not an overcoming of violence, a choosing of death. In the light of the killing of Jesus, we can see that victimage is an empty resolution of our troubles, a false identification of their source: victimage binds us to endless and futile repetition (Girard alludes to the idea in Hebrews 9 and 10 of the inefficacy of sacrifice to take away sin, though he regards the epistle as falling short of the necessary demystification of sacrifice as such).[40] Nothing purely immanent in the way of ritual can deliver us; which is why the knowledge of the arbitrariness of victimage ('secularisation') divorced from the concrete possibility of 'the Kingdom' is the occasion of impotence, despair and displaced violence in our age.

'That is indeed why the Son promises men that if they manage to behave as the Father wishes, and to do his will, they will all become sons of God.'[41] This comment exhibits very clearly the 'liberal Protestant' aspect of Girard, a reluctance to go beyond knowledge and behaviour in examining the workings of the Christian myth; but it also focuses our attention on a crucial point in the scheme, the redefinition of the divine in the life and death of Jesus. Jesus, in promising the Kingdom, speaks of a God who is without rivalry or partisanship: 'if the deity exists, it does not choose sides in the conflicts of doubles. There is no "Gott mit uns" in Heaven'.[42] The God of Jesus sends his rain upon just and unjust; what is more, he does not intervene to overthrow violence by force (by saving Jesus from death). He *cannot* be other than involved in the victim's powerlessness:[43] 'A non-violent deity can only signal his existence by having himself driven out by violence – by demonstrating that he is not able to establish himself in the Kingdom of Violence'.[44]

The identity of Jesus with a God who is *wholly* outside the processes of sacred violence is established by the death of Jesus. Girard seems to be saying that the powerlessness of Jesus is the 'evidence' for his divinity – i.e. his freedom from the arbitrary constructions of the human world. There are clear echoes here of Bonhoeffer as well as of Simone Weil (to whom Girard acknowledges his debt). God can only establish his reality as distinct from that of the world in his silence before the claims and the accusations of the world's powers; and so far from this being what has been called a 'sacralisation of impotence', it is the necessary ground for any action free from illusion and any power free from self-destructiveness. Only a negative theology of this sort can generate a theology that is genuinely about salvation rather than sacrificial repetition. It would be an intriguing exercise to follow up Girard's insight by comparing it with, for instance, Gregory Nazianzen's deployment of the traditional axiom that the divine knows no envy,[45] or – even more significant – Augustine's denial[46] that God loves us for anything we can 'contribute' to him. For both these theologians, a God who is ontologically unclassifiable is *ipso facto* not involved in mimesis: if he cannot be imaged (imitated), he does not imitate us. Our welfare is therefore not something to be wrested from God in Promethean fashion. It is his free gift.

If Girard's reading here is tenable, and, as a theologian, I believe it is, the specifications for our talk about God, the grammar of his absolute difference, are properly grounded not in metaphysical argument but in the realised possibility of a corporate human life free of victimage, the gift of non-violent relation – the experience of grace, I suppose the theologian would say. How tightly bound is this to the *Christian* story? Sandor Goodhart has underlined the roots of 'secularising' negative theology in the Jewish sense of God, the Jewish 'seeing to the end of the dramas in which human beings are engaged and learning when to stop', the conviction of the Exodus experience that 'in the place of the name of God is a promise'.[47] But I suspect Girard would still ask, How, except through the historic and historical narrative of the innocent victim, does such a God *specifically* manifest himself as the negation of violence? It must be by some concrete transaction that puts religion itself to the test that God as God, God free from religion, appears. And if that makes Girard sound unduly like Karl Barth, that too may suggest some further work of comparison . . .

'God free from religion': Girard is not, as we have noted, simply advocating a return to ecclesiastical Christianity *sans phrase*. He has no illusions about the degree to which Christianity has colluded with sacrificial violence and found ways of intensifying it. Yet he seems to be saying that a purely secular (in the usual sense of the word) social order is inconceivable. Either we face uncontrollable mimetic escalation, which can be halted only temporarily by reciprocal threat, or we relapse into the 'displaced' sacral violence of seeking for victim groups in society. Without a belief in an order that is free from mimetic confict and which therefore does not need violence to establish it, we are condemned to these despairing alternatives. Girard insists repeatedly that only because of the Christian story have we embarked on the process of secularisation, and that it is a nonsense to ignore this text. If we can reconnect the process with its origins, the logic of Enlightenment modernity will paradoxically complete itself and 'everything will tip over on to the non-sacrificial side'.[48] Girard is unashamed of speaking about a kind of historical logic, because he maintains that he is not going beyond the description of processes verifiable at least in principle. But it remains unclear what is to be done. We need the restoration of a transcendental referent, and the analysis of victimage provides the crucial criterion for knowing when we are *truly* speaking of the transcendent: the sacred as sacrificial can now be decisively named and rejected as the sphere of idolatry. 'Green' politics, of course, operates with just this awareness of a fundamental need for myth, but is reluctant to relate this at all to the Christian story;[49] thus, in Girard's terms, it fails to perceive the nature of the central problem of violence and becomes merely utopian. We are returned constantly to the necessity of a myth of victimage and its overcoming, a myth against myths.

And if, as Girard assumes, along with Hocart and other anthropologists, myth grows out of ritual, we are returned also, by the same token, to the need for a ritual against ritual; and so to the significance of the *community* created, founded, by the 'anti-sacrifice of Jesus, the community of reciprocity with its acknowledgment of the *difference* of others, the acknowledgment that the other *is* other, not simply a mimetic rival.[50] This community is pretty consistently a travesty of what it is meant to be, but without its *enactment* of the anti-sacrificial text of the Gospels in baptism and eucharist, the text remains a piece of information rather than a transforming discovery. The task of the sacramental community is thus less the making of individual converts than its own faithfulness to the self-critical task given to it of enacting, in sacrament and structure, the constantly necessary dismantling of sacral violence; and its critical engagement with the forms both of sacral violence and of conflictual mimesis in its context. It has become fashionable in theology of late to deplore the legacy of the Enlighten-ment and to seek alliance with 'postmodern' critiques of that legacy. Girard suggests, to one reader at least, that things are less clear-cut – that the theologian should be *claiming* the legacy of modernity, to prevent it becoming another form of sacral distortion.

'Let the church be removed, and the world will soon come to its end'. This remark of Newman's in the *Essay on development*[51] is given fresh force by Girard's thesis. If he is right, society will continue to stand in need of a community that offers an alternative foundational myth to that of sacred violence, since modernity can generate no myth of its own, by its very nature *as* modernity. What kind of belief in such a myth is now possible in our society and what kind of partici-pation in such a community remains, from Girard's viewpoint, an open question. But so long as the project of demystification remains both taken for granted and incomplete, modernity requires that myth and that community to halt its regression towards sacred violence. At a time when the project of modernity has produced cultural, moral and political sterility of an unprecedented kind on the one hand and fierce reaction towards the sacrificial economy on the other (racism, terror-ism, a politics of superstition and fetishism), Girard's voice needs to be heard.

Notes

1. Jacques Ellul, *Violence* (New York: Seabury, 1969) – mostly directed against Christian endorsement of revolutionary violence in the '60s.
2. Rollo May, *Power and innocence* (New York: Norton, 1972).
3. Ibid., 187.
4. Ibid., 183–5.
5. Ibid., 96.

6. There is some illuminating material in Mike Davis, 'Los Angeles: civil liberties between the hammer and the rock', *New left review* 170 (1988), 37–60.

7. May, *Power and innocence*, 185.

8. René Girard, *Things hidden since the foundation of the world* (London: Athlone, 1987), 7.

9. Ibid., 20.

10. See esp. Girard, *Violence and the sacred* (London: Johns Hopkins University Press, 1977), ch. 11, and *The scapegoat* (Baltimore: Johns Hopkins University Press, 1986), 130.

11. Girard, *Things hidden*, 32.

12. Ibid., 37.

13. Ibid., 51–68.

14. Ibid., 54–5.

15. Ibid., 111.

16. Ibid., 108.

17. Ibid., 112–25.

18. Ibid., 127.

19. Ibid., 129.

20. Ibid., 127–8.

21. Ibid., 311.

22. Ibid., 304–5.

23. Ibid., 413; cf. Girard, *The scapegoat*, 130.

24. Girard, *Things hidden*, 414.

25. Ibid., 255.

26. Ibid., 257.

27. Ibid., 258.

28. Ibid., 257–61.

29. Rowan Williams, *Star wars, safeguard or threat?: a Christian perspective*, CANA occasional papers 1 (Evesham: Clergy Against Nuclear Arms, 1987).

30. Girard, *Things hidden*, 258.

31. Girard, *The scapegoat*, 201.

32. Girard, *Things hidden*, 436.

33. Lucien Scubla, 'The Christianity of René Girard and the nature of religion', in Paul Demouchel (ed.), *Violence and truth* (London: Athlone, 1988), 160–78.

34. Quoted in ibid., 172.

35. Girard, *Things hidden*, 197.

36. Ibid., 202.

37. Ibid., 204; cf. Matthew 24.35.

38. Ibid., 206.

39. Ibid., 208.

40. Ibid., 228–9; Girard, *The scapegoat*, 200.

41. Girard, *Things hidden*, 215.

42. Ibid., 244.

43. Ibid., 219, 231ff., 269; Girard, *The scapegoat*, 206.

44. Girard, *Things hidden*, 219.

45. Gregory Nazianzen, *Second theological oration*, §11.

46. Augustine, *De doctrina christiana*, Bk 1.

47. Sandor Goodhart, ' "I am Joseph": René Girard and the prophetic law', in Dumouchel (ed.), *Violence and truth*, 53–74.

48. Girard, *Things hidden*, 436.

49. See, e.g., Trevor Blackwell and Jeremy Seabrook, *The politics of hope* (London: Faber and Faber, 1988).

50. Cf. Girard, *The scapegoat*, 21–2.

51. John Henry Newman, *An essay on the development of Christian doctrine* (Harmondsworth: Penguin, 1974), 146.

The suspicion of suspicion:
Wittgenstein and Bonhoeffer

I

Fergus Kerr's fine book, *Theology after Wittgenstein*,[1] devotes a good deal of space to expounding Wittgenstein's therapeutic dismantling of the myth of the solitary subject living 'inside' the visible body and goes on to suggest some of the possible consequences for religious thought of this demythologizing. We shall need to rethink much of what we habitually say about 'authentic' or 'interior' prayer, about acts and intentions, about mortality and eternal life; theology must rediscover itself as a language that assists us in *being mortal*, living in the constraints of a finite and material world without resentment. We are not, in fact, 'in' the world as selves contained inside some other sort of thing – the shell or husk of flesh: what we are *are* our limits, that we are here not there, now not then, took this decision, not that, to bring us here and now. And if this is true, understanding a person is understanding their limits, their materiality. Kerr quotes Nietzsche on the Greeks, who knew how 'to stop courageously at the surface, the fold, the skin, to adore appearance ... Those Greeks were superficial – out of profundity!'[2] And he continues after this quotation: 'the depth of the world is on the surface, so to speak: but also, what is most secret about the self is public knowledge'.[3]

We are frequently told that we live in a time of 'suspicion' in our thinking and interpreting. Paul Ricoeur[4] famously identified Marx, Nietzsche, and Freud as 'masters of suspicion', those who pressed the Cartesian doubt to its most extreme point, the doubting of consciousness as well as the doubting of things. All three assume that consciousness is in need of decoding: 'For Marx, Nietzsche, and Freud, the fundamental category of consciousness is the relation hidden-shown or, if you prefer, simulated-manifested'.[5] How are we to reconcile the imperative of decoding with a recognition of the profundity of surfaces? Is Ricoeur wrong, still trapped in the Cartesian framework at whose outer edges the three 'masters' stand? Or is Wittgenstein absurdly over-reacting to the Cartesian problem and asserting that all language, all 'presentation', must be taken at face value, so that we are left only with an essentially uncritical behaviorism?[6] Ricoeur is apparently endorsing a diagnosis of the post-Cartesian malaise in terms of insufficient scepticism; the remedy is an ascesis of thought by way of the suspicions of one or other of the masters, so that language ceases to function as a delusive protection against the unfathomable and uncontrollable world.[7] Wittgenstein refuses the terms of such a discussion, it seems, denying that we can usefully analyse consciousness (whatever that is) into simulation and truth: consciousness is not another object-to-be-known, it *is* what language shows (as the statue *is* what the stone shows, *is* the stone seen or recognized like *this*);[8] and what is shown is what we all know and all we know.

In what follows, I intend to explore this tension further, in an attempt to see whether it adds up to a contradiction. I shall briefly examine Wittgenstein's critique of Freud and his general attitude to the idea of interpretation as 'decoding'. And I shall try to elucidate what conception of 'interiority' remains after the demythologizing of the imprisoned self, with the help of another of the century's major critics of certain notions of the inner life, Dietrich Bonhoeffer (in the letters written from prison in his last years). The comparisons and contrasts with Ricoeur's project of Christianized post-Freudian suspicion can then be assessed with greater clarity, and the sense in which Wittgenstein and Bonhoeffer may justly be counted as *critical* thinkers will emerge. Perhaps we need not, as philosophers or theologians, be left with the bald alternatives of false naivete about ideological or pathological distortions of speech, and manipulative reductionism.

II

Wittgenstein's positive appreciation of Freud is in no doubt; both Rush Rhees[9] and Maurice Drury[10] record his conviction that Freud had 'something to say', particularly in *The interpretation of dreams*, and the conversations with Rhees and others testify to the degree to which he took Freud seriously. However, after a passing enthusiasm for the idea of practising as a psychiatrist (1934; though he had apparently begun to read Freud shortly after the First World War),[11] he both described himself as a 'follower' or 'disciple' of Freud and insisted that the father of psychoanalysis had misunderstood his own project.[12] By 1946, he believed that the 'way of thinking' represented by *The interpretation of dreams* was positively dangerous and needed the sharpest criticism.[13] A phrase in one of the 1943 conversations with Rhees indicates one reason for this hostility: Freud 'wanted to find the essence of dreaming'.[14] Dreaming is seen by Freud as a kind of language or, more accurately, a set of determinate symbols, 'a way of saying something' (I'd be inclined to underline *way* in this phrase). Given the correct tools, the dream can be decoded into 'ordinary speech'. Yet, as Wittgenstein points out, there is no means for reversing the procedure, for *encoding* 'ordinary speech' in dream symbolism: we cannot suppose that there is a content that can be indifferently expressed in ordinary and in oneiric language as two 'ways of saying'. This means, then, there may be no 'correct' interpretation of a dream: its detail resists assimilation to a single pattern, a controlling latent meaning that orders the symbolism of the dream. Does this mean that dreaming is a matter of chance, that we refuse to face the questions of scientific causality?[15] But why should we oppose chance and determination in this simple way? Of course, there may be *reasons* for oneiric symbolism of various sorts, and Freud's readings may have a good deal to offer; but why assume a single pattern? What if dreaming is simply something we do, like a children's game, like art, like ritual, like story telling – like speech itself?[16]

The attraction of systematic Freudian interpretation is precisely in its concentrated simplicity. Our lives, thoughts, acts, imaginings are not, after all, contingent, but have the nature of a dramatic script being enacted: 'it may then be an immense relief if it can be shown that one's life has the pattern rather of a tragedy – the tragic working out and repetition of a pattern which was determined by the primal scene'.[17] The same point is already made with some force in the earlier lectures on aesthetics: reductive explanation has 'charm'.[18] This attraction is at least twofold. The *hidden* is attractive to us, says Wittgenstein – the idea of things buried and uncanny, and also we are sufficiently afraid of self-deceit, sufficiently mistrustful of our speech and images, to be ready to embrace the 'ugly' or disedifying interpretation of what we do ('It is charming to destroy prejudice').[19] A Freudian interpretation of a dream is therefore essentially a rhetorical technique: it is about *persuasion*, not discovery, it is a practice intelligible only in the context of a performance by analyst and analysand.[20] The interpretation, as Wittgenstein says elsewhere,[21] is a 'solution' because it is agreed to be such.

> Someone seeing the unfolded picture might exclaim 'Yes, that's the solution, that's what I dreamed, minus the gaps and distortions.' This would then be the solution precisely by virtue of his acknowledging it as such. It's like searching for a word when you are writing and then saying: *'That's* it, *that* expresses what I intended!' Your acceptance certifies the word . . . as being the one you were looking for.

'Successful' analysis is in fact, so it seems for Wittgenstein, itself a game of sorts; its rules have to do with ritually offered and accepted transformations of selected narrative material. Like other kinds of systematic interpretation, it trains one in *ignoring* certain features of what is concretely present; which is why it does not in itself necessarily contradict or exclude other readings.[22] The claims to exclusive truth ('x is *really* y' or 'x is *only* y') cannot be sustained because the ideas of abstract convertible content in two kinds of utterance cannot be sustained (translation works only one way; we cannot establish reciprocally equivalent expressions for 'the same thing' in ordinary and oneiric language). This again recalls the more general point about aesthetics: a putative account of how a particular aesthetic sensation might be neurologically analysed and reproduced would not be capable of delivering the aesthetic stimulus, the artwork itself, in all its detail.[23] If analytic reduction of dreams or behaviour patterns is seen (correctly) as the playing out of a particular option among several interpretative strategies, it may open possibilities to us; if presented as the uncovering of a deeper and determinative truth, it deprives us of possibility.[24] And it does so by taking us away from the constraint of here and now and persuading us to ignore and discount the complexity of what determines that here and now. It is a claim to know independently of agreement (that is, of community and conversation) – to have a knowledge that is nobody's in particular.[25] What Wittgenstein seeks to combat in Freudianism is the flight from particularity and the endlessness of difference (concrete detail) and the inexhaustibility of social converse,[26] the flight that for him represents the bondage of European thought to an epistemological problematic that remains obstinately dualist and so obstinately discontented with finitude. Specific interpretations are always exercises in ignoring difference and uncontrollable converse;[27]

their danger lies in their potential for ignoring the fact of their ignoring.

In principle, the critique is applicable to any totalizing interpretation, Marxist, sociobiological, religious schemes of some kinds; and it is important to remember that Wittgenstein is not rejecting interpretation as such in favour of a passive reception of what presents itself but is rather defending the pluriform vitality of interpretation. The same notes of 1948 that contain his remark about the sort of Freudian exegesis of dreams that deprives us of possibilities also have a long and suggestive discussion about 'understanding and explaining a musical phrase'.[28] very reminiscent of certain passages in the lectures on aesthetics. You explain to someone that the phrase is like *this* (how? by gesture, by movement, by comparison). They say, 'Yes, I see' (but they don't have to). If they go on to perform the phrase in a way responding to what has been said, there has been an agreement in understanding – though what 'understanding music' means is only establishable in relation to how an entire life is lived, how hearing and performing music relates to what else is seen and done. Understanding, explaining, interpreting are not efforts of an individual to penetrate a surface: they are *social* proposals for common reading and common, or at least continuous, activity (a gesture or performance that in some sense goes on with or takes up from mine). They do not, therefore, see what is to be interpreted as setting a problem to be solved: interpretation is not designed to put an end to puzzlement for good and all, though it may remove specific puzzles ('When a dream is interpreted we might say that it is fitted into a context in which it ceases to be puzzling';[29] but, as the 1948 notes make plain, a final end to puzzlement – ' "Oh, *that's* how it was!" ' – is an end to potential stimulus).[30] The interpretative proposal is precisely one that is made at a point in time and space; it acknowledges the finite and so acknowledges other possible voices; it is, in fact, suspicious of a suspicion that looks for a determinate hidden content to consciousness or phenomena.

III

The same polemic is at work – with a more immediately recognizable Christian motivation – in Bonhoeffer's prison letters. In June and July 1944, Bonhoeffer wrote two letters to Eberhard Bethge in which he developed a critique of 'unaristocratic' apologetic.[31] With the withdrawal of God from the public sphere of human language, it had become necessary to look for religious meanings in the private, the interior; and a Christian apologetic faced with what seems to be a contented and self-sufficient human world struggles to persuade this world that it has a diseased *inner* life, a secret and hidden misery. 'Existentialist philosophy and psychotherapy have worked out some quite ingenious methods in this direction.'[32] This works on the assumption that the private sphere is of final, central significance. Just as the gutter press wants 'revelations' of the secret life of public figures and is suspicious of anything that looks like a guarded privacy, so the apologist hunts for the 'intimate' level – 'as if you couldn't adequately appreciate a good play till you had seen how the actors behave off-stage'. 'Anything clothed, veiled, pure, and chaste is presumed to be deceitful, disguised, and impure.'[33]

With a social confidence that rather takes aback the liberal reader, Bonhoeffer dismisses all this as 'the revolt of inferiority', the pervasive and pathological mistrust felt by the socially disadvantaged or isolated (echoes of Nietzsche's *ressentiment*, perhaps). The Word of God cannot be allied with this vulgarity, this urgency to know what is discreditably secret. Setting aside the unmistakable tones of the cultivated upper bourgeoisie of pre-Hitler Germany, there are at least two very serious points being made here. One is that the assumption of an equivalence between the 'inner' and the 'essential' is controversial and historically conditioned;[34] the other is that a large part of what conditions it is the development of cultures in which isolation has become an increasingly widespread experience. If we lack a properly common language, a properly public life, we shall be increasingly unsure of what (in both the simplest colloquial sense and the more philosophical sense) other people *mean*: we shall mistrust the other until and unless we have a key to unlock the secret chamber of their 'essential' selfhood, a technique of decoding. Before we can effectively say what we have to say to another person, we must be able to establish that it will be rightly and safely received, by setting in advance certain criteria of truthfulness that must be accepted by the other. If you won't listen, it's because of your hidden guilt or sinfulness; if you won't listen, we shall have to deal with your resistance; if you won't listen, it is because of ideologically induced false consciousness (any or all of these may be *true*, of course, but that is not the point: the 'audibility' of their truth can only emerge as a common, agreed world is actually shaped in the discourse between us). Bonhoeffer is alerting us to the fact, familiar enough now, rather less so in 1944, that the notion of an essential private self is a sociohistorical construct, and that hermeneutical suspicion arises from the universal 'modern' (post-Enlightenment or post-Renaissance) experience of cultural fragmentation and consequent mistrust. We constantly feel we need to know more of the other because some directness, some presence or certainty eludes us, and that lack menaces us. As Stanley Cavell puts it in the brilliant concluding section of *The claim of reason*, 'we are rather disappointed in our occasions for knowing, as though we have, or have lost, some picture of what knowing another, or being known by another, would really come to – a harmony, a concord, a union, a transparence, a governance, a power – against which our actual successes at knowing, and being known, are poor things';[35] we are tempted always to 'the conversion of metaphysical finitude into intellectual lack'.[36]

The second of these two summer letters to Bethge is followed by Bonhoeffer's poem, 'Who am I?'[37] – at first reading a slightly banal presentation of the outer and the inner person, concluded by an abrupt transition into piety. It is, in fact, a subtle commentary on the letter's argument. The calm and cheerful exterior that Bonhoeffer was aware of presenting to his jailers and fellow prisoners ('They often tell me / I would step from my cell's confinement / calmly, cheerfully, firmly, / like a squire from his country-house') is contrasted with the anger and impotence within, so that the question 'Which is the real me?' is raised; but it is raised to be itself exposed to suspicion. Why should the analysis be in terms of a false exterior persona cloaking a 'real' weakness; what if the truth is that the interior self is in flight from the 'victory already achieved' of the visible person? And all these are in any case 'lonely questions', the indulgence of a certain kind of solitude; whatever or whoever is there, he belongs to God. In other words, the question 'Who am I?' is not about an 'intellectual lack', to be filled by an account of the real (hidden) self: the private sense of self, in this case, humiliating and wretched, may represent another kind of fiction or evasion, a construct out of the chaos of passing emotions. But Bonhoeffer's flesh and blood were in the prison at Tegel, offering sanity and comfort to other prisoners: how if at all that indubitable victory (both the imprisonment and his manifest response to it) should be harmonized with his inner fears is essentially an abstract problem posed in an unnatural isolation. The 'answer' is the simple self-commitment to God: the wholeness of Bonhoeffer's selfhood lies in its belonging to God, a wholeness achieved in trust or hope rather than analysis. The pinning of knowledge, especially self-knowledge, to 'metaphysical finitude' is secured by putting the entire situation in the context of God. My own identity's 'ungraspable' quality thus becomes not an elusive level of interiority, but the unknowable presence of the creator's absolute affirmation, the mysteriousness of grace, past, present, and future, not of the 'true self' as a hidden thing. My unity as a person is always out of my field of vision (I can't see my own face), just as the divine condition for there being fields of vision at all, for there being a world or worlds, is out of my field of vision (I can't see my own origin).

This is further elucidated by some of Bonhoeffer's throwaway remarks on perfection. There are the cryptic notes of June 1944[38] on humanity, animality, and perfection, in which he implies that the human is irreducibly animal, resistant to the pathos of nostalgia, 'the delight in death' (yearning for the unmediated absolute): somehow the 'animal', though clearly not the whole of human identity, is our guard against *hubris*; which is why it is 'the perfect human form' that is the focus of – what? thought in general? theology in particular? 'The divine, not in absolutes, but in the natural form of man.' 'To meet again, then, is a God': Bonhoeffer cites this remarkable line from Euripides' *Helen* apparently to illustrate the manifestation of the gods *within* human converse, the encounter of speech-using animals. It is this encounter that decisively relativizes the inner *Sehnsucht* of the isolated soul. Perfection does not lie in this inner world; in July he writes, 'I should seek the "perfect" in the human, the living, and the earthly, and therefore not in the Apolline, the Dionysian, or the Faustian'[39] – not, presumably, in the static determination of a psychological type, but in the world of temporal engagement and growth.

A year earlier, he had written to Bethge of a friend's horror at the spectacle of 'a film that showed the growth of a plant speeded up; she said that she and her husband could not stand it, as they felt it to be an impermissible prying into the mystery of life'.[40] This occurs – strangely, at first sight – in the context of a discussion of honesty and reserve and the nature of truthfulness. As in the reflections of 1944, there is a distinctive blend of simple old-fashioned *pudeur* and philosophical and theological acumen. Since the Fall, concealment is necessary and good in the sense that there is plenty in human thought, feeling, and experience that *should not* be part of shared discourse. We are alienated, divided, and corrupted; but to bring this into speech (and to assume we thereby tell a better or fuller truth) is to collude with sin. This is less than perfectly clear in the 1943 remarks; but what Bonhoeffer wrote in 1944 suggests that it is precisely the self-isolation that regards the complexities of the 'inner life' as the primary reality that is the source of at least certain kinds of sin. The interior struggle should be hidden because, once brought into the light of speech, it is caught in the trap of mistrust, the fragmenting of discourse: 'I tell you that I am not what I seem; and so I know that you are not what *you* seem, and I shall not be able to hear you until you, like me, renounce semblance for truth (here, let me help you . . .).' Bonhoeffer finely sums up in 1943 with a surprising allusion: 'Kant says quite rightly in his *Anthropologie* that anyone who misunderstands or questions the significance of outward appearance is a traitor to humanity.'[41] And the last few words should be taken quite seriously in the light of the writings of 1944: we are capable of betraying the reality of what we in fact are, where we in fact stand, of body and speech, of the bonds of sociality that constitute us as human, discounting the tangible, utterable contingency of what is there for the senses, in claiming to strip (oneself and others) to what is held to be true and essential and which is, in fact, the product of certain alienating or fragmenting forces in the social and linguistic world.

The same principle, incidentally, is applied to history as a whole. Bonhoeffer declares his suspicion of a Hegelian philosophy of history on the grounds that any notion (Hegelian or otherwise) of history as a continuum is bound to be a distortion.[42] The 'essential' story of humanity is a scheme that always leads to the ignoring or misreading of the concrete phenomena of the past by forcing them into a pattern of *development*. We either absolutize or dismiss classical antiquity by categorizing it as 'primordial': perhaps 'classical values' are more accessible to us in other (medieval or modern) forms. Why should we suppose there is a single story to tell of humankind? 'Until we can see further into it, it will be as well to base our attitude to the past, and to classical antiquity in particular, not on a general concept of history, but solely on *facts* and *achievements*.' Thus there can be no facile reduction of the complexity of the past to a single 'inner' structure. Both relativism and systematic traditionalism are ruled out: we cannot distance the whole of the past as 'foreign' (any more than we can distance the contemporary foreign by calling it archaic),[43] nor can we say that the ways we differ from a 'classical' past are the measure of our decline and unseriousness, so that truth is discovered by stripping away the extraneous forms of contemporary life to return to fundamentals. Conversing with the human past is (in Wittgenstein's phrase) simply something we do, and, like other conversations, it has its unexpected convergences and its unexpected gulfs in understanding. The search for the single story of humanity reflects, once more, an age of alienation and mistrust, the flight from the risks of discourse.

There is, of course, much more that could be said about Bonhoeffer's analysis of faith and of Christian language from this point of view, the celebrated and much misunderstood 'nonreligious' interpretation of the gospel.[44] But enough has been said to indicate that Bonhoeffer as a theologian shares much of Wittgenstein's project of 'suspecting suspicion'. But it should also be clear that their commitment to the profundity of surfaces cannot be written off as a *faux naif* rejection of interpretation itself. Wittgenstein believed most emphatically in the possibility of deception and self-deception,[45] and he, no less than Bonhoeffer, was aware of living in a culture saturated with fundamental untruthfulness. It is precisely because our culture is fragmented in so many ways (by economic injustice, by nationalistic violence and threatened violence) that we are unable to speak truthfully with each other, and public language becomes a mountainous refuse heap of self-protective clichés. Starting from such a context, how can we not be suspicious? And how can we not have a certain longing for 'uncovering', for a language that will show us what is *really* happening? Yet that longing for a *unifying* discourse, to the extent that it urges us away from the particularities before us, colludes with our fragmentation, persuading us to ignore what is awkwardly or meaninglessly *there*. Because our speech and, therefore, our common life are so fragmented, we must be suspicious equally of the untruthfulness of what is offered us and of the untruthfulness of our own refusal of it (for we have no language or consciousness that has not been given us, and the great seduction is to think we can arrive at 'our' truth by isolation). In Kierkegaardian terms, irony reaches into the very heart of consciousness; it does not stop at the frontier of my liberated or autonomous selfhood.[46]

IV

If we now turn back to Ricoeur on Freud, it is something very like this pervasive irony that Ricoeur finally sees emerging from a sustained thinking through of the task of interpretation. Ricoeur begins, as we have noted, with the statement that modern critical hermeneutics assumes that the dialectic of concealment and manifestation is 'fundamental' to consciousness. However, his discussion of Freud leads him to the conclusion that Freudian interpretation carries within it a severe tension. Symbolization, for the later Freud, is both a 'making friends with necessity', a dealing with the imminence of death, and some kind of liberation, some affirmation of desire to which the imminence of death is immaterial.[47] Although Freud is sharply critical of the way in which the latter too easily and quickly offers resolutions that are, in fact, only possible by way of the former, he is not, Ricoeur claims,[48] entirely without sympathy for the lyrical, the aesthetic, and (in the widest sense) erotic claiming and transfiguring of reality in symbolic vision: the conclusion to the great 'Leonardo' essay seems to point in this direction.[49] But if this is so, symbolization is not in fact capable of the reductive reading Freud insists upon; in the terms Ricoeur uses, it is not simply a matter of the 'economics' of the psyche, the release of tensions, outlets for repressed forces. Symbolism is 'over-determined', not simply to be read as a single and 'real' language of the subconscious as opposed to the conscious, but a discourse in which both our origins and our final meaning (the goal of irreducible human desire) speak and are spoken of.[50] So the primary 'dispossession' or displacement or decentring of ordinary consciousness to show what it conceals does not finally yield another closed explanatory structure (the subconscious simply doing the job of pre-critically conceived rationality). The hidden voices are many and complex in their relations. They can only be heard in their fullness by listening again to the pluriformity of what is shown or articulated – back to the surface, in fact, to what Ricoeur calls 'the second naivete', a phrase peculiarly his own.

Ricoeur's proposal is carefully paradoxical: to think with or through symbols, they must first be unraveled or decoded, so that their over-determined, even chaotic complexity appears. They must be reduced to show their irreducibility, then 'reappropriated' in 'concrete reflection' and 'living speech', in the particularities of hermeneutics; and it is in the constant dialectic of the loss and the recovery of the symbolic particular that the symbol opens out on to the endless horizons of desire refining itself into the love of creation and creator.[51] In its return to the spoken word, reflection continues to be reflection, that is, the understanding of meaning; reflection becomes hermenuetic; this is the only way in which it can become concrete and still remain reflection.[52]

This comes close to saying (but doesn't quite say) that, at the end of the day, interpretation is simply responsive action: the creation in communicative behaviour of a new moment in the historical configuration, generated by a fruitful and irresoluble puzzlement at what this 'historical configuration' addresses us with. Wittgenstein can say that the most significant interpretation can be a gesture; Bonhoeffer looks forward to an unimaginable future religious language that (like Jesus' parabolic speech) will not offer a 'reading of the world, but will liberate and renew it'. Not interpretation, but change – a Marxist resonance that has not gone unnoticed by some readers of Wittgenstein[53] who have declined the facile and popular misinterpretation of Wittgenstein's dictum that 'philosophy leaves everything as it is'[54] (*philosophy* is not itself interpretation but the questioning about the conditions for intelligible, unmythological interpretation: it is not itself passion or action, faith, hope, or charity, and shouldn't try to be).[55] If there remains (as I think there does) a tension between Ricoeur and the two exponents of the profundity of surfaces, it is in the way in which his language can still be read as presupposing a privileged status for consciousness and for theory – though this is in some respects modified in later essays. Wittgenstein and Bonhoeffer more clearly presuppose that to interpret the symbolic, linguistic, and behavioral complex that 'addresses' us in the human world is to have one's own pattern of speech and action conditioned (not determined) by it, to be provoked (called forward) by the ways in which it touches, confirms, resonates, or questions what we have done and said. To interpret means interweaving a text (words or actions, words *and* actions) with our own human project, acquiring a partner, a pole of difference that refuses to allow our 'project' to return endlessly on itself, as if it were indeed generated from a well of unsullied interiority, 'self-consciousness'.

V

Are we then (if Wittgenstein and Bonhoeffer are right) simply to stop talking about the 'inner' life of persons? This would be an odd conclusion. Both are writers whose lives and words show the sort of patterns we associate with interiority: solitude, chosen or enforced, meditation or prayer, acute and painful awareness of injury or falsity in relationships (penitence), passionate and reflective reading, a struggle for openness or honesty of a kind (granted Bonhoeffer's hostility to the idea of honesty as merely unexamined candour, irrespective of what you might call the moral grammar of a society or a situation). If we gather up such patterns of behaviour under the term 'interiority', and if we want to avoid the idea that they are patterns stemming from a 'true' life beneath the surface of fleshly being in time, what is it that we are speaking of?

It may be that an analogy from visual art will help. Sometimes you will hear people talking about the 'life', even the 'inner life', of a picture: the sense that the viewer has of not exhausting the object when all its details have been taken in, a quality that can sometimes be called enigmatic, sometimes warm, spacious, or deep. A self-portrait by Rembrandt or a landscape by Turner or Corot or Nash or one of Klee's elusive linear statements would have this kind of 'interiority'. Now in this case, there is manifestly nothing there except the work itself: there is no *region* behind or beyond what is seen and sensed that would explain the 'inner life' of the work, nothing that is private or secret. Everything is 'on the surface', *is* the material surface, in fact. But, if we speak of its inner life as what teases and eludes us or what invites us simply to look and absorb, without 'results', without decoding, we mean, I think, that the picture strikes us as sufficiently solid, sufficiently realized in itself or worked through, that it resists being mastered and made to serve some function in our mental programme. It invites us to take time. Our relation to it isn't just spatial (eye to object, stimulation of the optic nerve in a sort of chronological vacuum, the speed of light) nor just a matter of a clearly determinate period (until I've found out what use this is, until I've solved/decoded this problem): we do not know what time is demanded of us, nor what it will issue in. We respond to the work as to a claim on our attention, of indeterminate scope; a presentation of multiple possibilities for assimilation and action.

Is interiority as a moral or 'spiritual' concept comparable to this? We show our 'inner life' not by the desperate effort to say everything, to externalize the stream of unspoken fantasy or dialogue that accompanies our material and public speech, but by so speaking and acting as to invite the taking of time. The person struggling with the former enterprise 'has become a virtuoso of confession, an entertainer with his suffering', *assuming* that the basic fact is the unwillingness of others to know him or her and so constructing an ideal identity that cannot and, in fact, is not really meant to reveal what is hidden: 'the very capacity for intimacy measures the fact of isolation; measures the depth of privacy unshared, i.e., refused'.[56] The confessional style can, at the end of the day, produce simply a spectacle, not an invitation, because it takes for granted the inadequacy of conversation, the fact of *learning* the nature of another human being. Cavell draws our attention to the tragic possibilities of taking for granted the inadequacy or falsity of such learning: there is the risk of ultimate terror and madness, the image of the other as lie, as contradiction, as threat, even while we know at the same time our bondedness with the other, our dependence and partiality.[57] At the end of *Othello*, 'the two bodies lying together form an emblem of this fact, the truth of skepticism. What this man lacked was not certainty. He knew everything, but he could not yield to what he knew, be commanded by it. He found out too much for his mind, not too little.'[58] Othello, in other terms, wants to know and to *have done with knowing*; but that enterprise is the death of the specifically human mind, a dream of final orgasmic possession that entails the voiding of one's own identity (limit, flesh, words, time).

My obscurity to myself, yours to me, and mine to you, are not *puzzles*, waiting for fruitful suspicion to uncover the real script, Marxian, Freudian, sociobiological (though all these stories *may* be true, need finding out). They are to do with the inescapability of taking time. 'I do not really know myself' must be heard as 'I don't yet know what to say; how to speak so that others listen and answer and build up in their words a way for me to go on speaking so that others may answer; how to become a partner in the world.' The sense of a choked or imprisoned or elusive interiority is, on this account, a sense of skills not yet learned and nourishment not given, of not knowing what it might be to be *heard* and so set free – which is why the resolution suggested by a religious believer like Bonhoeffer has such powerful pertinence: I have been 'heard' by God, and I have been given words – of praise and penitence and thanks – that direct me away from the question of how I shall 'know myself'.[59] I have been given time to learn what to say, with the help of the language of praise; because this is a language in which my finitude and limit are affirmed at the same time as my freedom and value, I may better learn from this how to speak to others without assuming their refusal, giving time to them and inviting them to give it to me.

Religious interiority, then, means the learning of patterns of behaviour that reinforce the awareness of my finite and provisional status, my being in time. It is neither a flight from relation, not the quest for an impossible transparency or immediacy in relation but that which equips us for knowing and being known *humanly*, taking time with the human world and not aiming to have done with knowing (and desiring). Religious language can be the ally of projects of 'suspicion' to the extent that they question the easy, restrictive social practice that discourages taking time (puzzlement, invitation, dialogue) – the kind of practice or discourse we label 'superficial'; the 'false consciousness' of the Marxist. The point at which suspicion itself is under criticism is when it comes itself to the point of discouraging the taking of time. The religious critique, as formulated by the writers we have been looking at (I have no qualms about seeing Wittgenstein's polemic as 'religious' in this context),[60] directs itself against the potentially tragic and inevitable self-and-other-diminishing fantasy of abstracting knowledge from attention and response, from a material history of action – from the world, in fact. But what sets it apart from pure humane pragmatism is that it proposes to us a self-description enabling us to set aside once and for all the illusion that our value or 'reality' depends on the success with which we can activate a suprahistorical knowing subject in penetrating to the hidden structures beneath the world of time and flesh. As Augustine memorably put it, we are driven at last to fling ourselves down upon the human mortality, the skin and bone, in which the Wisdom of God speaks to us so that 'in its resurrection we too shall rise'.[61]

Notes

1. Fergus Kerr, *Theology after Wittgenstein* (Oxford: Blackwell, 1986).
2. Ibid., 188.
3. For further discussion of this, see the four articles by Fergus Kerr in *New Blackfriars* 64 (1983) and the third part of his 'Rahner retrospective', 'Transcendence or finitude', *New Blackfriars* 62 (1981), 370–9, especially the quotation on p. 378 from Valéry, 'Le plus profond, c'est la peau.'
4. Paul Ricoeur, *Freud and philosophy: an essay on interpretation* (New Haven: Yale, 1970), 32ff.
5. Ibid., 33–4.
6. The use of Wittgenstein in theoretical discussion of psychoanalysis by Roy Schafer – for example, *A new language for psychoanalysis* (New Haven: Yale, 1976), *Language and insight* (New Haven: Yale, 1978) – has provoked accusations of this kind. See, for example, Roy C. Calogeras and Toni M. Alston, 'On "action language" in psychoanalysis', *Psychoanalytical quarterly* 49 (1980), 663–96, esp. 680–2, for the remarkable assertion that Wittgenstein believed language to be unfalsifiable.
7. Ricoeur, *Freud and philosophy*, 550–1.
8. Compare Stanley Cavell, *The claim of reason* (Oxford: Clarendon Press, 1978), 398.

9. Rush Rhees, introducing 'Conversations on Freud' in Wittgenstein's *Lectures and conversations on aesthetics, psychology and religious belief* (Oxford: Blackwell, 1966), 41.

10. Maurice Drury, 'Conversations with Wittgenstein', in Rush Rhees (ed.), *Recollections of Wittgenstein* (Oxford: Oxford University Press, 1984), 136.

11. Ibid.

12. Wittgenstein, *Lectures and conversations*, 41, 44, 49, 51–2.

13. Ibid., 41, 44, 50ff.; Drury, 'Conversations with Wittgenstein', 137.

14. Wittgenstein, *Lectures and conversations*, 49–50.

15. Ibid., 42, 49; cf. Wittgenstein, *Culture and value* (Oxford: Blackwell, 1980), 68.

16. Wittgenstein, *Lectures and conversations*, 49–50.

17. Ibid., 51.

18. Ibid., 24.

19. Ibid., 23–4.

20. Ibid., 27.

21. Wittgenstein, *Culture and value*, 68.

22. Wittgenstein, *Lectures and conversations*, 27: 'There are certain differences which you have been persuaded to neglect'; 23.

23. Ibid., 28ff., 37–40.

24. Wittgenstein, *Culture and value*, 69: 'it is really as though I have been deprived of something'.

25. A major theme of Cavell, *The claim of reason*, esp. ch. 8, 204–21.

26. Cf. Wittgenstein, *Lectures and conversations*, 27.

27. This is an area in which – as my phraseology might hint – I would agree with those who see *some* convergence between Wittgenstein and Derrida; but the shadow of idealism hangs far more heavily over Derrida insofar as the *physicality* and temporality of discourse is so imperfectly dealt with.

28. Wittgenstein, *Culture and value*, 69–70.

29. Wittgenstein, *Lectures and conversations*, 45.

30. Wittgenstein, *Culture and value*, 69.

31. Dietrich Bonhoeffer, *Letters and papers from prison*, enlarged edn (London: SCM Press, 1971), 339–42, 343–7.

32. Ibid., 341.

33. Ibid., 345.

34. Ibid., 346: 'The discovery of the so-called inner life dates from the Renaissance, probably from Petrarch' – a typically sweeping summary; one would need to look further at the difference between the medieval Augustinian tradition of entry into the depths of the self and the Renaissance idea. The former might be said to be the movement to awareness of the *fact*, not the experiential contents, of reflective activity, presence to oneself.

35. Cavell, *The claims of reason*, 440.

36. Ibid., 493.

37. Bonhoeffer, *Letters and papers*, 347–8.

38. Ibid., 331–2.

39. Ibid., 376.

40. Ibid., 158.

41. Ibid.

42. Ibid., 230.

43. The point is made by J. Fabian in his excellent and provocative study, *Time and the other* (New York: Columbia University Press, 1983), which argues that 'scientific' anthropology achieves control over the cultures it studies by denying that they and the observer share the same time: the object culture belongs to the past (as 'primitive') and so cannot be an interlocutor.

44. This is worth comparing with some of Wittgenstein's remarks to Drury in *Recollections of Wittgenstein*, 114.

45. Ibid., 174–5 on the dangers of self-deceit; compare Wittgenstein, *Culture and value*, 34.

46. See ch. 12 below on 'ironic' detachment as itself a cultural construct in need of being seen ironically.

47. Ricoeur, *Freud and philosophy*, 331–2.

48. Ibid., 333–5.

49. Ibid., 336–7.

50. Ibid., 494–5.

51. Ibid., 529–31, 536ff.

52. Ibid., 496.

53. Kerr, *Theology after Wittgenstein*, 66–8; cf. A. R. Manser, *The end of philosophy* (Southampton: University of Southampton, 1973).

54. Cf. Wittgenstein, *Philosophical investigations* (Oxford: Blackwell, 1953), I §§126, 128, 496; and also take careful note of the remarks on 'progress' in philosophy, *Culture and value*, 15, 86–7.

55. Wittgenstein, *Culture and value*, 53, 56, on 'wisdom' as distinct from 'faith'.

56. Cavell, *The claim of reason*, 464–5.

57. Ibid., 492–3.

58. Ibid., 496.

59. See Bonhoeffer's poems of summer 1944, *Letters and papers*, 347–56, and cf. 370–1, 391–4.

60. How else should we read *Culture and value*? The impetus of philosophical critique here is manifestly a commitment to the world *against* the fantasies of the will and the egotistic imagination – which I take to be one mark of what might count as religious. And – in the light of this last section – see *Culture and value*, 80: 'This is how philosophers should salute each other: "Take your time!" [or perhaps, "give yourself time" – "*Lass Dir Zeit!*"].'

61. Augustine, *Confessions* VII, 18.

11

Simone Weil and the necessary non-existence of God

Of two men who have no experience of God, he who denies him is perhaps nearer to him than the other.

The false God who is like the true one in everything, except that we do not touch him, prevents us from ever coming to the true one.

The 100 possible thalers in Kant. The same applies to God.

We have to believe in a God who is like the true God in everything, except that he does not exist, for we have not reached the point where God exists.[1]

These observations from Simone Weil's Marseilles notebooks are her most concise crystallisation of a theme which evidently preoccupied her a great deal in her last years; echoes are found throughout both the Marseilles and the New York notebooks, and – less clearly – in some of the published essays. It has not, to my knowledge, been systematically traced and discussed, and it presents all kinds of problems to the would-be interpreter. What follows is not the exhaustive treatment that this motif deserves, but an attempt to locate Weil's gnomic remarks on the non-existence of God in relation to other and better-known themes, and to suggest how the idea throws into sharp relief some of the central strengths and weaknesses of Simone Weil's vision – most particularly, her understanding of love, divine and human.

This essay is in no sense an attempt to reduce Simone Weil's vision to a cluster of contradictory and questionable principles. But I believe that, in her account of the grammar of the words 'God' and 'love', there are troubling points of tension. It is possible to read *Waiting for God* and *The need for roots* and to emerge with a very positive sense of her love for the world in its resistance to the desires and projects of the ego, a love both committed and purged from self-regard. Yet, even in these works, the vision is shadowed by other elements, which need

to be brought into focus if this resourcefulness is to be properly apprehended. Not to weigh these elements means not being able to understand why Weil's legacy is still so widely seen as morally problematic.
If the present essay seeks to do something of this job, it is not with the
aim of derogating from Weil's seriousness and significance: quite the contrary. Her thinking is neither merely edifying nor merely 'occasional'; it
is a powerfully comprehensive vision, none the less compelling for its
strains and its moral ambivalences. Depth is not coterminous with
consistency, in Weil any more than in Plato or Hegel.

I

The issue arises in the *Notebooks* in connection with the question of
what she calls 'concordant composition'. Human contact is fraught
with danger (moral danger) in that need and willingness to respond
appropriately to need seem to be systematically uncoordinated: one
person's need threatens the other and drives them away. There is no
time for the relationship to establish itself. 'Concordant composition'
seems to be a way of designating how circumstances might develop so
as to allow such need to be met; but, as we know, such a development
is not to be seen in the world we inhabit. Because human need is real
and urgent, our inclination is to *manufacture* a meeting of our needs,
reordering circumstances through our imagination; and this, Weil
claims, is an infallible way of blocking access to the true 'composition'
in which needs are truthfully or accurately met. From our necessarily
limited standpoint, it is impossible to know what such true concordance
between the time in which I am aware of my need and the time of the
world's process would look like; so my only choices are to accept discordance, unfulfilled need, in the present, or to lie. To accept discordance is
thus to accept that I cannot imagine the good (and must not try). In the
language she uses elsewhere, it is to accept 'the void',[2] to face the contradictoriness of our desires (we cannot realise simultaneously the conditions for attaining all that we desire as good). And this indefinite
deferral of a good that can be seen or imagined or understood is a
moment of contact with the 'supernatural', in the sense that it steps
aside from the realm of motivations determined by specific goals, particular states of affairs: it is a wanting of nothing in particular – or, to
put it more provocatively, it is a wanting of *everything*, a consent to
the ensemble of things. It is union with 'the will of God': 'A plurality

of distinct and convergent motives places the will [presumably by means of the acceptance of the necessary collisions between the plurality of goals] in contact with what is above the sphere of particular motives'.[3]

Thus the determination of desire by a specific state of affairs, wanting this rather than that, is a barrier to the 'supernatural', the realm in which alone desire is truly and truthfully met. For desire to open itself to a non-illusory fulfilment is for it to refuse to *imagine* fulfilment. The desiring or needy human subject must learn to conceive fulfilment, the 'concordance' of need and circumstance or time, as 'non-existent', at least at the level at which the mind normally perceives. 'Before placing oneself in the position where [concordant composition] may be felt, not by the sensibility, but by the higher part of one's being, one must have felt to what extent it is non-existent'.[4] These are the words immediately preceding the observations on God's existence with which we began, and the connection of thought is clear. To imagine God is, Weil implies, to conceive a state of affairs, a determination of circumstances, which will inevitably be conditioned by my needs, and will be a falsehood. Even if I imagine *as an object in my mental world* the God who is characterised by the selfless abandonment, the creative letting-go of reality which is, for Weil, the crucial element in truthful speech about God, I am thereby kept away from the God who can be truly talked about precisely because God has been brought into my mental world, in which all objects are – so to speak – tainted by the particularised wants of the unredeemed subject. So to 'believe' in God, if it is not to be the manufacture of a 'false concordant composition', becomes an intensely paradoxical affair: if God is in our minds, God must be 'imagined' as not existing, not involved in any real or imaginary circumstances. The *grammar* of our talk of God can appropriately be refined, so that we know what we are talking about – that is to say, there is a proper place for objecting, 'You can't say *that* about God', when faced with models of a vindictive or arbitrary divine power (such as Simone Weil identified in the Jewish Scriptures and in much of the rhetoric of the Catholic Church). But the assertion of God's existence cannot be part of this grammatical exercise – hence the allusion to Kant's dismissal of the ontological argument on the grounds that object and concept do not differ in *content* according to whether the object is real or possible ('The real contains no more than the merely possible. A hundred real thalers do not contain the least coin more than a hundred possible thalers'[5]). We are thus able to sort out what we must say about God in order to be talking about God at all; but we cannot affirm that this

God exists over against us, an agent within the system of agencies, a subject with whom I can converse, a particular determination of my own existence in the world.

'We have not reached the point where God exists.' The denial that God exists as a particular determination of the way the (my) world goes is itself a strategy that only makes sense in the context of a process not yet completed. We are to 'believe in', to put our trust or hope in, a God who, while not a particular determination of the world, represents that relation to the world towards which I aspire if I am at all interested in truthfulness – that is, if I am at all human. Weil believes that we are constituted as human by our hunger for the good as such, that hunger which prevents us from being content with the satisfaction of this or that specific need by a specific good and thus – if we let it – warns us that the search for specific goods will turn our desire back towards the ego and thus foster the manufacturing of illusory final fulfilments.[6] We want the good, and want it so badly that, on the one hand, we are unhappy with the specific goods we attain, and, on the other, we long to be able to tell ourselves that this or that good adequately meets our needs as we understand them; our temptation is therefore to reshape in our speech and thought what the world provides for us into a form acceptable to our account of our needs – and so to cut ourselves off from the good as such, which we reach only by recognising that our needs are not met in the terms we prescribe. There *is* (if our human being is not simply condemned to utter futility, if our deepest desire is not a misapprehension) a correct, an undistorting vision of, and relation to, the world, a way of receiving the good-as-such; and to speak of God is to speak of that possible relation to the world as real.

> I am absolutely certain that there is a God, in the sense that I am absolutely certain that my love is not illusory. I am absolutely certain that there is not a God, in the sense that I am absolutely certain that there is nothing real which bears a resemblance to what I am able to conceive when I pronounce that name, since I am unable to conceive God – But that thing, which I am unable to conceive, is not an illusion.[7]

And

> If God should be an illusion from the point of view of existence, He is the sole reality from the point of view of the good ... God exists because I desire Him; that is as certain as my existence.[8]

My desire for the good-as-such, which, to be fulfilled, must be, and can only be, an acceptance of the world as such, is – if it is not 'illusory' – the desire to occupy that 'place' where the creator stands in respect of creation. This is not a place *in* the world (let alone at the centre of the world).[9] If my love or desire, my longing to receive the good-as-such, is somehow 'grounded', not a self-serving fantasy, then there is such a 'place'; there is God. The rigorous purgation of our desire for this or that outcome, this or that determination of circumstances, is not asceticism for its own sake, but the sole possible means of testing whether desire can survive in the absence of specific objects; if it can, it cannot be self-serving, a matter of fantasy under the control of the needy ego. And to know this, presumably, is to know 'that my love is not illusory'. 'God exists because I desire Him' must mean something like:

> The desire for the good is utterly independent of any particular story of need and gratification; it is our *fundamental* relationship to what is not ourselves; we cannot *not* orient ourselves – once we have stopped lying about need and fulfillment – towards such a relationship, testing ourselves against what that relationship entails; but that relationship is not an 'ideal' towards which we strive or struggle, as if it needed to be brought into being; it is there *before* our wills get involved in anything.

The reality of God is the truth that the world can be, and in some sense already is, seen and affirmed, loved, as a whole; that it is possible to say yes to all that is or has been in the world, and that this possibility is entirely independent of what I or any other individual as a matter of fact can or does achieve. If the world may be seen as 'let' to exist, precisely as it is, God is what lets it be, and so is appropriately talked about in the kenotic mythology Weil habitually employs ('God renounces ... being everything ... to the extent of being nailed to the cross').[10] For me to love the world as it should be loved, unconditionally, requires me to see the world as an object of unconditional love *prior* to my own hoped-for growth towards love; and that is to see the world as loved from beyond the world, loved by a God who can be characterised as 'attention without distraction'.[11]

I do not want at this stage to comment on the connections of argument here, but it may be helpful to note a couple of possible misinterpretations of what Weil is saying. First, and most obviously, the divine 'position', the point at which 'concordant composition' is discernible, can sound like a position from which the world can literally be seen as a whole, and all its chains of circumstances traced and understood. This is clearly not what Weil means; such a position could only be a fantastic projection of our need to grasp patterns and explanations, precisely the kind of need which the ascesis of acceptance is meant to suppress. 'Composition', she says, is 'felt . . . by the higher part of one's being' – an unhelpful turn of phrase, but designed to separate out the sense of composition, the accepting love of the world, from the ego and its imaginings and demands for graspable satisfaction. The position of divine love is not one of total comprehension, but of total openness to reality beyond the self. Second, there are the apparent contradictions between Weil's different remarks about conceiving God. I must believe in a God who can be spoken of, who has the qualities of the true God and so can be the subject of, at least, 'grammatical' discussion; yet 'there is nothing real which bears a resemblance to what I am able to conceive when I pronounce that name'. The key, I think, is in the word 'nothing real'. What I am able to conceive in saying 'God', what I may conceive more or less accurately, intelligibly and consistently, depending on how carefully I do my grammatical work, is something that *cannot* be an object among others in the world inhabited by the needy ego. There is no thing in the world's reality to which the name 'God' applies. I cannot but conceive God as some sort of object, because I cannot (logically) conceive what is not in the world; the paradox is that the more faithfully I purify my conception, the clearer it should be that what I am talking about cannot 'exist' in worldly reality. The experience of faith is, as Weil says, the confidence that, in spite of this, my talking about God is not idle or vacuous – though it must be absolutely minimal if it is not to become so ('Not to speak about God . . . not to pronounce this word, *except when one is not able to do otherwise*').[12] But such confidence depends on the conviction that the world can be loved unconditionally, it depends on the possibility of the purification of my love – which has not yet happened ('We have not reached the point where God exists'). So: God is 'there' before us, in that the possibility of pure love is 'there', whatever happens to me, and God is not 'there', because the possibility has yet to be realised in me, the one who is trying to talk about God.

It seems, then, that while I am still on the way to learning love, I can only properly speak of the true God by refusing to recognise anything *in* the world as divine presence – i.e. as claiming our unconditional desire. No item or episode or person in the world, no determination of circumstances, can be the end of our desiring. But if I *had* reached the 'place' of unconditional love, I should not need to speak of God and indeed *could* not do so, since I should stand in God's place ('we have passed to the side where God is').[13] Thus there is never a moment when I can legitimately or intelligibly speak of God as 'existing', as a concrete reality over against me. But the last thing this means is that God is a fiction or a projection, or a tool to purify my spiritual consciousness. It is I who must become a 'tool', a passive instrument in the hands of love;[14] I must enter the process of 'decreation' so that between the world and unconditional love no barrier is set up in the shape of an ego with plural and specific needs or projects. If God is to be real, to 'exist' in a sense other than that in which determinations of the world exist, I must *cease* to exist – that is, I must cease to be an object to myself, a self-conscious reflector on my needs and projects. 'To say "I" is to lie'.[15] 'All the things that I see, hear, breathe, touch, eat, all the beings that I meet – I deprive all these of contact with God and I deprive God of contact with them to the extent to which something in me says "I"'.[16] So long as I have before my mind *images* of want and fulfilment, I am failing to see the whole, to love unconditionally: I distinguish between what I want and what I don't, and so fail to reflect the absolute impartiality of God in letting be a world which is absolutely silent about God, which allows no conclusions to be drawn about the divine nature from the way it goes (only from its bare existence). 'The image of the indifferent power of God is the passive obedience of the creature'.[17] The acting, choosing, ordering ego cannot be united with God, cannot love unconditionally. As long as it is in operation, it is necessary to deny God's existence as an item in the subject's consciousness; and when it has ceased to operate, God's existence does not need to be affirmed – it is simply the point from which I see. Not that it then becomes *manifest*: 'God is always absent from our love, as he is from the world; but he is secretly present in pure love. When the presence of God is visible in love, then it is the presence of something other than God'.[18] In other words, if I am a 'pure' or unconditional lover of the world, if God is present in my 'supernatural' virtue,[19] this does not mean that I become for some other hungry ego a sign of God, a determination of the world that speaks of God, my virtue is not an explanatory problem, a miraculous hiatus in the world. I am simply a means whereby love is made present. That this should be so requires, if it is to be properly interpreted (not explained) that we have to hand a language about unconditional love, about God, about the death of the ego and the reality of God's love in that 'moral space'; but having this language is itself part of the process of life in faith (it has no meaning otherwise), and so has nothing to do with any thing in the world that might be triumphantly pointed to as an epiphany of the divine.

Thus the *content* of the world, in an important sense, is not *changed* by love – that is, no new occult force is introduced into it as an extra item or datum for the mind. Grace is what happens when a self is entirely freed from self-assertion and the quest for gratification of needs, and this *makes a difference* to the world because it interrupts the transmission of violence from self to self which Weil sees as endemic in unredeemed creation (see the essay on the *Iliad*, for her finest treatment of this).[20] It does not bring in some specific 'power' not present before. If love sought to change the world in the sense of bending circumstances to the preferences and plans of a self, it would not be unconditional. Real love does what *must* be done, what circumstances impose.[21] Real love is therefore not bound by goals, since obedience is nothing to do with setting goals. It transforms by obeying the impersonal requirement of truthful seeing.

This brings us to a final set of ideas connected with the non-existence of God which I want to examine before attempting any assessment or development of the themes so far discussed. Real love is not love of anything in particular – or rather not of anything *as* particular.

> We cannot stop ourselves from loving. But we can choose what it is we love.
>
> We ought to love what is absolutely worthy of love, not what is worthy of it in certain respects, unworthy of it in others. (Plato)

> Nothing which exists is absolutely worthy of love.
>
> We must therefore love that which does not exist.
>
> But this object of love which does not exist is not devoid of reality, is not a fiction. For our fictions cannot be more worthy of love than we are ourselves, who are not.[22]

Compare:

> God alone is worthy of interest.[23]

And:

There are two objects for us to love. First, that which is worthy of love but which in our sense of the word existence, does not exist. And second, that which exists, but in which there is nothing it is possible to love. That is necessity. We must love both.[24]

And:

The appropriate object for love is God, and *every man who loves something other than God is deceived, mistaken*.[25]

Love finds no object that has an unconditional claim upon it; yet – Weil seems to assume – the grammar of love is such that uncon-ditionality is part of authentic love (could we say that this is so because love is not something exhausted by the gratification of any specific desire? because it is 'underdetermined' by objects?). Love must there-fore direct itself at what is not – at the reality of unconditional love itself, at the position of total acceptance 'outside' the world. 'If love finds no object, the lover must love his love itself, perceived as some-thing external. Then one has found God'.[26] But if love loves the possibil-ity/reality of unconditional love for the world, it is thereby returned to love of the world, to the love of 'necessity'. 'Necessity, in so far as it is absolutely other than Good, is Good itself':[27] if the good-as-such is unconditional love, it is the love of everything that is *not* the good-as-such; in loving itself, it loves its opposite, necessity, the God-forsaken world. The world is loveable through the medium of the good; indeed, there is a kind of to and fro movement between the necessary and the good which will (once again, if we *let* it) purify our love. Objects and goals in the world 'refuse' to be a final good for us, they retain their irreducible otherness, and so frustrate the will which wants to absorb them: this is the experience of evil and the root of our 'affliction', *misère*; but it is also 'the form which God's mercy takes in this world',[28] in that it can save us from the ultimate lie of believing ourselves satisfied. We must learn to love what will not, and cannot, be absorbed into ourselves. This is why, in Weil's justly famous essays, 'Forms of the Implicit Love of God' and 'Reflections on the Right Use of School Studies',[29] so much stress is laid on the training of the spirit by sub-mission to, and acceptance of, the specific structures of the world, the density of other persons, the given shape of intellectual disciplines: encounter with the given, the non-negotiable, is the painful defeat of the self, and therefore is grace. It instructs us that what can be given to us by the world is not what we want for our gratification. Our initial efforts at, and fantasies of, love (search and gratification, itch and scratch) are brought to nothing, and we are challenged to love not what we want but the sheer otherness of what is there – almost (in principle at least) an *undifferentiated* otherness, in the sense that it is indifferent with respect to my specific wants or articulated needs.

We can only be at home in the world when we have given up the search for that thing, that person, that set of circumstances that will secure our existence, guarantee our being at home.[30] To know that the world as necessity, as utterly and finally other than my will, as incapable of sustaining my love (in the form towards which my love aspires, the form of unconditionality) is the necessary condition of loving the world. I love the world properly only when I have found 'evil', resistance to my gratification, in every determination of the world. As Weil repeats so many times, God is found only in the experience and the understanding of divine absence, which is also the experience of the impossibility of love *in* the world. 'The appropriate object for love' is the sole *subject* of love – that which is not the world, which is not 'there', God.

II

So far, I have done no more than attempt to read and unravel Simone Weil's thoughts on God's existence and non-existence (well aware of the Weilian ambiguity of 'reading'). In the second part of this essay, I want to ask how far all this hangs together in Weil's own terms and in the light of some wider considerations, and what sort of things are being taken for granted in her vision. First, however, we should register the extreme importance for the philosopher of religion of Weil's pivotal observation that the more carefully you examine the grammar of 'God' in its traditional uses (God as creator, as 'last end' of creation, as Trinity, as source of unconstrained grace and mercy), the more it should be clear that we are not talking about an item in any possible list of objects, but about what is other than the world as such. And – a subsidiary point to this – the kind of reality appropriately ascribed to such a God is not an issue to be settled by attempts to prove that there is some determinate subject properly called 'God', but is only appropriately dealt with by way of a much more taxing set of questions. These questions have to do with the evaluation of lives purporting to be lived 'before' God. Are their goals and desires 'illusory' or not? Does the language of the divine serve self-oriented purposes or not? Are the changes or 'conversions' involved in such lives adequately characterised in terms of an immanent psychological economics or not?

Like all questions dealing with adequate interpretation rather than adequate explanation, they are incapable of definitive answers access-ible to universally agreed methods of inquiry. To borrow an idiom not particularly at home with Weil's normal discourse, they are irremedi-ably 'conversational' issues – matters in which interpretative talk and exchange will simply continue. If – for the interpreter of religious language – the possibility of God is bound up with the possibility of an undeceived life lived 'before' God, a life that can be argued to have integrity and not to be governed by fantasy, then – for the religious believer – the exposition and 'defence' of religious language will be bound up with the effort to provide expositions of what holiness might humanly entail.

So much, I believe, stands from Weil's argument, and it imposes a proper austerity on theological utterance, certainly in so far as it might presume to elucidate how divine action might proceed, as if we were dealing with a subject possessed of determinate goals and choices such as we have. But it is precisely this consideration about the necessary distance between what can be said of finite subjects, and what could be said of God, that prompts unease with Weil's analysis of love. She moves very rapidly from the facts of the mobility, fluidity, and discon-tent of human love to the conclusion that there is an *essence* of love that is unconditional. I want certain specific goods, and my ordinary living has in it a substantial amount of self-regard in that it looks for these goods to be provided, these needs to be fulfilled. If these needs *are* met, we are able to go on existing; but that is not enough, we did not want simply to go on, but to find rest or fulfilment.[31] Love is not satisfied by the meeting of needs, but goes on expanding. If our needs are *not* met, we are tempted to manufacture goods or to pretend that the goods we have attained are an adequate answer to our desires. This cuts us off from reality and so again has the effect of actually increasing our hunger. And if love is thus unsatisfiable, whether or not it achieves any specific goals it sets itself, it is oriented towards unconditionality.

The trouble with this analysis is that, like all essentialist accounts, it is damagingly abstract. It elides things that are habitually and reasonably distinguished in speech. I may have specific goals and desires of which I can intelligibly say that I shall know when they have been satisfied. Of many of these (feeling hungry at a particular moment, wanting to get on with writing a letter, and so on) I can say that, when satisfied, they have no further significance. There are circumstances in which 'ordinary' desires may take on a massive importance and fill our horizons. Normally, however, I know that not *everything* depends on this being fulfilled in some exactly specified way, and that there will be other things I shall need or want in much the same way at a future date. This level of desiring is properly irrelevant, I think, to Weil's argument. We should not – except very loosely ('I'd love a biscuit') – talk of love here as a rule. But the cases of ordinary wants taking on extra significance open the door to something closer to what Weil is interested in. To a starving person, the thought of food has ceased to be a casual or 'routine' desire: survival depends on it. And, more generally in human experience, people may come to believe that their survival – or at least their survival as self-respecting persons – depends on attaining some particular goal which to an observer looks trivial or dispensable. This binding of one's inner security or sense of identity to some external object or person or state of affairs normally indicates a profound affective disorder – so that success in gaining one's goal will by no means allay the underlying fear, need, and vulnerability. This is much more what Weil takes as her starting point; and if she says, in effect, that this condition is far more pervasive than we might like to think, we ought to take her seriously. After all, the state of the human world does not suggest that human beings have sorted out their desires and their sense of identity or security particularly well – René Girard's account of the fundamental role of 'mimetic rivalry' in socialisation and social relation might be adduced here.

Now there are certainly circumstances in which another person may be entangled in this binding of the self to something external; my value and security may come to depend entirely on my needs and wants being met by a particular kind of human relationship – by a variety of what we usually call human love. In pursuance of my interests (as I imagine them), I may manipulate or tyrannise over someone else, deny their right to be themselves or to have interests other than my supposed interests, and so do profound injury to them. In Weilian terms, I reduce them to something like the condition of an inanimate object in respect of my desires. Weil's claim is that this is endemic in ordinary human relations. If I love someone as a particular individual, this means that their particularity is attractive to me. *These* features of their reality meet or gratify my expectations, they are pleasing by my standards; my selection of them as objects of love means that I have found reason to ignore or discount other aspects of their reality and to withhold love from other individuals not possessed of the relevant desirable features. Thus my love of the individual as individual is *necessarily* an attempt to 'cannibalise' them, to bring them into *my* world on *my* terms. This is not, we should realise, meant to be an empirical observation about the prevalence of distorted or selfish motivations in human relations; it is designed to show what must be involved in 'loving' the particular and the temporal. And, because love has been defined as essentially unconditional, it is also meant to show that love of the individual as such is not really love at all. To think that it is is, as Weil says, a 'mistake' – not a sin, but a plain error, a misuse of words, a conceptual, and not just a moral, solecism.

Because this is the nature of the argument, it cannot be met simply by saying that not all relations are corrupt and self-serving in this way – though I believe it is legitimate to object to the characterisation of inadequate love as a 'mistake'. To say that *all* specific uses of the word 'love' to refer to human relations are misplaced, in the light of a highly controversial prescriptive redefinition of love as essentially unconditional, is to do a rather futile violence to language. If a word is *never* rightly applied in a specific instance, we could never actually learn how to use it, because learning to use a word involves learning to recognise *instances* where it does, and does not, apply. We could not learn how to use 'love' from a transcendental argument of the kind Weil presents. But if this is so, we do not and cannot begin with or argue from an 'essence' of love. Love is a word we are taught to apply to certain sorts of relationship, fraught with all the ambiguities characteristic of human relationships as such, relationships vulnerable to time, chance, forgetfulness, and corruption. Certainly we learn how to distinguish between kinds or even degrees of love, we develop ways of identifying, in ourselves and others, levels of self-interest or moral self-referentiality in love that are destructive; we learn, perhaps, how potent in human relations is the desire to be in control, to write scripts for others to perform. But the point is that we learn to distinguish more and less corrupt and damaging kinds of love precisely in the process of particular relationships; we learn about the way in which hidden or tacit, unacknowledged needs dictate our loves only if failure or impasse force us to reflection. And this means that a substantial part of what I learn about love is bound up with a growing clarity about my needs, a reduction in the number of illusions I nurture about myself. I become more capable of distinguishing between the reality of other people and the projections of my buried needs. This means that I am free to enter relationships knowing better what I am asking of another, and better able to see clearly what another person is in him or herself, not only as they relate to what I want. In short, I may learn how to engage with another person in both the respects in which they meet my needs, *and* the respects in which they do not. *Both* are inseparable from engagement with the particularities of an individual life; the alternatives are not the de-realising of another by reducing them to what serves my need, and the loving of the other as an impersonal 'given'. And understanding love in such terms is not separable from reflecting on, and learning from, my own affective history: exploring the development of my 'standpoint'.

Love as something learned from the constant and critical reappropriation of the history of my relationships is not imaginable as independent of a point of view, a place in the world. This should not, however, be taken to mean that we learn love from introspective recollection, or that love is a calculated 'plotting' of the ego on the world's territory, a highly self-conscious strategy. The recognition that it is bound up with a point of view (and thus a subject's and a body's history) is a recognition that what we call 'love' is tied to contingency, to the unpredictable convergences of my self-understanding, my language for and about myself, and the alien depths of other human beings. To purify love is to learn how egotistic fear and fiction work to smooth out the particular otherness of another person, so that my language remains uninterrupted, my control unchallenged, my involvement in time and chance unacknowledged. And to know this contingency in the event of love is precisely to retain and nurture an apprehension of the *difference* of this or that 'other', their own contingency; to be surprised, delighted, puzzled, hurt by them in a way which witnesses to their unassimilated reality, an independent hinterland to their side of the conversation (it is worth comparing Weil here with Levinas on the human face as the 'trace' of the transcendent, that which utterly resists mastering). At its most serious, when love involves a real and costly appropriation in imagination of another's standpoint – what we should call compassionate love – it involves a kind of 'analogical' skill, reading the history of another person through the medium of the possibilities of which my own contingent history has made me aware. If we can make observations about the grammar, rather than the essence, of love, they would have to include reference to a point of view, evolved in time: the 'place' of divine love, outside the world, is unimaginable, not because we are unmitigatedly sinful, or mistaken about the definition of love, but because we are finite, and our love is therefore necessarily temporal and positional. If, by grace or hard work or both, we manage to broaden the scope of our love so that we are able to give patient attention, to respond joyfully and generously, to the presence of a wide variety of others, this suggests not that we have abandoned a point of view, but that we have learned not to let our responses be totally dictated by what we believe to be our needs, and to accept, or even celebrate as a gift, what in another person is irrelevant to my imagined need or expectation.

Further: love is not, as we ordinarily understand it, a matter of attitude in the sense of a modification of our interiority. The 'responses' just mentioned are to do with behaviour. In that sense, we are right to be wary and rather sceptical about claims to universal love; we want to see what a pompous moraliser like Leigh Hunt's Abou ben Adhem actually *does* with particular people in particular circumstances. Weil is inclined to identify particularised love with particularised projects; but, in fact, when she writes about obedience to circumstances, she is effectively making the connection between love and response to specific needs in others. And that alertness to the specific – which saves her notion of love from the reproach of absolute quietism often levelled against it – is rather inadequately catered for by the definition of love as essentially non-positional and devoid of specific direction. There is certainly a tension here in her thinking. Love must be directed to the *whole* system of necessity; but necessity is, of course, precisely what is experienced in this or that encounter, precisely the raw otherness and resistance of this or that piece of the world's process. It is not simply 'otherness as such', not *simply* the generalised absence of God. Or again: a human being can only be loved unconditionally 'if one loves an attribute of him which is indestructible';[32] yet unconditional love does not love *any* attribute, any feature which is deemed deserving of love.[33] What is to be loved is surely the absolute contingency, the mortality, of a person: the object freed from the future that our egotistical imagination longs to project,[34] the object or person as radically vulnerable to destruction by time and chance.[35]

The nature of the tension in Weil's thinking arises, I believe, from an awkward duality in her understanding of 'submission to time' ('Renunciation is submission to time. Suffering causes time and space to enter into the body ... The mortal soul is subject to necessity').[36] On the one hand, she insists that we have no alternative to loving necessity – the world of limits and particularities – if we are to love truly at all;[37] and this means renouncing the power we should love to have over the future and coping with the limit imposed by a present situation, task or person. In this sense, submission to time suggests an acceptance of the temporally conditioned character of my response, as well as of the object (task, person . . .), because I could not truthfully or appropriately respond to a temporal object without letting its temporality shape my own part in the relation. On the other hand, we have seen that Weil can speak as if the temporal conditioning of love were a matter of error and corruption, an obstacle to unconditional love. It seems as if we can only properly love the particular by having no *attitude* to it in its particularity whatsoever. Such a love is safe from the corruptions of the particular: it is a 'submission' to the fact that detached love for the particular is impossible in the world, and thus an acceptance of death. 'One must place one's life in something one cannot touch on any account. It is impossible. It is a death. It means no longer being alive. And that is exactly what is wanted'.[38] Thus the love for which we aim should be invulnerable, indestructible; such love is only possible in the attitude-less relation to the world of a dead consciousness, a non-consciousness. Death is the ultimate submission to time.

The paradox here is that the dead consciousness is, *as such*, no longer submissive to time, but free of temporality; it is not simply a pure passivity of awareness (whatever exactly that would mean), receiving without judgment or projection what the world proffers, but beyond both action and passion. Or, to put it another way, the problem is that the 'dead' consciousness only does the work Weil wants it to do if its deadness is some sort of willed strategy on the part of a living consciousness; otherwise, there is a hopeless contradictoriness in speaking of deadness as the paradigm for love of, and submission to, the temporal. But this suggests a 'death' which is precisely a work of the imagination, a seizing of the future: suicide is an assertion, an act of *force* (compare Weil's rather startling paragraphs on the will as a 'principle of violence; which must be made to do violence to itself' – a model which she is obviously aware of as being in tension with the bare acceptance of 'desires and aversions, pleasures and pains' that she has just commended).[39] She has rightly grasped that love from no point of view is not a possible position for a finite subject. She has attempted to surmount the impossibility by – effectively – identifying loving consciousness with no consciousness at all. And I cannot see how this can conceivably be a way of talking about an ideally receptive mode of consciousness – quite apart from the moral ambiguity of the 'strategy of suicide' on Weil's own principles. These tensions are very suggestively and sympathetically explored in an essay by J. P. Little;[40] but I should like to look a little beyond the 'presenting' points of strain to some possible sources for them.

Let me propose, tentatively, that there are at least two rather wider problems in Weil's thought and idiom which intensify her difficulties over the love of particulars. The first is discussed by Peter Winch in his book, *Simone Weil: the just balance*. He argues, correctly, I believe, that Weil's account of the relation between work and thought is askew in its insistence (at least in some texts) that the paradigm of successful work is something like the solution of a mathematical problem. Such a process is totally free of the 'accidental', it cannot be interrupted by the unpredictable history of the world. Now, as Winch points out,[41] this works as a *grammatical* observation about what counts as a mathematical problem and its solution, but not as a description of what it is like for a specific person to solve a problem at a specific point in time: 'while geometrical figures are independent of contingencies, the mind that thinks about them is not'.[42] The action of the mind in working on a mathematical problem is not, in fact, all that different from the action of the mind in working on any kind of problem: it belongs to all our discourse about the mind's action to involve reference to the struggle with historical and material circumstance, with the uncontrollable. Weil herself is clear enough about this in certain contexts.[43] But her language repeatedly slips towards the notion that the interruptions of circumstance somehow *corrupt* or *distort* the mind's conceptions and purposes.[44] It is not simply that we are always enmeshed in the business of overcoming obstacles; the world of contingency is, as such, an obstacle, over against the freedom of the mind, a freedom shown in our capacity to form 'pure' mathematical conceptions.

My suggestion is that what Simone Weil has to say about the love of particulars and the imperative towards 'purity' of response reproduces the difficulties she runs into with her account of the mind's work. The subject is, in both cases, conceived as fundamentally beyond *conditions*: seeing the forms of geometry or the structures of mathematical proof is, *more Platonico*, bound up with seeing the form of the good (unconditional letting-be), since both can be said to survive unscathed whatever in particular may happen in the world. Furthermore, in both cases, the mind or subject as pure or unconditioned, and thus supremely active and free, is, in concrete terms, powerless; it cannot form the world to its conceptions, and falls into error if it mistakes any worldly outcome for its eternal object. In the activity of mathematics, this error is unavoidable once particular figures are constructed (as they must be).[45] In the moral life, however, as we have seen, there *is* the possibility of escaping error, by a mode of response to the world from which the ego, the will oriented to temporal ends, is absent ('We are not defiled by actions from which we are absent').[46] When this occurs, the relation between situation and response is simply one of congruence. What needs to be done is done – just as in the case of the mathematical operation. When the body in the world can perform only one action in response to a situation, we have 'equilibrium', 'true balance'[47] – at least when that 'inevitable' response is the fruit of a conscious policy of withdrawing from the situation the force of the ego, a fully willed submission.

If we reflect a little further on the implications of Weil's understanding of the willing self as both unconditioned and powerless, we come to the second source of her difficulties. This is, admittedly, a more speculative suggestion. Recent discussion of the post-Cartesian development of epistemology (and I think particularly of Stanley Cavell's work) has characterised this history as the quest for a place where no 'claims' are made, no *interest* is involved. It should be possible to identify the pure case of knowing, where the cognitive subject registers a state of affairs without distorting mediation: hence the significance of self-presence as a paradigm of knowledge in this tradition, from Descartes's *cogito* to Moore's 'This is a hand'. Is it possible to see Weil's language here as a kind of ethical and spiritual transcription of this canonisation of cognitive disinterest? Truth is attained only in a position devoid of particularised interest, self-serving or self-reflecting perspectives, mediation through the minds and words of others. Weil's moral truthfulness, her encounter with the reality determinative for the life of the spirit, likewise pulls towards a suspicion of mediation's capacity to block vision, and a search for a position without location in respect of affective relations. Mediation is wholly central to her characterisation of being in the world, yet it is also the source of 'infinite error'. The moral and spiritual task is so to live with mediations that they become the means of eradicating the errors inseparable from being in a position in the world. The subject's position is irretrievably tragic.

If it is true that the Cartesian and post-Cartesian subject is meant to stand to the world in the relation of an effectively absent God, as the vantage-point of freedom from particular determination which only that which is quite other than creation can enjoy, we have a further elucidation of Weil's understanding of the non-existence of God. The same holds for the reverse – that is, if the God of modern abstract theism is conceived as doing the job of the Cartesian ego. The epistemological claim is that, even without God, there is the possibility of a point from which things may be seen truly or justly. Weil accepts the 'modern' conclusion of God's absence from the world, and claims that there is still the possibility of a point from which things may be *loved* justly. But for her the establishing of that possibility is a genuine re-establishing of God, since we must love what is not the world before we can rightly love the world, and we cannot love what is only the creation of our minds. Thus the transcription of the 'view from nowhere' aspiration from the epistemological to the spiritual sphere has the effect of overcoming atheism without reinstating a divine object: modernity overcome by modernity, perhaps. Whether or not anything like this is part of Weil's *conscious* project, this particular philosophical problematic may be worth considering as a possible locus for her subtle discussion of God's 'existence'. Indeed, the profoundly Kantian nature of her delineation of God's reality shows quite plainly where she is most at home: as in the second Critique, God is the 'invisible' condition for the possibility and intelligibility of our moral aspiration being realised. The logic of our moral life is such that what we hope for must be conceived as capable of actualisation. To conceive our hope in this way, not as an account of what any individual may hope to attain, but as a standing reality beyond the history of phenomena, *is* to conceive of God, God 'on the side of the subject and not on that of the object'.[48]

We are left with a tantalisingly uneven and paradoxical picture. So much of the energy and resourcefulness of Weil's thought, especially in the published essays in *Waiting for God* and *On Science, necessity and the love of God*, comes from a sense of the positive value of the finite – the good life as the fruit of contemplative attention directed to the otherness and uncontrollability of the world, free from the urge to coerce the world into patterns the ego can cope with. This side of her vision assumes that to be human is not to be an absolute initiator or an independent and self-regulating mental substance.[49] Yet her speculation is haunted, most clearly in the late notebooks, by the sense that the necessarily frustrated subject, the limited point of view, is somehow the source of error, a corruption of some potentially divine subjectivity only thinkable for us in terms of negation, passivity, absence, death.

Thinking (or acting) in the first person, that is, out of our finite point

of view, is slavery;[50] liberty is when the 'I' is not there, and God loves
God, me and the world in one single unconditioned, unspecific, eternal,
indiscernible action (or non-action, perhaps). There is no truth or value
in the particular point of view I have as observer, or in the position or
stance of what is observed: 'In the universe as seen from a point of
view there can only be imaginary forms of balance and plenitude, and
thanks to an unlimited exercise of the imagination'.[51] Hence, too, we
cannot and must not love ourselves except 'because God loves us'[52] –
and thus, presumably, *as* God loves us, that is, unconditionally and
impersonally, as part of the whole fabric of the necessary. God loves
that particular perspective of creation which can only be had from the
spot where I am; but only when I am absent from it – i.e., not really as
a *subject's* perspective. Any other love of God for me as an individual is
not conceivable, especially when 'I feel so clearly that even the affection
which human beings evince for me can only be a *mistake* on their
part'.[53] But perhaps the most revealing remark on this side of the
balance is in the New York notebook: 'creation is a fiction of God's'.[54]
The otherness of creation to God is reduced to a kind of divine play,
in which the *purpose* of creation is decreation: God 'cannot create
anything which is God, and . . . cannot be loved by anything which is
not God';[55] God is loved to the extent to which creation is destroyed
(as subject). Our acceptance of this condition for loving God is our
absolution of God for the 'crime' of creation,[56] for letting-be a world
destined for dissolution, and working towards that dissolution in the
process prodigal of terror and pain.

As suggested already, the problem here may be that, in her interest
in the uncontrollable otherness of world and context, the specificity of
that otherness, so superbly evoked in *Waiting for God* and *The need
for roots*, slips away into concern with otherness-as-such – a 'resistance'
to the ego which can be abstracted from the labour of working with
this or that bit of unyielding environment. A profoundly suggestive
philosophy of work[57] is entangled with a rather different project –
alterity overcome by the dissolving of the positional subject, so that
otherness is no longer to be *negotiated* (the term is meant to recall
Levinas once again).

When she writes in this vein, it is certainly a dissolution she envisages,
not some kind of *Aufhebung*. She echoes Hegel to the extent of envisag-
ing the 'essential' position of finite spirit as identical with that of infinite
spirit; but is about as far removed from Hegel as possible in absolutising
the alienation of subject and world (there can never, in Weil, be an

identity between the process of the world and the activity of the spiritual subject). And the paradoxical effect of remaining at the stage of the 'unhappy consciousness' is that there is no positive evaluation of what consciousness is conscious of, no story of spirit becoming itself in material encounters. Yet something like this would certainly be a possible way forward from the more constructive elements in the Weilian analysis, once something like the Hegelian dissolution of the individual mental substance has been digested. This is simply to put in the terms of her own philosophical formation what can be more adequately pursued in terms of the Wittgensteinian critique of the privileges of mental privacy. But the mention of Hegel is also meant to draw attention to the possibility of talking about the overcoming of the individual perspective, not by the denial or dissolution of points of view, but by a consistently relational and dialogical account of the shaping of human awareness – which would also take seriously the formation of any particular awareness by history, that dimension so often elusive in Simone Weil's thinking. Pursuing this further would lead us into the intriguing area of Weil's aesthetics. Consider for example her insistence that the beautiful in verbal art must be like the visually beautiful, a wholly *contained* movement, a point in space rather than a duration in time, let alone an indeterminate duration in time (i.e. something leaving emotional or interpretative 'loose ends', something with imperfect formal closure), or a set of non-contingent relations, as in music. But this would take us too far afield for the present.[58]

It is hard to attempt any conclusion. Weil's analysis of how God is to be spoken of remains one of the most difficult and challenging of this century, and for that very reason it is important not to canonise it or domesticate it. I have tried to show that, as she presents it, it collapses under a weight of contradictory pressures. How much it helps to propose psychological or sociological explanations for the enormous problems she has with the possibilities of self-love or love of the particular I am not sure, though the questions are worth posing. What, as a woman, is she culturally 'allowed' to think about her body? What on earth is going on in her extraordinarily vitriolic and silly comments on Judaism – a real demonisation of her own heritage? These issues are mercilessly raised by unsympathetic readers like Giniewski';[59] and those convinced (as I am) of Weil's significance and seriousness should not be allowed to brush them aside. However, I have not attempted to tackle them directly in these pages.

If there is a general observation to be made, perhaps it is this: the identification of an imperative to love (as a finite being) with an imperative to take the stance of the creator towards the world is a sure way of undermining the intelligibility of what we can say about love itself (certainly in a religious context; but not exclusively). It is also, theologically speaking, a misunderstanding of the logic of creation. For thinkers like Augustine and Aquinas, the relation of the world to the agency on which it depends, considered in the light of the whole context of revelation, tells us that God wills that there be goods, interest, goals, not identical – even formally – with the good of self-contemplation that God as God enjoys. God wills what is not God, and so wills a world in which creatures are called to move towards their own immanent goals – certainly within an ordered system in which the highest good is the creature's conscious or 'rational' relation with the creator (so that the interests of self-aware beings are more significant and comprehensive than others), but not in such a way that any specific interest, any legitimate 'natural' need, is dispensable or negligible. The good of the self-aware creature is union in love and knowledge with God, but within the limits imposed by the nature of creaturehood – temporality, changeability: the complete grammatical break between what is properly said of God and what is said of the creature means that union with God is intelligible only as a *process* of transformation within the order of creation, and never (even 'in heaven') amounts to an identity of subject. Hence the love appropriately given to the self and to objects in the world is (for Augustine at least) a quite complex affair, the struggle so to understand the interests of self and others that they may be woven in to the fundamental and decisive interest of the reasonable subject – the need to be moving further into that trust in God which enables the particular human subject to become a sign of divine trustworthiness to others, and thus to be at one with God's love towards the world. This model is no less serious than Weil's about the impossibility of identifying God or grace as a determinate item for consciousness.

The exposition of this doctrine, of course, raises problems of its own; but what it does succeed in doing is establishing the reality and legitimacy of interests other than God's 'interest'. In simpler terms: to reflect upon and assess the particular needs of myself or anyone else is not a moral catastrophe so long as it is done within the framework of a synoptic sense of the good of creatures made for the love of God. Thus, such reflection and assessment may lead to all sorts of re-visioning of what we think are needs and goods, but will *not* attempt to discard entirely the significance of the variety of personal goods. Because of this, it will be painfully vulnerable to the tragic collision of interest, to the destructive misconceiving of needs, and so on. But this 'fragility of goodness', to borrow the title of Martha Nussbaum's profoundly perceptive and imaginative study, is not a matter of global moral failure, not a *mistake*, not a humiliatingly wrong place for the moral consciousness to be. This is what moral and spiritual life *is* – just as mental life *is* the negotiation of unforeseen (historical) circumstance.

Simone Weil often writes as if she so believed, and yet repeatedly reintroduces the spectre of the 'pure' subject, free from place and time; she thus makes it increasingly hard for herself (the last notebooks contain some of her harshest observations on this) to give an intelligible account of loving what is transitory in its own terms. The only valid interest is eternal – the paradoxical interest of securing a non-position in the world, so that even action apparently directed towards the need of another is really an allowing of the balance of things to remain in position, rather than the fruit of reflective (and fallible) assessment of needs. If we are to take seriously those ways in which Weil helps us to grasp and reflect on the necessarily finite and vulnerable standpoint of moral thought and action, we need to understand also as fully as possible what it is that pushes her argument in the direction of what I think is a morally and intellectually ambiguous, if not unsustainably paradoxical, account of what it is to love God and the world. Without disputing most of her observations on the grammar of 'God', on the existence of God as something other than a particular determination of circumstances in the universe, it is, I think, possible to challenge the assimilation of this grammar to that of the finite moral subject in a state of grace. This also suggests that what Weil implicitly proposes as the controls for our language about God might also need to be challenged. As noted earlier, Weil effectively argues that the ungraced soul *cannot* truthfully speak of God, since it will inevitably conceive God as object, while the graced soul will not speak of God because it has no position over against God's. Words about God can only legitimately be uttered in the process of clarifying what is involved in the difference between the soul's state with and without 'grace' (the acceptance of death for the ego). But if the intelligibility of moral finitude is better preserved by a rather more densely textured account of creation and the relationship between infinite and finite, then the systematic prohibition against saying 'I' to God[60] can properly be broken in a language both of praise and of repentance – the acknowledgment of creation as the establishing and sustaining of a non-divine point of view precisely in its vulnerability and unfinishedness.

Notes

1. Simone Weil, *Notebooks* (London: Routledge and Kegan Paul, 1956), 151.

2. Cf. ibid., 148, 153, 198, 204, 410–11, 431, 491, 545, etc.

3. Ibid., 239.

4. Ibid., 151.

5. Immanuel Kant, *The critique of pure reason* (Hampshire: Macmillan, 1929), 505.

6. Weil, *Notebooks*, 487; *On Science, necessity and the love of God* (London: Oxford University Press, 1968), 159.

7. Weil, *Notebooks*, 127.

8. Simone Weil, *First and last notebooks* (London: Oxford University Press, 1970), 157.

9. See, e.g., Simone Weil, *Waiting for God* (New York: Harper and Row, 1951), 158–60.

10. Weil, *Notebooks*, 193, among many other instances.

11. Weil, *First and last notebooks*, 141.

12. Weil, *Notebooks*, 234; cf. 326.

13. Simone Weil, *Intuitions pré-chrétiennes* (Paris: La Colombe, 1951), 153.

14. Weil, *First and last notebooks*, 132, 243–4, etc.

15. Ibid., 132; cf. 337–8.

16. Weil, *Notebooks*, 378f.; cf. 364, 404, etc.

17. Weil, *First and last notebooks*, 130.

18. Ibid., 275.

19. Ibid., 111, 145, 339, etc., and *Waiting for God*, 149–50, etc.

20. Simone Weil, *The Iliad, or the poem of force*, Pendle Hill Pamphlet 91 (Wallingford, PA: Pendle Hill, 1981).

21. Weil, *Notebooks*, 29–30, 57; cf. the remarks on the *Bhagavad Gita*, esp. 80–94, and the notes on war, 32–5; how are we to 'obey' the need to take up arms in defence of human freedoms and yet show in our conduct of war that desire for unconditional acceptance that alone can preserve peace? How do we fight not for power, but in order to change the mind of the enemy towards the possibility of – powerless – acceptance as a goal for both sides?

22. Weil, *Notebooks*, 220.

23. Weil, *First and last notebooks*, 126.

24. Ibid., 324.

25. Weil, *On Science, necessity and the love of God*, 104.

26. Weil, *First and last notebooks*, 260–1; the reference to Augustine, *Confessions* 3.1, substantially misunderstands the import of that text – though Weil might have found grist to this particular mill in the *De Trinitate*.

27. Weil, *Notebooks*, 424.

28. Ibid., 495.

29. Weil, *Waiting for God*, 83–142 and 57–66.

30. Weil, *Notebooks*, 469.

31. Ibid., 494–5.

32. Weil, *First and last notebooks*, 282–3.

33. Weil, *Notebooks*, 220.

34. Ibid., 553.

35. Ibid., 218–19; cf. 483 on God's 'infinite love for finite things as such'.

36. Ibid., 221.

37. Ibid., 492.

38. Ibid., 484.

39. Ibid., 428ff.

40. J. P. Little, 'Simone Weil's concept of decreation', in Richard H. Bell (ed.), *Simone Weil's philosophy of culture: readings toward a divine humanity* (Cambridge: Cambridge University Press, 1993), 25–51.

41. Peter Winch, *Simone Weil: the just balance* (Cambridge: Cambridge University Press, 1989), 96–7.

42. Ibid., 98.

43. Ibid., ch. 6.

44. See Winch's remarks, ibid., 73ff., on the curious idea that any geometrical figure constructed in the world involves a *mistake* when compared to the ideal form.

45. Cf. Weil, *Notebooks*, 237, on 'error as a source of energy'.

46. Ibid., 57.

47. Ibid., and many other instances.

48. Ibid., 358.

49. The positive contribution of uncontrollable otherness is admirably developed in Richard H. Bell, 'Reading Simone Weil on rights, justice and love', and Eric Springsted, 'Rootedness: culture and value', both in Bell (ed.), *Simone Weil's philosophy of culture*, 214–34 and 161–88.

50. Weil, *Intuitions pré-chrétiennes*, 153.

51. Weil, *Notebooks*, 146.

52. Ibid., 278.

53. Ibid., 364, my italics.

54. Weil, *First and last notebooks*, 218.

55. Weil, *Notebooks*, 330.

56. Weil, *First and last notebooks*, 94–5; cf. 140 and 263.

57. Lucidly set out in Winch, *Simone Weil*, and Clare B. Fischer, 'Simone Weil and the civilization of work', in Bell (ed.), *Simone Weil's philosophy of culture*, 189–213.

58. Weil, *Notebooks*, 4–5; cf. her remarks on tragedy, 620: 'Shakespeare's tragedies are second-class with the exception of *Lear*' because *Lear* alone succeeds in containing its dramatic movement in a formal way, being a play essentially about power, death, and justice.

59. Paul Giniewski, *Simone Weil ou la haine de soi* (Paris: Éditions Berg International, 1978).

60. Weil, *Notebooks*, 173.

12

'Religious realism': on not quite agreeing with Don Cupitt

Don Cupitt's contribution to theology and the philosophy of religion in this country has not often met with unqualified welcome from his colleagues, so perhaps it will not be surprising that I have subtitled this paper as I have done. It will probably become fairly clear that my disagreements are in some respects fundamental. And yet I am perfectly serious in saying 'not *quite*', and in wanting to offer a real – if still qualified! – welcome to the challenges he presents. He has reminded all of us who attempt some kind of professional reflecting on the notion of God that we are very ready to evade and elide the more obstinate problems posed by our own tradition. At one level, Cupitt's target is not really so much the language of Aquinas or Gregory of Nyssa as the lucid dissolutions of the starker paradoxes of classical theism in much contemporary Anglo-Saxon philosophy of religion (Richard Swinburne would, I think, represent a great deal of what Cupitt most objects to,[1] and some aspects of process theology might come under the same strictures) – and the dramatic personalist and narrative theologies of continentals such as Moltmann.[2] Cupitt is concerned to repudiate any talk of God which suggests that we have to do with an exceptional spiritual individual, a person with a story: theology cannot be the analysis of God's states of mind or the record of his adventures with creation. And while Kant and the Buddha may be the figures foremost in much of Cupitt's implicit and explicit polemic in this area,[3] he is entirely conscious of standing firmly within a Christian tradition of negative theology, to which he makes powerful appeal. In fact, to those who believe themselves to be defending a 'traditional' version of Christian theism, Cupitt can retort that the tradition itself – in its completeness – subverts much of what it appears to be saying. There are long-standing uncertainties about the rightness or adequacy of treating God as an object, an individual to whom acts and properties can be straightforwardly ascribed. Eckhart, John of the Cross and Simone Weil are to be taken seriously; and if taking them seriously interferes with the Cleanthean simplicity of Swinburne's natural theology, for instance, so much the worse for the latter.

Perhaps you could characterize Cupitt's presentation by saying that it is an attack on any idea that God is *interesting* – 'interesting' as my own ego is interesting, as the foibles of another personality are interesting. We are fascinated by selves as we understand them, and so find it practically impossible to conceive of a relation to God which is not comparable to a relation to a self – an ensemble of impressions, memories, emotions, reactions. Like those souls deplored by Auden's King Herod, we demand that God 'be interesting and weak like us'.[4] And Cupitt reiterates, in reply, what is perhaps the most central insight of the Buddhist tradition – that this kind of fascination is essentially corrupt and destructive: it is a bondage to the limited and the particular, the endless accumulation of meaningless contingent fragments, the feeding of a curious and self-indulgent ego with transitory stimuli. Religious practice claims to offer liberation: but if God is conceived as yet another bundle of stimuli for the greedy self, and if our relation with God takes on the 'interesting' character of a personal love affair (longings and raptures, rows and reconciliations) how on earth can it liberate? It pretends to transform us, but does it not in fact merely shift the dramas of the ego on to a new and more satisfactory level?

Thus far Buddhism and, if I read him correctly, Cupitt. Critics of Cupitt may question his appeal to a self-evidently irreversible evolution of 'modern' consciousness, or they may complain that he caricatures the personalist language of Christians about God; and they are probably right to so object. But the essence of Cupitt's argument is not here, but in the profound challenge he offers to the intrinsic corruptness (as he sees it) of projecting what belongs to the realm of interacting egos into our religious language. Salvation is – in a quite strict sense – disinterestedness: neither God nor myself may be an object of fascination, delighted probing, *care*. The dramatic, the personal, the narrative in religious speech may in some contexts be unavoidable; but they are essentially irreligious – hugely complex and successful tools for maintaining infantile narcissism. The only escape from the seduction of this kind of religious speech is, for Cupitt, the recognition that, in order to do what it is meant to do, talk of God must be purged of any implication that we are seeking to describe the nature and disposition of a transcendental self – or any kind of 'transcendent object' at all. All we may seek to do is to educate our wills to detachment.

I suspect that we are being presented with a false dichotomy here, and my aim in these pages is to question some of what it seems to take for granted. But I should say that I am not at all sure that Cupitt can be 'refuted', insofar as he offers less a sustained argument than a particular kind of vision of the moral and spiritual world. I think that his presentation of this vision is actually weakened by the unsatisfactory character of some of his own argumentative machinery: he tends to overbid his hand by appealing repeatedly to the self-evidence of what he is saying in respect of the contemporary consciousness,[5] thus leaving his critics ample scope for pointing out that this sort of cultural determinism goes rather badly with the radical voluntarism he defends. The *force* of what he says is: 'In such a world as ours, what can we now do?' The *form* in which it is said is too often, 'In such a world as ours, all intelligent persons will agree what can be done' – which is a far feebler address. So what follows is not designed to 'disprove' something like this second sort of appeal, but rather to ask whether the vision commended is quite as consistent, attractive, and liveable as it is made out to be, and whether the choices with which we are confronted in developing a credible spirituality are as sharply defined and distinct as Cupitt would have them.

I

It is time now to look in more detail at what Cupitt actually says about the nature of moral and religious life and speech. Here, then, are three key-statements, each of which I have tried to expand and paraphrase in order to bring out their connections.

(a) 'A world in which people have become active creators of religious value is what I mean by the Kingdom of God'.[6]

I.e.: the Kingdom of God is that state in which human beings have quite ceased to be passive, moulded by their (physical or intellectual) environment. They have, in other words, become *responsible*; they are answerable for the shape and direction of their lives. Their projects are initiated freely, not dictated from beyond. Thus they are answerable for their *values*; these are not imposed on them by the world, but created as a means of transcending the world.

(b) 'A morality that deserves to be adopted must be rational, consistent and impartial'.[7]

I.e.: a responsible morality is precisely one in which action is not determined from moment to moment by impulse or desire. These things are conditioned, time-bound, and ultimately ego-directed. Moral action does not just happen, it is enacted in full consciousness; it is a stranger to passion, and thus to all the 'interesting' quirks of the self and its preferences. Thus moral purpose must be universal in its import, since it cannot be determined by the conditions of any one individual's psychological state.

(c) 'A morality that seriously concerns itself with motives and with psychology is inevitably led in the direction of religion'.[8]

I.e.: as we imagine a harmonious moral world of fully responsible agents, we are made more painfully aware of our present experience of corruption and self-deceit in moral living. It is not enough to present the moral demand as demand alone: it must be transformed into another kind of requirement, the invitation to a passionate and faithful commitment to disinterestedness. The historical form of such a commitment is religious living, which represents the moral goal to us in terms of an unchanging reality utterly independent of our desires and fantasies, whose stability acts as a constant energy-bestowing point of reference and criticism. In the presence of this objectivized goal, we grow steadily in the disciplines of unsparing self-appraisal.

Cupitt adds that it is inevitable that such a representation of the moral goal will take personal and mythical forms – partly because we as human beings need narrative structures to understand ourselves.[9] We are moving, growing, becoming, and we cannot make a once-for-all leap into the austerity of a purely timeless conceiving of God. But the morally and spiritually mature person recognizes this for what it is – a necessary subterfuge in language, whereby we are first drawn away from sheer infantilism by a story of God's dealings with us, which gradually enlarges our horizons. If we attend to it properly, we shall see how it subverts its own surface anthropomorphisms.

Cupitt's case is richly and subtly presented. The problem with its presentation, though, should be apparent from the quotations I have used. As several critics have observed, there is a blurring of categories which enables him to move from 'values should not be imposed' to 'values must be *created*'; from 'morality must not be determined by the self and its passions' to 'morality is a policy decided upon quite independently of need or desire'. The question which must be pressed here is one to do with the *ground* of moral life. It is possible to elucidate (which does not necessarily mean to justify) a moral option with reference to how I believe things to be with myself and the world at large or humanity as a whole. Indeed it is quite hard to see how, in normal moral discourse, we avoid such elucidation. Why (I might be asked) do I trouble myself about apartheid? about torture? Part of my reply is likely to be that I *perceive* the sufferer as a human being whose interests are like mine: I cannot look on their privation or agony any more complacently than my own. I *see* myself and my own experience meshing with theirs ('if this happened to me, what I should feel is what they now really feel', 'if I should be outraged at my oppression, they have every right to be so', and the next step, 'I have every right to be outraged on their behalf'). I am not a lonely and incomparable soul: at the very least I am reminded of my vulnerability by the wounds of others. There is more than one possible response to this kind of perception – which we might call for convenience a perception of human solidarity: I might say, 'I must shield myself as much as possible from such reminders' or 'I must do all I can to secure myself against such a fate'. But the fact that a perception does not *compel* a particular moral response does not mean that it can be ignored when we try to explore the response we do in fact make.

The point is that 'I *choose* to concern myself with apartheid etc.' is a rather peculiar moral remark. A puzzled interlocutor might say, 'Of course you do, I can see that. But have you any reason for choosing: because if not, the relative importance of moral issues will depend wholly on an individual's whims.' In the same way, if we are trying to elucidate a moral attitude we now hold, we may well do so partly by adverting to a kind of experience which has led us to this point. 'Why are you, as a Christian, indulgent towards divorce (or homosexuality, or whatever)?' may well be answered with, 'If you had seen what I have seen and felt something of the demonic complexities and tensions of sexuality, you might judge likewise.' There is nothing necessarily irresponsible in the admission that I judge thus because my experience prompts me to; because this is how I see the world goes; because I see human well-being thus and not otherwise.

In other words, moral judgment is *learned* – as we discover our own inner knots and limitations, what can be expected of others, what are the effects of time, mindfulness and forgetfulness; as we experiment with models of what it is to be human. The moral life is not something initiated by my choice; I am ensnared in moral 'tradition' as soon as I begin to relate consciously and reflectively to the world around me. And if this is so, it is impossible to see what a quite unconditioned and contextless 'creation of value' would mean. Some of Cupitt's language seems to suggest that moral evaluation is only properly itself when it is purely an assertion of naked will against what is the case, and that moral community only emerges as diverse individuals together come to make detached and universalizable or impartial judgment. But what is this naked will, abstracted from the growing and desiring of particular persons in particular circumstances, persons who reflect and talk morally simply because they are already social beings, perceiving and judging as their language makes them able, members *already* of moral communities? Moral development is not plausibly represented as an advance towards the condition in which a will with no (acknowledged) history invents its values and determines its policies in a social vacuum.

Cupitt evidently does not want to defend any such insupportable notion, though he sometimes sounds as if he does. Like any other serious moralist, he allows that will is formed by perception – or, better, that *willing* is a movement of the self that cannot be made sense of without the idea of an object desired – and thus of a perceived world of possibilities.[10] Thus Cupitt can write, 'One must seek a higher purity and intensity of consciousness, *because* consciousness itself – and perhaps all biological life – is a teleological striving'.[11] 'Because' relates the option to a vision. Whatever exactly it means, this exhortation does not speak of an ungrounded generating of values, spirit affirming itself against the world; it carries with it a perception of intelligent life as necessarily purposeful, which is far from uncontroversial.

The same could be said of Cupitt's favoured myth of European history up to the present as a story of the gradual purifying of self-awareness; or of the insistence that the moral ideal is necessarily one of social harmony.[12] But the point is perhaps clearest in the moving and potent accounts in *The world to come*[13] of the gospel of Jesus as a response to the vision of human life on 'the edge of the abyss'. When we see the emptiness from which we come and into which we go, we grasp our freedom to choose *what to be*. Nothing constrains us except the truth that nothing constrains us; and from this vertiginous perception, the gospel of the possibility of life 'in the Kingdom' is born.

Cupitt writes eloquently here about 'the Void' which is the context of our world (and again the Buddhist allusion is important): the unillusioned person will look at the reality around, see its absolute refusal to deliver any promise of meaning and so conclude that meaning can only be the issue of a deliberate assertion of will in the face of a silent universe. That very silence and meaninglessness may be productive of a chastened awe (Cupitt can even write, with a rare detour into the sombre purple of Edwardian agnosticism, of 'the peace and silence of the Ineffable').[14] Yet this vision of 'the void' pre-empts the judgment about values: it is already a way of seeing, a *tradition* of seeing – not simply what is left when metaphysics retires. Even in its native Buddhist territory, the term is not a straightforward one: for the Māhāyana, especially after Nāgārjuna,[15] 'the Void' is not the emptiness 'beyond', with which we are confronted; it is the recognition of the world as nothing but pure process, energy and interaction, the absence of fixed essences. Reality *is* the Void, the plenum-void, as some would call it; and the 'saving' response is not a heroic act of the will (who is there to do the willing? a Buddhist might ask), but that acceptance of conditionedness which frees me from the fantasy that I can 'own' the world, and so liberates me from the wheel of desire and suffering. This is a way of living *in* the endlessly interconnected, interdependent world – not a Promethean challenge to the spirit in bonds.

'The Void' for Cupitt is part of a *tragic* vision: he will say elsewhere that our 'destiny' is extinction.[16] And that is a very different proposition from both 'I shall die' and 'the human race will not survive indefinitely'. It is here that he (like his beloved Nietzsche) most shows himself the child of that dramatic Christian (especially Protestant) personalism he so vigorously attacks (redeemed spirit in battle with the downward drag of passive nature). The free creator banished from heaven is incarnate in us;[17] but we cannot create the world of matter which conditions and binds us: our creating therefore is in the realm of will, in the positing of groundless value.

But what is important, if we are to take such a stance as this, is that we recognize the *dependence* of what we will on what we see, and allow that our 'seeing' cannot be itself the creation of a world *ex nihilo*. The language we learn already encodes for us certain ways of perceiving, of 'arranging' the world. It is strictly unimaginable what it would be like to arrive at a way of seeing free from linguistic conditioning (language is not a *hindrance* to understanding, a veil between the mind and truth).[18] And if this is so, moral integrity, maturity and responsibility do not consist in the assurance that nothing at all conditions the motion of the will (for what could this mean?). They have nothing to do with the Sartrean effort to constitute a unique moral style for the individual or with Raskolnikov's fantasies of demonstrating power by performing a moral outrage (see how many things I can *choose* to do!). Maturity is better seen as the expansion of understanding and imagination; responsibility is being answerable for one's choices *in terms of* being prepared to own and explore one's perceptions.[19] These are qualities which make sense only if we see the moral life as the process in which 'given' perceptions are tested and modified in the painful crucible of our own experience – and vice versa: moral vision enlarges its interpretative scope as tradition and personal discovery or response criticize each other.

This returns us to the 'narrative' dimension of ethics mentioned earlier. In a variety of ways (some of which I see and some of which I can only suspect), what I can do depends on what I have done and what has been done to me; and what I now do limits what I can see or do in the future. This is the context in which willing occurs. There are no blank states, no neutral perceptions leaving the will in a vacuum. And if this is true, moral maturity must involve a significant element of the passive or receptive – which Cupitt seems so to deplore.[20] It requires acceptance of our finitude, of the truth that what I can desire or determine is limited – by individual and corporate history, by society, by the possibly injured or diminished psyche, by the mere fact of being a body. Acceptance of this sort, acceptance of what Simone Weil calls 'necessity', does not mean the abrogation of action, nor even the passing of a *morally* complaisant judgment on the way things are. It is simply to begin the purgation of fantasy in our moral life by grasping that consciousness is not self-created and therefore will cannot be a straightforward absolute.

II

Cupitt does not, on the whole, write nonsense, and it would be unjust to ascribe to him the sort of fantasies about the will which I have castigated. His concern is to rule out servility and naked eudaemonism in ethics, and it is a proper concern. But it is essential to ask whether the sub-moral is to be excluded only by a massive reconstruction of what we commonly mean by the moral itself, in such a way that morality is sharply divorced from vision and desire only to be wedded to *power*. The risks of this over-compensatory reaction in Cupitt's work will already have emerged; but they can be most clearly illustrated if we look at the vexed question of 'heteronomy' in ethics, a major concern of *Taking leave of God* in particular. Cupitt presents this fairly clearly in terms of a conflict about power. He will describe the prophetic experience as one of 'being summoned by an alien and almighty commanding will',[21] and contrast this with the recognition of moral law as 'autonomously authoritative', to be 'imposed' only by myself on myself.[22] Heteronomy is fundamentally opposed to disinterestedness, and so to the 'higher consciousness' at which the moral life aims.

But the difficulty with all this (a difficulty skilfully detected and pursued by Keith Ward in his response to Cupitt)[23] is the confusion which it entails between (i) the formal or 'grammatical' observation that moral discourse is autonomous in the sense of being irreducible, (ii) the substantive assertion that moral behaviour is only genuinely moral when arising from an autonomous consciousness generating its own values. It is quite possible to say 'Moral judgments are not the same as and don't depend on considerations of a non-moral kind (success, self-preservation, social harmony, etc.), they are what they are – like artistic judgments, they are concerned with matters not quantitatively measurable' – and at the same time to say, 'The moral standards I invoke are real or valid independently of any particular person's adopting them.' Of course it is extremely hard to say exactly what this latter statement means. 'Moral facts' is an uncomfortable expression, and few modern writers have made themselves wholly clear on what 'moral realism' might involve.[24] But the force of the statement is that moral language is not *formally* 'about' my state of mind or will: moral judgments and goals can rightly be specified in terms not reducible to desired states of mind, and moral pressure can rightly be characterized as something not simply generated from within.

One of the important functions classically fulfilled by language about 'the will of God' in Christian ethics (or the *dharma* in the Indian traditions, or even the historical dialectic in Marxism) is that it expresses in morality the need for detachment from the primacy of interest or appetite and for avoidance of an obsessive concern with the condition of my will. Choosing to obey or conform to or be faithful to a vision of the moral world may involve a choice to be a certain sort of person. But choosing to obey, etc., *for the sake* of being that sort of person is a good deal more ambiguous. I may commit myself to a particular vision, 'not knowing where it will lead' – meaning by that that I recognize the danger of undermining moral and spiritual life by picturing in advance what sort of person I should like it to make me. 'Religion *has* to give one wit, levity and command', writes Cupitt.[25]

Why? If this is true, 'religion' has signally failed to function in the lives of rather a large number of allegedly religious persons, from Jesus in Gethsemane to a good many inhabitants of geriatric wards and mental hospitals. It is conceivable that exposure to a certain kind of moral vision might in practice be ruinous; certain forms of religious and moral life are capable of making different people both more intensely human and rather less than human (the problem of Judas has something to do with this). Yet this cannot provide a *moral* reason for refusing commitment.

Moral action is not a tool for the production of certain sorts of consciousness. 'Morality may call a man at any moment to surrender the most promising avenue to his own moral perfection':[26] the pressure of vision may lead us, 'divert' us, into compromising and unclear areas – politics, administration, the ordained ministry of the Church – because it illuminates needs and calls to which we can only respond by jeopardizing in some measure both our own honesty and our freedom (as we presently see them). But if my moral concern is with the production of an 'autonomous' consciousness, a disinterested will, the already agonizing choices involved here become still more complex. We should need to speak of being detached from our own detachment, disinterested in our own possible interestedness, and so on. In fact, by a circuitous route, we return to just that absorption with the fascinating twists and turns of the ego which Cupitt wishes to reject. He quotes with approval Goethe's (and Spinoza's) dictum, 'If I love you, is that your concern?' and insists that disinterested love does not seek to 'change its object'.[27] Yes, in the sense that love may persist independently of its *achieving* anything. But if there are finally no moral goals outside the self or the will, the definition of disinterestedness becomes very problematic. Cupitt's position sounds uncomfortably like saying that the meaning of any 'moral' action I perform is provided by its relevance to an ultimate normative state of will or consciousness. All ostensibly external ends (feeding a hungry person, attempting to change a government by some sort of political action, sexual fidelity, or what have you) are instrumental to the development of 'higher consciousness'.

If this is so, a good deal of confusion is introduced into the business of constructing orders of priority among possible courses of action, or even reflecting on the choice between action and inaction. But the most tangled knot comes in seeing the disinterestedly free state of consciousness or will as the keystone of moral intelligibility. It makes sense to say that one struggles not to let choices and goals be determined by selfish, consoling or indulgent considerations. But if *disinterestedness* is itself the goal, if there are not goals beyond the self, how do we distinguish this from an ultimate narcissism, from the kind of elevated eudaemonism Cupitt occasionally lets slip?[28]

Given the pressure of vision, moral action can take on the character of witness; the imitation of God in Christ, or fidelity to the *dharma*, suggests an ideal moral condition of 'transparency' to an independent truth, whose beauty may attract and bring pressure upon others. This is the primary sense (for instance) of the obedience of Jesus to the Father as presented in the Fourth Gospel.[29] But this represents a moral/spiritual attitude whose focus or object is never the state of the self; it is a condition of attending simultaneously to the vision that draws us and to the particularities in which it must be worked out, the obstinate contingent realities of the world about us. Disinterestedness can only issue as a by-product of the moral life: as a goal in itself, it cannibalizes all other goals, and enjoins that we attend to ourselves (including our possible future selves).

It is to escape from this trap that Cupitt appeals to the language of religion. He is, in fact, fully aware of the limits of moral possibility, and of the dangers of fantasies about the ultimate consciousness to which we aspire.[30] The value of religion, for him, is that it expresses the authority of the moral ideal *independently* of its being achieved by me or anyone else.[31] 'God' personifies a fully realized spirituality, awareness and liberty, the ideal spiritual state. He (or it) is to be sought and longed for quite irrespective of my fate or my chances (realistically speaking) of 'reaching' him.

The idea is that this allows us to represent disinterestedness as a moral goal without landing us in the impasse of seeing it as a goal for any individual. But I am not sure that this *does* work as a way out. There are, after all, no such things as states, spiritual or otherwise, without people or affairs being 'in' them. If we talk of a state of consciousness, as our last end, we are still speaking of a goal for a real or possible *self*. To say 'God is to be loved for his own sake' and mean 'the state of absolute spiritual liberty is to be desired for its own sake' does not solve the problem of how we may disinterestedly pursue purity of heart. We know perfectly well (according to Cupitt) that there are no moral constraints external to the will, and so no moral goals external to the self. In the last analysis, we shall still evaluate our acts and choices according to how much nearer they bring us to 'divine consciousness'; we are still acting *for the sake* of our own purification.

Cupitt in fact accepts that disinterestedness best makes sense when moral striving is provided with an imaginative focus beyond our present self-consciousness. But how can this be effective when such a focus is acknowledged to be simply a fantasy of what I might in principle be?

Cupitt insists that only by way of the disinterested consciousness do we become capable of self-giving love;[32] but this does not really resolve the difficulties. We have seen that this love is the 'concern' only of the lover – i.e. it is primarily, once again, a state of the deified will. It may represent an almost unimaginable kind of selfhood, 'almost like egolessness',[33] yet it is still only imaginable *as* a form of selfhood. There is a risk of love itself being implicitly converted into narcissism if we so stress its role as one of the necessary components of the divinized consciousness and detach it wholly from heavenly and earthly objects, from *relatedness* or intentionality. Cupitt evidently considers the classical theistic language about God's self-sufficiency and self-love to be a 'coded' description of the detached condition for which we seek. But a more traditional Christian might want to say that this language has actually worked in theology as a way of blocking off the aspirations of finite consciousness to aseity or 'self-creation', not as a way of feeding them; and also, even more importantly, that classical Christianity has always qualified the pure Aristotelean doctrine of God as the object of his own contemplative love with the trinitarian conception of God loving himself as 'other' than himself, the idea that God's love is itself a giving and a receiving.

The trouble is that Cupitt's scheme renders the idea of God almost exclusively *functional*. 'God' is introduced into moral discourse as a rhetorical device to break the impasse of a threatened solipsism – though how exactly this is to be done if we *know* the word is such a rhetorical device, I do not know. 'God' is there in order to facilitate the 'purification' of my consciousness. Thus those traditional expressions which are clearly of some importance to Cupitt – 'for God's sake', 'for the love of God', *ad majorem Dei gloriam* – lose their real sense and role. Their normal use is as *final* or irreducible terms in any discussion about the reasons for action; if they are admittedly coded ways of saying, 'in order to become a certain kind of self-aware person', their essence is gone. The German Catholic philosopher, Robert Spaemann, sums it up admirably: 'An interpretation of the idea of God in functional terms ... which thinks of God as good for something, annuls the very concept of God. That for which God fulfilled a function would be greater than God. Either something is good for God, and functions are prescribed by God, not fulfilled by him, or one should not speak of God at all.'[34]

Insofar as this is true of Cupitt's use of God-language, I believe his account of religion is profoundly irreligious. I have suggested so far that he (at least) flirts with a view of the will which is dangerously coloured with Promethean fantasies; and that his discussions of heteronomy and disinterestedness confuse formal and material considerations and lead him back to the kind of self-obsessed scrupulosity which he claims to repudiate. 'God' comes in to break the solipsistic circle; but God is no more than a final device of the will for its own salvation. Paul Ricoeur memorably says that, in religious and moral reflection, 'We too often and too quickly think of a will that submits and not enough of an imagination that opens itself.'[35] But to start from here, with some kind of interweaving of the moral and the aesthetic, is to put many of Cupitt's questions into a very different perspective. It suggests that a God conceived as independent of my will need not represent a rival claimant for power, a Feuerbachian diminution of human spiritual stature. My most fundamental difficulty with Cupitt is the predominance in what he writes of a rhetoric of power: if we are to avoid seeing ourselves as puppets of the divine will, it seems, God must become the tool of the finite will. However, to explore this problem more adequately, we must look in more detail at what Cupitt has to say directly about God and spirituality. To this we shall turn next.

III

The fourth chapter of *The world to come* offers an intriguing analysis of the common religious use of the word 'God'. It designates: (i) 'the Ineffable', the sum total of what in the universe remains (and will remain?) unknown to us; (ii) 'the Ideal', the personification of the spiritual requirement in terms of an achieved reality; and (iii) the mythological person to whom prayer is addressed, the imaginary interlocutor of *Taking leave of God* ('the invisible companion', 'possibly connected with the bicameral anatomy of the brain').[36] The first of these leaves open the door for some kind of mysticism and what is elsewhere called '(non-cognitive) worship'.[37] The second we have already begun to examine. And the third is a necessary but transitory *praeparatio evangelica* 'for enabling ordinary people to enter upon and participate in the spiritual life'.[38]

The connection between (i) and (ii) is what is set out in the account in *The world to come* of the message of Jesus: we realize the unconquerable dark and emptiness by which we are spiritually and physically surrounded, we realize that our only possible positive response is disinterested morality, with the religious myth as an aid to this. Vision and choice are thus related only negatively; one is as it were a protest against the other. But this rules out a very great deal of what has commonly been thought to be 'religious' response to the world. Kolakowski has argued[39] that to speak of 'the Sacred' at all is to designate 'a special kind of perception' in which the 'moral and the cognitive aspects of the act of perception are so blended that they are indistinguishable from each other . . . It is not the case that the believer separately "knows" that God is Creator and concludes that he ought to obey him (such reasoning being logically illicit, anyway): he "knows" both in an act of acceptance.' Or consider that kind of religious language which speaks of *gratitude* as a motive for the moral or spiritual life (I do not mean that rhetoric which says 'You ought to be good because you ought to be thankful', which is a logical and psychological quagmire): the world is seen as speaking of gift, gratuity, generosity, it evokes praise and celebration, a gratuitous response, and the impulse to act in a way which accords with an attitude of grateful celebration or reverent delight. To refuse to recognize this as religious is surely eccentric.

The reply might be, though, that all this is to make religious faith dependent on seeing the world in one particular *mood* – and one which in fact has all the signs of a comforting illusion. Cupitt is, in contrast, preoccupied with the Pascalian terror of infinite indifferent space. Petru Dumitriu puts it vividly: 'you must imagine the earth returned to its Ice Age, humanity long since dead, life extinguished; and *then* believe in God, if you can, *then* try to love God'.[40] But it is the same writer who insists that joy or gratitude in respect of the order of the world remains, on any showing, something incommensurable with the experience of loneliness, corruption or mortality. To have seen the world as a place to be 'at home' in is not an *argument* for God; but it remains a fact obstinately unassimilable into the contrary vision of the universe as hostile or indifferent. It remains *surprising*, and its oddity is, for Dumitriu, a fundamental element not in proving religious faith and speech but in simply grasping why it should persist at all. Joy proposes a world that can be 'read' as gift, and so remains a question, a challenge, in wretchedness or dereliction – can this too be embraced as gift? There are echoes here not only of Simone Weil on embracing 'necessity' as an indispensable testimony of God's grace (because he permits what is not himself, an order of Godlessness, to exist in its own integrity), but also of Arthur Koestler or Iulia de Beausobre[41] on the paradoxical irruption of joy and world-affirmation in a person under sentence of death.

'Being itself', writes Dumitriu, 'the ensemble of what is given, known or unknown, is our homeland. God is our homeland; or rather: that narrow and slippery region between joy and desolation, that zone which only God can inhabit, is our homeland.'[42] 'It is in this sense that God is our Father, says one of Wittgenstein's entries in his *Notebooks*, for June 11th, 1916.'[43] The allusion to Wittgenstein is interesting. The early Wittgenstein's cryptic remarks on 'mysticism' suggest that, like ethics and logic, the language of religious vision does not express any state of affairs which *happens* to be so. It is, like ethics and logic, one way of seeing the world *as* a world – as interconnected, self-continuous: of seeing things as a whole.[44] God is 'how it is with things in general'[45] – not, 'the way things go', certainly not 'the sum total of states of affairs', but that which enables us to imagine unity in our shared mortal experience, not simply at the level of intelligible communication (like the propositions of logic) but at the level of the meaning or purpose of act and desire.

Here again, we are close to Kolakowski's 'the Sacred', an area of discourse in which acts may be understood and judged according to their relation to the truth of things, as directed or not directed to the manifesting of wholeness and continuity; an area of discourse in which acts can be spoken of as more than isolated happenings. And the later Wittgenstein writes of belief as sustained *passion*, in which we are 'educated' by life itself when driven to a certain depth, as in extreme suffering, for instance: a passion which (it is implied) is precisely a commitment to seeing human experience whole.[46] Most strikingly, perhaps, Wittgenstein compares the 'existence' of God to the 'existence' of colour in the visual field. The question, 'what difference does colour make?' cannot be answered with reference to some particular; and there is no graspable 'essence' of colour abstracted from its role in our perceiving. Its essence is its existence: what we mean by colour as such is established only by the fact of its all-pervasiveness in our discourse. And so with God.[47]

This is not, of course, to imply that God is to be *identified* with some bit of our psychological equipment. That is not how Wittgenstein's examples work; in this case he points to an analogy which enables us to see how the grammar of God-talk operates, to see that it is structurally more like talking about some 'grid' for the understanding of particular objects than talking about particular objects in themselves. As also with – say – a tonal system in music, it is futile to ask, 'What difference does it make?' The answer could only be an unhelpful 'Everything or nothing'. What distinguishes God-talk from the language of colour or of tonality is that the former sets the *whole* business of our knowing and perceiving against the measure of an all-inclusive vision and an all-inclusive affirmation; it is part of the process of coming to love the world-as-a-whole by a growth towards (or into) a perspective like that. *Consenting* to the order of finitude, to limitation and contingency, the endless recalcitrant singularities of things, is (to paraphrase Simone Weil yet again) the only image we could ever have as finite beings of what it might mean for God to create an independent world, to let the world be. It is not a bid for absolute understanding (certainly it requires the risk of choice), nor is it an attitude of passivity or uncritical approbation towards what happens. As a religious interpretation of things, it commits itself, on the basis of the elusive hints we have that we *may* be at home in being-in-the-world, to seeing the complexity or ambiguity or tragedy of the world as possible signs of a radically generative love.

If maturity in religious and moral terms is bound up with consent to time and finitude,[48] this suggests that the proper destiny of the will is to embrace its own inevitable frustration by the order of things, and to find in that frustration the occasion of truthfulness and even hope. But this happens only by that prior acceptance of the world as beauty, as a home, as a stimulus to desire.

'We have to try to cure our faults by attention and not by will':[49] morality follows in the wake of *eros*, consent or delight in the world, the response of longing and affirmation which the will cannot generate out of its own powers.[50] Classical Christian (and non-Christian) speech about God has offered a context in which morality and eros can be united, by proposing that we take with entire seriousness that attitude to the world which we can call contemplative or even (weak though the world is) aesthetic. Cupitt, on the contrary, by placing the contemplative and the ethical in sharp disjunction (the world as cold and indifferent, the will as protest), the Ineffable and the Ideal confronting one another, simply dismantles a fundamental aspect of religious vision as it has commonly been seen. And how do the amputated joints of *The world to come*'s analysis of God-language come together to make possible the response of 'thanksgiving and love' commended in *Taking leave of God?*[51] As soon as the aesthetic and non-voluntarist dimension is allowed a foot in the door, ethics begins to be coloured by 'love of the world'; and a bridge is built back to that vision of the world as expressive of gift which is contained in the doctrine of creation. I am still not quite sure whether Cupitt wants this bridge to be there or not.

The recurring difficulty (which leaves this question so tantalizingly unresolved) is Cupitt's conviction that a God who is other than a function of the will can *only* be an object, an individual with a will in competition with our own. A religious morality, in this perspective, can *only* be prudential, and Cupitt wants to hold on to that strand in the tradition which stresses the *internal* connectedness of ethical behaviour and love of God; they do not 'happen' to coincide. Cupitt interprets this to mean that God can (*must*) have no 'extra-religious reality'.[52] He is not to be spoken of outside our speaking about religious forms of life, he is not neutrally demonstrable, not *there* independently of religious will.

But as in the whole discussion of morality, so here – whether by carelessness or sleight of hand – there is a muddling of formal and substantive considerations. Non-religious folk may use the word 'God', even a scientist of a certain kind may like to play with it,[53] but such uses do not specify or constitute the fully and strictly religious sense of the word (which will involve the 'passionate' aspect to which Wittgenstein alludes). There cannot be religiously acceptable extra-religious *inducements* to be committed to God. But within religious discourse, things are slightly different: the grammar of faith has to do with yielding self-interest to God's glory, with praise, the ascription of worth to what we have no control over. A religious discourse which denied not the extra-religious, but the extra-subjective, reality of God would hardly be intelligible. The element of praise would vanish, and the dimension of gratuity – or even what we might call play. The observance of monastic life, the decoration of the mediaeval cathedral, the nursing of the senile, the lighting of a candle, or even the study of pure mathematics all in diverse ways say something about the potential improvidence of religious devotion. All such actions are radically changed if performed with the sake of intensifying my own spirituality (as they are if performed with the predominant motive of recognition or reward).[54] How are we to characterize them if not with that puzzling phrase, 'for the glory of God'? They are performed not with the motive of winning salvation, not in obedience to a command, but as expressions of the desire and pursuit of the beauty of God.

I suggested earlier on that moral language collapses upon itself when it tries to treat disinterestedness as a moral goal. So too religious language collapses upon itself when it tries to make spirituality a religious goal. Eckhart, Tauler, John of the Cross, Fr Baker and many more unite in denouncing the idea that the goal of the spiritual life is to be more spiritual. To be what it is it must give up reserves and conditions in surrender to the dark purpose of an unknown God: as we have noted, it cannot safely image the condition to which it aspires. God as that to which the silence and abandonment of contemplation is directed abides as a corrective to subtle forms of complacency and spiritual eudaemonism. And so a functional reduction of 'God' to the status of a corrective *designed* as such by the aspiring will simply cannot work.

Cupitt insists frequently and passionately on the unimaginable nature of the spiritual goal and the importance of the death (not just the suffering or attenuation) of the self in face of the 'religious requirement': he is clearly concerned to avoid any simplistic picture of self-improvement as the crowning spiritual goal. The irony is that, in rejecting the extra-subjective reality of God, he has effectively deprived himself of any way of doing justice to his concern. Objectification for him *must* be a repressive and self-alienating mechanism.[55] And this also leads him into an obstinate conviction that those figures who use 'objective' language about God and yet seem to inhabit the kind of spiritual space he himself is interested in *must* be crypto-voluntarists. The obvious case is John of the Cross.[56] It is true that John 'does not give a philosophy of God, nor a theory of man's knowledge of God', but it is simply not true that John reduced faith to a matter of will alone. On the contrary, faith is for him the mode of *understanding* proper to the contemplative life (as love is the proper mode of willing): it is what happens to the *intellectus* when there is nothing particular for it to understand, a trustful directedness towards that wholeness of vision which eludes us. For John, 'meaning' is always elusive and unmasterable, we glimpse it and share it only as we grow in love (hence the significance for him of a renewed vision of creation in the unitive state); nothing could be further from a simple conception of meaning as the fruit of will.

The more consistent a voluntarist Cupitt is, the more he assimilates religious symbolism to the status of tools for the will; the harder it becomes to give a satisfactory account of what has been and might be meant by loving God, and the love or 'glory' of God as a motive for action; and the more religious contemplation comes to seem self-reflexive only. So far from allying himself with the tradition of the *via negativa*, Cupitt is led (despite his own professed concerns) towards a mere evacuation of the really complex problems of moral and spiritual life by discounting whatever suggests an element of response to or exploration of a given. He is so (understandably) eager to repudiate the notion that we can speak 'neutrally' of God, that God could be an object for investigation and intellection, that he leaves no room for any kind of unity between intellect and will, or knowledge and love, and so belittles the significance of vision and consent in both faith and morality. But this leaves the would-be critic with a very tangled set of problems about the reference of religious words; and we need now to pay some attention to the difficulties of 'theological realism'.

IV

If 'realism' is exactly what Cupitt suggests it is, a good many fairly traditional theologians might find themselves uneasy with it. I don't think that anything so far in this essay, for instance, would commit me to a belief that all theological statements accurately depict some states of affairs in another world, that God can be established as an 'objective' entity by neutral enquiry, that morality and spirituality are calculated to earn everlasting repayment, or even that 'eternal life' primarily designates an indefinitely prolonged post-mortem existence. 'Realism' in this sense is an Aunt Sally. On the other hand: I want to say that the grammar of faith is irreducibly intentional and not reflexive, that it is proper to do certain things, irrespective of the comfort and apparent welfare of myself here and hereafter, for the gratuitous love of God, that religious belief and practice are never independent of stimulus, attraction and desire, and that functionalism in the reading of religious symbols is a self-subverting strategy. Is this 'realism'?

Space forbids an extended discussion of the endlessly ramifying problem of reference in not only the philosophy of religion, but logic, the philosophy of science, psychoanalytic theory, and other areas.[57] Critics of realism have often been accused of reducing various realms of discourse to arbitrary constructions, uncontrolled by any external (non-linguistic) constraints. They have defended themselves by pointing out that, while no language can logically state its own relation to what is not language, this need *not* involve us in saying that language is 'only' about language (which is logically just as difficult). We are still able to use the words 'true' and 'false', 'justified' and 'unjustified' intelligibly; but that there is a relation called 'reference' between a word and a determinable object-out-there cannot be maintained. A cautious realist might respond by saying that all we need to know is that language offers *access* to something other than itself,[58] the anti-realist will still object that we cannot 'know' that except within the conventions we have already settled on.

Cupitt gives his readers very little sense of the range of intellectual options involved in this debate. In *Taking leave of God*, he tends to take for granted a simple dichotomy between descriptive-scientific-objective language and symbolic-noncognitive-arbitrary language. In *The world to come* he has become more alert to the difficulties of the philosophy of science, but still assumes that we have a straight choice between simple descriptive reference and the most drastic constructivism. This is neither adequate nor illuminating. The scientific world on the whole shows that it is possible to be at very different points on the spectrum between naive realism and (equally naive?) constructivism and still agree that they work under constraints, that their task is a discipline. If asked whether they thought what they were doing had any relation to 'truth' or 'reality', they might well reply – with some asperity – 'What does it *look* like?' What are disciplines, procedures, conventions of communicating *for* if not to express the answerability of what I do and say to what is outside 'me' as an individual and perhaps even 'us' as a scientific community? Settling the problem of realism may be less important than understanding what a certain kind of life-commitment *shows*.

So I wonder whether our theological discussion is best couched in terms of realism versus constructivism, intellectualism versus voluntarism. If the martyr or the contemplative, Schweitzer, Merton, Maksimilian Kolbe, Mother Teresa, were asked about the relation of their lives and deaths to 'reality', they too might reply, 'What does it look like?' Confessing the objectivity of God may have more to do with this than with the ability to demonstrate beyond argument (how, anyway?) that our theological language refers. The use of claiming that it *does* refer is connected to the need to see it as not just arbitrary or revisable at will,[59] and there may be circumstances in which we speak about its 'reference'. But the question of objectivity or intentionality in religious language is certainly not resolved by such a claim. We need rather to ask what is *shown* in lives purporting to be religious, and in this way to keep open the question (which Cupitt seeks to foreclose) of the relation between meaning and being, the eternal and the contingent.

What if the life of the saint were not just an admirable achievement, but a fitting or harmonious response to 'how it is with things'? We cannot simply or securely 'know' this to be so; but I think some very strange things would be happening to religious and imaginative language if we *never* asked some such question.

In this light, Cupitt's programme risks a disturbing diminution of human possibilities. It does not render disinterested love or martyred witness unthinkable (though it certainly makes problems for the former, as we have seen), but it does rule out a committed use of language about acting for the glory of God. And, although in the history of Christian spirituality, the exponents of the 'pure' love of God have run into inextricable theological tangles, they have witnessed to a need (and a *right*?) somehow to give expression to the idea that God is to be loved whether or not I am 'saved'. Of course this is hopelessly muddled as a theological notion: loving God as he is to be loved and being saved are not separable. But we need some vehicle (however conceptually absurd) to give expression here to the fact that 'I want nothing but Jesus and to see him at peace in Jerusalem' (the prayer of Hilton's 'pilgrim') means something other than 'I want to be a fulfilled autonomous spiritual subject.'[60]

Further, Cupitt (as I have already suggested) is the prisoner of a rhetoric of power. Creative will stands forever over against conditions, givenness (which necessarily means domination); freedom or autonomy over against receptivity and participation (which again means domination and alienation); spirit against nature. The level of participation in our lives, our belonging in a context, our social and natural being, is to be overcome, because it denies us power, 'The work of religion is to celebrate the *triumph* of universal, free and *sovereign* consciousness, *emancipated* from and *lord* over nature'.[61] Faith is thus presented as the enemy not only of belonging but of need – even of finitude, it sometimes appears. No amount of appeal to the necessities imposed by the 'contemporary' consciousness can conceal the fact that this is one of a wide variety of positions emerging from an engagement with post-Enlightenment European thought. To begin from a hermeneutically innocent or 'privileged' belief in the absoluteness of will is not a self-evident starting point; and to treat it as such disastrously isolates religion from those other sorts of humanistic discourse which are prepared to deal seriously with the aesthetic and the imaginative (arts and sciences alike).

Two final points emerge from this. Cupitt distinguishes religion from art as a mode of symbolic mediation because religious symbolism is 'community-building'.[62] What exactly can this mean, in the overall context? Religious symbols are indeed the stuff of community life; but community life is just that realm of belonging, inheriting language, and, with it, ways of perceiving, from which Cupitt seems so consistently to wish to escape – not simply in critical distance as a stage towards deeper engagement, but in some decisive liberation. He returns frequently to the notion of irony, partly as a means of reserving the rights of the private realm. But it remains one of the deep ambiguities of Kierkegaard that his 'irony' is more or less explicitly a flight from the menace of participation, the corruption and bad faith of the public realm. We have to ask how far this traps us in the mythology of a pre-linguistic core of pure selfhood, untouched and unformed by being part of a linguistic community. Irony as a means for removing the barrier between the self and the truth hidden by language and society, a retreat into a reality which the public realm cannot corrupt, is a dangerous – as well as a conceptually difficult – resort. Perhaps we need a deeper level of irony which would enable us to see even the thinker's ironic solitude as a cultural construct – a dialectical irony, slipping back and forth between bland images of participation and seductive, dramatic images of autonomy. Acknowledging our inescapable insertion into community and what some awkwardly call 'linguality' is not automatically to settle for bad faith. It is rather a condition for the necessary realism (in the looser sense of the word) which shows us ourselves as neither wholly finished nor wholly free, as having a body, a language *and* an imagination: a presence to nature and society, *and* a capacity for history and personality.

And last: I have emphasized throughout that Cupitt generally subordinates the contemplative to the functional, and he is quite right to see this as part of the intellectual story of post-seventeenth-century Europe (though not *all* of it). But that intellectual story is part of a wider one, the story of our socio-economic inheritance, of *capitalism*. 'Functionalization . . . involves: Fundamental interchangeability of anything for anything, definition of things in terms of their exchange value, i.e. as commodities, with capital as the standard form of property and planning as the standard form of interaction.'[63] In the functional world, I have meaningful existence as a producer of serviceable and exchangeable goods; my value is my producing capacity, and my liberty is my mastery of it. What I do not produce thus represents a threat to my liberty, and a challenge to extend my mastery.

I am not playing the popular game of reducing a philosophical proposal to its supposed economic base, nor do I think that such an exercise constitutes a decisive refutation. But if we want to *understand* Cupitt, this too is part of the agenda. I have already noted that one of the important questions raised by Cupitt's book is about the kinds of life we value, want to be committed to, or simply want to see continuing as human possibilities; and we may get a better grip on this if we bear in mind that there may be social and political correlatives for Cupitt's theological positions. Whether he would commend or identify with what they imply, I am not sure.

We are, after all, disagreeing about the hopeful or meaningful conduct of human lives in a world from whose day-to-day processes we can draw precious little comfort. We agree in seeing the question of God as something which cannot be settled by supposedly neutral observation, and language about God as something not readily intelligible if treated as description of an individual or object. Part of our difference is, I think, that Cupitt actually cuts the Gordian knot of the 'objectivity' of God, where I should wish to go on tracing its several strands and trying to see *why* it has taken these particular contours. I don't believe, though, that we can dissolve our problems just by an analysis of the supposed diverse roots of the concept of God (we should by now have learned that from the heroic failures of Frazer, Freud and others). And because we are disagreeing about the shape of possible lives, I think there may be more to this than a mere difference of taste. I suspect Cupitt (who is nothing if not a powerful preacher of the way of salvation as he sees it) might agree about that, too.

Notes

1. See Richard Swinburne, *The coherence of theism* (Oxford: Clarendon Press, 1977); *The existence of God* (Oxford: Clarendon Press, 1978); *Faith and reason* (Oxford: Oxford University Press, 1981).

2. See Cupitt's very severe review of Moltmann, *The future of creation* (London: SCM Press, 1974) in *Theology* 83 (1980), 215–16, querying the ontological status of Moltmann's mythological language.

3. Juxtaposed in Don Cupitt, *Taking leave of God* (London: SCM Press, 1980), 8; Kant is Cupitt's authoritative precedent in the moral sphere, Gautama in the religious. See also the valuable but rather inconclusive essay on 'Kant and the negative theology', in Brian Hebblethwaite and Stewart Sutherland (eds), *The*

philosophical frontiers of Christian theology (Cambridge: Cambridge University Press, 1982).

4. W. H. Auden, 'For the time being', in *Collected poems*, ed. E. Mendelson (London: Faber, 1976), 302.

5. Thus *Taking leave of God*, 'Introductory: the spirituality of radical freedom', presents 'internalization' and 'autonomy' as the two irreversible and non-negotiable fruits of the (European) historical process.

6. Don Cupitt, *The world to come* (London: SCM Press, 1982), xiii.

7. Cupitt, *Taking leave of God*, x.

8. Ibid., 149.

9. Ibid., 166.

10. The grounds for the classical Thomist view of intellect's primacy over will; see, e.g., *Summa theologiae* I.80.2 and 82.4. The question is well discussed by Hannah Arendt, *The life of the mind II: willing* (New York: Harcourt, Brace, and Jovanovich, 1978), ch. 3.

11. Cupitt, *Taking leave of God*, 121, my italics.

12. See, e.g., Cupitt, *The world to come*, 49.

13. Ibid., 88–9, 118–20.

14. Ibid., xvii.

15. Nagarjuna, by identifying *nirvana* with the world of appearance (i.e., by denying that they are two separable states for 'reality' to exist in, or that there is something beyond the phenomenal universe) makes it clear that 'voidness' is to be understood as the total interdependence of contingent phenomena: we cannot ever isolate a nondependent stable individual substance. See Nagarjuna's *Dialectical method*, ed. K. Bhattacharya (Delhi: Motilal Banarsidass, 1978), and T. R. V. Murti, *The central philosophy of Buddhism*, 2nd edn (London: George Allen and Unwin, 1960), ch. 9.

16. Cupitt, *The world to come*, 112.

17. A familiar theme in the work of Thomas Altizer; see 'History as apocalypse', in T. J. J. Altizer et al., *Deconstruction and theology* (New York: Crossroad, 1982).

18. On the contrary, it is only in language that 'private' experiences ever become accessible – to us as well as to others. The frustrating inadequacy of language as a whole to produce unimpeded communication (whatever exactly that is) is not a problem comparable to the inadequacy of a *particular* person or group's linguistic skills. See – amongst an enormous literature – D. R. Hofstadter's 'Reflections' on a paper of Thomas Nagel's in D. R. Hofstadter and D. C. Dennett, *The mind's I: fantasies and reflections on self and soul* (Brighton: Harvester, 1981), esp. 413–14. Cf. some of D. Z. Phillips's remarks in *Death and immortality* (London: Macmillan, 1970), 4–10, 14–15 ('Our language is not a poor alternative to other means of communication' – p. 15).

19. This I take to be part of the force of Stanley Cavell's impressive argument in *The claim of reason: Wittgenstein, skepticism, morality and tragedy* (Oxford: Clarendon Press, 1978), parts 3–4, see esp. 309–12, 324–6, 370–83.

20. Cupitt, *Taking leave of God*, 17.

21. Ibid., 85.

22. Ibid., and passim.

23. Keith Ward, *Holding fast to God* (London: SPCK, 1982), ch. 4, 41–9.

24. For one very searching and fruitful recent attempt, see Mark Platts, 'Moral reality and the end of desire', in Platts (ed.), *Reference, truth and reality* (London: Routledge and Kegan Paul, 1980), 69–82.

25. Cupitt, *Taking leave of God*, 14, my italics.

26. J. L. Stocks, *Morality and purpose* (London: Routledge and Kegan Paul, 1969), 29.

27. Cupitt, *The world to come*, 120, 137.

28. E.g., Cupitt, *Taking leave of God*, 161.

29. Powerfully developed in the theologies of Karl Barth, esp. *Church dogmatics* IV/1 (Edinburgh: T&T Clark, 1956), and Hans Urs von Balthasar – see, most conveniently, *The von Balthasar reader*, ed. M. Kehl and W. Löser (Edinburgh: T&T Clark, 1982), 132–5, 162–6, 170–9.

30. Cupitt, *Taking leave of God*, 142–8 and chs 7, 9 and 12 – despite passages like that already quoted from ibid., 14.

31. Ibid., chs 8, 12 and conclusion.

32. Cf. ibid., 101.

33. Ibid., 87.

34. Robert Spaemann, 'The question of the meaning of the word "God"', *International Catholic review (Communio)* 1 (1972), 39. To avoid confusion, it should perhaps be made clear that 'prescribed' here does not mean ordered or imposed *ab extra*: Spaemann is arguing for 'God' being the *determinative point of reference* in debates about value, a point not itself determined with respect to something else.

35. Paul Ricoeur, 'Toward a hermeneutic of the idea of revelation', *Essays in biblical interpretation* (London: SPCK, 1981), 117.

36. Cupitt, *Taking leave of God*, 133; the reference is to the argument of Julian Jaynes, *The origin of consciousness in the breakdown of the bicameral mind* (London: Allen Lane, 1979) – a case whose implications are as subversive for Cupitt's approach to religion as for a more traditional one.

37. Cupitt, *The world to come*, 66.

38. Ibid., 71.

39. Leszek Kolakowski, *Religion, if there is no God* (London: Collins, 1982), 174ff.

40. Petru Dumitriu, *Au Dieu inconnu* (Paris: Seuil, 1979), 76. There is an English translation – *To the unknown God* (London: Collins, 1982) – but I have preferred to make my own versions, as the published renderings are regrettably awkward.

41. See Constance Babington Smith's memoir, *Iulia de Beausobre: a Russian Christian in the West* (London: Darton, Longman & Todd, 1983).

42. Dumitriu, *Au Dieu inconnu*, 65.

43. Wittgenstein's *Notebooks 1914–1916*, 2nd edn (Oxford: Blackwell, 1969), 70 (and cf. 74). These and other passages are illuminatingly dealt with in R. Spaemann, 'Mysticism and enlightenment', *Concilium*, NS 5 (1973), 70–83.

44. See, e.g., 6.45 of Wittgenstein's *Tractatus logico-philosophicus* (London: Routledge and Kegan Paul, 1961), 148–9.

45. Wittgenstein, *Culture and value* (Oxford: Blackwell, 1980), 33, 56, 62.

46. Ibid., 85–6.

47. Ibid.

48. Cf. the excellent essay by D. Z. Phillips, 'Knowledge, patience and Faust', in *Through a darkening glass* (Oxford: Blackwell, 1982), 89–112.

49. Simone Weil, *Gravity and grace* (London: Routledge and Kegan Paul, 1952), 105.

50. Cf. Thomas Aquinas, *Summa theologiae* I.IIae.34.4.

51. Cupitt, *Taking leave of God*, 82.

52. Ibid., 9, 10, 96, etc.

53. A familiar example is Einstein's 'God does not play dice.' Is this a religious utterance or not?

54. Cf. David Lodge's witty characterization of the problems faced by a traditional Catholic in acquiring a plenary indulgence – *How far can you go?* (London: Secker and Warburg, 1980), 8: 'But there was a catch: You had to have a "right disposition" for the indulgence to be valid, and a spirit of calculating self-interest was scarcely that.'

55. On the fallacy of seeing all objectification as alienation, see Nicholas Lash, *A matter of hope: a theologian's reflections on the thought of Karl Marx* (London: Darton, Longman & Todd, 1982), 83–4, 180–6.

56. Cupitt, *Taking leave of God*, 138–9.

57. A good guide to the state of the debate in some areas is Platts (ed.), *Reference, truth and reality*; on the problem of psychoanalysis, see, e.g., Roy Shafer, 'Narration in the psychoanalytic dialogue', in W. J. T. Mitchell (ed.), *On narrative* (Chicago: University of Chicago Press, 1981), 25–49.

58. The expression 'epistemological access' is used by Richard Boyd, defending a chastened realism in 'Metaphor and theory change: What is "metaphor" a metaphor for?', in A. Ortony (ed.), *Metaphor and thought* (Cambridge: Cambridge University Press, 1979), 356–409.

59. Cf. Rush Rhees, *Without answers* (London: Routledge and Kegan Paul, 1969), 132: 'You might think that I meant that the language about God was just a sort of beautiful pretence; or perhaps that it was just a part of the formality of a ceremony, like after-dinner speeches. I do not mean anything of the sort, of course, and if I wanted to avoid *that* I might say that the language about God certainly does refer to something. But then I should want to say something about what it is to "talk about God", and how different this is from talking about the moon or talking about our new house or talking about the Queen.'

60. See the excellent treatment of desire and detachment in the spiritual life in Alain Cugno, *St John of the Cross: the life and thought of a Christian mystic* (London: Burns and Oates, 1982), esp. chs 3–4. In a quite different key, some remarks by Mary Hesse – 'Retrospect', in A. R. Peacocke (ed.), *The sciences and theology in the 20th Century* (London: Oriel, 1982), 284 – are perhaps relevant: 'These theological virtues may *not* be the conditions which have survival value in the sociobiological sense ... God in his wisdom may have ordained values which are consistent with earthly extinction; to suppose otherwise is to embrace some form of materialism.' There are difficulties with this formulation, but the point is worth pondering: is eudaemonism in respect of the 'higher' human consciousness exempt from strictures like these? This is not designed as a prosecuting counsel's question: I am far from sure how it might be candidly answered.

61. Cupitt, *Taking leave of God*, 156, my italics.
62. Cupitt, *The world to come*, 21.
63. Spaemann, 'The question of the meaning of the word "God" ', 39.

13

Redeeming sorrows: Marilyn McCord Adams and the defeat of evil

In a paper delivered in Claremont in 1991, Marilyn McCord Adams presented an analysis of Maurice Wiles's 1986 Bampton Lectures, and in particular his discussion of the character and activity of God and of the problem of evil.[1] Her overall critique of Wiles is full of interest and deserves consideration in its own right, but there are two areas where I find her paper unsatisfactory in terms both of philosophical analysis and of moral adequacy to the question of suffering – especially the kind of suffering she describes as horrendous, suffering that gives reason to doubt whether the sufferer's life as a whole can be regarded as a 'good' for him or her. I intend to look first at the whole matter of how evil, especially of the extreme kind discussed, might be understood as offset or defeated in the general economy of the universe, then at the concepts of divine action invoked to underpin the thesis of the paper.

There are evils 'on which traditional Free Will and Big Picture theodicies founder', not merely because the evils in question are too frequent or widespread, but because they are too *intense*. 'I have tried to articulate this intuition,' Adams says,

> by identifying the class of horrendous evils as evils participation in which (either as victim or as perpetrator) constitutes *prima facie* reason to doubt whether the participant's life can (given their inclusion in it) be a great good to him/her on the whole ... Such evils constitute *reason* to doubt whether the participant's life can be worth living, precisely because it is so difficult humanly to conceive how such evils could be overcome. My own view is that horrendous evils exhibit such a disproportion to any and every package of created goods that only appropriate relation to the incommensurate goodness of God could overwhelm them.[2]

I take this to mean that there are evils such that, after enduring them, the sufferer's sense of worth and hope is so damaged that no particular experience of the finite world could restore it. And, as the argument develops, it seems that 'appropriate relation' to the divine goodness is to be conceived in two ways. From the perspective of the onlooker, such evil is defeated by being placed in a broader context, in which the divine self-identification with mortal suffering in the person of the incarnate Word demonstrates that God 'honours' the experience of any and all human suffering by being present in it. Theologians of different persuasions, she argues, whether process thinkers, Chalcedonians, fellow travellers with Wiles, or mystics, may speak in different ways of God's identification or intimacy with human suffering.

> Outdistancing the Stoics, Christian theologians could consistently claim that the *facts* of such identification and/or intimacy, *whether or not they are recognised by the created participant in horrors*, constitute an immeasurable honour and endow the worst that creatures can suffer, be, or do with great positive meaning, and defeat both the concrete and symbolic negative value of such conditions by integrating them into their relationship with God, which is of immeasurable symbolic value.[3]

From the perspective of the sufferer (who may have no access to this perspective of 'symbolic defeat'), there must be a concrete defeat, consisting in a promised post-mortem beatitude, where the incalculable excess of divine goodness over any and all experience of pain obviates any concern over an uneven distribution of finite goods. The generosity of God is 'incommensurate' with the need or injury of a finite sufferer, and can therefore never fall short of the capacity to restore a full sense of worth and hope.

I

My first worry is over these notions of proportion and incommensurateness. In so far as they have a natural home, it is in the realm of a certain kind of aesthetics; and this tends to slant the way in which the issue is considered, privileging the observer's point of view. If we speak of 'proportion', we seem to be presupposing an ideal state of relation between elements of our experience: just so much of this, and no more.

And this in turn implies that it would be sensible to speak of a proper or fitting quantity of suffering in a life, the sort of amount that could be offset without too much trouble and integrated within an overall story that came out well, that did not leave too many moral loose ends. Now I know that those who use the language of 'disproportion' here are not explicitly committed to anything quite so crude, and that their aim is to register the fact that there are kinds of suffering so intensely destructive that we cannot imagine a process whereby they could be healed and lived with. There is a difference between even the worst attack of toothache and the memory of twelve years of continuous sexual abuse as a child. But is the language of 'proportion' the right one for this distinction? That is to say, is the relation between destructive and constructive experiences properly conceived as one in which a certain quantity of the one balances a certain quantity of the other?

The situation is more complex, surely. As Adams recognises,[4] people respond in widely diverse ways to what happens to them: 'one bears easily what crushes another'. But this ought to suggest that we abandon the pseudo-aesthetic mode in talking about such matters. What makes an experience bearable for one person and the final and intolerable blow for another is, of course, in large measure what they have been made by previous experience. That is to say, we cannot take 'experiences' as psychological atoms that can be assessed on a scale of proportionateness to each other and to an imagined whole. There is, philosophically speaking, no such thing as 'an' experience, capable of being unproblematically isolated and assessed. Rather, our interaction with what we do not choose or control, our environment, develops and modifies what we sense and say of ourselves; and we do not know in advance what a new stage of this interaction will do to our linguistic and narrative construction of who we are. We do not know what it might be that would silence or paralyse the whole process of self-construction to the point where we had no desire or energy to continue to 'present' ourselves to ourselves. Nor can we easily say what could or would restore this. In small measure, most of us recognise the impossibility of correlating 'experiences' when we are in a state of extreme pain or unaffected delight. The Roman general at his triumph had his slave at his shoulder to whisper, 'Remember you are human', but it is hard to imagine what strictly affective difference this might make. And all this, I take it, is what Wittgenstein wanted to draw our attention to in saying that the world of the happy and that of the unhappy were not the same world.

This should in turn make us cautious about accepting too hastily the conclusion that no finite outcome could heal the effects of appalling injury. It must be emphasised that there is and can be no way of theorising this without blandness and dishonesty; but I am concerned that the notion of humanly unhealable hurts should not be used as a device to bring in the need for divine (unmediated?) consolation. Just as we cannot tell what experience of suffering or humiliation will destroy the hope of an apparently serene person (it may be something which, because of deeply buried personal history, has a significance utterly obscure to the observer, something that may look relatively slight to anyone other than the subject), so we cannot simply state that 'horrendous' evil resists all finite outcomes for good. Towards the end of *King Lear*, a play that deliberately invites us to look at extremes of suffering and the arbitrary way in which they are both inflicted and resolved or accepted, Lear imagines for a moment that his dead daughter is alive:

> She lives! if it be so,
> It is a chance which does redeem all sorrows
> That ever I have felt.[5]

Leaving aside the (useless) question of whether Lear's experience counts as 'horrendous', the point is that the bare fact of Cordelia's survival is being regarded as an adequate element in healing a memory of acute suffering. The question of whether it is 'proportionate' to the suffering is not asked and could not be answered. But the way in which the whole matter is treated here should remind us of the incalculable elements in talking of injury and restoration. Let me take another example from the literary imagination: Robertson Davies's novel, *World of Wonders*,[6] describes the life of a master conjuror, a man whose adult career has been a triumph of sophisticated illusion – the illusions of his trade, and the magnificent fiction of his professional autobiography and public persona. We are allowed to hear from him his true autobiography, as related to a group of friends and colleagues; and it is a record of the 'horrendous' that makes very painful reading indeed. He is abducted as a child from his village in rural Ontario by a drug-addicted paedophile who works in a travelling circus (the 'World of Wonders' of the title), and for the whole of his childhood and early adolescence is a virtual slave to his kidnapper; he is forced to spend endless hours imprisoned in a mechanical figure that is part of the circus entertainment, manipulating its works; he has no life outside the sad troupe of minor criminals and inadequates that make up the circus, and, of course, he continues to be routinely abused by his original captor. Now what could we say about a 'package of created goods' adequate to make of this a bearable story? The reader (and the listeners to the story in the book itself) will be inclined to say that this is a triumph of evil; but Davies does not let us get away with any simple moralisings. Magnus, the conjuror, has created a life that is for him worth living, as a result of a wide range of events, interior and exterior. Is he a 'whole' person? In a number of important ways, no. Yet it would make no sense to say that the appalling evil of his childhood experience could be touched only by the direct hand of God.

I do not quote these examples to imply that 'horrendous' evils needn't be as bad as they seem; far from it. My problem is with the calculus of good and bad experiences suggested by the language of proportion, a calculus that appears to be a long way from what happens in the ways people attempt to make sense of their lives. As I said earlier, such talk privileges the observer's standpoint, turning the question of how evil is to be lived with into the question of how a satisfactory object can be constructed. While there is a long tradition, going back at least to Augustine and Plotinus, of discussing the question of evil in aesthetic terms, we ought, I believe, to be suspicious of the whole discourse in so far as it makes the problem more mine than the sufferer's and misconceives the nature of 'experiences'. I do not see how there can be a calculus of values for discrete experiences that would allow the observer/theorist to assess the worthwhileness of a life as a whole; and I do not believe that the subject whose suffering is under discussion will naturally think in such terms. Even in aesthetics, the language of balance or proportion is massively more complicated than the rather odd observation on appreciating a painting in Adams's paper suggests. Adams draws on an argument by Roderick Chisholm in order to make a distinction between

balancing off (which occurs when the opposing values of mutually exclusive parts of a whole partially or totally cancel each other out)

and

defeat (which cannot occur by the mere addition to the whole of a new part of opposing value, but involves some 'organic unity' among

259

the values of parts and wholes, as when the positive aesthetic value of a whole painting defeats the ugliness of a small colour patch).[7]

In a note, Adams qualifies her agreement with Chisholm:

> In my judgement Chisholm is wrong to make defeat and balancing off *exclusive* relations: for example, the ugliness of some square centimetres in a Monet painting might be both balanced off by a greater number of pretty square centimetres and defeated by the aesthetic value of the overall design of the painting of which they are integral parts.[8]

I can make no sense whatever of the notion that we evaluate the overall aesthetic quality of a work by balancing its 'ugly' and 'pretty' [*sic*] parts. Why should we call an isolated square centimetre of a Monet painting 'ugly' (and what on earth are we doing looking at square centimetres, anyway)? What is it 'ugly' *as*? It isn't meant to be a painting in its own right, and has no existence simply as a square centimetre in the abstract. By what imaginable criteria could we make any aesthetic judgement at all about it, and why ever should we want to? In fact, exactly the same problem arises here as with the notion of discrete things called experiences; the inadequacy of the language in the aesthetic sphere should already be alerting us to the inadequacy of the whole of this sort of aesthetic analogy.

It will be clear by now that I am not happy with the idea of 'symbolic defeat', to the extent that it still stays with the observer's perspective. If we look at what Adams says about the symbolic defeat of evil by way of God's identification with the experience of human suffering, we find this expressed pretty clearly: the fact of God's presence in suffering, whether or not the sufferer is (or could be?) aware of it, gives incalculable meaning or positive value to suffering because it constitutes the suffering in question integral to a relation with God. This is rather sketchily put, but it deserves some unscrambling. I take it that the point is something like this. God in Christ assumes not only humanity in general but humanity specifically in its vulnerability. Because the life of God incarnate is worked out, articulated, in a human biography in which acute physical and mental suffering occur, such suffering cannot be held to be of itself an absolute obstacle to perfect and conscious union with God; indeed, it may seem as part of the concrete working out of God's will, not in the sense that God actively wills particular sufferings, but because the way in which sufferings are endured be-comes an aspect of the way in which the love and generosity of God are made concrete and historical. So far, I shouldn't want to disagree. It is the next stage that seems to me problematic. Here, it appears, we are invited to draw two doubtfully warranted conclusions. There is first the notion that God might be said 'literally' to experience whatever agonies human beings endure and, second, that the experience of pain can be a moment of identification with the 'inner life of God'.[9] While these are only possible options for the theologian, as presented in Adams's paper, they are clearly meant to bear some apologetic weight. The first is puzzling on two counts: we need an extra argument to say that because God in some sense suffers in Jesus Christ, God suffers in (presumably) the same sense in every finite intelligent subject; and, following on from that, to say that God literally suffers everything that we suffer founders on some very obvious problems, such as the fact that God is not a historical or material agent. While we may say as much as we like about divine knowledge of and compassion for our pain, the one thing we cannot say without either trivialising our talk of God or departicularising our talk about human suffering is that God endures human pain exactly as any human subject does. I shall come back later to the wider question of how we should speak of divine action (and passion), but for now wish only to register a grave objection to the imprecisions and potential nonsense involved in taking these proposals as they stand.

As for the second conclusion, this also seems to founder on two serious obstacles. It risks (once again) treating experiences as isolable units: x has experience e, God also has experience e, therefore God and x share a single experience; for God, experience e is part of an indivisible life of bliss, so for x, experience e can also in principle be integrated into a life of bliss. This ignores the point made a little while back, about experience's location within an evolving story of self-awareness and self-presentation. It also leaves open the question of how the integration moves from being a potentiality to being a reality for the subject. Can the affirmation of the possibility alone of integration or the conferral of meaning serve even for the observer as an adequate account of the 'defeat' of an evil whose problematic nature lies precisely in the injury done to a subject? The added unclarity of saying that suffering can be ('literally' again) an insight into the inner life of God should be noted: is this claiming that suffering becomes intrinsic to being divine? That would be an eccentric conclusion, both in terms of the arguments actually presented here, and in terms of the ways in which classical Christology, up to the end of the Middle Ages, laboured to avoid any account of the union between God and humanity in Jesus that licensed a direct ascription of suffering to the divine person of the Word *qua* divine. But that is an issue that would lead us far afield. What remains obscure to me is how any of this argumentation justifies talking about symbolic defeat. The involvement of the incarnate Word in suffering, in traditional Christology, most emphatically allows us to say that it is possible to interpret one's suffering as not only compatible with but intrinsic to one's own unique living-out of the calling to realise God's likeness in the flesh. But this surely, as an interpretative resource, depends on acts of interpretation, themselves dependent for their specific possibility upon the history of the subject of suffering, the linguistic resources available, the images opened up by the tradition in which he or she lives, and so on. The passion of God incarnate is certainly a given for the Christian, a central point of reference and critique; among other things, it challenges any account of divine action that simply assimilates it to the supremely successful exercise of power as normally understood, and warns us that we shall find more to say about God by talking of vulnerability than by talking of the unqualified triumph of a sort of individual will over recalcitrant circumstances. But this is not to authorise fantasy about the 'feelings' or 'experiences' of God (it ought not to be necessary to underline the absurdity of this). Nor is it to produce a theory that allows us to believe that all forms of destructive evil will be 'overcome' simply in virtue of the direct proximity of the divine life to them. The passion of Christ, as an inexhaustible resource of possible meaning and healing, is one thing; I cannot see that it can be generalised into a universal principle that confers value on suffering irrespective of the sufferer's own account.

The discussion thus slips over into discussion of 'concrete defeat', with Adams arguing that

> Christian religion usually advertises divine goodness to created persons as guaranteeing them lives that are great goods to them on the whole and in the end – along concrete as well as symbolic value-dimensions. If symbolic defeat of horrors is to be achieved via integration into the creature's relationship with God, Christian religion has preached how 'the sufferings of this present life' will resolve into incomparable joys of recognised beatific intimacy with a Heavenly Lover.[10]

Once again, I want to distinguish two phases of the argument, the earlier of which I can understand, the latter of which I find unacceptable and doubtfully intelligible. For the subject, symbolic defeat is not enough; thus we must think of further concrete experiences that will restore the sense of worthwhileness to a scarred life. As we have seen, we should not leap to the conclusion that nothing but divine presence without mediation will do this job. But it is perhaps reasonable to say that, given an unlimited time scale, more and more possibilities arise for developments in what I have called the self-awareness and self-presentation of a subject, such that there would at least be resource for healing. If theologians speak at this point of the significance of post-mortem existence, it is not to justify or explain suffering, but to try and imagine a context ample enough for the subject of profound injury to grow into a different kind of self-perception. Such contexts exist in our ordinary experience, in therapeutic relationships, new kinds of communal life, and the sheer unpredictable range of stimulus that might or might not effect a transformation. For those whose death cuts them off from any such possibilities, theology can only point to its fundamental belief in a God who is faithful and eternal, and say, 'if there is hope, it lies there'. If it knows its business, it will not want to go much further. But even if we allow such a minimal appeal to the post-mortem dimension, what we have to say is that the subject remains what he or she has become as a result of the experiences of this life; the possibilities that lie open are defined by a particular history – as they would be in a 'normal' therapeutic situation. Otherwise, we should have to suppose that the post-mortem identity had suddenly ceased to be the identity constructed by this history and no other. This would resolve the problematic nature of destructive evil by a kind of eschatological dissolution of the particular subject as such: in the light of eternity, the suffering of the abused child or the victim of torture is no more 'difficult' to heal than that of an academic who fails to get the job they wanted or a theatrical producer whose grant from the Arts Council has been halved.

I don't think this will do. What I am not clear about is whether this is what Adams is really proposing. I can see the point of saying that no one is going to 'grudge' the different length of time it has taken to arrive at 'concrete defeat' for different subjects, once we are all enjoying the beatific vision. But that is hardly the point. If the love of God is simply an overwhelming tide of 'positive experience' that can be guaranteed to swallow up any and all specific negative experiences, we are left with nothing to say about the particular ways in which suffering damages the self and the particular needs that are to be met in healing it. The 'indifference' of divine love is in danger of becoming an abstraction that ultimately devalues particular histories, and the promise of a specific healing or wiping away of tears is reduced to the promise of a maximally positive experience for all one day. And – to go back a little in the argument – this is also the ground for my unease with the idea that the resolution of earthly pains of a specifically acute kind must lie in an unmediated experience of the divine love – as if the love of God could now be bestowed on an individual subject without the intervention of a 'world'; as if we could make sense of a notion of experience that bypassed the world – our entire environment, our history and language, our essential interconnectedness with other subjects. Here there raises its head the familiar spectre of a kind of philosophical ethos that regards the world as a regrettable barrier between the subject and truth.

But this brief evocation of post-mortem developments is, in Adams's essay, part of a justification for particular acts of (interventionist) divine providence. If 'divine goodness to created persons requires the concrete defeat of horrendous evils within the context of the individual participant's life',[11] we need not only the promise of post-mortem bliss, but also 'particular divine providence':

> Given our record to date, for God to continue a radical non-interference policy would be to turn the alleged divine aim at loving and creative relationships from an intention to a pious hope or idle wish.[12]

God, for reasons that are, I suppose, systematically inaccessible, elects to provide specific experiences of nurture or guidance for some finite subjects; and, because of the ultimate equivalence of everyone's experience of the divine love, there can be no place for resentment that one receives this and not another. In the long run, we all have the same guarantee. Is there, then, any rationale to the divine intervention? We can, it seems, answer this only in general terms, by way of an analysis of human moral agency, which brings out the character of such agency as exercised in 'impaired freedom'. There are no finite 'ideal agents', since we are all moulded by the experience and upbringing we have had: 'our childhood adaptational strategies continue to distort our perceptions and behaviour'.[13] God's agency, in contrast, is incommensurably greater (I know this phraseology is problematic, and shall come back to it shortly); it cannot be in competition with ours, so that its presence never threatens our limited liberty.[14] It thus makes sense to conceive God's agency as one that enables our own in whatever ways are appropriate.

> Just as developmental psychology understands the infant's emerging personality as an interactive product shaped by the characteristics and the many and varied responses of mother and child, so the formation of our identities as spiritual beings and disciples is a collaborative process involving give and take on both sides, but one in which the Holy Spirit functions as an agency-enabler and developer rather than an agency-obstructor or manipulator.[15]

There are welcome recognitions here, notably the more nuanced account of the evolution of a subject and the acknowledgment of incommensurability between divine and human action. However, the argument is developed in a way that actually undercuts these points, especially the latter. It appears that for some subjects the ordinary historical environment for human growth is inadequate: it must be supplemented by divine intervention. What Adams in particular does not make clear in her admirable evocation of the Holy Spirit as enabler of our Christian freedom is how we are to differentiate between the action of God's Spirit in the usual mediating forms in which Christians speak of it and special or additional actions intervening in the processes of the created order: the phraseology of this discussion suggests that part of the 'normal' process of the formation of Christian freedom in us is the presence of specific actions by God the Holy Spirit. So is the Spirit's action an emergency intervention or a normal interweaving of divine agency with the processes of human growth? A little earlier, we have had an appeal to the necessity of particular providence on the grounds that the world's condition is far too gravely askew for finite agency to be able to resolve its difficulties. 'The scope God has already allowed creatures "to do their own thing" has made a mess far too big for human beings to clean up all by ourselves (although it will be our vocation to make some contribution).'[16] This might mean – as an orthodox theological commentator of a broadly Thomist orientation would probably say – that the predicament of fallen humanity is such that the incarnation is required to overcome the evil consequences of Adam's sin; the 'intervention' here would be God's assumption of human nature and the gift of the Holy Spirit in the fellowship of the

Church, Christ's Body. But is this what is being said? It sounds more as if the world is in need of constant divine intervention, especially in a century as bad as ours. If we turn back to the later discussion of the role of the Holy Spirit as enabler, we are left rather in the dark as to whether we are to envisage a regular series of interventions rather than the somewhat different case of a particular worldly history (Israel, Jesus and the Church) being 'read' as communicating transformative divine action. The difference is significant because it affects what we say about divine action; and, at long last, I shall turn to this second area of major unease with Adams's paper.

II

What is disturbing in her account of providence is that it suggests that providential divine action has something of the nature of crisis management – that is, it is essentially reactive. It becomes more necessary the worse things get. The implication is that, as human history evolves, it is quite likely that we shall need increasing supplements of direct divine intervention to save us from even worse disasters than we currently experience. If I understand the drift of the argument correctly, the character of this intervention is to do with the fostering of holy lives, rather than with spectacular modifications in the course of historical events. But the difficulty remains that the world requires, increasingly, more than the 'natural' can provide. I shan't comment here on the strictly theological problems of a view that might imply that the work of Christ is inadequate to the task of renewing the world, or that God will always act to prevent a worst possible outcome of the consequences of human sin and irresponsibility. I prefer to concentrate now on the conceptual difficulties arising from the implied picture here of divine action. While we are told that this action is incommensurable with ours, the gist of the discussion in fact suggests that it is not strict incommensurability at all that is at issue, but incalculably large quantitative difference. The comparison of the distance between God's action and ours to that between parent's and infant's rather suggests as much; but the essential point is that God is conceived as reacting to a situation which we have to suppose God failed to provide for in advance. How else are we to read the curious statements about God stepping in 'after' we have been allowed a certain amount of exercise of our created liberty? We are, in fact, returned to the most crude and basic form of the protest to which theodicy seeks an answer: could God have made a better world? Is the divine action in creating somehow deficient or incompetent? If God has continually to intervene when created choices become (disproportionately?) destructive on a large scale, is the world as originally created incapable of realising the divine purpose? And if God is capable of the endless damage limitation apparently envisaged here, is God not capable of creating an environment where this sort of intervention is less necessary? And so on. But the deeper problem lies in the notion of God's action as resting on punctiliar decisions to step into a crisis, or to intensify our awareness of the 'personal environment' sustained by the Holy Spirit. And this leaves us with a God whose action is not really incommensurable in relation to ours, but very like ours in character, though utterly different in scope. It is action that has to weigh circumstances and assess the seriousness of situations, action involved in decision-making, conditioned by what it responds to.

There is one passage in particular which highlights the problem. Adams mentions Maurice Wiles's suggestion that divine *presence* lures us

> into alignment with God's unifying purpose for the universe without exercising any particular providence at all. Of course, *for all we know*, divine being may be like a complex symphony or painting, so rich that – quite apart from God's *doing* anything in particular – our acts would open us up to some sort of implicit awareness of first one aspect and then another, each evoking novel responses which 'change our lives'. My counter-point is that *for all we know* this is not the case. Nothing in our spiritual *experience* requires us to say so. However defeasible, Scripture and tradition pull in the opposite direction.[17]

This is a startling refusal to engage in any properly philosophical discussion of what is involved in saying that God acts. Plenty of theologians and philosophers have pointed out that, if God is conceived as acting in a punctiliar way, the divine action is determined by something other than itself; likewise if God is conceived as 'reacting' to anything. If either of these conceptualities gets a foothold in our thinking about God, we ascribe to God a context for God's action: God is (like us) an agent in an environment, who must 'negotiate' purposes and desires in relation to other agencies and presences. But God is not an item in any environment, and God's action has been held, in orthodox Christian thought, to be identical with God's being – that is, what God does is nothing other than God's being actively real. Nothing could add to or diminish this, because God does not belong in an environment where the divine life could be modified by anything else. God is the empowering source of anything other than God being real, that is, the ultimate 'activator' of all particular agency. This is the heart of Aquinas' doctrine of God, and it has been given eloquent restatement in David Burrell's remarkable monograph *Aquinas: God and action*.[18] Burrell is particularly good at showing how, in order to speak of God's causal relation to the universe, we do not need to imagine 'an' activity by which some change is effected: we need only point to the fact of dependence ('if it weren't for *a*, there wouldn't be *b*'; or 'the occurrence of *x* in *b* is the action of *a* in or on *b*').

This suggests that the discussion of divine action in both Wiles and Adams is misplaced. We do not have to choose between God acting primitively to create, then acting by suasion or attraction, on the one hand, and God acting to create and subsequently supplementing that action with new actions on the other. God is eternally and actively real – in classical Augustinian and Thomist terms, God is active in knowing and enjoying what it is to be God. In making the world, God neither performs a single and unrepeatable action, nor initiates a series of actions. All we can say is that it is the case that the range of possible ways in which God's being, knowing and loving might be reflected or 'imitated' by beings other than God (that is, beings whose action is not identical with their nature, but who realise or articulate what they are in processes) is actual. We might say that God 'decides' to create, if we like, but we'd better be aware that, while we have no other obvious way of saying that no one and nothing 'made' God create, we cannot attempt to understand this 'decision' as if it were a decision comparable to the ones we make – at particular moments, faced with a range of options. And what creation then means is that the single divine act on which everything depends activates a variety of patterns of action in the differentiated and time-taking system that exists as other-than-God.

How, in such a perspective, do we talk about divine action or particular providence? The answer can only be in terms of the character of the finite system as a whole. If there are moments when the act of God is recognised more plainly than it is in others, or when the subject senses a closeness to the underlying act of God that has the effect of prompting, warning, reassuring or guiding, we are not to think of the fabric of the finite order being interrupted, but rather of the world being such that, given certain configurations of finite agencies, the texture of the environment is more clearly transparent to the simple act of divine self-communication. It is as if, to use a rather faulty metaphor, the created order is a texture of uneven thickness. The flaw in the metaphor is that it could be taken as meaning that the created environment is a kind of obstacle between the spiritual subject and God; and I have already noted the inadequacy of that way of seeing things. But the basic model of a 'timelessly' ordered system, in which the more evident presence of the divine action was not an intervention but the foreordained result of certain finite outcomes, at least allows us to hold off the mythological notion of a God who reacts to circumstances. What I have in mind is, of course, spelled out in one (memorable) way by Simone Weil, for whom divine action is only perceptible when the ego renounces or displaces itself. This is when grace occurs; not that it can be produced by performing particular actions or acquiring certain dispositions, because it is always and necessarily impossible to predict what exactly it would involve in any complex situation for divine action to be more effectively present; nor that the divine activity can be counted on to 'tidy up' any moral loose ends hanging around. Weil would indignantly reject any use of this model of divine action for the production of a theodicy. But she sees the point that, in a different idiom, is fundamental to the classical doctrine of God: if God is not in an environment, God's action can never have the form of an episode intruding into the history of created causality or finite agency. It must not be in competition for a shared logical space (and this is, I suppose, why a theologian like Augustine can so firmly reject a view of miracle that regards it as a direct divine interruption of finite agency, as opposed to an extraordinary realisation of possibilities inherent in finite agency itself; but that is another matter).

This is what is involved in treating divine action as really 'incommensurable' with human (or finite in general). And this is why the alternatives of Wiles's austere limitation of divine action to the bare positing of the finite order and Adams's commitment to the possibilities of multiple interventions represent a false dichotomy. It does not answer to say of the latter option that for all we know it may be the case. We have to do what the theologians of the tradition have always done: to take the undoubtedly punctiliar and anthropomorphic language of scripture and piety in talking of God's agency and ask how it can be read in the light of the doctrine of God to which the system of doctrinal and biblical speech overall points. Since there is at the heart of this speech a conviction that God is that on which every particular depends, the one who creates from nothing, the logic of our discourse about God's action must observe the constraints imposed by the implicit prohibition against describing God as an agent among others. And I hope this can be said without inviting the lazy response that this is an imposition of alien metaphysics on the personalist idiom of the Bible.

Where does this leave us as regards the problem with which we began in this paper? If God's action is strictly incommensurable with finite agency in the way I have argued, we have even less hope of deploying God as a 'balancing' factor in the aesthetic/moral equation that would allow us to judge the final worthwhileness of a sufferer's life. God is never going to be an element, a square centimetre, in any picture, not because God's agency is incalculably greater but because it simply cannot be fitted into the same space. To pursue the Christological issues raised here and elsewhere by Adams, it is like the concern of high scholasticism in particular that the presence of the Word as incarnate in Jesus should in no sense be conceived as 'competing' with the full created subjectivity or identity-as-subject of Jesus. We cannot say that, where 'packages of created goods' fail in the potentiality for healing the effects of unspeakable outrages, we can call on the infinite good of divine attention, involvement and beneficence to supply what is missing. It is simply not that sort of problem, and to treat it in such terms lands us, I have argued, with a dry and philosophically eccentric view of human experience and how identity is constructed by conscious subjects, and with a dubious doctrine of God's agency. I believe we should hold out for genuine incommensurables: the incommensurability of the worlds of the happy and the unhappy, and the incommensurability of God's agency and ours.

This leaves the question of the healing of outrages unresolved, of course. But I do not think that we can properly or intelligibly draw distinctions between evils that are in principle capable of resolution by way of created goods and evils that require nothing less than direct divine response. If my sub-Thomist analysis of divine action is correct, then in any imaginable created order the love of God is actively present in particular configurations of finite causes. In heaven, however we are going to understand that, we perceive (following the insight of a Bonaventure or a John of the Cross) not 'naked deity' but God in ourselves and in all things. Thus the problem of 'offsetting' appalling evil is no different in principle in this world and in the world to come; and the recognition of this, along with the difficulties raised for how we are to conceive the processes of 'self-awareness and self-presentation', should warn us off the whole project of looking for factors to balance and overcome negative experience. Human biography doesn't seem to work like that. The non-'horrendous' evil may be the final breaking point in a long history of the attrition of someone's sense of worth; and the apparently inadequate 'created good', the bare survival of a child, the acquisition of confidence, the triumph of will (deeply ambiguous as that is, as in Robertson Davies's story), will sustain a sense of worthwhileness, of life as a recognisable good. These matters are resistant to any kind of generalisation. But it is this resistance that relativises the whole issue of theodicy. So often, as we are all aware, the problem of theodicy is not experienced as such by those for whom, according to all the discussions, it ought to be an agonising primary question. That it is not a problem tells us nothing that makes it easier to reflect on the suffering of others; it doesn't even make it easier to think about or look at the suffering of those who don't find their suffering a problem. We are brought back constantly, in thinking about this, to the uncomfortable question of who theodicy is being done for.

So much of the language of Adams's treatment, which is far from insensitive to the gravity of the issues involved, like so much of the language of the whole tradition of theodicy, seems to presuppose that the purpose of theodicy is to make the world of human experience capable of being contemplated without despair. The trouble is that, if this really is the agenda, two seductions of the spirit will always haunt the enterprise: either there will be pressure to argue that the situation is not as bad as it seems, or there will be the urge to arrive at a perspective that is in principle not accessible to us, a position where we are not obliged – as here and now we are – to know suffering as unhealed and, often, humanly unhealable as far as we can see (it is always salutary to think of the quantity of human lives, in past ages and our own, totally without access to means of healing or sense-making). Perhaps it is time for philosophers of religion to look away from theodicy – not to appeal blandly to the mysterious purposes of God, not to appeal to any putative justification at all, but to put the question of how we remain faithful to *human* ways of seeing suffering, even and especially when we are thinking from a religious perspective. Part of the task of a good theology and of a candid religious philosophy is, I believe, to reacquaint us with our materiality and mortality. And part of that is the knowledge of suffering as without explanation or compensation – and also the knowledge, of course, that there are unpredictable, unsystematisable integrations of suffering into a biography in the experience of some. But this is to say, I think, that we should be worrying about seeing suffering always in its historical particularity: this, here, for this person, at this moment, with these memories. This might make us pause before ascribing all the world's pain 'literally' to God; for if God is compassionate towards the world, this is not self-pity, but the exercise of that radical love which is attention to the other in its difference, not its kinship; thus in its specificity within the world that is not-God. Being aware of this becomes a morally important matter in a context where love is always in danger of being redefined as natural solidarity (an aspect of this whole area that I have tried to address elsewhere).

In plain English, I suspect that it is more religiously imperative to be worried by evil than to put it into a satisfactory theoretical context, if only because such a worry keeps obstinately open the perspective of the sufferer, the subject, for whom this is never a question of aesthetics, however imaginatively and discriminatingly pursued. What might be called the 'mortal' knowledge of suffering, the knowledge of it as contingent and thus potentially unconsoled, matters not because our intellectual hubris needs bridling (though it doubtless does), but because it insists that certain things are known by 'testimony' – which means by converse, exchange, sociality, by attending to a perspective that is not and could never be one's own. Now in fact, as the philosopher ought to know, this is really an observation about knowledge as such; it is just that some kinds of knowing are less patient than others of reduction to the terms of the ego ambitious for self-sufficiency. And the pain of others is perhaps foremost among such items of knowledge. Thus my earlier insistence on the need to query the observer's perspective here is not just a piece of intellectual squeamishness. I want to insist on this as a condition for religious thinking of any sort, which, if it is serious in articulating the contemplative ideal which I think is fundamental to religious perception and talking, is bound to the task of attention to perspectives that remain irreducibly different – even if that difference entails a self-dispossession and recovery of the self through the other, as for Hegel (I am still convinced that Hegel is a basically Christian philosopher!). The suffering of a historically particular other must be a paradigm for the kind of knowledge that will not allow us to stop listening, because we cannot completely internalise or domesticate it.

In that sense – and that alone? – knowing about suffering might be a way into knowing about God. But this has to go on avoiding the pietistic reduction of such a vision to the idea that suffering is a 'mystery' that teaches us humility, and also the fashionable but, I believe, deeply questionable notion that suffering offers access to the heart of a suffering God. The subject's account of their pain most basically reminds me that the world is a world of differences and so of converse and so of listening. If I learn this, I may have learned a bit of what classical theology wants to say about God – that it is impossible to give God an essential definition or to map God on a conceptual scheme, because what God is, the world isn't. And I shall not know God without acknowledging what my own knowledge is like, historical and situational; so that I know God as supremely what I must listen for and can never domesticate.

Even the best and subtlest of theodicies cannot but seem a strategy for evading most of this. 'Who is it for?' is a question very close to 'In whose presence is it done?' If the answer to that is, 'In the absence of the perspective of the sufferer as subject or narrator', how can it fail to evade – to evade not only humanity, but divinity as well?

Notes

1. Marilyn McCord Adams, 'Evil and the God-who-does-nothing-in-particular', in D. Z. Phillips (ed.), *Religion and morality* (New York: St Martin's Press, 1996), 107–31, discussing Maurice Wiles, *God's action in the world: the Bampton Lectures for 1986* (London: SCM Press, 1986).

2. Adams, 'Evil and the God-who-does-nothing-in-particular', 113.

3. Adams has explained the distinction between 'symbolic' and 'concrete' earlier in the paper: 'Briefly, symbolic value is the value a thing has by virtue of what it symbolises ... Any given action or event, condition or state of affairs may have multiple, sometimes contradictory dimensions of symbolic value (for example, Christian religion sees the cross of Christ, intended as a symbol of shame and degradation by the Roman government, as transformed by God's intentions into a sign of glory). With this we contrast, in a "rough and ready" manner, "concrete" value for persons, which has to do with pleasure and pain, with health, wealth, and material well-being.' Ibid., 114–15.

4. Ibid., 113.

5. *Lear*, Act V, Scene 3.

6. Robertson Davies, *World of wonders* (Harmondsworth: Penguin, 1977).

7. Adams, 'Evil and the God-who-does-nothing-in-particular', 114, referring to Roderick Chisholm, 'The defeat of good and evil', in Marilyn McCord Adams

and Robert Merrihew Adams (eds), *The problem of evil* (Oxford: Oxford University Press, 1990), 53–68.

8. Adams, 'Evil and the God-who-does-nothing-in-particular', 130, n. 44.

9. Ibid., 116: 'While insisting . . . that God could have existed without any creatures at all, Christians might still maintain that God *literally* feels or experiences the *same* pain or agony that we feel, or that what creatures experience as pain or agony are literally visions into the inner life of God.'

10. Ibid., 117.

11. Ibid., 118–19.

12. Ibid., 119.

13. Ibid., 120.

14. Ibid., 121: '[T]he radical disproportion between divine and human agency prevents God from being a member of our moral community, enmeshed in our networks of rights and obligations.'

15. Ibid., 123–4.

16. Ibid., 119.

17. Ibid., 124, referring to Maurice Wiles, *God's action in the world*, 102.

18. David Burrell, *Aquinas: God and action* (London: Routledge and Kegan Paul, 1979).

14

Maurice Wiles and doctrinal criticism

'Doctrinal criticism is the critical study of the truth and adequacy of doctrinal statements.' With this quotation from a highly influential essay by G. F. Woods,[1] Maurice Wiles, in 'Looking into the sun', his inaugural lecture at King's College, London,[2] signalled the opening of his own discussion and development of Woods's programme. This programme he summarizes as including the following:

> Examination of the relation of any doctrinal statement to its historical situation; the analysis of any doctrinal statement into its component parts; investigation of the varying uses of analogy in the various terms employed in any doctrinal statement; distinction of the differing types of proof to which appeal is made; recognition of the variety of ways in which doctrinal statements are combined into systematic wholes; consideration of what point has been selected as the fundamental starting-point of a doctrinal system and for what reason.[3]

The task is clearly conceived, by both Woods and Wiles, on the analogy of biblical criticism; we have lost our innocence in respect of the biblical text, and have learned to look beyond the surface of narrative and rhetoric. We have become sensitive to the varieties of genre and idiom, to the historical interrelation of different texts and portions of texts, to the process by which texts are produced and the social and ideological conflicts they embody and encode. The text tells us both more and less than we thought: more about the history of its own production and about its world of reference, less about what it *purports* to tell us of a distant or relatively distant series of events. A critical reading is one which knows what sort of information to look for. So, it is suggested, with the 'text' of Christian doctrine as well. We must lose our innocence, learn to see what doctrinal propositions really tell us (about the conditions of their production, about what counted as argumentation in the context in which they were produced, what connections between different bits of Christian language appeared natural and obvious and why, and so on), and what they cannot tell us (facts about a transcendent and intangible realm). But the Christian theologian undertaking this task is not trying to dissolve the substance of the believer's central commitment, any more than the biblical critic – properly understood – is a threat to faith. He or she is only pointing out that traditional doctrinal formulations, rooted as they are in social and intellectual milieux that are not ours, cannot tell us authoritatively what they purport to tell us: 'I am not in a position either to affirm them or to deny them; I cannot give any satisfactory sense to them *in that form*'.[4] But the analytic enterprise yields 'insights' about the character of belief and the object of belief, insights which may be profitably brought into conversation with the theologian's 'patient, continuing study of the world around' him or her.[5]

This inaugural lecture exemplifies all that is most attractive and stimulating in Maurice Wiles's work. It says a great deal in a brief space, with complete clarity and an absence of what might be called intellectual tribalism (the sending out of signals by the use of jargon). It both commends and embodies a commitment to honesty, patience, and humility in the study of the evolution of Christian language. It is reticent, for the most part, about its author's own confessional position, yet somehow indicates a paradoxical but perfectly real loyalty to an enterprise which is certainly conceived as being in continuity with the thought and prayer of earlier ages. Its programme has been variously worked out in Wiles's later writings, all of which exhibit the same qualities – rare enough in theology to command much gratitude. For there can be no doubt that Wiles has succeeded in placing on the map of Anglophone theology a set of issues of the first importance, largely by the care and tentativeness of his own style. Anyone now discussing theological method in the British context – to mention no others – will sooner or later have to come to terms with the Wilesian question, a question which might be summarized like this: if, as is surely the case, traditional doctrinal statements make claims about what is actually true about the universe, how do we respond to those claims in an intellectual climate in which they cannot possibly be *legitimated*? This is a different issue, I think, from that of the possible *verification* of religious claims by agreed secular methods: Wiles is not a positivist with a pious gloss, looking for simple, universal proofs. The problem is rather that an examination of the history of Christian doctrine uncovers a bewildering range of criteria appealed to in establishing the validity of credal or confessional statements, few if any of them recognizably resembling the kind of appeals we might now allow in testing the validity of inferences.[6] If this is so, then whatever doctrinal statements tell us, we cannot assume that it is simple information about states of affairs. But (and this is where the paradoxical loyalty comes in) Wiles will have no truck with the idea that doctrines were never meant to convey propositional truths in the first place: he has expressed considerable scepticism about the proposal that we should treat doctrine as 'regulative',[7] seeing in this the prospect of another and deeply corrupting sort of positivism, a passive assent to the *de facto* deliverances of ecclesiastical authority.

The issue of doctrinal criticism is thus a position formally agnostic about the truth-claims of particular classical doctrinal statements – but in practice sceptical or negative. For if a doctrinal statement might be telling us the truth, but we were incapable of articulating any coherent criteria for deciding whether it were doing so or not, the one thing the doctrine surely could *not* be telling anybody would be 'saving' truth. Assuming that any truth which purported to be of decisive and transforming relevance should be capable of being *known* to be true, of being asserted with confidence in its sustainability or legitimacy, the truth claims of doctrinal utterances, in so far as they employ means of legitimation unrecognizable or unacceptable to us, must be at best matters of secondary interest. What is significant now is the experiential impulse behind the doctrinal formulae. In the case most frequently discussed by Wiles – the doctrine of the Incarnation – we can say that the doctrinal enterprise reveals, not the propositional veracity of what it actually claims, but the 'transforming impact' of the life, death, and resurrection of Jesus:[8] as Wiles admirably puts it, the first believers were not

> rationalist theologians, drawing firm deductions from fixed and detailed patterns of expectation; the categories in which it was natural for them to think of Jesus were extended and outgrown by the immensity of the experiences in which they were caught up, and which they associated with him as risen Lord.[9]

The critical study of doctrine, then, delivers two things: negatively, an awareness of the fragility of the epistemological foundation on which doctrinal claims may rest; positively, an enhanced appreciation of the intensity of an experience dramatic enough to produce such extraordinary, strained, and finally unsustainable claims. The impulse is to maximize the status of Jesus so as to ground ontologically the sense of a 'transforming impact'; but the pressure towards such an ontological grounding is not necessarily derived wholly or even primarily from the nature of faith itself. It owes a great deal to factors in the intellectual culture in which Christian faith developed. This point is explored in some detail in the celebrated essay of 1970, 'Does Christology rest on a mistake?'.[10] Here the commitment to Jesus' ontological uniqueness is seen as dictated by prior assumptions about the punctiliar character of the creation[11] and the fall. The action of God and the condition of sinful humanity are taken to be bound up with identifiable episodes in the history of the universe: thus the saving action of God reversing the fall is understood analogously. But the former linkage is mythological – indeed, *fallacious*;[12] thus the consequence is equally an error about logical entailment. Similar readings of the roots of incarnational doctrine recur, though their emphasis is more generally on the effect upon Christian language of current expectations of decisive (punctiliar) divine intervention.[13] I have a strong suspicion that Wiles came to recognize that the way in which the point is made in the 1970 essay is vulnerable to a number of serious criticisms, from the viewpoint of New Testament theology (can Paul's second Adam typology be the source of quite so much and bear so much weight in the argument? and does anyone in the early Christian period actually, concretely, *argue* like this?), and from strict logic (is the linkage of fallenness with a historical fall actually a *logical* question at all, and can we then convict Paul or whoever of mistakes about logical necessity?). None the less, the overall point is clear enough: there are factors quite extrinsic to Christian commitment as such which lead to the confusions of classical incarnational language. The Church may long have 'felt the need to say something more'[14] than that Jesus opens our eyes supremely or decisively to the nature of God's relation to the world, 'illuminating, as no other life, the significance of the whole story',[15] but that feeling rests on a sort of category mistake, the search (prompted by adventitious circumstances) for a clear ontological substrate beneath the naturally exuberant expressions of devotion which emerge in response to what the life of Jesus effects – and which remain quite legitimate in their proper sphere.[16] That there *is* a sort of ontological substrate Wiles is prepared to grant, rather surprisingly;[17] but its relation to the mythological or metaphorical language of the doctrinal tradition is oblique.

This summary does less than justice to a wide-ranging, flexible, and always elegantly expressed case, but I hope it accounts for its main themes. I believe that something like the task identified as that of the doctrinal critic is indeed a proper theological job; but I shall argue in the rest of this essay that Wiles's version of it will not quite do. My queries fall under four main headings. First of all, I have doubts about the brisk assimilation here of doctrinal to biblical criticism. Second, I find the actual definition and categorization of classical doctrinal statements unsatisfactory. Third, I think that Wiles's account of the relation between doctrine and experience contains a substantial *petitio principii*. And finally, I have a question about the whole model of critique and the concept of establishing legitimacy employed by Wiles and a good many others in discussing doctrinal truth claims. If I can at all emulate Wiles's fairness and patience with positions other than his own, I shall be paying him tribute enough.

I

Biblical criticism can operate at several levels, but, for the purposes of the present discussion, I want to focus on two major aspects. At the simplest level, a 'critical' reading of the biblical text is any reading that is capable of discerning things over and above 'surface' meaning; and, in this sense, biblical criticism goes back to the earliest ages of the Church. To read comprehensively and adequately is to know something of how a text works in its setting – to be sensitive to idiom and genre, so that we do not mistake metaphor for literal description or deliberate fiction for reportage.[18] Apparent absurdities are thus removed, and the text is allowed to establish its own world of reference instead of being forced into ours and judged inadequate by standards it does not set out to meet.[19] This is the common coin of patristic and medieval hermeneutics: modern criticism works on much the same basis, though with a far sharper sense of the radical nature of historical and cultural difference. The main point of this exercise, whether in its classical or its modern form, is to make sure that we do not derive from the text information it is not designed to give. The more sensitive we have become to the genre and location of various bits of scriptural narrative (aetiological myth, wisdom tale, catechetical pericope, etc.), the less we shall look for bare documentation – in other words, the more sceptical we become about simply reading all scriptural narrative as historically veracious in the modern sense, though scholars may reasonably differ quite widely over how much history they can recover. Most of the familiar styles of biblical criticism (source criticism, *Formgeschichte*, redactional analysis) assume that this sensitivity to genre is a substantial part of their task, even if it is not the only one.

However, they also have a more complex agenda, which has come increasingly into focus in the twentieth century (though it is anticipated, albeit crudely, by Reimarus, Baur, and others). This is what is sometimes called *Tendenzkritik* – though it might also be seen as *Ideologiekritik*. In whose interest does this text work? On whose behalf is it claiming authority (whom does it legitimate)? Although this has been an element in most modern critical discussion, it has now emerged with far greater clarity in the hermeneutics of liberation theologies – most recently in feminist exegesis.[20] Form criticism, in looking at narratives from the point of view of the needs of communities in specific situations, and redaction criticism, asking about the shaping influence of authorial theologies, both employed the notion of reading with an eye to *Tendenz*; but it has taken the more robust and controversial methods of liberationist hermeneutics to draw out the potential consequences of such reading. A surviving text is a successful text, on the whole – which means that it has served what turned out to be a successful interest. To understand it fully, we need to be aware of what it does not say, what it controverts, what it represses or suppresses. We must do some (potentially subversive) decoding, and we can turn our first-level skills at reading with a sensitivity to idiom and genre into tools for this tougher and riskier task. And while 'first-level' criticism has a pedigree stretching back to the patristic era, this latter style is more obviously the result of the post-Enlightenment challenge to non-accountable authority. Its only classical antecedent is perhaps the view of certain gnostic groups that the Hebrew Scriptures, being written in the interest of the world-creator, repressed and distorted the true history of salvation whose heroes are the serpent, Cain, and so on.

How do these enterprises compare with doctrinal criticism as envisaged and practised by Wiles? As to the former, it is not clear that we can analyse doctrinal statements quite so readily into genres, especially narrative genres. Evidently there are doctrinal utterances that have a loosely narrative form – the second article of the Creed is a case in point – and it is possible to say, as theologians have long granted, that some aspects of liturgical and hymnodic language have to be read in the light of more general and programmatic principles. Since at least the third century[21] theologians have appealed to various kinds of regulative pressure in Christian language reminding us of the risks of anthropomorphism or mythology.[22] As I shall try to show in more detail later on, the *doctrine* of the incarnation in the strictest sense is not identical with a simple narrative of a divine agent embarking on a fresh episode in his biography; nor is it simply a sort of explanatory device to make sense of unusual features in the life of Jesus. It may at times work in such ways, but they cannot be said to exhaust the scope of the doctrine overall or to be determinative for its interpretation. A similar point might be made about the doctrine in Catholic Christianity of a 'real presence' of Christ in the consecrated elements;[23] piety and semi-theological rhetoric deploy a number of images and idioms (the highly materialist imagery of the 'Mass of Saint Gregory' legend or some of the byways of the Grail tradition, the Byzantine language of the descent of the heavenly Emperor borne up on the shields of the angels, like the earthly emperor and his guard at a coronation, the baroque metaphor of the 'Prisoner of Love' in the tabernacle, and so on) which, taken as they stand, offend against any number of wider theological concerns. But neither they, nor indeed the conceptualization of the belief in terms of a specific ontology (transubstantiation), tell us adequately what the doctrine claims and exactly how it works – nor have they been seriously thought to do so by theologians. To put it briefly: 'doctrine' is a text already differentiated, already showing cognizance of its own ambiguities. Criticism here is not a matter of determining on analytic (literary and historical) grounds how to distinguish the information we appear to be deriving (from the 'surface' sense) from the information genuinely available. Our misunderstandings of the propositional content of doctrinal formulae cannot be put down to ineptitude in the reading of conventions with which we are no longer familiar; judgement on the lack of straightforward informational content must rest on other grounds – as indeed is the case in Wiles's 'Does Christology rest on a mistake?', where the procedure is in fact very much *unlike* that of the biblical critic in so far as it looks for a direct error in reasoning, thus questioning the legitimacy of the idiom it seeks to interpret. A better case could be made for the significance of cultural misunderstanding with regard to the alleged association of incarnational language with apocalyptic, where we might reasonably appeal to the inaccessibility of an idiom in arguing to the unintelligibility of a doctrine formulated in its terms; but more would then have to be done to show that the connection between apocalyptic and any statement of incarnationalism was such as to warrant this move. If apocalyptic is an element among others in the formation of the doctrine, an element which can recede without being missed, the argument is less telling. We could appeal to a sense of what *must* have been the initial and determinative impulse, but we are then speculating – and doing so in a way which runs all the risks associated with any search for a *single* explanation of a historical phenomenon.

The second aspect of the critical enterprise offers far better analogues. *Tendenzkritik* of scripture and of doctrine may well run along similar lines; and once again, feminist theology brings the issue into very clear focus.[24] Not only doctrines of creation, fall, and incarnation, but the very regulative principles of doctrinal talk about God (divine aseity and impassibility, in the traditional framework) come under question here in respect of the interests they serve and legitimate. Wiles has had relatively little to say of this kind of *Kritik*, but I suspect that it poses far more serious difficulties for doctrinal traditionalists than the rather nebulous idea that doctrine is a matter for conventional literary-historical decoding. One of the greatest positive elements in the programme Wiles sets out is, of course, the recognition, painfully slow to dawn on theologians, that doctrine really does have a history;[25] and *Tendenzkritik* reminds us further that human history is a history of conflict, the contesting of the power to define situations and mould them accordingly. Doctrine is implicated in power if it is implicated in history.

What we have here is not so much the possibility of misjudging the sort of information offered by a text as the possibility of a reader's failure to derive from the text the information it actually carries, information about its own production and use. And what poses serious questions here for the student of doctrine is much the same point that Wiles makes in a rather different context: it becomes possible to see how factors extraneous to the business of Christian believing itself can shape the argument and direction of a doctrinal tradition. I do not think that there is any simple or general response which would blunt the edge of this sort of criticism. Any defence of the viability of a particular bit of doctrinal language in the face of a strong demonstration of its interest-laden character would have, once again, to argue against the propriety of single global explanations for a start; but that would mean demonstrating in any given case that a doctrinal idiom or formulation is 'underdetermined' by the interest it may serve – i.e. that it preserves themes and elements either irrelevant to or even subversive of that interest. There is also the epistemological consideration that the truth and sense of a proposition cannot be derived solely from an account of the purposes it is made to serve (and so its truth cannot be denied solely by arguing against the legitimacy or propriety of the interest in which it works unless that interest could be shown to be wholly and exclusively formative of its structure).[26] Thus the truth or falsity of Marxist claims about economic relations could not be settled by reference to the iniquities of Eastern European state socialism; and the truth or falsity of incarnational doctrine could not be settled by reference to the oppressive patriarchalism of a Church which explicitly or implicitly deploys the maleness of the person of Jesus in defence of its practice. So long as it can be shown that other trajectories are possible, that other motifs are embodied in the tradition which make for its *self*-critique, the analysis of doctrine as simple and monolithic ideology is inadequate.

Tendenzkritik alerts us to the questionable character of a text rather than displaying directly and incontrovertibly the non-sustainability of its claims – that is to say, it begins rather than ending critical discussion. It underlines the hybrid nature of texts, their determination by factors beyond what the first, 'innocent' reading shows, and so prompts consideration of questions that seem both futile and compulsive about 'essential' meanings. Where both scripture and doctrine are concerned, this can produce a search for pure sources, religion uncorrupted by the world,[27] the gospel before culture. But the lesson of criticism is precisely that of the radically historical nature of all religious utterance: there is nothing untouched by culture and the contestation of power. This is acknowledged rather strikingly in an undeservedly neglected discussion of biblical hermeneutics by Karl Barth in the introduction to the third edition of his Romans Commentary.[28] Here he dismisses Bultmann's efforts to identify *in* the text the authentic Word of God differentiating itself from the products of the human spirit: *all* the words of scripture are human, compromised, and inadequate, and *all* are potentially the vehicles of the Word.

> There are in the Epistle no words at all which are not words of those 'other spirits' which he calls Jewish or Popular-Christian or Hellenistic . . . Rather it is for us to perceive and make clear that the whole is placed under the KRISIS of the Spirit of Christ.[29]

What might this mean in the study of doctrinal history? The conclusion might still be a Wilesian one; but if so some other difficulties would also need to be dealt with. In particular (as we shall see later), the question has to be resolved of how to avoid the kind of historicizing and relativizing of doctrine that simply replaces traditional formulations by some unthematized commitment to the developing stream of Christian life and reflection in a way which makes the self-critique of the tradition practically impossible to articulate (a position which I do not think Wiles would find congenial). For the moment, it is enough to recognize that *Tendenzkritik* is quite as grave a challenge to doctrinal assertion as it is claimed to be – indeed, arguably more serious than Wiles's very muted version of it might suggest; but that neither it nor the simpler styles of genre critique can settle the truth and intelligibility, the intellectual legitimacy, of doctrinal propositions with any decisiveness.

II

In his London inaugural, Wiles takes as his example of material for the doctrinal critic 'the church's conviction about the uniqueness or finality of Christ'.[30] Here and elsewhere, it is reasonably clear that he means the whole complex of strategies by which Christians have tried to latch their sense of Jesus' significance on to a reality beyond what is tangibly and historically given, so as to *ground* the apprehension of that significance in a statement of how things are with the universe. This covers, of course, a great variety of statements: as the Christology essay of 1970 implies, it includes the 'second Adam' typology of Paul and Irenaeus; but it extends equally to the very formal and abstract idiom of Chalcedon. It would be appropriate, surely, to spell out the sorts of *Kritik* suitable to the different idioms involved here, and this has not, I think, been fully carried through in Wiles's work. In respect of the 'second Adam' language, or perhaps the transferring to Christ, in Colossians I, of attributes associated in Jewish speculation with the pre-existent Torah, we can quite evidently and properly discuss the context in which metaphors develop and shift: in Paul's universe there are indeed a number of available schemes for ascribing to something supreme and decisive meaning, generative and authoritative import. He (and the author of Colossians if it is not Paul) works at least partly in a context in which primordiality is one such scheme: if the Law is the decisive communication of God's purpose, it must be 'with' God at the beginning of all things. It cannot be a contingent event in the world. In a different context, different strategies would be appropriate (as with those Chinese Christians who have proposed identifying Jesus as the embodiment of Tao). These moves are informal, pre-dogmatic, and it is not in dispute that the intelligibility of certain metaphorizations depends on the intelligibility of their context. Good critical reading of a text like Romans 5, 1 Corinthians 15, or Colossians I will show how a metaphor works in greater depth than any reading which merely takes the language for granted – let alone the sort of reading which does not even spot the presence of a metaphor at all. Similarly, a critical reading of a text like Anselm's *Cur Deus homo?* will display the ways in which a metaphor shapes the argument – and perhaps how problems arise in interpretation when neither author nor pre-critical reader acknowledges the metaphorical character of certain premises or moves in the argument. This, I think, is very much how Wiles sees the paradigm of doctrinal critique at its most basic.

But this could be taken to imply that all doctrinal utterances are, or are reducible to, rhetorical strategies (metaphor as a communicative device), and that doctrinal formulation, credal or conciliar as well as systematic or 'descriptively didactic', to borrow Schleiermacher's term,[31] is generally characterized by a misprision or forgetfulness of its metaphorical origins (understood in terms of vivid communicative strategy). Yet the history of doctrinal controversy in the early Church is in large part a record of the struggle between metaphorical or narrative modes of tracing and evoking God's action and a set of diverse considerations, some philosophical, some soteriological, which pointed up the tensions within these modes and sought to resolve them, or at least contain them by surrounding them with warning signs and insisting on the rigorous purging of anthropomorphism.[32] Thus: the generation of the Word is not an event in the life of God preceded by some other state of affairs; the Word of God does not supply the missing motor in a defective human vehicle; the story of Jesus is not one in which a human individual collaborates with a divine individual, intermittently yielding full control to the latter – although all these notions were respectably current in the idiom of Christian rhetoric up to 451 (and beyond). In short, while Christological language may employ metaphor, it also carries a measure of 'immanent critique' of the unexamined metaphor and an awareness of the potential contradictoriness and inadequacy of metaphor when treated either as an explanation in its own right or as a mere illustration of a simpler and more primitive idea. As I put it earlier, this is a 'text' already cognizant of its own ambiguities.

The Church's conviction about the uniqueness or finality of Christ is thus, as already intimated above, a manifold, nuanced, and self-reflective business. Early and diverse metaphorizations of this conviction are not superseded or crudely translated into 'literal' language, but qualified by the application of regulative considerations: doctrinal definitions, Chalcedon above all, and the subsequent Christological clarifications of the Byzantine period, are indeed not *simply* regulative stipulations (no more ontologically bold than the rules of tennis), but the result of applying regulative principles to the more chaotic language of pre-dogmatic *doctrina*. Given a commitment to the truthfulness of the whole complex of practices, verbal and non-verbal, moral, imaginative, devotional, and reflective, which embody 'the Church's conviction' about Jesus, dogmatic Christological definition sets out to establish the conditions for telling this truth in the most comprehensive, least conceptually extravagant, and least idly mythological language. *Pace* Wiles and many others, including nearly all of the contributors to *The myth of God incarnate*, incarnational doctrine is not to be reduced to the narrative of a heavenly being coming down from his native habitat, uneasily combined with an undifferentiated assertion of *identity* between Jesus of Nazareth and the divine Word. No professional theologian from 451 to (say) 1850 would have recognized that as an account of what the doctrine claimed.[33]

Now the Wilesian doctrinal critic might well respond that the critical element in doctrinal formulation is neither here nor there: it is simply the sophisticated articulation of a basic misconception, which vitiates any attempts at refinement. If the fifth-century theologian acknowledged the need to qualify the metaphors of piety, he was still under the illusion that these metaphors were part of the process of bringing to speech a single focal truth about Jesus' relation to God, a truth not to be stated in any way except one that expressed the unsurpassable character of that relationship. Everything rests on the belief that the 'impact' of Jesus is to be construed in a certain way; and if the critic is right to see this construal as dependent on a set of cultural and intellectual assumptions we can no longer make, the refinement of the initial belief by 'immanent critique' will not help us. This at once raises a point of the most fundamental importance as to how we are *now* to identify or to characterize the initial experience of Jesus' 'impact' in such a way as to make it clear that the traditional construal is in some sense a mistake. I shall return to this in a moment; but before leaving the question of how 'doctrinal statements' are being defined in Wiles's argument, it is, I think, worth registering that his account of the doctrinal critic's task depends quite heavily on what looks like a reductive and undifferentiated view of what doctrine consists in, a view that, on the showing of his various essays in Christology, tends repeatedly to search for some originary miscalculation or wrong turning, some category error about the status of the language used. What I have been trying to suggest in this section is that, if the history of doctrine is in fact both messier and more self-reflective than Wiles appears to allow, the critic needs to query whether this kind of search is really the essence of the job, and attend more to how exactly the tensions between dogma and metaphor are negotiated under different kinds of pressure from different historical contexts.[34] It is not enough to assimilate all doctrinal utterance to metaphorical elaboration unconscious of its own questionable status, as though 'Once in royal David's city' and the beginning of Duns Scotus' *Opus Oxoniense III* were comparable enterprises.

III

The most problematic area of Wiles's discussion lies in his attitude to the relation between the fundamental (or, better, foundational – not just a nit-picking distinction) moment of Christian experience and its articulation in terms of what is truly the case in the universe. There can be no doubt at all of Wiles's own commitment to the belief that Jesus – the Jesus of flesh and blood, ministering and crucified – makes a decisive, perhaps even uniquely authoritative, difference to how we speak of God and God's relation to the world (the human world at any rate): this is expounded eloquently and movingly in the chapter on 'Jesus and the Way of Faith' in *Faith and the mystery of God*[35] but it is in evidence in all that Wiles has written on Christology. Jesus is the (or 'a'?) supreme case of an event in which God is active in the only way we may properly expect God to be active: in the creation of 'new possibilities', and in summoning men and women to transforming decisions. His life functions as a parable, in so far as parable may be thought of (following Eta Linnemann) as 'an event which decisively alters the situation'.[36]

However, as Wiles elaborates the point, it seems that the parabolic quality of the story of Jesus, above all the death of Jesus, amounts to something rather less than Linnemann's words might suggest. The narrative of the crucifixion, taken together with the whole record of the ministry, shows us how God deals with evil: 'the parable of the cross points the human imagination to a vision of God as participant in the continuing conflict with evil, identifying himself at whatever cost with both the perpetrators and the victims of that evil. It is through the cross that he is most clearly seen as the God for whom nothing is expendable except himself'.[37] This insight invites us to decision – to recognize the evil in ourselves and to begin the work of our own transformation. This is very finely said indeed; but is it all? It seems here as if *the* basic Christian experience were that of acknowledging an insight into the divine character. But this is some way short of Linnemann's idea of a moment in human language which concretely alters the possibilities in a situation by (at least) reconstituting our sense of ourselves, our responsibility, our guilt or complicity, our hope. And how exactly do we move from the story of Jesus to the language Wiles uses about divine involvement and divine cost – language which is in fact dramatically anthropomorphic, even mythological? What does the powerful phrase about God's 'expendability' actually *mean* for a theology which has elsewhere entered severe proscriptions against presuming to talk about the divine life in itself? It might be said, in the light of Wiles's excellent discussion of metaphor earlier in the same book, that there are matters which can only be spoken of in metaphorical idiom, and that we can and must not press for an answer to the question of what 'exactly' such a turn of phrase as this refers to. This is entirely correct; but I do not think it answers the difficulty here, which is that in Wiles's own terms we have no grasp of how the metaphor is generated or how the move to a strong narrative statement about God can be explicated (let alone legitimated). God's 'expendability' is a good instance of a robust metaphorical move standing in profound tension with (Wiles's) regulative principles for talk of God: it is, to use the terms I proposed earlier, pre-dogmatic and informal, an agendum for reflection.

We could deal with this, perhaps, by saying that the story of Jesus somehow confirms and deepens what we already know of the nature of God's action from thinking about the world in general or the lives and words of those who seem to live very close to God: Jesus 'lives out' the pattern of divine action and compassion, the divine denial of force, so radically, to the point of death, that we become aware as never before of what is involved in believing in a compassionate God. But if this is true, it is something of an overstatement to say that this story 'decisively alters the situation'. Should we say, then, that Jesus, by speaking for the love and mercy of God in his ministry, requires of us that we see the same love in his passion as in his action, thus introducing into our grasp of God's love the element of true vulnerability? This is more promising: but it still involves a considerable leap from the detail of Jesus' life and death to ascribing to God a kind of cost or privation, let alone the identification alike with perpetrators and victims of evil of which Wiles speaks. We should need to spell out too why it is that Jesus' speaking and acting for the mercy of God have sufficient distinctiveness and authority to warrant the belief that this suffering shows us a suffering in God *in a way that other martyrdoms in the Jewish world did not or do not.* How is a story of unjust suffering patiently and unresistingly borne transformed into a story of *God?*

I do not want to dismiss or dismantle Wiles's vision, only to draw attention to its profoundly tantalizing character. Our situation, it is claimed, is changed by an insight about the nature of God's action and love whose precise relation to the story of Jesus is difficult to state with clarity. It could also be noted that the form in which this insight is expressed is quintessentially twentieth century, taking for granted the intelligibility of the radical vulnerability of the divine person in a way quite alien to all preceding generations of belief, including the world of the New Testament (a point elsewhere raised by Wiles in criticizing putatively orthodox accounts of incarnational doctrine among some contemporary theologians). Is the narrative of Jesus *constitutive* of this insight (and if so, in virtue of what, and 'by what authority') or is it *illustrative* of a more generally available understanding (in which case, can it bear the full 'parabolic' weight of creating the conditions for a genuinely transforming decision)? Then there is the question of how the insight privileged in Wiles's account actually relates to what we can say about the historically primary sense of the impact of Jesus, to which implicit appeal is made in the critique of doctrinal formulation. This is to bring into focus the distinction hinted at earlier between foundational and fundamental experience: is the historically primary sense, the foundational experience, demonstrably one with the central insight afforded, in a modern theologian's eyes, by the life and death of Christ, the fundamental, distinctive contribution of the Christian vision? The New Testament falls some way short of saying that the life and death of Jesus provide a manifestation of the character of God's love in the sense of giving us a supremely full human analogue, in death as well as life, of that love: if they manifest God's love, it is because they *are* the action of God, moving towards the restoration and the universalizing of God's people, or the adoption of human beings as children of the

Father. In other words, for the New Testament writers overall, the difference Jesus makes is *first* concerned with how and with whom God may be called upon, a difference in language and community, and only derivatively a difference in how God is to be thought about. It makes some sense to consider Jesus as constitutive of an understanding of God if Jesus is first the one who precipitates into existence the restored community of Israel, a community whose prayer and practice slowly and traumatically separate it from the historic Israel. Before we come round to reflecting on the difference Jesus makes to understanding God, he has made a difference encoded in the tangible difference of the *ekklēsia* from both Jews and Gentiles.[38] And this unmistakably suggests that the language of reconceiving God in the light of Jesus is irremediably parasitic on a prior apprehension of the life and death of Jesus as divine action, not on the basis of discovering analogues between the character of Jesus and the character of God, but in the light of the kind of transformation already begun in the social reality of those who called themselves God's people.

If the assumption is that the *essence* of the difference associated with Jesus is the provision of a new and undoubtedly challenging and radical picture of God, it is quite intelligible to conclude that doctrinal formulation focused on the person of Jesus is in an important sense misconceived. But such an assumption runs a real risk of foreclosing on the results of 'doctrinal criticism', importing into the understanding of the first believers a kind of 'pre-doctrinal' (not only pre-dogmatic) and innocent kernel of belief (Jesus shows us the truth about God) which is in fact dependent upon, the deposit of, a highly developed chain of reflection. Wiles does not claim that the essence of primitive Christian belief included the vision of a vulnerable God (the very vocabulary necessary for formulating this is only born in the course of complex and very robust incarnational debates in the fifth and sixth centuries); but his exposition in *Faith and the mystery of God* suggests that this is a proper extrapolation from the 'vision' of God's action and purpose first conveyed through Jesus. There is a certain circularity at work here, not necessarily vicious, but not much easier to handle than the traditional doctrinal idiom. What can now be salvaged from a chastened doctrinal heritage must be something like what impelled the Christian enterprise in the first place; and the chastening of the doctrinal heritage is itself spurred by a recognition of the distance between foundational experience and its supposedly mythological articulation. It is a little bit as if the devout imagination could make us coeval with Jesus and the first believers, so that we can lay hold of the buried pearl of Jesus' 'impact' and yet remain free of those cultural pressures that lead inexorably towards the errors of doctrine. Remember that a *mistake* is something recognizable in a community of people sharing the same world-construction, the same rules: if Christology rests on a mistake, we must be able in some way to share the rules and aims and horizons, the definitions, of the first makers of Christianity, so as to be able to say, 'That is not a legitimate move (however predictable or intelligible in the light of circumstances)'. And that is possible only if our experience of Jesus is at least potentially on all fours with that of the first believers, if we can find an experiential essence in common (allowing, of course, for some measure of nuancing and development in the passage of time).

The problems here are manifold. We have to consider not only Troeltsch's critique of Harnack, but also Kierkegaard's argument in the *Philosophical fragments*[39] that the experience of the believer contemporary with Christ furnishes the occasion or condition of subsequent faith, not its normative content. What prompts and forms belief is not the 'raw' event of the life of Jesus, but that event as witnessed to – as already mediated. If we have to make ourselves contemporary in imagination with the first believers, reconstructing an 'impact', our faith will constantly come to rest either in speculative projections or in inoffensive generalities. We have no way of saying what *we* would see as contemporaries of Jesus and the apostles: the 'impact' of Jesus is itself embedded in a world of image and expectation not our own, and we could not ever be in a position to evaluate this more satisfactorily than Jesus' contemporaries – having the experience (as Eliot might have said) but *not* missing the meaning. It is not simply that the importance of Jesus is misconstrued: what the experience of Jesus as significant actually amounts to is, as a historical question, answerable only in the terms of his contemporaries. He was important for first-century reasons, not important for timeless reasons distorted by confused first-century minds. I suspect that Wiles is here not enough of a historical relativist![40] It is difficult to work out how far he is really committed to the implied view that the first-century believer and the twenty-first-century believer are engaged in the same task, making sense of the historical effect of another man's biography, but there is enough in what he writes to generate the difficulties I have tried to indicate. And my doubts about whether we should find Jesus significant *as a historical figure* for good twenty-first-century reasons are not, I should add, a recommendation of some sort of programmatic scepticism about the

Gospel record, or a dismissal of the theological importance of the Jesus of history, but merely a recognition that Christology is not *first* a task of historical assessment of a chronicled individual. A good deal of recent criticism of classical incarnational doctrine seems to be based on the complaint that there is not enough evidence to justify dogmatic conclusions, and Wiles's interpretation assumes such a gravamen. But what if the entire enterprise is not about *historical* evidence and (incommensurable) dogmatic conclusions at all?

The model of 'experiencing' Jesus discernible in Wiles and others in this connection is problematic. The New Testament writers and their congregations did not (as Wiles himself agrees) make deductions from an overview of the facts of Jesus' life and the impression made by him. What their language actually says is that, in his ministry *and* now, Jesus is the form which God's judgement takes; that he, then and now, makes real the welcoming mercy of God in the Lord's Supper; that the believer is united with him, that the death and resurrection of Jesus in particular constitute the condition of there being a new humanity of unrestricted *koinōnia* so that if we 'enter into' the dying and rising of Jesus by baptism and in daily conversion, we come to stand where he stands, in full intimacy with the Father, and the barriers separating us from other human beings fall away. The relation of the believer to Jesus here is not that of an observer, however deeply or lastingly impressed, but what Paul and John conceive as 'indwelling', being where he is. How exactly can we relate all this to the assessment of Jesus' significance as a historical human individual? For these are the words and images which say what the difference is that Jesus makes – what the 'experience' involved is. You may say that they are unintelligible, but not that they represent a simple misunderstanding. And both within and beyond the New Testament, the basic intra-Christian impulse to doctrinal reflection lies here: what is to be said of a human life that is creative and definitive of a new frame of reference in speaking of God and the world by establishing a new social reality in which God is spoken of – a human life which is believed, rightly or wrongly, to be present and active, still being lived, for and in the Christian, a life not perceived as something that can be talked of as an episode in the past?[41] If we want to say that the essential core of all this is still an *evaluation* of the impact of Jesus, we are saying that we understand the early Christians' experience so much better than they did that we can discount the greater part of what they concretely said not only as metaphor but as misplaced or dispensable metaphor. Is it enough to say, with Wiles, that the early believers had experiences which they 'associated' with Jesus as risen Lord (but which might in principle be intelligibly detached from that association)? To sustain itself in this connection, Wiles's thesis would need to be very much refined, to avoid either the Harnackian anachronism of thinking that what we find attractive and important in Jesus was itself the foundational experience, or the implication that we stand alongside the first believers, striving to interpret an experience not previously mediated.

IV

Very briefly: I have used words like 'legitimacy' and 'legitimation' quite frequently in this essay, partly as a reminder of how much critical activity is bound up with a kind of *legal* paradigm. What is allowed to count? Can we agree on what people have a right to expect will be accepted or understood as valid currency? In a very interesting passage of the first *Critique*,[42] Kant spoke of his aim as being to deliver us from the 'natural' state of war, where assertions are contested and sustained by force alone, and to establish a quasi-legal authority: 'The critique . . . arriving at all its decisions in the light of fundamental principles of its own institution, the authority of which no-one can question, secures to us the peace of a legal order, in which our disputes have to be conducted solely by the recognized methods of *legal action*.'

Legal settlement is universally and eternally valid, in that it does not depend on the outcome of messy and protracted negotiations between arbitrarily distinct interests (as between nations in the aftermath of war). We are delivered from the Hobbesian 'injustice and violence' of pre-rational nature[43] by the establishing of an authority whose credibility and legitimacy are beyond the disputes of mere interest and locality and are accessible to all reasoning minds. The hope of being able to settle disputes without recourse to contests of power is a noble and persistent one (most recently and fully defended by Habermas); but it is a hope that is easily confused with the fantasy that there might be a form of human discourse free from local and personal pasts, from standpoints. The universal tribunal envisaged by Kant is meant to be in everyone's interest and to be distorted by no 'local' constructions of reality. But the history of post-Enlightenment thought has left us, at the very least, a legacy of scepticism about these universal juridical claims, and a tendency to think more about how different local constructions can engage 'critically' with themselves and each other in the purging of violent and untruthful exclusivisms and the negotiating of the tensions between real difference and possible new forms of communality.

These are the commonplaces of recent epistemology (and anti-epistemology). To say that there is no universal tribunal, that pluralities of perception cannot be settled by 'legal action', is not necessarily to doom ourselves to irrationalist relativism. It is, though, to acknowledge that what is sustainable, what can be asserted without arbitrariness (if that is a proper paraphrase of what legitimacy means), has more to do with how particular perceptions cope with and absorb contesting claims and maintain elements of critical 'listening' provisionality within their own frameworks than with meeting foreordained universal conditions of legality. In our specific case, I am uneasy that Wiles follows Woods so faithfully in assuming that the 'truth and adequacy of doctrinal statements' can be tested in a fundamentally historical and analytical discipline. Wiles here comes curiously close to Pannenberg – not usually his favourite theologian – in implying that the truth of revelation should be accessible to supposedly neutral study;[44] or to Lonergan's confidence that 'dialectics' can deal with the truthfulness of doctrinal propositions as part of a continuum of analysis slipping easily from history to system-atics.[45] Wiles's appeal[46] to 'economy and coherence' in the assessment of doctrinal validity or viability makes little allowance for how *transitions* in understanding extend and outgrow (in his own words) currently available conventions of making sense within an existing tradition, let alone within the canons of some general normative rationality.

To the task of doctrinal criticism, the following, I believe, may be granted: the rigorous exploration and testing of conceptual structures for points of strictly logical inadequacy, the attempt to identify concepts imperfectly defined or focused; the examination of the role of metaphor, and the attempt to discern places where it might be leading an argument by the nose in unconscious (uncriticized) ways; and the search for interest or *Tendenz* in doctrinal utterance. All this is more or less included in Wiles's basic proposals. But I have tried to suggest in these pages that dealing with these issues can easily be tied in with settling issues of truth if we are not careful, in ways which are actually inattentive to the concrete history and operation of doctrinal formulation. Such a connection can only be defended by recourse to a very full-blooded abstract universalist rationalism, which I do not think Wiles really professes, though he may come pretty near it at times. Our disagreement is ultimately, I should say, about how to 'read' the difference made by Jesus. If Jesus is finally *illustrative* of truths about God which are in principle independent of this particular life and death, doctrine will be above all the process of transmitting these truths (with all the resources of image and symbol to which Wiles grants increasing importance), and the exact place occupied by Jesus may quite properly vary from one bit of Christian pedagogy to another. If Jesus is *constitutive* for Christian language about God and for the present reality of the believer's relation to God, in such a way that what is said, done, and suffered is strictly unintelligible without continuing reference to Jesus in a more than historically explicatory way, doctrine will be an attempt to do justice to the way in which the narrative and the continuing presence (or presence-in-absence, if you want to nuance it further) of Jesus is held actively to shape present horizons, in judgement and in grace. The disagreement is not over whether doctrinal utterances are or are not to be received uncritically, but over whether any kind of critical method can settle the legitimacy of the distinctively *doctrinal* enterprise itself as generally conceived by Christians, an enterprise resting as it does on the conviction, variously and often very confusedly articulated in our primary texts, that our world of speech and corporate life has been comprehensively remade, so that new conceptualities are brought to birth. *Kritik* can look hard at those conceptualities, with a wide variety of suspicions; but not all Wiles's reasoned eloquence should persuade us that it is in a position to disallow the underlying unsettlement of our thought: the question, 'What is it that is true of Jesus of Nazareth that would make some sense of the Church's commitment to new imaginings of God and humanity and of the possibility of new relation to God and humanity?' I believe that this is in fact the question that arises from taking with full seriousness the notion of parable which Wiles finds so attractive – an event which interrupts us and compels us to take up new positions by showing us quite unexpectedly where and what we are in respect of an unforeseen reality set down before us; something more than an extended simile. Wiles is far from insensitive to this priority of *krisis* over *Kritik*; but how can his model of doctrinal criticism allow it its proper weight?

Notes

1. G. F. Woods, 'Doctrinal criticism', in F. G. Healey (ed.), *Prospect for theology* (Welwyn: James Nesbit, 1966).

2. Maurice Wiles, *Working papers in doctrine* (London: SCM Press, 1976).

3. Ibid., 152.

4. Ibid., 161.

5. Ibid., 162.

6. This is the conclusion of a very early (1957) paper, 'Reflections on the origins of the doctrine of the Trinity', republished in *Working papers in doctrine*, 1–17, and the point is reiterated in 'Christianity without Incarnation?', in John Hick (ed.), *The myth of God incarnate* (London: SCM Press, 1977), 1–10, esp. 3–6, 8–9.

7. This position is now associated with George Lindbeck, in the wake of his book on *The nature of doctrine* (Philadelphia: Westminster, 1984). For Wiles's views on this, I am dependent on conversation with him, and on an unpublished paper delivered to the late Hans Frei's seminar at Yale.

8. The phrase is used in Wiles, *The remaking of Christian doctrine* (London: SCM Press, 1974), 52.

9. Ibid., 53.

10. Wiles, 'Does Christology rest on a mistake?', in *Working papers in doctrine*, 122–31.

11. There is actually some confusion here: Wiles does not distinguish between the idea of creation *ex nihilo* as an absolute and unrepeatable beginning (i.e., creation in the strict traditional Christian sense), creation as a punctiliar 'event' in the sense of something occurring in time (a view generally rejected by theologians at least since Augustine, and the subject of considerable philosophical discussion in late antiquity – see Richard Sorabji, *Time, creation and the continuum* (London: Duckworth, 1983), and my *Arius: heresy and tradition* (London: Darton, Longman & Todd, 1987), 181–98), and the creation of the human species by special intervention (a more thorny point, on which it is difficult to pin down many classical theologians, because they are capable of using both the language of a discreet act of creation and something more like a doctrine of the divine simultaneity of the entirety of the creative process). Only in respect of the third is Wiles's argument strictly pertinent, and this uncharacteristic unclarity makes the article in some ways hard to evaluate.

12. Wiles, *Working papers in doctrine*, 125, 127.

13. See, e.g., Wiles, *The remaking of Christian doctrine*, 54; 'Christianity without Incarnation?', 4.

14. Wiles, *Working papers in doctrine*, 129.

15. Ibid., 128; cf. *The remaking of Christian doctrine*, 113–15; 'Myth in theology', in Hick (ed.), *The myth of God incarnate*, 161.

16. Wiles, 'Christianity without Incarnation?', 9; cf. Wiles, *Faith and the mystery of God* (London: SCM Press, 1982), on the uses of metaphor.

17. See, e.g., Wiles, 'Myth in theology', 161, on 'the union of human and divine at the heart of the human personality' as the ontological substrate for the

myth of the Incarnation. This is a far from straightforward statement: it clearly has little to do with the primitive connection of incarnational language with the perception of an event of global change in the world (a connection which Wiles regards as the effect of the apocalyptic milieu); how then does it relate to the initial experience of Jesus by his contemporaries, and how could we know or guess that this was what the doctrinal language was 'really' trying to say? I return to this problem later in the present essay. And what precisely is the nature of the 'union' here spoken of? The union with God of which the New Testament speaks is almost uniformly a union whose character depends on the notion of a relationship defined by and communicated in the person of Jesus and the Spirit of Jesus, a relation to the source of the world as to a father. Is Wiles talking about this, or about something more monistic?

18. This is the burden of Augustine's *De doctrina christiana* (esp. book 2); cf. also Thomas Aquinas, *Summa theologiae*, I.1.9–10.

19. On this, see Paul Ricoeur, *Interpretation theory* (Fort Worth, TX: Christian University Press, 1976), ch. 4, and *Hermeneutics and the human sciences* (Cambridge: Cambridge University Press, 1981), esp. ch. 4.

20. Cf. the examples accessibly located in Ann Loades (ed.), *Feminist theology: a reader* (London: SPCK, 1990), part 1, and Letty Russell (ed.), *Feminist interpretations of the Bible* (Philadelphia: Westminster, 1985).

21. See, e.g., Origen's discussion of what it means to call God 'spirit' (*pneuma*) in an intellectual context where the word had highly specific philosophical (materialistic) connotations, in his *De principiis* I.1.

22. A very significant example would be Athanasius' insistence that the language of begetting or sonship used of the relation of the Logos to the Father must be carefully purged of any suggestion of the temporal, physical, and mutable associations of the terms in ordinary use; see, e.g., *Contra Arianos* I.26–7.

23. An instance is discussed in Wiles, 'Christianity without Incarnation?', 2.

24. For a recent analysis of Christology in the context of feminist critique, see Daphne Hampson, *Theology and feminism* (Oxford: Blackwell, 1990), 1 and 2 – a very nuanced querying of the possibility of salvaging Christology from patriarchy, granting, paradoxically, that such a task would be easier with patristic than with much modern Christology, but assuming that the intellectual structure of the former is not available to us.

25. For a discussion of how this issue was seen by some of the Church of England in the early 19th century, see my 'Newman's *Arians* and the question of method in doctrinal history', in Ian Ker and Alan G. Hill (eds), *Newman after a hundred years* (Oxford: Clarendon Press, 1990).

26. A good discussion of the issues arising here may be found in David McLellan, *Ideology* (Milton Keynes: Open University Press, 1986).

27. See e.g. Elizabeth Schüssler Fiorenza, *In memory of her* (London: SCM Press, 1983), for a very sophisticated essay in this genre. This learned, moving, and profoundly creative work does not quite, finally, escape the temptation of setting up a primitive and 'innocent' Jesus-movement as that against which the corruptions of the canon and the later churches may be judged, despite the disclaimer on p. 92. But it must also be granted that Schüssler Fiorenza's understanding of the task of historical reconstruction is a complex one, and does

not necessarily involve any claims about a primordial community *achieving* the emancipation it presages in its structure and language.

28. Karl Barth, *The epistle to the Romans* (Oxford: Oxford University Press, 1933), 16–19.

29. Ibid., 16–17.

30. Wiles, *Working papers in doctrine*, 154.

31. Cf. Friedrich Schleiermacher, *The Christian faith* (Edinburgh: T&T Clark, 1928), §§15 and 16.

32. Cf. n. 22 and Wiles, 'Christianity without Incarnation?', 2.

33. Some defenders of the doctrine of the Incarnation have apparently assumed that what has to be vindicated is precisely something like an identity statement, and have produced accounts of the doctrine quite considerably removed from, say, the major medieval discussions of it. A most striking example is Thomas V. Morris, *The logic of God Incarnate* (Ithaca, NY: Cornell University Press, 1986).

34. E. A. Peterson's celebrated *Der Monotheismus als politisches Problem* (Leipzig: Hegner, 1935) begins to do something like this. Recent years have seen several studies of Marian doctrine and Eucharistic practice which have raised these sorts of question; an application of this method to Christology on a wide historical front, setting side by side the characteristic metaphors and visual images of a period with the language of doctrinal debate, would be of great significance.

35. Wiles, *Faith and the mystery of God*, esp. 60–3.

36. Ibid., 70.

37. Ibid., 72.

38. Ibid., 60.

39. Søren Kierkegaard, *Philosophical fragments and Johannes Climacus* (Princeton, NJ: Princeton University Press, 1985), §§IV and V, esp. 99–105.

40. He may be contrasted in this respect with Dennis Nineham whose 'Epilogue', in John Hick (ed.), *The myth of God incarnate*, 186–204, and discussion of the wider issues of history and faith in *The use and abuse of the Bible* (London: Macmillan, 1976) take for granted the radical historical inaccessibility of Jesus, and concentrate on elaborating a theology of the Church as carrier of an experience of God *occasioned* in some sense by Jesus, but not given specification by any particular facts about him. Wiles is sometimes quite close to such a position (for example, it appears to be implied in his essay 'In what sense is Christianity a "historical" religion?', *Theology* 81 (1978), 4–14), but in practice (as in *Faith and the mystery of God*) he continues to see the narrative of Jesus as having some kind of normativity for faith in a way which is not obviously entailed by Nineham's account.

41. See Herbert McCabe's discussion of *The myth of God Incarnate* and subsequent correspondence with Wiles in his collection of essays and sermons, *God matters* (London: Chapman, 1987), and in particular his statement on p. 71: 'It is in the contact with the person who is Jesus, in this personal communion between who he is and who I am, that his divinity is revealed in his humanity, not in any, as it were, clinical objective examination of him.'

42. Immanuel Kant, *The critique of pure reason* (London: Macmillan, 1933), 601.

43. On the philosophical and theological problems of the assumption that the

state of nature is a state of violent conflict, see John Milbank, *Theology and social theory* (Oxford: Blackwell, 1990), 278–325.

44. See, e.g., Wolfhart Pannenberg, 'Dogmatic theses on the concept of revelation', in *Revelation as history* (London: Sheed and Ward, 1969), esp. 135–9.

45. Bernard Lonergan, *Method in theology* (London: Darton, Longman & Todd, 1972).

46. Wiles, *The remaking of Christian doctrine*, 17.

Index